Exploring Communication Theory and Research

A Reader

Isabelle Bauman

Dan Peterson

MISSOURI STATE UNIVERSITY™

(name effective August 28, 2005)

KENDALL/HUNT PUBLISHING COMPANY
4050 Westmark Drive Dubuque, Iowa 52002

Contents

Why? An Introduction

Why are you reading this book? Most likely because it is required for a Communication Theory class you are taking. This begs the question, why are you taking the class? We would like to think it is because you have an interest in communication theory, but recognize that such a class may be a requirement for your degree program. Our experience is that some students become interested in the Communication discipline because they feel that enhancing their communication skills will improve their career prospects, their personal lives or both. Others enter the discipline because they are already effective communicators and want the credentials to use those skills professionally. Regardless of why you entered the field of communication, you may be wondering how a class in *theories* can help you achieve your goals. Your associations with the study of theory may include words like "boring," "irrelevant," "hard," and "not practical."

In addition, you may have had classes where instructors asked you to read journal articles. If you are like our students you may have found these articles to be very difficult to read. We frequently have students ask "Why can't they just write what they mean? Why do they have to make it so complicated?" You may also have wondered why you should spend your time reading journal articles at all. In many ways, we wrote this book to address these important concerns. Let us tell you a little bit about ourselves and then explain why we think it is worth your time and energy to read both theories and journal articles.

About Us

Isabelle has been teaching communication theory at both the graduate and undergraduate level since 1991. She received her Ph.D. in communication from the University of Wisconsin-Madison and did her undergraduate coursework at the University of Puget Sound in Tacoma, Washington. She considers working with communication theories to be equivalent to playing in a mental sandbox; she gets to use different theories to play with ideas about communication and see what happens as a result. Besides theory, she also teaches courses in quantitative research methods, interpersonal communication, gender and other diversity issues at Missouri State University (name effective August 28, 2005).

Dan received his Ph.D. in organizational communication from Ohio University in Athens, Ohio. He completed his undergraduate degree and Master's degree work at Brigham Young University in Provo, Utah. He believes that communication theory should be taught not just as an abstract idea, but as an applied concept for everyday life. He teaches courses in organizational communication, leadership, public speaking, and communication theory at Missouri State University (name effective August 28, 2005).

About Theory

Why Study Theory

Many learners ask themselves why the study of communication theory is important for them as students and later as organization members. Thus, an understanding of "why" is an important hurdle to overcome so that students not only understand theory but also appreciate it. This section will provide several reasons for why the study of communication theory is important, not only for theory novices, but also for experts.

An Inquisitive Stance

Humans are inquisitive and creative beings. We want to understand and to make sense of the world around us. When something does not make sense to us, we usually try to create an understanding. Although we tend to take it for granted, we are inquisitive theory creators in our everyday lives. For example, a person might create a theory about how to distinguish a good restaurant from a bad one. This theory might be based on the dinner salad and might sound something like—

> If the salad is good, then the entrée will also be good. However, if the restaurant cannot prepare something as simple as a salad effectively, then the meal that follows will usually not be satisfactory.

When we become inquisitive about the communication and interactions we are a part of every day, theories for why things happen follow naturally.

Studying formal theory makes us even more inquisitive. How so? There are three sides to theoretical curiosity—comprehension, critique and creation. In order to make sense of and then critically analyze a theory you must first seek to describe the theory, then to interpret its meaning, and ultimately evaluate it by both its positive and negative points. To describe and interpret the theory, you must read carefully about it, investing time to truly understand its meaning in the correct context. One question you might ask in this process is how the theory applies to your experiences and those of others. Once you have described and interpreted the theory, it can be critically evaluated by the merits of its positions. Each of these steps is part of a process of being inquisitive. You may even find that such theoretical exploration opens your mind to greater understanding of communication and human interaction.

Unfortunately, what often tends to occur in the study of theory is that students evaluate a theory first without understanding it fully. This creates a mental block and makes interpretation and analysis difficult. In such a close-minded case, it is not surprising that theory seems pointless and unimportant. As you consider the theories in this book with an open mind, seeking first to understand and then evaluate, you will see your level of inquisitiveness grow for not only the study of communication, but also the theory. In general, learn to appreciate, yet be critical of the creative and inquisitive stance taken by the authors of each of the articles in this reader.

Locate Connections

Part of making theory enjoyable is making connections. Connections can be made in many ways, but we will focus on three—connections from theory to your major, connections between theory and your everyday life, and connections from one theory to another. One pragmatic reason for studying communication theory is to better understand how it relates to your specific major. Most students who complain about taking a communication theory class do so because they do not see its connections with their major. Once students start to make these connections, an appreciation for communication theory grows. Even better, students who refine their understanding of communication theory, quickly begin to see connections between the theories specific to their major and the more general theories studied in a communication theory course.

Look at the theories studied in this course. Compare them with your own experiences. Students tend to be most passionate about the theories that apply to their lives most directly. In contrast, if you see theory as irrelevant to what you are experiencing, you may disregard it. With each theory you study, you can highlight its relevance by locating connections to your life. You most assuredly will find connections once you develop close understanding of the theory. Figuring out how to link experience and theory is one of the most important benefits of this kind of study.

You should also spend time looking at how the theories in this course are interconnected. Some of the theories grew out of similar foundational theories but have taken different directions because of varying philosophical approaches. Other theories are complete departures from the way communication was studied at that period of time. As you begin to understand historical relationships between theories, you will become savvy in your ability to critique, create, and use theory about communication.

Assumptions Theorists Make

Any time we make a statement about communication (or anything for that matter), we have made some assumptions about the world and about our knowledge of the world that will be implicit in that statement. For example, if we make the statement "people who are lying don't make eye contact" what are we assuming? Well, first of all we are assuming that something we call "lying" exists in the world. If something exists in the world, presumably, we can say what is true or not true about it, such as that it (lying) is related to eye contact. We can then verify that relationship through observation. In other words, we may be able to "discover" what is "true" about lying. These are the kinds of assumptions made by scholars who may be identified by one or more of the following labels: "objective or objectivist" (Baldwin, Perry, & Moffitt, 2004; Griffin, 2003), "post-positivist" (Miller, 2005), and "foundational-empirical" (Anderson & Baym, 2004).

What kinds of things would we be assuming if we made the following statement: "persons-in-conversation create and recreate meanings?" You may be thinking "Yikes! What does that mean?" but bear with us for a moment. Part of what makes this example complicated is some unfamiliar-looking terminology. "Persons-in-conversation" is not a phrase you hear everyday, but what does it imply? One implication is that people's most important area of existence is in interactions with other people. Thus, this statement focuses less on observable qualities like eye contact and more on subjective or individual experiences of people as they talk to each other. Because people who are talking to each other are likely to have different points of view, there may be more than one perspective on "truth." Knowledge, then, would consist in coming to understand various social meanings and experiences, rather than discovering truths. These are the kinds of assumptions made by scholars who may be identified as "interpretive" (Griffin, 2003; Miller, 2005), "subjective" (Baldwin et al, 2004), or "reflexive-empirical" (Anderson & Baym, 2004).

Of course, the actual range of assumptions made by communication theorists is much wider and more complex than we have just presented. However, it should be clear that, in making theory, scholars also make assumptions about the world and about knowledge. These assumptions affect what the theories each scholar produces look like. The range of these assumptions also explains why there are so many theories of communication. You will be able to see some of the impact of differences in assumptions in this book. There are two articles on communication relating to sexual behavior, one takes a more "objectivist" approach to theorizing (Bevan, 2003) while the other takes a more "interpretive" approach (Dougherty, 2001). There are also two articles on communication related to health issues. The more "objective" approach is taken by Freeman and Spyridkis (2004) using the Elaboration Likelihood Model of persuasion. The more "interpretive" approach is taken by Kenny (2001) using Dramatism. In each case, the assumptions made by the scholars affect the topics they choose to focus on, the methods they use to do their scholarship, and the conclusions they come to.

How This Book Fits

We intend this book to help you make the connection between the theories you read about in your Communication Theory textbook and/or hear about in class and the published scholarship related to those theories. We hope it will help you see some of the many ways in which theories can be used. In addition, we hope it will help you understand more about the process of theory development. One of the difficulties in teaching a course on communication theory is the sense that these ideas occur in a vacuum. Theories tend to be presented in their current form as stable "truths" about communication. The reality, of course, is that theories emerge and change over time. They have a history. They occur in a particular intellectual, disciplinary, and social context. They are written by people with varying experiences and perspectives. While we can't cover all of these elements for the theories discussed here, we can give you examples that represent points in time in the development and use of each theory. Our hope is that this process will help the theorizing process become more alive for you.

About Journal Articles

Kinds of Scholarship and Publications

Within this reader you will experience communication scholarship from a variety of perspectives. Theory, however, is an underlying principle that binds the approaches together. In fact, the most versatile theories presented here are useful in a variety of contexts some of which are identified in this section. In addition, we will be discussing the difference between types of publication outlets. By understanding how application context and publication outlet affect theory development, you will become a savvier consumer of research.

Contexts of Communication Study

Researchers study communication in a variety of contexts. Those included in this text are interpersonal relationships, persuasion, health, organizations, and cultures. Some general or foundational communication theories seem to reach across all these areas of study. For example, critical theory, which emphasizes power and influence has been studied in each of the areas above, but through theoretical exploration and innovation, the theories are shaped to fit the situation being studied. Also, each area has specific theories. For example, the theory of organizational socialization is one that relates strongly to the context of organizational communication, but less so in other areas.

Types of Publications

Theory is presented in a number of outlets including journal articles, books, magazines, trade publications, and Internet websites. The readings in this text consider academic journals exclusively. Why we have chosen this emphasis will better be explained in this section as the different types of publications are reviewed. Three criteria will be used to distinguish the different publications: editorial rigor (the number of editors who review a manuscript before it is published), peer review (the manuscript is reviewed by other researchers and experts in the particular field of study), and research orientation (the amount of research used for background and support for the claims in the manuscript, and/or the presentation of original scholarship).

Journal Articles. A journal is a collection of research-based scholarly studies based on both theoretical and applied research. Both *Human Communication Research* and *Journal of Applied Communication* are examples of journals in this field. Journals are mostly published monthly, quarterly or bi-annually. Articles in a journal tend to have the most editorial rigor of all the publications. In fact, if you turn to the beginning of a journal, you will see a long list of editors from universities and organizations. Many of these editors review potential journal articles before they are published. The list of editors also demonstrates the peer review process. Each of the editors listed is an expert in his or her field and as such is qualified to evaluate the theoretical premises made in the article. The process of having a journal article accepted for publication is competitive. Only the best articles based on the peer review process are accepted into journals. Many articles are sent to journals, but because of peer review and editorial rigor, they are not published. When an article is published, because of the peer review process it is seen as a credible document. Journal articles tend to be more research-based than the other types of publications. This is one reason why many journal articles cite numerous sources and have long reference lists.

Books. A book is a publication, usually divided into content specific chapters that go into greater depth than other publications. Books are not published on a periodical time schedule, although it is not uncommon for a new edition to appear every few years with updated research and material. The shear volume of a book enables much more information to be shared than can be in a journal article with limited space. Like journal articles, books are also reviewed by editors, however, these editors may not be experts in the specific topic(s) covered in the book. While an excellent source of information, books tend not to be reviewed by peers to nearly the same degree as a journal article. The peer review of the book usually comes after it has been published and is often based on the number of copies sold, or on subsequent book reviews. As a result, the process of having a book published is usually not as competitive as a journal article. The amount of research in a book versus a journal article is difficult to distinguish, except that as a book grows older, so does its research, but journal articles, because they are published more quickly and frequently, provide constant updating of research as theories are extended.

Trade Publications. A trade publication is an industry specific periodical with practical articles, information, and advertisements intended for a particular trade, for example, *Public Relations Tactics* or *Advertising Age*. A trade publication is usually printed monthly or bi-monthly. On the surface, some trade publications can appear quite similar to journals, especially if the trade publication refers to itself as a journal. However, using the criteria for this chapter, some clear differences exist. Editorial rigor is not the same. An article appearing in a trade publication might be reviewed by two or three editors before it is published. Frequently, although not in all cases, manuscript topics are given by editors to writers paid by the publication to produce an article about a topic important to readers. Although writers and contributors are often experts in their field, documents do not pass through a peer review process. Articles are researched, although the works cited in the text and the references at the end are usually not as extensive. Probably most importantly, however, is that trade publications usually rely on other publications as sources of research and rarely present original research results.

Magazines. A magazine is a collection of interest specific articles and information that is primarily driven by advertising dollars, for example *Cosmopolitan, Time Magazine,* or, *Sports Illustrated*. Articles written for magazines are assigned by editors to writers who research a topic and construct a manuscript. Magazines are usually published weekly, bi-monthly or monthly. Like a trade publication, manuscripts are reviewed by a limited number of editors, so they cannot claim the same editorial vigor as a journal. Because of the quantity of articles that must be produced by writers, the peer review process is limited or non-existent in this kind of publication (outside of editorial review) because writers are responding to the request of an editor. Research is completed for each article, but in most cases that research is not based on scholarly literature. Original research is virtually never presented in magazines. Sources may be referenced in the body of the text, but a list of references at the end of a magazine article is uncommon.

Internet Websites. The Internet contains a vast array of information. In fact, you can find journal articles, books, trade publications, and magazines all online. Because of advanced search engines and programs, information is readily available to those seeking it. However, users of this resource must check the credibility of each source they find on the Internet. Obviously, the Internet is neither a peer reviewed outlet, nor one with editorial vigor. That said, research that is peer reviewed and editorially stringent can be found on the Internet (i.e., *The Electronic Journal of Communication*), but individuals using the information must take the extra step of being sure it meets the criteria discussed in this section. One way to do this is to use reliable search engines, to look for a reference page at the end of a text, search for source citation in the text, and check for the rigor of peer and editorial review.

Because journals are in many ways the benchmark of scholarly excellence we have chosen to focus on this type of publication. All of the journal articles selected for this book fit the criteria of editorial rigor, peer review, and presence of strong research grounding. Although relatively recently published, each article extends a previously published theory, demonstrating theoretical application and progress.

How Publication of Scholarship Relates to Theory

Most generally, publication is a major way in which knowledge is disseminated. For knowledge of a theory to be spread, it needs to be published. For knowledge of research to be spread, it needs to be published. For knowledge of practical applications of theory to be spread, you guessed it, it needs to be published. Publication of theories and research findings allow these different forms of knowledge to influence each other, leading to further knowledge development.

The process of publication also serves as a quality control measure to assure the validity of our knowledge base, either directly or indirectly. Because journal articles are usually subject to peer review, we can be reasonably confident of the validity of those ideas. When theories or research are published in forums that are not peer-reviewed, we don't have the same assurances, at least not directly. Indirectly, we can establish the quality of an idea by looking at how frequently people use it and cite its source. People tend to use exciting, thought-provoking, high quality publications more often than those that are boring or problematic. Work that is used more often (cited in other publications, talked about in textbooks, references in trade-journals, etc.) tends to stay active. Work that is not used tends to die.

Finally, when scholars develop or modify theories, they base their ideas on already published research and theory. Ultimately publication relates to theory in that it forms the building blocks of new theoretical developments.

About This Book

As should be clear by now, our goal for this book is to help you read and understand journal articles and how they relate to theory so you can see for yourself where the ideas developed in theories come from and appreciate connections between theory, research, and your life experiences. In order to do this, we have included the next chapter which gives some guidelines for reading research-based journal articles. This chapter is accompanied by a sample article that we will use to illustrate the various points we make. Each following chapter focuses on a specific journal article related to a communication theory. We will give a brief introduction to the article that includes some background of the theory, a summary of the structure of the article, and a couple of distinctive points about the article that we want to highlight for your attention. We also include a few questions to help you make connections to the theory and research presented. The book concludes with a summary section to help you reflect on what you have learned from your experience with communication theory and research.

Our suggestion would be that you begin with the chapter on how to read a journal article, followed by the article by Bevan. We assume that you also have a more traditional textbook on Communication Theory and we suggest that for each of the following chapters you read about the theory in that textbook first, then read our introduction and then the journal article. While our introductions are written assuming that you have read the prior chapters in this book, they should still be understandable if read in a different order. More than anything else, we encourage you to take the time to read the journal articles from beginning to end. Allow yourself *time* to do this. Especially at first, this kind of reading may be difficult, and rushing through it will only lead to confusion and frustration.

Reading journal articles is a skill. As with most skills, it gets easier with practice. This reader is intended as a kind of guidebook to help you make that practice more efficient and less frustrating.

References

Anderson, J. A., & Baym, G. D. (2004). Philosophies and philosophic issues in communication, 1995–2004. *Journal of Communication, 54,* 589–615.

Baldwin, J. R., Perry, S. D., & Moffitt, M. A. (2004). *Communication theories for everyday life.* Boston: Allyn and Bacon.

Bevan, J. L. (2003). Expectancy violation and sexual resistance in close, cross-sex relationships. *Communication Monographs 70,* 68–82.

Dougherty, D. S. (2001). Sexual harassment as a [dys]functional process: A feminist standpoint analysis. *Journal of Applied Communication Research, 29,* 372–402.

Freeman, K. S., & Spyridkis, J. H. (2004). An examination of factors that affect the credibility of online health information. *Technical Communication, 51,* 239–264.

Griffin, E. (2003). *A first look at communication theory, (5th edition).* Boston: McGraw Hill.

Kenny, R. W. (2001). Toward a better death: Applying Burkean principles of symbolic action to interpret family adaptation to Karen Ann Quinlan's coma. *Health Communication, 13,* 363–385.

Miller, K. (2005). *Communication theories: Perspectives, processes, and contexts (2nd edition).* Boston: McGraw Hill.

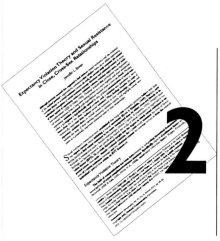

2 A Map of New Territory or The Theory Student's Guide to Journal Articles

Our experience with students making their first attempt at reading journal articles is that they find it at least as confusing as navigating in a foreign city without either a map or an interpreter. The purpose of this chapter is to provide a basic map of journal articles and some rules of thumb for interpreting some of the standard elements you will find there. If you have some experience reading journal articles, you may still find this chapter useful in directing your attention to aspects of articles you may not have noticed before or in helping you understand why things are laid out the way they are in these publications.

Throughout this chapter we will be using a journal article by Jennifer Bevan (2003) as an example. Her article is reproduced following this chapter and you will notice that we refer to specific elements of her work using page numbers to guide you to the correct section of the article. As will be the case any time we cite an article reproduced in this book, any page numbers listed will refer to *this book, not the page numbers from the original publication.* For citations that are not reproduced in this book, any page numbers refer to those of the original source. Let us make one other note about Bevan's article before we move on. You may notice that it is an example of what is called "quantitative" research (because it relies on statistical analysis for part of its argument). Not every journal article you will encounter uses the quantitative format, so throughout this chapter, when relevant, we will note ways that other types of articles might differ from our particular example.

Journal Articles as Argumentation

To understand why journal articles are written the way they are it may be helpful to think of them as pieces of argumentation. Other scholars have suggested that constructing high quality research methods is analogous to constructing high quality arguments (i.e., Merrigan & Huston, 2004). We would extend that idea to any form of scholarly publication, but specifically to journal articles. Authors of journal articles are submitting a piece of reasoning for your evaluation. They want to convince you that what they are claiming in their article is correct or useful. So, in order to understand journal articles, it may be helpful to look at how different features of the article contribute to developing the author's argument. One model of argumentation suggests that any argument has three basic components: claims, data, and warrants (Toulmin, 1983). The claim is the point the author wants to support. The data is the evidence the author uses to support the claim. The warrant is the part of the argument that shows how the data and the claim are related. For example, imagine the following discussion:

(1) Sandy: Mountain Dew is more popular with college students than any other drink. (claim)
(2) Chris: How do you know?
(3) Sandy: Well, there are more slots for Mountain Dew than for anything else on our campus's beverage machines. (data)

In line 1, Sandy makes a claim about the beverage that is most popular with college students. Before agreeing with that claim, Chris asks for evidence. Sandy suggests a piece of evidence in line 3, but do you think Chris will accept the argument?

(4) Chris: What do beverage machine slots have to do with the popularity of Mountain Dew? (Chris is asking for a warrant explaining how the data provided is related to the claim being made.)

(5) Sandy: Well, vendors provide more slots for drinks that sell more. If there are more slots for Mountain Dew, it probably sells better than anything else. The only reason I can see why it would sell better is that students like it better than anything else, which means it's more popular. (warrant)

Now, this particular warrant is probably pretty self-explanatory and you may be thinking that Chris is an idiot for even needing to ask. It is true that some warrants are so taken-for-granted that they are never stated. Other times, the warrant is made explicit.

Using Toulmin's model we can see a journal article as a series of claims, backed up by data with warrants connecting the data to the claims. In order to look at how these ideas play out in Bevan's article, we will first consider ways authors use overall article structure to help clarify the parts of their argument. Then we will look at how you might recognize claims in the article. Finally, we will consider the different forms of data authors draw on and the warrants that connect data to claim.

Journal Article Structure

Most authors of journal articles are making fairly complicated arguments, so they use a system of headings and a fairly standard order to help the reader follow the points they are making. You can expect research articles to be structured in the following order:

1. *An abstract.* This is a paragraph summarizing the journal article. It is usually located at the very beginning of the article and frequently printed in a different font than the rest of the article. This is a good place to begin identifying some of the author's central claims.

2. *An introduction.* This may be as short as one paragraph or it may be a couple of pages. Here the author identifies the topic of the article and presents justification of its importance.

3. *The literature review.* Here the author will summarize past research on the topic and introduce any theories being used to frame the research. Initial claims being made by the author will be set up in this section. Stylistically, authors won't talk about each of the sources they draw on separately, rather they will probably use several sources in each paragraph to make and support their claims. Please note also that the abstract, introduction, and literature review sections may or may not actually be called, for example, the "literature review" in the article. Authors may, instead, use content themes to label material in these sections.

4. *Methods.* This is the section where the author describes what was done to collect the data being analyzed. The basic claim here is that the researcher did a good job with the data collection so that conclusions drawn from the data will be believable. Articles where data isn't collected, such as those presenting rhetorical analysis (see Chapter 8) or examples of practical applications (see Chapter 3), won't have methods sections, per se. Since data wasn't collected, the author doesn't need to describe the data collection process and the primary reason for a methods section disappears.

5. *Results.* Here is where the findings of the study will be presented. In quantitative research articles, the results will typically take the form of statistics, as is the case in the following article by Bevan (2003). In qualitative research articles, the results will typically be presented as sample quotations from the data. These quotations will be followed by some interpretation of their meaning and/or implications for the study (see the article included in Chapter 4 for an example). This is one difference in the structure you might expect from quantitative versus qualitative research. In quantitative research, interpretation of the findings will be done in the discussion section. In qualitative research, results and interpretation are typically presented together.

6. *Discussion and Conclusion.* In quantitative research articles, this section provides an analysis of what the statistics presented in the prior section mean. Usually these results will be tied together with material and claims presented in the literature review. In qualitative articles this interpretation will already have happened in the prior section. In both types of research, the final section of the paper will usually discuss potential limitations of the study. Articles will usually conclude with a discussion of how the findings might apply to practical problems, modify theory, and/or direct future research.

Authors use headings to signal the structure of their article. Generally, headings that are centered on the page signal larger topical groupings. Within those larger groupings authors will use side-headings to signal subtopics and paragraph headings for topics within the subtopics. For example, Bevan uses the heading "Sexual Resistance as an Expectancy Violation" (p. 18). Within this section, she identifies two factors expected to make a difference in the expectations regarding sexual behavior and sexual resistance. These two factors are labeled in the two side-headings *"Relational Context"* (p. 18) and *"Message Directness"* (p. 19). Bevan uses paragraph headings in her methods section to identify the three different measures she used in her study. The *"Measures"* section is marked by a side heading (p. 21) and each type of measure is discussed in its own paragraph with a separate paragraph heading. For example, "perceived violation of expectancy" heads the paragraph in which these measures are discussed (p. 22).

Claims

Any assertion of a conclusion made by an author can be considered a claim (Toulmin, 1983). As such, you can expect to find claims in any section of a journal article however the content addressed by the claim will vary depending on where in the article the claim is located. We have identified seven content areas that describe a range of journal article claims. These may not be the only possible contents of claims, but they seem to be some of the most common.

Claims about what is known or believed to be true about a topic. Most journal articles are situated in a particular topic area, for example, organizational communication, romantic relationships, conflict, etc. In order to talk about that topic, authors need to make assertions about what they believe to be true. The very first sentence of Bevan's article is an example of this kind of claim-content. "Sexual resistance researchers have established that long-term romantic partners believe that they can expect success when initiating a sexual encounter" (p. 17). Note the specific wording of the claim, here. She is not claiming that romantic partners will always be successful with initiating sexual encounters, but only that there is evidence partners believe they are likely to be successful. Claims referencing this type of content will most often be found in the introduction and literature review sections of the journal article.

Claims about a theory. Authors may make assertions about the concepts used in a theory, how those concepts are defined, what claims or propositions the theory makes, what relationships it proposes, what assumptions it makes, and/or how the theory has changed over time. For example, Bevan makes some claims about how the term "expectancies" has been defined in several publications relating to Expectancy Violation theory (p. 18). Claims of this sort will also tend to be found in the introduction and literature review sections of the journal article.

Claims about limitations or criticisms of past theory or research. One way that authors can argue for the importance of their work is to point out problems in the existing literature. On page 18, Bevan claims that there is an omission in the literature on expectancy violations.

> Despite recent research on expectancy violations in cross-sex friendships (Afifi & Faulkner, 2000) and romantic relationships (Afifi & Metts, 1998), little is known about the effect of relational context on the interpretation of the violation (see Burgoon & Hale, 1988 for a comparison between friends and strangers).

In the next sentence she makes a claim about Expectancy Violation theory suggesting why this omission is problematic. "Such a query is important, as relationship aspects are important factors throughout the expectancy violation model proposed by Burgoon and Hale" (p. 18). This pair of sentences shows one example of how claims from different content areas (claims about a theory and claims about limitations or criticisms of past theory) can be sequenced together to form more complex arguments. As with the prior two content areas, claims about limitations or criticisms tend to be found in the introduction and literature review sections of articles.

Claims about the expectations for and/or importance of the conclusions of this article/study. In some ways, claims of this sort can be considered the central claims of a journal article. In quantitative research articles these claims may take the form of hypotheses and are usually found in the literature review. You will find Bevan's hypotheses on pages 19 and 20. Please note that hypotheses are not the only way claims of this type are stated.

Claims about the procedures and measures used in the study. These claims are typically found in the methods section of an article. They cover statements about who or what was studied, how the study data were gathered, how concepts were measured, and possibly how data were analyzed. Examples from Bevan include the claim that "participants read one of eight sexual resistance scenarios and then answered items intended to measure the realism and frequency of occurrence of the scenario in their own close relationships and items assessing perceived message directness and strength" (p. 21). This is a claim about the procedures followed in the study. An example of a claim about who was studied is found in the statement "Data were collected from a college-age sample taking introductory and advanced speech communication classes at a large, southern university" (p. 20). In both cases, Bevan is asserting something about the procedures used in this study.

Claims about the strengths and/or limitations of the study methods. Claims of this sort can take a variety of forms and tend to be found in either the methods or the discussion sections of articles. Claims about reliability or validity of measures and/or study procedures would fall under this content-area. For example, Bevan states "Because combining the realism items ($\alpha=.91$) and the frequency items ($\alpha=.88$) both resulted in internally consistent scales, two separate composite measures were computed" (p. 22). In this case, Bevan is both making a claim about the quality of the measures of realism and frequency and a claim about data analysis procedures. She claims both these measures to be internally consistent (a good thing), which is the claim about procedural strength. She then claims that the analytic procedures was to compute these two measures as separate scales and justifies this move based on the prior claim of internal consistency. An example of a claim about study limitations can also be found in Bevan. She states "the current study's failure to assess the impact of follow-up requests for sex or subsequent sexual resistance messages suggests that actual behavior in sexual resistance situations may not have been captured accurately" (pp. 27–28). This claim forms part of the discussion section argument and functions to qualify or set limits on the conclusions of the study.

Claims about what the study found and what those findings mean. In quantitative research articles claims about study findings will be found in the results section. Claims about the meaning of these findings will be found in the discussion section. In qualitative research both sorts of claims may be found in a combined results and interpretation section of the article. In Bevan's article, the statement "hence, H2 [Hypothesis two] was partially consistent with the data" (p. 25) is an example of a claim about the study's findings. While the statement "mounting evidence suggests that, across relational contexts, sexual resistance from a relational partner is fairly negative and unexpected for the resisted individual, regardless of the level of message directness employed" (p. 27) is an example of what the findings related to Hypothesis 2 in this study mean.

Data and Warrants

Authors draw on data and warrants to justify their claims, regardless of content area or type of claim (Toulmin, 1983). Data are the "facts" which form the basis of the claim. A warrant is "that part of an argument which authorizes the mental 'leap' involved in advancing from data to claim" (Golden, Berquist & Coleman, 1976, p. 289). Different forms of data and different types of warrants are used to justify different types of claims. In particular, the data and warrants supporting claims relating to research methods and results are topics elaborated on in classes and textbooks devoted to the study of research methods. As we cannot cover every possible form of data or type of warrant here, we will give you a sample of common types as a way of helping you understand what to look for in this part of an article's argument.

Source citations. With regard to truth claims, claims about a theory, and claims asserting criticism or limitations of past research or theory, citing other sources constitutes a major form of data. For example, when Bevan claims "when one violates a partner's expectations, the partner is likely to be more attentive toward future messages relating directly to the nature of the relationship" (p. 18), she cites LePoire and Burgoon, (1994) in parentheses following the statement of the claim. The argument here is that the publication by LePoire and Burgoon (1994) provides the evidence for Bevan's claim. The warrant, or reason why this link between data and claim is compelling, is based on the rule of thumb that published research is of good quality (remember the quality-control function of the peer-review process). In this case, the strength of the argument may also be affected by the reader's knowledge that Judee Burgoon was the original author of Expectancy Violation theory and that Beth LePoire was her student.

Statistics. With regard to claims about study findings and the strength or limitations of those findings, authors of quantitative research may use statistical presentations as ways of summarizing their data. For example, Bevan makes the claim "results indicated that dating partners perceived the sexual resistance message to be a violation that was significantly more negative than did cross-sex friends" (pg. 24). The data supporting this claim are presented in Table 3 on the same page (information about how to interpret the table can be found in the note directly underneath the table). The specific evidence relative to this claim is that the Mean Violation Valence for dating partners was higher, (M = 5.11) than for cross-sex friends (M = 4.73). These numbers mean that dating partners said that sexual resistance messages were more negative than cross-sex friends. The warrant connecting these means to the claim involves tests of statistical significance presented immediately following the claim "$F(1,294 = 8.07, p < .01, \eta^2 = .03$" (pg. 24). Now, this is a reader about communication theory, not a reader about statistics. So, suffice it to say that this line of numbers is intended as the statistical justification that this data does, in fact, support this claim.

Quotations from participants. Qualitative research tends to draw on interviews and focus groups for data rather than numerical responses to questions. Space limitations preclude authors from including transcripts from all the interviews conducted for a study. So, authors use sample quotations as evidence to illustrate and support the claims they make about themes or meanings present in the complete interview data-set. To the extent that the reader agrees with the author's interpretation of the given example, the claim made by the author is assumed to be supported.

Examples. When authors make claims about the procedures used in a study, one common form of evidence supporting those claims is to cite examples of those procedures. Bevan uses examples of questions from her questionnaire as evidence supporting her claims about the measures used in her study.

> Specifically, three items assessed how realistic the situation was (e.g., "How realistic do you think this situation is?"), and two items measured how often or frequently the participant had actually experienced a similar situation (e.g., "How often has this situation occurred in your own cross-sex friendship/dating relationship?"). (p. 21)

There are actually two pieces of argumentation going on here. The obvious one is that by providing an example measurement item as data, Bevan is demonstrating that she, in fact, had such a measure. Less obviously, Bevan is also providing evidence about the strength of her study's results. To the extent the reader agrees that the examples are good measures of the concepts in question, the reader is more likely to agree that Bevan's claims are based on high quality data.

Summary

The intent of this chapter has been to provide you with a road map, of sorts, for understanding journal articles. Hopefully you have also come to understand some of the process by which scholars articulate and justify theoretical and research arguments using a series of claim backed up by data and justified by warrants. We have used Bevan's (2003) article as an example throughout and in a few pages you will have a chance to read that article in full. Before you go on, however, we want to provide you with the same kind of introduction to Bevan's article that we will be using with the rest of the chapters in this book. Please note that the title of this section gives you a preview of the basic claim we will be making about this article. What forms of data do you see us using?

Expectations in Research: Mutual Influence of Research and Theory

Ways that sexual activity impacts on communication and relationships is the subject of increasing research interest (e.g. Afifi & Lee, 2000; Hughes, Morrison, & Asada, 2005; Motley & Reeder, 1995). The article by Jennifer Bevan extends Expectancy Violation theory to this growing research area.

Background of Expectancy Violation Theory

Expectancy Violation theory was developed as a way of understanding interaction dynamics regarding personal space (Burgoon & Jones, 1976; Burgoon, 1978). It is similar to several other theories (e.g. Communication Accommodation theory, Giles, Mulac, Bradac, & Johnson, 1987; Discrepancy Arousal theory, Cappella & Greene, 1984; Interaction Adaptation theory, Burgoon, Dillman, & Stern, 1993) in its assumption that we adapt to others as we interact with them. Burgoon's original formulation of this theory argued that we have predictions (called *expectancies*) about how another person is going to act in an interaction. When these predictions are not met, the theory says we have had an *expectancy violation*. The outcome of such a violation will depend on whether we see the violation and/or the person we are interacting with in a positive or a negative light. As can be seen in Bevan's article, Expectancy Violation theory has since been extended beyond its original personal space context to verbal and relational forms of communication.

Article Structure

The article begins with a summary of key terms from Expectancy Violation theory. It highlights a recent development in understanding how expectancy violations is interpreted and provides definitions of three concepts in this area: *violation valence, violation expectedness, and violation importance*. The next section of the paper develops Bevan's argument that sexual resistance constitutes an expectancy violation. She develops specific hypotheses that both relationship type (dating relationship or friendship relationship) and message directness will affect evaluations of violation valence, violation expectedness, and violation importance. Watch for how she justifies these predictions based both in aspects of EVT and in prior literature on sexual resistance. The rest of the article follows a standard format reporting on methods used in the study, results of the study, and a discussion of the results. In the discussion section, notice that Bevan explores the implications of her findings both for EVT and for our understanding of sexual resistance in relationships.

Distinctive Points

This article is a good example of how research is cumulative and how research and theory development are related. The specific 'news' of this article, as highlighted in the final paragraph of the article, is based on the distinction between the three violation dimensions. Bevan indicates that this work was initiated by Afifi and Metts (1998). Bevan's citation of this work as well as her citations of other studies done on sexual resistance demonstrates how prior research impacted on her study. In addition, by validating the conceptual change Afifi and Metts (1998) suggest for EVT, Bevan demonstrates how research findings can lead to changes in theoretical concepts. Articles like this are one reason why good theories don't stay the same—they change with new information in order to become more accurate and more useful.

References

Afifi, W. A., & Lee, J. W. (2000). Balancing instrumental and identity goals in relationships: The role of request directness and request persistence in the selection of sexual resistance strategies. *Communication Monographs, 67,* 284–306.

Afifi, W. A., & Metts, S. (1998). Characteristics and consequences of expectation violations in close relationships. *Journal of Social and Personal Relationships, 15,* 365–392.

Bevan, J. L. (2003). Expectancy violation theory and sexual resistance in close, cross-sex relationships. *Communication Monographs, 70,* 68–82.

Burgoon, J. K. (1978). A communication model of personal space violations: Explication and an initial test. *Human Communication Research, 4,* 129–142.

Burgoon, J. K., Dillman, L., & Stern, L. A. (1993). Adaptation in dyadic interaction: Defining and operationalizing patterns of reciprocity and compensation. *Communication Theory, 4,* 293–316.

Burgoon, J. K., & Jones, S. B. (1976). Toward a theory of personal space expectations and their violations. *Human Communication Research, 2,* 131–146.

Cappella, J. N., & Greene, J. O. (1984). The effects of distance and individual differences in arousability on nonverbal involvement: A test of discrepancy-arousal theory. *Journal of Nonverbal Behavior, 8,* 259–286.

Giles, H., Mulac, A., Bradac, J. J., & Johnson, P. (1987). Speech accommodatin theory: The next decade and beyond. In M. McLaughlin (Ed.), *Communication yearbook 10* (pp. 13–48). Newbury Park, CA: Sage.

Golden, J. L., Berquist, G. F., & Coleman, W. E. (1976). *The rhetoric of western thought, 2nd edition.* Dubuque, IA: Kendall/Hunt Publishing Company.

Hughes, M., Morrison, K., & Asada, K. J. K. (2005). What's love got to do with it? Exploring the impact of maintenance rules, love attitudes, and network support on friends with benefits relationships. *Western Journal of Communication, 69,* 49–66.

LePoire, B. A., & Burgoon, J. K. (1994). Two contrasting explanations of involvement violations: Expectancy violations theory versus discrepancy arousal theory. *Human Communication Research, 20,* 560–591.

Merrigan, G., & Huston, C. (2004). *Communication research methods.* Belmont, CA: Wadsworth.

Mongeau, P. A., & Carey, C. M. (1996). Who's wooing whom II? An experimental investigation of date-initiation and expectancy violation. *Western Journal of Communication, 60,* 195–204.

Motley, M. T., & Reeder, H. M. (1995). Unwanted escalation of sexual intimacy: Male and female perceptions of connotations and relational consequences of resistance messages. *Communication Monographs, 62,* 355–382.

Toulmin, S. (1983). *The uses of argument.* Cambridge, England: Cambridge University Press.

Expectancy Violation Theory and Sexual Resistance in Close, Cross-Sex Relationships

Jennifer L. Bevan

Although previous research has suggested a link between sexual resistance and the violation of the resisted partner's expectations, communication scholars have yet to utilize expectancy violation theory in a sexual resistance context. As such, the current study examines the resisted individual's perception of sexual resistance message directness and relational context in terms of three aspects of expectancy violations: violation valence, violation importance, and violation expectedness (Afifi & Metts, 1998). Findings indicate that participants view hypothetical sexual resistance from a long-term dating partner as a more negative and more unexpected expectancy violation compared with hypothetical rejection from a cross-sex friend. Further, when a participant is hypothetically rejected by way of direct communication of sexual resistance from his or her close relational partner, such a violation was perceived as more relationally important than indirect sexual resistance. These findings broaden the scope of expectancy violation theory to include sexual resistance in close relationships, replicate and validate the study of three separate expectancy violation aspects, and highlight sexual resistance as a potentially important relational event in close relationships.

Sexual resistance researchers have established that long-term romantic partners believe that they can expect success when initiating a sexual encounter (Byers & Heinlein, 1989). Further, new dating partners find sexual resistance to be more unexpected than do either cross-sex friends or individuals in ambiguous male–female relationships (Metts, Cupach, & Imahori, 1992). Despite these findings, no known research has specifically linked the study of sexual resistance to expectancy violation theory (EVT). To provide theoretical insight into the degree to which sexual resistance is expected across close male–female relational contexts, the current study examines the level of directness of a sexual resistance message and the relational context the message occurs in from the resisted individual's perspective within an EVT framework.

Expectancy Violation Theory

The field of communication has been instrumental in integrating theoretical foundations into investigations of sexual compliance/resistance situations. Specifically, aspects of politeness theory and facework (Afifi & Lee, 2000; Metts et al., 1992), uncertainty reduction theory (Edgar, Freimuth,

---

From COMMUNICATION MONOGRAPHS, VOL 70, ISSUE 1, MARCH 2003 by J.L. Bevan. Copyright © 2003 by Taylor & Francis Ltd, http://www.tandf.co.uk/journals. Reprinted by permission.

Jennifer L. Bevan (PhD, University of Georgia) assumed her duties as Assistant Professor at the Hank Greenspun School of Communication, University of Nevada at Las Vegas, on 1 August 2003. The author wishes to thank Jerry Hale, Jennifer Monahan, Kenzie Cameron, and the anonymous reviewers for their helpful comments on the manuscript. An earlier version of this paper was presented in 2002 at the annual meeting of the National Communication Association in New Orleans, LA, where it was awarded Top Student Paper in the Interpersonal Communication Division. Contact information: 4505 Maryland Parkway, Box 455007, Las Vegas, NV, 89154-5007; e-mail: jenbev34@ yahoo.com

Hammond, McDonald, & Fink, 1992), and planning theory (Afifi & Lee, 2000) have been examined in relation to sexual compliance/resistance. Consistent with this theoretical interest in communication and sexual resistance, the current study utilizes an EVT framework.

Generally, expectancies can be conceptualized as framing devices that help both to characterize and structure interpersonal interactions and affect consequent information processing, behavior, and perceptions (Burgoon, 1993; Burgoon & Hale, 1988). Communication expectancies denote "an enduring pattern of anticipated behavior" and can be individualized to a specific person or relationship (Burgoon, 1993, p. 31). An expectation of another is violated when that behavior differs from what is typical or expected (Afifi & Metts, 1998). Such a violation results in cognitive arousal and a sequence of interpretation and evaluation that aids an individual in coping with the other's unexpected behavior (Afifi & Metts, 1998). Moreover, when one violates a partner's expectations, the partner is likely to be more attentive toward future messages relating directly to the nature of the relationship (LePoire & Burgoon, 1994).

In the interpretation stage of the EVT model the valence of an expectancy violation is established and contributes to the overall assessment of how rewarding an interaction will be (Burgoon, 1993; Burgoon & Hale, 1988). Afifi and Metts (1998) have recently expanded EVT to include three separate, but related, aspects of how expectancy violations are interpreted: (a) *violation valence,* involving the extent to which the behavior is seen as positive or negative, (b) *violation expectedness,* defined as the extent to which the behavior varies from the range of expected behaviors, and (c) *violation importance,* characterized as the impact that the behavior will have on the relationship. This study extends these dimensions to the realm of sexual resistance.

Sexual Resistance as an Expectancy Violation

No known research has extended EVT to the study of sexual resistance between close relational partners. Nevertheless, Afifi and Lee (2000, p. 299) note that "sexual resistance is likely a task that produces considerable uncertainty, cognitive demands, time-constrained information processing, and online adaptation," characteristics that are similar to the cognitive arousal, interpretation, and evaluation that often accompanies a partner's unexpected behavior (Afifi & Metts, 1998). Further, sexual resistance is a situation that is highly vulnerable, volatile, emotionally sensitive, and accompanied by heightened emotional states and unique physiological changes (Edgar & Fitzpatrick, 1988, 1990). Choices in sexual situations (such as resisting a close partner's advances) could be caused by differing sexual goals and often result in conflict, frustration, and embarrassment for one or both partners (Edgar & Fitzpatrick, 1988, 1990; Sprecher & McKinney, 1993). These characteristics of sexual resistance suggest strongly that its occurrence will result in the resisted parties believing that their expectancies have been violated. Two aspects of the sexual resistance situation—relational context and message directness—are particularly salient when considering sexual resistance as an expectancy violation because they have been useful concepts in previous sexual resistance research (e.g., Goldenberg, Ginexi, Sigelman, & Poppen, 1999; Metts et al., 1992) and because relational characteristics and communication behavior represent two important considerations in EVT (Burgoon & Hale, 1988).

Relational Context

Despite recent research on expectancy violations in cross-sex friendships (Afifi & Faulkner, 2000) and romantic relationships (Afifi & Metts, 1998), little is known about the effect of relational context on the interpretation of the violation (see Burgoon & Hale, 1988 for a comparison between friends and strangers). Such a query is important, as relationship aspects are important factors throughout the expectancy violation model proposed by Burgoon and Hale. Specifically, relational characteristics such as prior history and liking are considered when one partner decides whether or not the other's behavior is an expectancy violation (Burgoon & Hale, 1988). One relational characteristic that seems important throughout the EVT process is the type of relationship the partners share. Put differently, societal and individual definitions of the relationship, acceptable behaviors between the partners, and implicit relational boundaries will likely play a significant role in how one interprets an expectancy violation. Thus, the role of relational context in the interpretation (i.e., violation importance, valence, and expectedness) of expectancy violations logically advances knowledge both about EVT as a theory and the consideration of expectancy violations as three separate aspects.

Though not specifically examining sexual resistance, Afifi and Faulkner (2000) found that the presence of sexual activity in cross-sex friendships varied in impact according to both the violation valence ascribed to the behavior and the extent to which the friend's feelings and intentions after the sexual episode were known. Specifically, cross-sex friends tended to use positive politeness strategies to resist sexual advances, possibly both to maintain the friendship and communicate sexual disinterest (Lee, 2001). Metts et al. (1992) found that sexual rejections occurring in new dating relationships were less expected, more face threatening, and more uncomfortable than rejections occurring in established, long-term cross-sex friendships and ambiguous male–female relationships. The current study extends Metts et al.'s research by comparing two long-term close relationships, and by considering sexual resistance as an expectancy violation instead of as a face threat. Overall, sexual resistance between cross-sex friends is likely to have a significant impact because sexual interest and activity are moderately frequent but often ambiguous and confusing for both partners (Metts et al., 1992).

When considering long-term romantic relationships, Byers and Heinlein (1989) found that co-habiting couples were more likely than spouses to initiate sexual intercourse. Further, Quinn, Sanchez-Hucles, Coates, and Gillen (1991) found that males in long-term relationships would stop sexual advances such as overt attempts to kiss and fondle their partners more readily than those in short-term partnerships. Thus, preliminary evidence suggests that long-term romantic partners exhibit unique sexual compliance/resistance patterns. Little is known, however, about how long-term romantic partners perceive sexual resistance within their relationships.

When comparing dating partners and cross-sex friends, sexual resistance between dating partners should be more negative, unexpected, and relationally important compared with cross-sex friends. Because individuals in long-term romantic relationships were rarely *unsuccessful* in sexual initiations and are aware of their partners' response to a sexual advance (Byers & Heinlein, 1989), long-term dating partners will likely initiate a sexual encounter when they think the chances of success are high. In contrast, cross-sex friends are likely to view sexual resistance as a less negative, more expected, and less relationally important violation than daters because their relational definition does not include sexual behavior and their knowledge of friends' receptivity to sexual advances is likely to be fairly limited. The first hypothesis explores this possibility:

H1: Those being resisted by a dating partner will perceive sexual resistance as an expectancy violation that is (a) more negative, (b) more unexpected, and (c) more important than will those being resisted by a cross-sex friend.

Message Directness

In addition to relational context, message directness is relevant to the application of EVT to sexual resistance situations. Direct strategies in sexual situations indicate messages with clear intent and no ambiguity about what the persuader would like to occur, whereas indirect sexual tactics leave more room for doubt about the persuader's intentions, providing him or her with plausible deniability (Edgar & Fitzpatrick, 1990). Both Afifi and Lee (2000) and Metts et al. (1992) have found that participants preferred using direct sexual resistance messages that were also instrumental in protecting the face of the resisted individual (i.e., "I'm not sure that we're ready for this").

In his language expectancy theory Burgoon (1995) proposes that individuals hold expectations about language that can affect whether or not they accept or reject a persuasive message. Consistent with this idea, the level of message directness from the individual resisting another's sexual advance is believed to be a potentially important consideration for the resisted individual when interpreting an expectancy violation. Learning about the relationship between message directness and expectancy violation interpretation in the sexual resistance context is important for two reasons. First, comparing direct and indirect sexual resistance messages potentially expands the scope of EVT to include a new communicative antecedent of the expectancy violation process. Second, research by Mongeau and Carey (1996) on date initiation and expectancy violation theory suggested that whether one person initiated the date indirectly (i.e., hinting) or directly (i.e., asking) was partially responsible for the other's expectancy violation with regard to the amount of sexual behaviors enacted on the date. This research suggests that a more focused inquiry into message directness and EVT is justified.

When considering the relational implications of sexual resistance message directness, Goldenberg et al. (1999), in comparing sexual resistance patterns in males and females and American and Japanese cultures, demonstrated the positive relationship between use of indirect refusal strategies and the continuation of one's new dating relationship. Goldenberg et al. focused upon new dating relationships and the participant cultural and gender differences when exploring sexual resistance message directness, which differentiates their research from the current project. Pertinent to EVT, Mongeau and Carey (1996) reported that males had significantly higher sexual expectations when females directly asked them on a date, compared to the female indirectly hinting at date initiation. Even in long-term relationships, how directly sexual resistance is communicated can be related strongly to how that expectancy violation is interpreted. Thus, indirect sexual resistance should be perceived by long-term relational partners who are sexually resisted as a violation that is less negative, more expected, and less relationally important compared with direct sexual resistance. The second hypothesis examines this relationship:

> H2: Both cross-sex friends and dating partners who are resisted will perceive partners' use of a direct sexual resistance message to be an expectancy violation that is (a) more negative, (b) more unexpected, and (c) more important compared to indirect sexual resistance messages.

Method

Participants

Data were collected from a college-age sample taking introductory and advanced speech communication classes at a large, southern university. The initial sample size was 342, but the elimination of individuals who did not respond to, or incorrectly answered, manipulation check items resulted in a final sample size of 307. Approximately 57% of the sample was female ($n = 174$), with two individuals not reporting gender. The average age of the sample was 21 years ($SD = 2.63$, range = 18–50). Almost 89% of the sample classified themselves as White ($n = 272$), 6% classified themselves as African American ($n = 19$), almost 2% indicated that they were either Asian ($n = 5$) or Hispanic ($n = 5$), and 1% placed themselves in the "other" category ($n = 4$). Two participants did not report their ethnicity.

All participants reported that they were either straight ($n = 306$) or bisexual ($n = 1$). Almost 39% of the sample reported being single and not dating ($n = 119$), 27% indicated that they have been involved in a committed relationship for more than 1 year ($n = 82$), 15% stated that they were single and dating one person ($n = 45$), 10% reported that they were single and dating many individuals ($n = 31$), and 9% indicated that they were in a committed relationship for less than 1 year ($n = 29$). One participant did not provide current relational status information. Finally, 69% of the sample reported that they had previously engaged in vaginal sex ($n = 213$) and almost 30% reported that they had not yet had vaginal intercourse ($n = 91$). Three participants did not respond to this item.

General Procedures

Participants received course research credit for taking part in the research. Their participation was voluntary and anonymous. Participants read and signed the consent form, and were then given the opportunity to ask questions about the project. To ensure privacy the researcher asked participants to not speak to one another while they were answering the questionnaire and also not to look at other students' surveys. Participants then were given the written questionnaire, and told to take as long as they needed to complete it (15 minutes was typical).

Participants read one of eight sexual resistance scenarios and then answered items intended to measure the realism and frequency of occurrence of the scenario in their own close relationships and items assessing perceived message directness and strength. The relevant dependent variable scales (violation valence, violation expectedness, violation importance) followed, along with two manipulation check items that measured the gender and relational context of the rejector in the resistance scenario, items measuring participants' level of sexual experience, current relational status, and demographic information. After they had completed the instrument, participants were given a debriefing form and an opportunity to ask questions about the research before being thanked and dismissed.

Research Design and Pilot Test

The investigation employed a 2 (relational context: long-term cross-sex friend vs. long-term dating relationship) $\times$ 2 (message directness: indirect vs. direct) factorial design. The message directness independent variable was replicated so that a total of eight hypothetical scenarios were distributed randomly to participants, resulting in relatively equal distribution across conditions.

The scenarios, adapted from Metts et al. (1992), asked participants to imagine that they are either friends with or dating an individual named Chris, and then detailed a situation in which the participants feel a sexual desire for Chris, attempt to initiate a sexual encounter, and are resisted. The use of hypothetical scenarios was employed to avoid participant biases in the recall and memory of actual sexual resistance situations that often accompany retrospective recall techniques, and to measure simultaneously participants' immediate and direct response to the relational event of interest and provide control over the specific situations the participants were to consider (Knobloch & Solomon, 2002).

To select four resistance messages that were fairly equal in levels of strength and directness for each manipulation, a total of 10 resistance messages classified previously as direct or indirect by a variety of sources (Garcia, 1998; Metts et al., 1992; Motley & Reeder, 1995; Muehlenhard, Andrews, & Beal, 1996) were pilot tested using undergraduates taking speech communication classes at a large, southern university ($N = 50$, 50% female). Each participant was asked to read six of the 10 potential messages and then indicate how direct and strong they found each message to be, using 7-point, Likert-type scales (e.g., 1 = "not at all direct", 7 = "completely direct"). The number of participants who were exposed to each potential resistance message ranged from 25 to 30.

A series of t-tests revealed that two indirect messages produced levels of strength that were statistically equivalent to one another and significantly more indirect than the direct messages: (1) "It's getting late"; and (2) "He/she does not appear to notice your advances and instead asks you to change the channel on the television." Further, two direct messages proved to have statistically equivalent amounts of strength and were also significantly more direct and strong than each of the indirect messages: (1) "Please don't do that"; and (2) "I don't want to do this." Thus, these four resistance messages were used in the main investigation.

Measures

Scenario realism and frequency of occurrence. A number of items about the sexual resistance situation itself, adapted from Bevan (1999) and Canary, Cody, and Marston (1987), were presented. Specifically, three items assessed how realistic the situation was (e.g., "How realistic do you think this situation is?"), and two items measured how often or frequently the participant had actually experienced a similar situation (e.g., "How often has this situation occurred in your own cross-sex friendship/dating relationship?"). All items were measured on 7-point, Likert-type scales (e.g., 1 = "not at all realistic", 7 = "very realistic"). As Table 1 depicts, participants found each of the eight scenarios to be re-

TABLE 1

Means and Standard Deviations by Experimental Condition for Scenario Realism, Frequency of Occurrence, Directness, and Strength

CONDITION	REALISM	FREQUENCY	DIRECTNESS	STRENGTH
Cross-sex, "I don't want to do this."	5.53[a,b]	2.00[a]	5.61[b]	2.59[b]
	(1.74)	(1.32)	(1.70)	(1.61)
Cross-sex, "Please don't do that."	5.60[a,b]	2.54[a]	5.80[b]	2.57[b]
	(1.72)	(1.59)	(1.43)	(1.43)
Cross-sex, "It's getting late."	5.79[a]	2.23[a]	4.32[a]	3.74[a]
	(1.65)	(1.33)	(1.68)	(1.37)
Cross-sex, watches TV to ignore advances	5.24[a,b]	2.52[a]	3.74[a]	4.42[a]
	(1.81)	(1.33)	(1.54)	(1.31)
Dating, "I don't want to do this."	3.80[b]	1.56[a]	5.71[b]	2.00[b]
	(2.21)	(1.02)	(1.77)	(.927)
Dating, "Please don't do that."	5.33[a,b]	1.71[a]	5.49[b]	2.43[b]
	(1.88)	(1.22)	(1.77)	(1.37)
Dating, "It's getting late."	5.21[a,b]	2.30[a]	4.15[a]	3.67[a]
	(1.41)	(1.64)	(1.73)	(1.43)
Dating, watches TV to ignore advances	5.00[a,b]	2.17[a]	3.60[a]	3.58[a]
	(1.90)	(1.46)	(1.52)	(1.58)
Marginal	5.21	2.10	4.78	3.13
	(1.81)	(1.36)	(1.85)	(1.57)

Note. N = 307. Within columns, means with superscripts in common do not differ significantly at *p* < .05. Values in parentheses represents standard deviations. Higher values (on a 7-point scale) indicate greater amounts of realism, actual occurrence, perceived message directness, and lower amounts of perceived message strength.

alistic and easy to imagine, but did not experience these resistance situations frequently in their own close relationships. Because combining the realism items (α = .91) and the frequency items (α = .88) both resulted in internally consistent scales, two separate composite measures were computed.

Sexual resistance message strength and directness. Strength and directness of the resistance messages were measured using items from Cameron (1998). One semantic differential item assessed message directness on a 7-point scale (1 = "indirect", 7 = "direct"). Two semantic differential items measured message strength on a 7-point scale (1 = "strong", 7 = "weak"). Because the internal consistency for the two strength items was strong (α = .90), a composite measure of message strength was computed (see Table 1).

Perceived violation of expectancy. Three scales developed by Afifi and Metts (1998) were used to measure perceived violation of expectancy. All expectancy violation items were measured on 7-point, Likert-type scales such that higher values indicate that the violation is more unexpected, more important, and more negative. Violation valence (e.g., "Chris's behavior was a very positive/ very negative behavior") was measured by a four-item scale (α = .86) and violation importance (e.g., "Chris's behavior was a minor/major relational event") was measured by two items (α = .79). Violation expectedness (e.g., "Chris's behavior was completely expected/completely unexpected") was originally measured using three items but a typographical error for one item resulted in incorrect measurement of the variable, and this item was removed from further analysis (α = .78). Three composite expectancy violation variables were then computed for analysis.

Results

Preliminary Analyses

Combining the message directness conditions. To determine if the eight sexual resistance messages could be combined into four total message directness conditions, two one-way ANOVAs were conducted, each with experimental condition as the fixed factor and either the message directness item or the combined message strength item as the dependent variables. Results showed that significant main effects were present for message directness, $F(7, 338) = 13.23$, $p < .0001$, $\eta^2 = .22$, and for message strength, $F(7, 338) = 13.68$, $p < .0001$, $\eta^2 = .22$.

Post hoc tests (all of which utilized the Tukey HSD technique) found that each of the four indirect conditions did not significantly differ from one another, but were perceived by participants to be significantly less direct and significantly weaker in strength than the four direct message conditions, which did not significantly differ from one another. Thus, the message conditions were collapsed within direct and indirect conditions and four combined experimental conditions—dating partner/direct, dating partner/indirect, cross-sex friend/direct, and cross-sex friend/indirect—were examined.

Manipulation success. A one-item manipulation check revealed that 95% of the original 342 participants ($n = 324$) correctly identified Chris as a person of the opposite sex, and only those individuals were retained for data analysis. Additionally, a second one-item manipulation check asked participants to identify the type of relationship and it was found that 94% of the original sample identified correctly the relational context identified in the scenario ($n = 321$). Again, only these participants were retained for data analysis. The size of the remaining sample was 310.

Next, the success of the message directness manipulation was assessed. Two two-way analyses of variance with relational context and type of message as the fixed factors and either the message directness item or the message strength composite variable as the dependent variable were conducted. For message directness, a significant main effect for message type was observed, $F(1, 303) = 81.64$, $p < .0001$, $\eta^2 = .21$, such that the direct messages were viewed as significantly more direct than the indirect messages. Significant effects were not observed for either relational context, $F(1, 303) = .48$, $p = .49$, $\eta^2 = .002$, or the relational context-message type interaction, $F(1, 303) = .03$, $p = .86$, $\eta^2 = .00$. For message strength, the main effects for both relational context, $F(1, 303) = 6.70$, $p < .05$, $\eta^2 = .02$, and message type, $F(1, 303) = 83.03$, $p < .0001$, $\eta^2 = .22$, were significant. The direct messages were significantly stronger than the indirect messages and the dating partner messagges were significantly stronger than the cross-sex friend messages (though the effect size for relational context was weak). The relational context-message type interaction was not significant for message strength, $F(1, 303) = .09$, $p = -.76$, $\eta^2 = .00$ (see Table 2). Because three participants did not answer the message directness item and were deleted from subsequent analyses, the final sample was 307.

TABLE 2

Means and Standard Deviations by Combined Experimental Conditions for Message Directness and Message Strength

	MESSAGE DIRECTNESS		MESSAGE STRENGTH	
CONDITION	M	SD	M	SD
Relational Context Condition				
Cross-Sex Friend	4.87[a]	1.80	3.33[b]	1.63
Dating Partner	4.73[a]	1.90	2.92[a]	1.53
Message Directness Condition				
Direct Resistance	5.63[a]	1.67	2.40[a]	1.37
Indirect Resistance	3.95[b]	1.63	3.86[b]	1.46
Marginal	4.78	1.85	3.13	1.59

Note. $N = 307$. Within columns, means with superscript letters in common do not differ significantly at $p < .05$. Higher values (on a 7-point scale) indicate greater amounts of perceived message directness and lower amounts of perceived message strength.

Analysis Plan and Covariates

Because almost one third of the sample had not yet had vaginal intercourse ($n = 99$), whether or not the participant had engaged in vaginal intercourse was entered as a covariate.[1] Hence, univariate ANCOVAs were performed for all analyses. Only statistically significant covariates are reported in the text.

Hypothesis One

H1 predicted that those whose sexual advances were resisted by dating partners would perceive that such an expectancy violation would be (a) more negative in valence, (b) more unexpected, and (c) more relationally important than those who were resisted by cross-sex friends. Three univariate ANCOVAs were conducted to test these predictions, with type of relationship as the fixed factor, number of vaginal intercourse partners as the covariate, and violation valence, violation expectedness, or violation importance as the dependent variables.

Results indicated (see Table 3) that dating partners perceived the sexual resistance message to be a violation that was significantly more negative than did cross-sex friends, $F(1, 294) = 8.07$, $p < .01$, $\eta^2 = .03$. In addition, results suggested that dating partners also viewed sexual resistance as a violation that was more unexpected than did cross-sex friends, $F(1, 294) = 7.31$, $p < .01$, $\eta^2 = .02$. Effect sizes do suggest, however, that these effects are small. For H1c, cross-sex friends were found to perceive sexual resistance as a significantly more relationally important violation than did dating partners, $F(1, 294) = 6.99$, $p < .01$, $\eta^2 = .02$, a finding *opposite* of what was predicted. The relational importance covariate was significant, $F(1, 294) = 4.18$, $p < .05$, partial $\eta^2 = .01$. Therefore, the data were consistent with H1a and H1b, but not with H1c.

Hypothesis Two

The second hypothesis stated that direct sexual resistance messages received from both cross-sex friends and dating partners will be viewed as (a) more negative, (b) more unexpected, and (c) more relationally important than indirect sexual resistance messages. H2 was analyzed by way of

TABLE 3

Means and Standard Deviations by Independent Variable and Experimental Condition for Expectancy Violation Importance, Valence, and Expectedness

	VIOIMP	VIOVAL	VIOEXP
Relational Context Condition			
Cross-Sex Friend	5.29[a]	4.73[b]	4.23[b]
	(1.15)	(1.04)	(1.23)
Dating Partner	4.93[b]	5.11[a]	4.79[a]
	(1.43)	(1.30)	(1.92)
Message Directness Condition			
Direct Resistance	5.45[a]	4.88[a]	4.65[a]
	(1.22)	(1.33)	(1.79)
Indirect Resistance	4.72[b]	4.96[a]	4.39[a]
	(1.42)	(1.05)	(1.53)
Marginal	5.11	4.92	4.52
	(1.29)	(1.16)	(1.60)

Note. $N = 307$. VioImp = Violation Importance, VioVal = Violation Valence, VioExp = Violation Expectedness. Within columns and conditions, means with superscripts in common do not differ significantly at $p < .05$. Values in parentheses represent standard deviations. Each mean was on a 7-point scale, with higher values indicating violations that are more negative, more important, and less expected.

three univariate ANCOVAs with type of message as the fixed factor, number of vaginal sex partners as the covariate, and either violation valence, violation expectedness, or violation importance as the dependent variables.

Results revealed that levels of violation valence did not significantly differ, $F(1, 294) = .42$, $p = .52$, $\eta^2 = .001$ according to whether the sexual resistance message was direct or indirect. Further, levels of violation expectedness did not vary significantly according to the directness of the sexual resistance message, although the means were in the predicted direction, $F(1, 294) = 1.81$, $p = .18$, $\eta^2 = .006$. Results showed that levels of relational importance did significantly differ, $F(1, 294) = 22.64$, $p < .0001$, $\eta^2 = .07$, such that those exposed to direct sexual resistance messages viewed the expectancy violation to be more relationally important than those receiving the indirect sexual resistance messages. Hence, H2 was partially consistent with the data.

Discussion

The main purpose of the present investigation was to examine sexual resistance as an expectancy violation in close male–female relationships. Specifically, this investigation was motivated by three overarching goals: (a) to assess the influence of relational context and message directness in the resisted individual's perception of the partner's resistance within the structure of expectancy violation theory, (b) to examine the three separate aspects of expectancy violations in a sexual resistance context, and (c) to gain deeper insight into sexual resistance in close relationships. Encouraging results were attained for each of these goals and are discussed in detail below.

Aspects of Expectancy Violations

Because preliminary research suggested that both nonromantic relational partners (Metts et al., 1992) and long-term dating partners (Byers & Heinlein, 1989) might view sexual resistance as a violation of expectations for the partner and the relationship, these relational contexts were applied to three violation dimensions arising from expectancy violation theory. Further, as communication message characteristics have consistently been associated with differential perceptions of expectancy violations (e.g., Afifi & Faulkner, 2000; Burgoon & Hale, 1988; Mongeau & Carey, 1996), the directness of the sexual resistance message was investigated from an EVT perspective. The predictions made about relational context and message directness expand the scope of EVT to include sexual resistance in close relationships. Specifically, both the relational context and message directness concepts proved fruitful for understanding and expanding the scope of the expectancy violation process.

For the resisted individual similar patterns were observed between relational context and perceptions of violation valence and unexpectedness. In contrast, message directness was only significantly related to the violation's importance to the relationship. Specifically, daters found sexual resistance to be a more negatively valenced and unexpected violation than cross-sex friends. Cross-sex friends, however, found sexual resistance to be more relationally important than did dating partners. For message directness, direct sexual resistance was interpreted as significantly more important to the relationship than indirect resistance. No variations in violation valence or expectedness were observed for message directness.

Afifi and Metts (1998) report conceptual distinctness between violation importance and violation expectedness; the current results replicate this difference and extend it to the realm of sexual resistance. Yet, Afifi and Metts did not assess similarities between violation valence and the other two violation aspects. The present findings indicate that, in sexual resistance situations, patterns for violation valence and unexpectedness are similar to one another and both are distinct from violation importance. Whether these associations between the violation aspects are unique to the sexual resistance situation or consistent across contexts is unknown. Other expectancy violations (i.e., the support and confirmation or acts of devotion violation types described by Afifi & Metts) might be positive but unexpected and thus be conceptually distinct under different circumstances. Future research should attempt to extend the relationships found here into these different communication contexts.

Relational Context

The current research introduces relational context as a useful consideration in the EVT sequence. Specifically, those resisted by dating partners viewed such a situation as an expectancy violation that was more negative (H1a) and unexpected (H1b) than individuals resisted by cross-sex friends. These findings are consistent with the idea that cross-sex friendships are not inherently defined by romance or sexuality (e.g., Afifi & Burgoon, 1998; Monsour, 2002), and are also consistent with Metts et al. (1992), who reported that being sexually resisted by a new dating partner was more unexpected and uncomfortable than being resisted by a cross-sex friend. H1a's and H1b's results can be explained by the idea that, because romantic partners believe that they know when and when not to initiate a sexual encounter (Byers & Heinlein, 1989), dating partners who are resisted are likely to view it as particularly unexpected and negative. In other words, sexual resistance between dating partners is more unexpected and negative than for cross-sex friends because dating partners believe that they are well acquainted with each other's "red lights" and "green lights" when initiating a sexual encounter. Overall, the tenets of EVT appear useful in better understanding previous research on sexual resistance in both cross-sex friendships and romantic relationships.

In contrast to H1a and H1b cross-sex friends found sexual resistance to be a *more* relationally important violation than did dating partners (H1c). Consistent with the idea that sexual involvement between cross-sex friends can have negative implications (Afifi & Faulkner, 2000), sexual resistance from a cross-sex friend is an expectancy violation that might be important to the resisted individual's view of the relationship. The decision to initiate a sexual encounter with a cross-sex friend is probably considered ahead of time and only attempted when the chances of success appear high. Upon resistance, one or both friends may ask themselves if the friendship will be able to overcome such an uncomfortable situation.

Communication that is out of character for an individual can threaten another's face (Cupach & Metts, 1994) or create an uncomfortable situation that immediately changes the nature of an interaction (Goffman, 1959). As such, impression management and facework are useful theoretical concepts in interpreting these data and should be employed in future expectancy violation and sexual resistance research. However, compared with these theories, EVT uniquely explains these findings because it accounts for the relational impact of sexual resistance (i.e., relational importance).

H1c's findings are also better understood when considered in terms of attribution theory. Recent research has found that expectancy violating changes in affectionate behavior in same- and cross-sex friendships tended to be attributed to external, uncontrollable causes (Floyd & Voludakis, 1999). Similarly, the resisted dating partner may attribute the sexual resistance by the other partner to an external cause rather than an internal reason (i.e., "My partner is too tired from working so hard" versus "My partner is not sexually attracted to me"). Put another way, compared with cross-sex friends, it is less likely that a single instance of sexual resistance would cause dating partners to be concerned about the future status of their relationship. Both Floyd and Voludakis' findings and the current interpretation of H1c suggest that future research employing attribution theory to explain expectancy violations, such as sexual resistance, will be fruitful.

This study's finding that relational context is more important than message directness both defies the focus on message impact in previous sexual resistance research (e.g., Goldenberg et al., 1999; Lee, 2001; Muehlenhard et al., 1996) and supports the continued study of how the type of relationship sexual resistance occurs in relation to the perception of resistance. The type of relationship in which a violation occurs is instrumental throughout the EVT process (Burgoon, 1993; Burgoon & Hale, 1988), but the specific role of relational context had not been investigated. The importance of relational context as an antecedent variable is logical and informative for the understanding of how expectancy violations are perceived and interpreted and can logically be extended to include additional relational outcomes of sexual resistance such as sexual and relational satisfaction, relational closeness, topic avoidance, and patterns of sexual communication and interpersonal conflict.

Message Directness

Message directness findings also provided insight into expectancy violation theory. Varying levels of violation unexpectedness and valence are not associated with level of sexual resistance message directness (H2a and H2b). Closer scrutiny of Metts et al. (1992) revealed no significant differences in the amount of predictability (a concept similar to expectedness) between a direct sexual resistance message (i.e., participants were told that a hypothetical partner was not sexually attracted to them) and an indirect resistance message identical to one used in the present study (i.e., the relational partner ignores the participant's sexual advance and changes the television channel). A similar line of reasoning can be applied to the valence of the sexual resistance message. Thus, mounting evidence suggests that, across relational contexts, sexual resistance from a relational partner is fairly negative and unexpected for the resisted individual, regardless of the level of message directness employed. Further, this failure to detect differences in violation valence and expectedness according to message directness levels again emphasizes the importance of relational context in one's evaluation of being resisted by a long-term relational partner.

H2c found that a partner's use of a direct sexual resistance message in a close relationship is a more relationally important violation compared with an indirect message. Overall, research suggests that direct resistance messages have the potential to be fairly damaging. Namely, direct resistance messages have the potential to be more face threatening (Afifi & Lee, 2000; Metts et al., 1992) as well as more of a threat to the continuation of one's dating relationship (Goldenberg et al., 1999) compared with an indirect resistance strategy. The resisted partner's interpretation of direct sexual resistance as a more relationally important expectancy violation than an indirect message can also be considered as a negative implication of directly resisting one's partner.

In sum, these findings establish message directness as an additional communication variable that is employed when interpreting another's behavior as an expectancy violation. Moreover, because the majority of the messages examined in the current study were verbal in nature, EVT can be extended to explain both verbal and nonverbal components of a sexual resistance interaction. Future research should consider the role of both relational context and message directness in all aspects of the EVT process.

The Impact of Sexual Resistance in Close Relationships

Edgar and Fitzpatrick (1988, 1990) speak of sexual compliance/resistance situations as potentially embarrassing, volatile, emotional, and conflict laden for one or both partners. Consistent with this claim, those who were hypothetically resisted by close dating partners or cross-sex friends believed sexual resistance constituted a moderately negative, unexpected, and relationally important expectancy violation in their relationships. Though specific hypotheses were not forwarded, means for each of the three violation dimensions were significantly higher than the scale's 4.0 midpoint, violation valence $t(306) = 13.68$, $p < .0001$, violation expectedness $t(306) = 5.40$, $p < .0001$, violation importance $t(306) = 14.15$, $p < .0001$.

Though strong conclusions cannot be drawn from this set of findings, preliminary evidence supports the idea that even long-term partnerships are negatively impacted from one instance of sexual resistance. Such an event could potentially be characterized as a negative turning point in the partners' relationship (Baxter & Bullis, 1986). If such behavior becomes a consistent pattern, sexual resistance could become a significant relational event that leads to decreased relational satisfaction, interpersonal conflict, the creation of a taboo topic, or even relational termination. Therefore, how close relational partners communicatively manage sexual resistance should continue to be an important focus of future sexual resistance research.

Limitations and Conclusions

A number of limitations must be kept in mind when considering the findings of the present investigation. First, the current study's failure to assess the impact of follow-up requests for sex or subsequent sexual resistance messages suggests that actual behavior in sexual resistance situations may not have been captured accurately. As with recent research (e.g., Afifi & Lee, 2000), future research should measure request persistence as well as continuing attempts to resist sexual advances.

A second limitation involves the nature of the sample examined. Approximately one third of the participants reported never having engaged in vaginal sex, suggesting that many respondents may not have had the capacity or experience to place themselves into the sexual resistance scenarios. Although attempts to correct this limitation were undertaken in the present study, subsequent research should gather a sample of individuals who have had sufficient sexual experience.

A final limitation concerns the low levels of statistical power for the significance tests. These levels of power (which ranged from .10 to .43) could have prevented significant findings from emerging. Despite low effect sizes, some statistically significant effects were found for every dependent variable. Future research should increase the statistical power of significance tests so that one may have more confidence in the null findings if they recur.

In sum, the study of sexual resistance in close relationships was informed by its application to expectancy violation theory. Specifically, the current results supported the idea that a single instance of sexual resistance is indeed an expectancy violation that can affect the resisted individual's view of the relationship. Further, conceiving of sexual resistance from an expectancy violation theory lens both expanded the theory's scope and provided a useful framework for understanding how the type of relationship and the way resistance is communicated are related to the resisted individual's interpretation of the violation. The current results both validate Afifi and Metts (1998) three violation dimensions as separate theoretical constructs and introduce avenues for future theoretical inquiry into sexual resistance in close relationships. Most importantly, these findings contribute useful knowledge to the growing theoretical interest from communication scholars with regard to sexual resistance.

Footnote

1. To further ensure that participants' experience of vaginal sex did not have an effect upon the dependent variables, a MANOVA was conducted with relational context, message directness, and experience of vaginal sex as fixed factors and each of the three violation aspects as dependent variables. Though the MANOVA detected a significant main effect for the vaginal sex variable, simple effects were not observed for any of the dependent variables, *Wilks A* = .974, $F(3, 294)$ = 2.66, $p < .05$, η^2 = .03. No interactions involving the vaginal sex variable were significant.

References

Afifi, W. A., & Burgoon, J. K. (1998). "We never talk about that": A comparison of cross-sex friendships and dating relationships on uncertainty and topic avoidance. *Personal Relationships, 5,* 255–272.

Afifi, W. A., & Faulkner, S. L. (2000). On being "just friends": The frequency and impact of sexual activity in cross-sex friendships. *Journal of Social and Personal Relationships, 17,* 205–222.

Afifi, W. A., & Lee, J. W. (2000). Balancing instrumental and identity goals in relationships: The role of request directness and request persistence in the selection of sexual resistance strategies. *Communication Monographs, 67,* 284–305.

Afifi, W. A., & Metts, S. (1998). Characteristics and consequences of expectation violations in close relationships. *Journal of Social and Personal Relationships, 15,* 365–392.

Baxter, L. A., & Bullis, G. (1986). Turning points in developing romantic relationships. *Communication Research, 12,* 469–493.

Bevan, J. L. (1999, November). *Understanding the role of interpersonal uncertainty in the experience and expression of jealousy in cross-sex friendships.* Paper presented at the annual meeting of the National Communication Association, Chicago, IL.

Burgoon, J. K. (1993). Interpersonal expectations, expectation violations, and emotional communication. *Journal of Language and Social Psychology, 12,* 30–48.

Burgoon, J. K., & Hale, J. L. (1988). Nonverbal expectation violations theory: Model elaboration and application to immediacy behaviors. *Communication Monographs, 55,* 58–79.

Burgoon, M. (1995). Language expectancy theory: Elaboration, explication, and extension. In C. R. Berger & M. Burgoon (Eds.), *Communication and social influence processes* (pp. 33–52). East Lansing, MI: Michigan State University Press.

Byers, E. S., & Heinlein, L. (1989). Predicting initiations and refusals of sexual activities in married and cohabitating heterosexual couples. *The Journal of Sex Research, 26,* 210–231.

Cameron, K. A. (1998). *The suasory effect of affective and cognitive messages: A test of conflicting hypotheses.* Unpublished doctoral dissertation, Michigan State University.

Canary, D. J., Cody, M. J., & Marston, P. J. (1987). Goal types, compliance-gaining, and locus of control. *Journal of Language and Social Psychology, 5,* 249–269.

Cupach, W. R., & Metts, S. (1994). *Facework.* Thousand Oaks, CA: Sage.

Edgar, T., & Fitzpatrick, M. A. (1988). Compliance-gaining in relational interaction: When your life depends on it. *Southern Speech Communication Journal, 53,* 385–405.

Edgar, T., & Fitzpatrick, M. A. (1990). Communicating sexual desire: Message tactics for having and avoiding intercourse. In J. P. Dillard (ed.), *Seeking compliance: The production of interpersonal influence messages* (pp. 107–122). Scottsdale, AZ: Gorush Scarisbrick.

Edgar, T., Freimuth, V. S., Hammond, S. L., McDonald, D. A., & Fink, E. L. (1992). Strategic sexual communication: Condom use resistance and response. *Health Communication, 4,* 83–104.

Floyd, K., & Voludakis, M. (1999). Attributions for expectancy violating changes in affectionate behavior in platonic friendships. *Journal of Psychology, 133,* 32–49.

Garcia, L. T. (1998). Perceptions of resistance to unwanted sexual advances. *Journal of Psychology and Human Sexuality, 10,* 43–52.

Goffman, E. (1959). *The presentation of self in everyday life.* New York: Doubleday.

Goldenberg, J. L., Ginexi, E. M., Sigelman, C. K., & Poppen, P. J. (1999). Just say no: Japanese and American styles of refusing unwanted sexual advances. *Journal of Applied and Social Psychology, 29,* 889–902.

Lee, J. W. (2001, July). *Stop! In the name of love: Face management in sexual resistance.* Paper presented at the annual joint meeting of the International Network of Personal Relationships/International Society for the Study of Personal Relationships, Prescott, AZ.

LePoire, B. A., & Burgoon, J. K. (1994). Two contrasting explanations of involvement violations: Expectancy violations theory versus discrepancy arousal theory. *Human Communication Research, 20,* 560–591.

Knobloch, L. K., & Solomon, D. H. (2002). Intimacy and the magnitude and experience of episodic relational uncertainty within romantic relationships. *Personal Relationships, 9,* 457–478.

Metts, S., Cupach, W. R., & Imahori, T. T. (1992). Perceptions of sexual compliance-resisting messages in three types of cross-sex relationships. *Western Journal of Communication, 56,* 1–17.

Mongeau, P. A., & Carey, C. M. (1996). Who's wooing whom II? An experimental investigation of date-initiation and expectancy violation. *Western Journal of Communication, 60,* 195–204.

Monsour, M. (2002). *Women and men as friends: Relationships across the life span in the 21st century.* Mahwah, NJ: Lawrence Erlbaum Associates, Inc.

Motley, M. T., & Reeder, H. M. (1995). Unwanted escalation of sexual intimacy: Male and female perceptions of connotations and relational consequences of resistance messages. *Communication Monographs, 62,* 355–382.

Muehlenhard, C. L., Andrews, S. L., & Beal, G. K. (1996). Beyond "Just saying no": Dealing with men's unwanted sexual advances in heterosexual dating contexts. *Journal of Psychology and Human Sexuality, 8,* 141–168.

Quinn, K., Sanchez-Hucles, J., Coates, G., & Gillen, B. (1991). Men's compliance with a woman's resistance to unwanted sexual advances. *Journal of Offender Rehabilitation, 17,* 13–31.

Sprecher, S., & McKinney, K. (1993). *Sexuality.* Newbury Park, CA: Sage.

FOLLOW-UP QUESTIONS AND EXPLORATION PROJECTS

1. The Toulmin Project is a web-based project from the University of Nebraska-Lincoln. It is designed to help students understand Toulmin's model of argumentation more fully. Go to the home page and read more fully about the theory. http://www.unl.edu/speech/comm109/Toulmin/

2. Identify a claim Bevan makes that we haven't already used as an example. Into what content area does this claim fall? What data does Bevan use to support this claim? What warrant justifies the claim-data link? Given the evidence, do you buy the claim? What role does this claim play in Bevan's overall argument? What would happen to her argument if this claim proved to be invalid?

3. One of the sources Bevan cites is by Mongeau & Carey (1996). Find this citation in her reference list. Find the place where she cites the article in her paper. What part of her argument does she use this article to support? If you can, find a copy of this article and read it. Do you agree with her use of this article? What implications do Bevan's findings taken together with those of Mongeau & Carey have for communicating about sexual activity in dating relationships?

4. How did Bevan measure expectancy violation valence, importance, and expectedness? How did she measure the effect of relationship context and message directness? Given these measures, do you think this study is a fair test of EVT? Why or why not?

5. How does Bevan account for any variations between her findings and what she hypothesized based on EVT and the sexual resistance literature? Would you say her findings support or contradict EVT? Why?

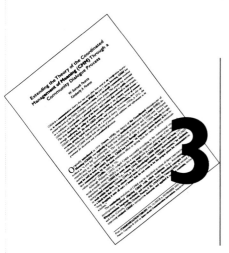

3 | Its Not "Just a Theory": Real-Life Interventions

What happens to a theory after it has been developed? One of the most common ways that theories get used is to guide research. We already saw an example of this use in the past chapter where research hypotheses were based on Expectancy Violation theory. Based on this research as well as comparison to other theories, the concepts of the theory may be refined or elements of the theory may be changed, eliminated, or elaborated. A theory may also be extended to new topic areas and combined with other theories. Again, we saw examples of this kind of work in the prior chapter when the Expectancy Violation theory was extended to help understand sexual resistance situations. But theories may also be extended by developing practical applications based on the theory, which is what we will see in the following article which extends Coordinated Management of Meaning (CMM) to develop processes of community dialogue.

Background of Coordinated Management of Meaning

This theory was originally developed in the 1970s at a time when, predominately, the theoretical and research orientation of the Communication Discipline was objectivist or social-scientific. Coordinated Management of Meaning went in a very different theoretical direction from most of the theories of the time. It followed philosophical developments arguing that social reality is created in interaction and focused on theorizing how that social construction process might work. Students sometimes find some of this theory's terminology to be difficult or awkward. Phrases such as "persons-in-conversation," "serpentine model," and "transverse view" make it difficult to think of this theory as practically applicable. Part of this terminological difficulty comes from the fact that we are used to talking about communication in terms of 'conveying information' or 'being accurate' or 'clearly received messages.' As you will see, these are phrases consistent with a Transmission Model of communication that CMM critiques. In order to substitute a new model of communication, CMM must change our language for talking about communication and, as with any new language, the terms will seem awkward and unfamiliar at first.

Article Structure

This article begins by situating itself within the body of literature on Coordinated Management of Meaning and introducing the circumstances in which this theory came to be applied to developing public dialogue in context of ethic conflicts in Cupertino, California. This first section concludes with an overview of ways that CMM theory affected the practice of public dialogue in this context. Each of the following sections of the article, indicated by a bolded heading, considers a specific concept from CMM as it was applied and developed within the Public Dialogue Project.

Distinctive Points

One of the ways this article is different from all the other articles in this book is that it is an example of an emerging theoretical tradition called "Practical Theory" (Cronen, 1995). Under this view, theories are not seen as abstract descriptions or explanations or understandings of the world, rather they are seen as ongoing conversations between theorists, practitioners, and people who are participating in whatever project is being undertaken. The goal of the theory is for each of these conversationalists to be able to use the theory to answer questions like "What's happening in this situation?" and "What could be done next?" (Pearce & Pearce, 2001). The following article takes terms from Coordinated Management of Meaning and uses them to develop answers to such questions.

References

Cronen, V. E. (1995). Practical theory and the tasks ahead for social approaches to communication. In W. Leeds-Hurwitz (Ed.) *Social approaches to communication* (pp. 217–242). New York: The Guilford Press.

Pearce, K. A., & Pearce, W. B. (2001). The public dialogue consortium's school-wide dialogue process: A communication approach to develop citizenship skills and enhance school climate. *Communication Theory, 11,* 105–123.

Extending the Theory of the Coordinated Management of Meaning (CMM) Through a Community Dialogue Process

W. Barnett Pearce
Kimberly A. Pearce

CMM is a communication theory that has most often been used as an interpretive heuristic in interpersonal communication contexts. Within the past 5 years, however, CMM has guided the work of the Public Dialogue Consortium, a not-for-profit organization involved in a multiyear, citywide collaborative community action project. This project has extended CMM from an interpretive to a practical theory and from interpersonal to public contexts. This essay describes the coevolution of the theory and practices that occurred in that project, strongly confirming the utility of treating communication as the primary social process— CMM's central thesis. Six other CMM concepts, including coordination, forms of communication, episode, logical force, person position, and contextual reconstruction, were also significantly elaborated. Appropriately for a practical theory (Cronen, 1995a, p. 231), the extensions of CMM include both new forms of practice and additions and refinements to its grammar for discursive and conversational practices.

Originally introduced in 1976 (Pearce, 1976), the theory of the Coordinated Management of Meaning (CMM) was explicitly grounded in an intellectual movement that Langer (1951) described as "a new key" in philosophy. Both that intellectual movement and CMM have developed considerably in the intervening years. The constellation of ideas on which CMM was based has moved from the periphery toward the center of scholarly thought (if contemporary scholarly thought may be said to have a center). Further, CMM has become "an impressive macro-theory of face-to-face communication, by far the most ambitious effort to spring from the ranks of speech communication scholars" (Griffin, 2000, p. 75).

Although Philipsen (1995) judged CMM successful according to the conventional criteria of social scientific research (ability to account for a statistically significant percentage of the variance of dependent variables), CMM has more often been employed as a heuristic in interpretive studies of interpersonal communication (e.g., Pearce, 1994). However, CMM theorists have not been content to work within the lines. Cronen (1991, p. 49) acknowledged some critics' characterization of CMM as a black hole that sucks in almost every issue of human existence. "CMM's creators," he admitted, "keep dragging it into all sorts of issues that do not seem to be the proper place for communication scholars."

The continuing evolution of CMM may be described in terms of three trajectories. One line of development involved aligning CMM with other traditions (e.g., American pragmatism; Wittgensteinian language analysis) and reconsidering basic theoretical concepts such as language and rules (Cronen, 1995b; Cronen, Pearce, & Xi, 1989/1990; Pearce, 1993). A second evolutionary trajectory retained CMM's interpretive character and applied it to other contexts, including public communication (Branham & Pearce, 1985; Narula & Pearce, 1987; Pearce, Johnson, & Branham, 1991; Pearce, Littlejohn, & Alexander, 1987; Weiler & Pearce, 1991).

This essay continues the third trajectory: a shift from interpretive to practical theory, in which CMM functions as a guide for practitioners and comprises a grammar that makes coherent a tradition of practice (Cronen, 1995a). As a practical theory, CMM was initially applied to the familiar interpersonal communication processes in mediation (Shailor, 1994) and therapy (Cronen & Pearce, 1985; Cronen, Pearce, & Tomm, 1985). However, starting with the Kaleidoscope Project in the late 1980s (Pearce & Littlejohn, 1997, pp. 197–208), CMM began to be applied as a practical theory to public discourse about controversial issues. The work reported here consists of elaborations of CMM's grammar based on participation in a multiyear, collaborative citywide "public dialogue" project.

In the mid-1990s, a group of communication scholars and practitioners grounded in CMM formed the Public Dialogue Consortium (PDC), a not-for-profit organization dedicated to improving the quality of public communication. The PDC began by renewing and then critiquing the Kaleidoscope Project. Although pleased with some of Kaleidoscope's accomplishments, we at PDC found several features inconsistent with the grammar of CMM. We were concerned about its format (a one-shot intervention of complex social processes), location (only on college campuses, although dealing with society-wide issues), framing (as having only two sides of an "undiscussable" issue), and structure (positioning ourselves as expert interventionists).

In 1996, the PDC approached the city manager of Cupertino, California, and proposed a collaborative project designed to identify the most pressing issue in the community and incorporate it in a productive form of communication. After considerable discussion, the city manager and members of the city council agreed to the project. Subsequently named the Cupertino Community Project: Voices and Visions, the project has continued into its fourth year (see Spano, in press, for a comprehensive description).

A rapid change in the ethnic composition of the city was the issue about which residents felt most concern. The project began in summer 1996, with many residents describing ethnic diversity as "a powder keg, waiting to go off" (Krey, 1999, p. 4) and being unwilling to speak of it publicly, fearful of providing the spark. Although several events and issues that could have ignited ethnic conflict occurred subsequently, there has been no explosive confrontation. Rather, the city has increased its capacity to handle this and other sensitive issues and has improved interethnic relations. In response to an open-ended question about issues confronting the city in a survey conducted in April 2000, only 2% of the stratified random sample mentioned race or ethic diversity. Eighty-two percent agreed or strongly agreed that the city "is doing enough to ensure that members of all ethnic groups feel welcome in Cupertino." The largest change between the 1998 and 2000 surveys in responses to relevant items was the number (from 28% to 49%) who said that the increase in ethnic diversity made "no change in how I feel toward people of other races." When providing this information, City Manager Don Brown (personal conversation) interpreted these results to mean that the residents had finished "working through" the issue and that increased diversity is "an accomplished fact of life."

In addition to the unwanted events that did not happen, markers of the success of the project (see Spano, in press, for details) include (a) an unusually sophisticated public meeting in which residents discussed how "hot topics" involving ethnicity had been handled and should be handled in the future (Pearce & Pearce, 2000); (b) the continuing activities of the "5Cs"—the Citizens of Cupertino Cross-Cultural Consortium; (c) the establishment of the "Collaborative"—an organization of high school and K-8 school districts, De Anza Community College, and the city government committed to promoting multiculturalism; (d) the creation of the position of assistant to the city manager for neighborhood relations; (e) the creation in the sheriff's office of a position of which 75% is devoted to community liaison; (f) presentation to the city manager of the League of California Cities' 1999 Managers Award for the Advancement of Diversity (Krey, 1999, p. 8); and (g) the feeling of ownership residents and city officials felt toward the project.

Following the grammar of CMM, we engaged in reflexive assessments of our practice at every opportunity, bringing in outside observers whenever possible. Consistent with Cronen's (1995a) description of practical theory as a coevolutionary process in which traditions of practice inform and are informed by grammars of discursive and conversational practices, we found that CMM both informed our participation in the Cupertino Community Project and was extended by what we learned in the project. Our experience increased our confidence in the central feature of CMM—treating communication as the primary social process—and led to significant extensions of six concepts, including coordination, forms of communication, episode, logical force, person position, and contextual reconstruction.

Communication as the Primary Social Process

The "communication perspective" (Pearce, 1989, pp. 23–31) consists of a knack of viewing the events and objects of the social world as made, co-constructed by the coordinated actions of, to borrow gratefully a term from Harré (1984), persons-in-conversation. This perspective involves a radical shift in what is foregrounded when perceiving social reality. We focus on mundane issues of who talks to whom, who listens when they do, how people speak and listen, and what language they use. The communication perspective is grounded in the belief that what persons-in-conversation actually say and do in relation to each other is the "stuff" that makes what otherwise might seem dominating realities such as class, gender, ideology, personalities, and so forth.

This perspective stands in contrast to more traditional top-down social theories and is aligned with theories of so-called microprocesses such as ethnomethodology. Rather than arguing which perspective is best or better warranted, like the good pragmatists that we are, we explored the consequences of our position.

The communication perspective led us to take a principled commitment to process rather than to desired outcomes or initial conditions in the Cupertino Project. We focused our efforts on creating conversations where they otherwise would not have existed and shaping these conversations in specific ways. As a result, the project differed from conventional wisdom and practice in at least three ways.

First, we set ourselves to manage the architecture of conversations about the issue, focusing on their inclusivity and quality. Conspicuously absent were such familiar political procedures as identifying "supporters" or "opponents" on the basis of the positions they affirmed, taking polls to assess the support or opposition of specific decisions, "counting the votes," persuasive speeches, rallying supporters, targeting the uncommitted, and disempowering those who disagreed.

Second, we treated "talk" as a form of action, not as a substitute for it. After the October 1996 town hall meeting (see Spano, in press), one participant expressed his amazement that so many people could talk for so long without taking any action. He described it as a wasted opportunity. To the contrary, we understood that meeting as having accomplished several objectives in the early stages of a continuing process, the most important of which was that residents saw a model for and experienced talking productively with members of other ethnic groups about a previously undiscussable issue. Later in the project, other residents wanted to go "beyond" talking about the issue and to "do" something about it. Again, we were impressed by how much had been accomplished and wondered what they perceived as missing. Our interpretation was that we had achieved our goals without some traditional markers of "victory," such as the thrill of heated confrontations, vilification of an enemy, and the publicly displayed pain of defeated adversaries. In our view, creating certain kinds of talk—we called it "public dialogue"—was itself the necessary and sufficient condition of success.

Third, we inadvertently developed an alternative model of the function of city government. The currently preferred model features city government providing quality "customer service" to residents (Osborne & Gaebler, 1993). Other models position city government as allowing individuals to accept responsibility for their own conditions, as providing solutions to social problems based on professional diagnosis and service provision, and as facilitating community self-help activities (Lappé & Du Bois, 1994). In this project, however, the city government accepted the responsibility of creating the architecture of and then participating in conversations about residents' concerns, their visions for the future, and the actions that they saw as bringing about desired futures. These conversations have occurred in annual town hall meetings sponsored by the 5Cs with city support, in semiannual meetings of the Collaborative, and elsewhere.

The city government was willing to accept this new responsibility because key leaders recognized that familiar forms of political process and public participation were insufficient for the most vexing issues. The city manager (Brown, in press) asked,

> How do political leaders deal with an issue that is generating strong community feeling but is not being openly talked about? How do professional managers tackle an issue that cannot be defined and any potential solution involves risks that it could blow up in your face?

He noted that most communities have taken

> the traditional approach of responding to problems after the fact with proposed actions. Examples include establishing human relations commissions that receive complaints and develop responses. These responses range from some form of mediation to legal prosecution of illegal discrimination or hate crimes.

These conventional practices are usually reactive, occurring after unpleasant or tragic events; remedial rather than preventative; and divisive because they perpetuate discursive structures of blame and victimage. Because taking a communication perspective enabled us to create something different and better than conventional practice, our confidence in the central thesis of CMM increased.

Coordination

The CMM concept of coordination differentiates it from many other theories of communication. Rather than using understanding or effect as the criterion for successful communication, CMM envisions persons as engaging in proactive and reactive actions intended to call into being conjoint performances of patterns of communication that they want and precluding the performance of that which they dislike or fear (see Pearce, 1989, chap. 2; Pearce, 1994, chap. 3). For heuristic purposes, the term "coordination" names this process; it does not imply that persons always or even usually achieve the conjoint enactment of the episodes they intended or desired. The point is that whatever episodes occur are nonsummative products of the interaction of many forces. For this reason, the crucial question for communicators is "what are we co-constructing together"?

One of the virtues of CMM is the richness of the heuristic it provides for understanding the meaning of each act in a conversation. CMM locates each act simultaneously within a series of embedded contexts of stories about persons, relationships, episodes (the "hierarchy model") and within an unfinished sequence of co-constructed actions (the "serpentine model"). Figure 3.1 consists of a simplified transverse view of a single act in a conversation. As shown in the figure, the meaning of the act derives from its placement in interpretive systems and in sequences of actions, rather than or in addition to features of the act itself. (Echoes of Wittgenstein's, 1967, dictum that "meaning is in use" are deliberate.) All of this occurs within a field of logical force (Cronen & Pearce, 1981) or a "local moral order (Harré & van Langehove, 1999). For our purposes, the most important implication is that the meaning of any act is not under the full control of the actor and is not finished when it is performed. "Our" acts move the meaning of the previous acts toward completion, and thus we participate in the determination of what "they" did, and vice versa. Shotter (1993) expressed this eloquently in his concept of "joint action" and the "rhetorical-responsive" process.

In this project, we moved this concept from a heuristic function for interpersonal communication to a guide for action in public discourse. Versions of the model presented in Figure 3.1 enabled us to reframe and sometimes redirect events that occurred during the project. For example, several people acted in ways that might easily be interpreted as mean-spirited, obstructionist, or opposi-

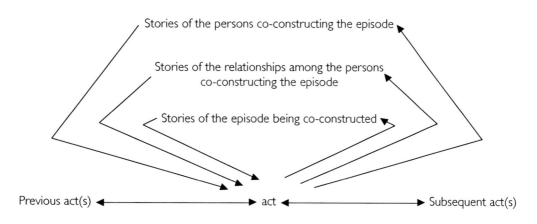

Figure 3.1. A Heuristic Model of the Meaning of an Act in a Conversation

tional. Remembering that the meaning of their acts were unfinished, we deliberately disregarded the others' intentions and the conventional interpretations and acted in such a way that, for example, "disagreements" became "welcomed identification of sites for further exploration and understanding." When offered acts clearly intended as insults, we responded as if they were welcome offers to be engaged with the project. We saw our responses as part of the process that moved the meaning of what others said and did toward completion and, sometimes, enabled us to change the intended meanings into something that would further public dialogue.

We had to extend our understanding of coordination when we were confronted by the realities of unequal distributions of power. Our purpose was to create a public dialogue process, and we quickly realized that, as Kingston (1999, p. 3) said,

> Politics and dialogue are not at all the same thing; and politics has to do with the exercise
> of power, a contest in which there are winners and losers—who are powerless. And there
> is no dialogue between the powerful and those without power.

We deliberately set ourselves to substitute the concept of power as co-constructed in ongoing, unfinished interactions for the more conventional notions that power is a thing, that people have more or less of it, and that power relations necessarily dominate all other possible relationships. We focused on the patterns of interaction involving those who were named as having and not having power and envisioned each act in terms of CMM's serpentine model, which depicts each subsequent action as simultaneously responding to the previous act and eliciting the subsequent act, and CMM's hierarchy model, which sees every act as simultaneously in several contexts, each of which may frame it as having a different meaning. This deep reading of the multiple, unfinished meanings of each act enabled us to see power as only one of many possible interpretations and helped us to identify openings for interventions that would transform power relations into collaborative participation in dialogic communication. For example, in addition to being careful to invite all stakeholders to our meetings, including some who would not normally be in conversation with each other, we were careful to frame the meetings in strategic ways and used trained "table facilitators" who intervened to ensure that the most dominant, extreme, or simply talkative participants did not dominate the group discussions.

The question, "What are we making together?" became something of a mantra, and, changing the metaphor, our catechism was completed by using the serpentine and hierarchy models as heuristics for the answers. To help us stay with an emphasis on coordination, we developed the contrast between CMM's notion of communication and that of the transmission model shown in Figure 3.2 (the figure is an extension of Pearce, 1994, p. 19). Among the contrasts between these concepts of communication are shifts from focusing on individuals to what Harré (1984) called "persons in conversation"; from single messages to what Shotter (1993) called the "rhetorical-responsive" process;

TRANSMISSION MODEL	CMM MODEL
Definitions: The popular transmission model describes communication as a tool used for exchanging information. "Good communication" occurs when meanings are accurately conveyed and received. In this model, communication works best when it is odorless, colorless, and tasteless, a neutral tool for describing the world.	**Definitions:** The CMM model claims that the events and objects of our social worlds are co-constructed in communication. The form of communication, fully as much as the content of what we say, sustains or destroys our personalities, relationships, and institutions.
How communication works: What is said? What is meant? What is understood? • How clear is the information? • How accurately is it heard? • How completely is it expressed? • Is the "channel" effective?	**How communication works:** What do we make together by what is said or done? • What contexts are created for the other? • What is prefigured by the language used? • What form of speech is elicited? • What tones of voice are elicited? • Who is included and who is not? • Who is addressed and who is not?
The work communication does: What gets done? • Is the uncertainty reduced? • Is the question answered? • Is the issue clarified? • Is the problem resolved?	**The work communication does:** What gets made? • What speech acts? (insults, compliments) • What relationships? (trust, respect) • What episodes (collaboration, conflict) • What identities? (shrill voices, reasonable persons, caring persons) • What cultures/worldviews? (strong, weak, or no democracy)
The role of the facilitator: To create a context in which defects in communication processes will not interfere with other, more important, processes of decision making, coalition forming, deal making, and persuading.	**The role of the facilitator:** To shape emerging patterns of communication so that multiple voices and perspectives are honored and the tensions among them are maintained.

Figure 3.2. Two Concepts of Communication

and from individual intentional or interpretive "meaning" to what is conjointly "made" in the process of communication.

Forms of Communication

The earliest presentations of CMM set its understanding of communication against the idea that communication either is or should be a colorless, odorless, tasteless vehicle for thought and action. Extending the idea that people make their social worlds, Pearce (1989) developed the concept of "forms of communication" and argued that there is a reciprocal, causal relationship between them and various historical and cultural "ways of being human."

A number of social analysts have distinguished debate, discussion, deliberation, dialogue, positional bargaining, interest-based bargaining, collaboration, and so on. Our work was based on conceptualizations of cosmopolitan communication (Pearce, 1989, 1993; Oliver, 1996) and transcendent discourse (Pearce & Littlejohn, 1997). Neither concept had previously been applied to a citywide, multiyear process, but we took from them a series of principles, such as to include everyone as much as possible; to value listening at least as much as speaking; to help others—particularly those with whom we disagree and find disagreeable—to be heard and understood; to incorporate appreciative and inclusive language rather than deficit and exclusionary language in our meetings; and to treat disagreements as welcomed sites for exploration rather than obstacles to progress.

City Manager Brown (in press) eloquently described the desired form of communication that was the driving force of the project.

> The "light bulb" moment for me came when I realized that this project was not about changing people's minds, but that it was about giving people a way to talk about tough issues. I also realized that people's fears and concerns are real and legitimate and that they need a way of talking about them without the fear of being branded a racist. . . . One of the most rewarding concepts . . . is that people are allowed to "stand their ground." We are not in the business of getting everyone to think the same way. Our aim is to provide a place where strongly held views can be given and received in a respectful manner. At the least, this will improve the clarity of our respective views. At the best, through this increased clarity, we may find that we share more common values about our community than we thought.

As the project continued, we refined our understanding of public dialogue. Pearce and Pearce (2000) differentiated among several "flavors" of dialogue, including those whose work is stimulated by David Bohm and those in the tradition of Martin Buber. In the Bohmian tradition, "dialogue" is a noun naming a distinct communication episode that a group might "do." In a dialogue, participants ignore relational issues in order to think together by performing a series of virtually identical speech acts. In the Buberian tradition, it is more appropriate to use the word "dialogic" as an adverb or adjective, describing the manner in which people relate to each other and in which they perform all possible speech acts. Building on Buber's perspective, we (Pearce & Pearce, 2000) developed the idea that public dialogue occurs when there is a "charmed loop" (Cronen, Johnson, & Lannamann, 1982) between stories of "self" (standing one's ground), "relationship" (being profoundly open to the other), and "episode" (co-constructing a sequence of actions that invites participants to remain in the tension between self and relationship). In the continuing evolution of our thinking about forms of communication, the cutting-edge question is how, dialogically, to do all of the rich array of communication acts that occur in politics, community building, public planning, zoning, and the other contexts of public discourse.

Episode

In CMM, "episodes" are thought of as bounded sequences of acts, with a beginning, middle, and end. They have a coherent narrative structure; communicators usually can name the episodes that comprise their lives (e.g., having an argument, dinner with friends, performance evaluation interview) and ensconce them in stories (Harré & von Langehove, 1999; Pearce, 1994, chap. 4). Although the length of episodes is defined by the participants, with a few exceptions, CMM researchers and theorists have usually thought of them as relatively short, uninterrupted patterns of interaction in face-to-face interaction, such as the phases of mediation or therapy sessions. The Cupertino Project required us to think on a very different scale, both in terms of the temporal extension and number of people and groups involved.

We were not the first to use the metaphor of "conversational architecture" as a way of thinking about the social system in which we are working. Our distinctive twist on this idea builds on the concept of episodes. We integrated the concept and the metaphor in a three-level public dialogue process model that has been invaluable in our work while stretching the notion of episode far beyond its original function in CMM.

We integrated the concept and the metaphor in a three-level public dialogue process model that has been invaluable in our work while stretching the notion of episode far beyond its original function in CMM.

Strategic Process Design

The strategic process design is the "largest" episodic concept. It is the plan for a deliberately chosen sequence of events that respond to existing conditions and lead to a desired outcome. The strategic process may last from a few weeks to several years, and the design will certainly change during the process.

Conceptualizing public processes as episodic structures enables us to differentiate public dialogue from other designs. For example, Yankelovich (1991) describes a "public education" design in which those he calls the "elite" spend such time as is necessary to learn and decide about an issue and then attempt to convince ("educate") the public to agree with them with less information and insufficient time. A popular description for the resulting coordinated episode between government officials and the public is "DAD"—an acronym for "decide-advocate-defend"—and its unwanted consequences include public cynicism and official burnout. In contrast, the strategic design for a public dialogue episode typically includes these steps: getting initial buy-in from relevant stakeholders, hearing all the voices, enriching the conversation, deliberating the options, deciding and moving forward together. Some of the differences in these strategic designs involve the placement of "deciding"; the timing of the public's involvement; and the array of actions and communication skills required by and developed by both officials and members of the public. Satisfaction with the process and willingness to accept the product also differ.

Event Design

Each step in the public dialogue strategic process is accomplished by one or more "events." Events are sequences of activities that occur within a single meeting; they may last from less than an hour to several days. Many types of events, deliberately sequenced, may occur within a public dialogue strategic design. Typical events include focus groups, town hall meetings, study circles, public deliberations, future search meetings, and guided group discussions.

The thinking that led to this three-level model began when we observed public participation events that stood alone, with little preparation or follow-up. Participants in these events frequently asked about next steps and received vague answers. With the notion of episodic structure in mind, we immediately saw the need for each event in the strategic process as completing the preceding event and prefiguring the next. That is, if we substitute strategic process design for episode in Figure 3.1, then each event may be seen in the place of an act.

Communication Facilitation Skills

The success of any event depends in part on the ways that facilitators act or respond, in the moment, to what the participants do. One level of facilitation skills includes conventional practices such as timekeeping, providing supplies, recording conversations, and ensuring that all participants have sufficient "air time." A second level of facilitation skills consists of (re)framing comments by using circular, reflexive, and dialogic interviewing procedures; positioning participants as reflecting teams and outsider witnesses; and coaching participants in dialogic communication skills. We differentiate among these levels because some public participation practitioners have a principled objection to this form of work. However, we think that this level of facilitation is crucial to a public dialogue process. We believe that what happens in the minute-to-minute process of events is important. The success of the event as public dialogue hinges on such subtle things as the difference between asking a question or making a comment at a particular moment, or the way a question is phrased, or the timing with which it is asked. One way of expressing our belief is that these skills percolate up into the events and strategic processes, determining whether they are successful. Another way of expressing it is to say that the strategic process and event designs are intended to create the preconditions for just this kind of intervention and the resulting form of communication.

Logical Force

Logical force is a distinctive concept of the "necessity" in social theory (Cronen & Pearce, 1981). As described in CMM, it is both complex and mutable; it describes persons in webs of perceived "oughtness" or, technically, a deontic logic implicating what they should, must, may, or cannot do in specific situations. As we reflected on our work in the Cupertino Project, we were struck by how far this concept had migrated in our practices.

Perhaps unduly influenced by its use among logicians, we originally constructed quantitative and qualitative ways of translating into research the deontic operators of obligatory, permitted, prohibited, and irrelevant. Because we were dealing with situated acts rather than timeless relations among propositions, we introduced the distinction between future and past in the form of the dichotomy between "causal/because of" and "intentional/in order to" attributions of motives. Using the serpentine and hierarchy model, we developed a complex array of "logical forces" that constitute the moment in which each act occurs, and we distinguished among contextual, prefigurative, practical, and implicative forces. However, we never really got beyond various permutations of oughtness.

Our work in the Cupertino Project, however, led us to describe logical force in a variety of ways, and we only subsequently thought through the conceptual implications of the shifts we had made. For example, some prevalent stories were determinedly rooted in an orientation to the past (Cupertino was once comprised of vast orchards and a few farms), whereas others were determinedly present/future looking (with over 90% of its residents having Internet access, Cupertino is on the leading edge of technological development even within Silicon Valley). This really was not so much a matter of oughtness as we had originally conceived of logical force but more a matter of discursive habits. These habits, however, had the same kind of effect of shaping how people were thinking and acting and constraining their ability to co-construct desired episodes with others who had other habits.

In addition, we became very sensitive to the habits people have of framing situations as problems and blaming others for the results of their own behavior. Elspeth MacAdam (personal conversation) wondered why people seem so susceptible to what she called the "acquired fascination with deficit language syndrome." Whatever the cause, the effects of these habits are similar to that of particular configurations of deontic logic, but these habits do not seem equivalent to permutations of oughtness.

In our practice, we became insistent about avoiding "problem talk," framing issues appreciatively (Hammond, 1996; Srivastva & Cooperrider, 1990), disrupting discourses featuring blame and victimage, and focusing on the positive visions that underlie even the most persistent complaints. In our articulations of CMM, we have become less insistent on equating logical force with deontic logic. Our concept is now more general. We speak of the "local moral order" (Harré & van Langenhove, 1999, p. 1) and the "grammar" of specific stories and ways of storytelling (Pearce & Pearce, 1998).

The Person-Position of the Facilitator and the Reliance on Ordinary Language

Like Wittgenstein (1967), Shotter (1989), and Harré and Grillett (1994), CMM takes into account the different sets of rights, duties, and privileges that adhere to the first-, second-, or third-person positions in the grammar of ordinary language. In the Cupertino Project, however, we often found ourselves facilitating or teaching others to facilitate, and this role does not quite fit any of these person positions.

In our event designs, facilitators' responsibilities include (a) helping the group follow a useful episodic sequence; (b) remaining neutral (actively aligning one's self with all of the participants, creating a climate of reciprocated trust and respect); (c) listening actively and helping participants listen to each other; (d) helping participants tell their own stories (taking a not-knowing stance, expressing curiosity, asking systemic questions); and (e) helping participants tell better stories by introducing appreciative and systemic perspectives through questions and reframing, weaving participants' stories together. Although this role is somewhat like a first-person position in that the fa-cilitator is a participant in the conversation, it is also somewhat like a third-person position because the facilitator maintains a heightened sense of awareness of the episode being co-constructed and ac-cepts the role of guiding it. It is somewhat different from all of these in that the facilitator's own opinion should be excluded from the conversation.

We became aware of the complexity of this role when some residents we trained withdrew as facilitators of small-group discussions at a town hall meeting. They explained that they wanted their own voice to be heard more directly in the meeting than it would be if they facilitated. As we reflected on their decision, we realized that the role of facilitator was more than a shift among the three posi-tions in ordinary language; it is a move to a stance of indirect influence.

The theoretical implications of this stance are enormous for social constructionists and others who believe that "ordinary language" comprises the limits of our social worlds. Either we must aban-don the basic principle or begin to explore much more of the subtleties of language than has been done in the literature to this point. We believe that both alternatives should be explored, but the "con-servative" approach is to extend our exploration of linguistic resources.

Most of the discussion of language among social constructionists has dealt with vocabulary (e.g., the difference made by describing a person as a "patient" or a "client"), parts of speech (e.g., the rights, duties, and responsibilities attached to person position as evidenced by pronominal use), and case (e.g., "I statements" that accept responsibility). Perhaps we should explore other parts of speech (e.g., prepositions) and the tense, mood, and voice of verbs. The "middle voice" that was a part of classical Greek expresses clearly and comfortably what requires awkward hyphenated expres-sion in either the active or passive voice, such as co-construction and coevolution. Another avenue of exploration follows McNamee and Gergen's (1999) insistence on the primacy of relationship in a social constructionist perspective. If valid, then prepositions should be a part of ordinary language that we explore for its philosophical and social implications because these are the words that describe relationships.

Exciting prospects for continued theoretical development result from connecting this idea to CMM's claim that ways of being human are reciprocally causally related to forms of communication. The process of more fully exploring the possibilities in the grammar of ordinary language, as well as the limits of language, may be seen as an exercise in describing and perhaps inventing ways of being human that have been underdescribed or underresourced. The rights, duties, and responsibilities of a facilitator, like those of therapist and process consultant, seem to adhere to a person position in the subjunctive mood and middle voice, with an affinity for inclusive prepositions. Would increased clar-ity in describing these roles have practical value in developing training programs, making personnel assessments, and developing social theory? Clearly, this is an exploration that we have begun but likely will not finish in our lifetimes.

Contextual Reconstruction

In some of the interpretive and critical work based on CMM, we noted that all actions occur in a context, and usually our rhetorical task is that of acting in such a way that what we do fits the context. However, there are times when we are committed to performing an action that runs against the grain of contextual prefiguration, and we must reconstruct the context so that it fits our action. Contextual reconstruction is a particularly interesting and challenging form of communication (Branham & Pearce, 1985); we found it a recurring form of life in the community dialogue project.

The need to act in ways that bring new contexts into being required us to integrate three ideas that had been developed separately in CMM: implicative force, game mastery, and cosmopolitan communication. In our work on logical force, we had been long aware of the effects that an act can have in changing the contexts in which it occurred. We called this "implicative force," and it is the basis of the idea of contextual reconstruction. However, Branham and Pearce (1985) had conceptu-alized this only from the perspective of a rhetor and then only from the perspective of a single act such as a public speaking event.

When working with a whole community during an extended period, we found it necessary to engage with a diverse set of people over an extended time. No single act should be expected to be sufficient to achieve contextual reconstruction. Among other things, this was one of the lessons we drew from the critique of the Kaleidoscope Project. This brought to mind the concept of game mastery, originally developed in the context of interpersonal communication (Pearce, 1994). Exhibiting game mastery, a participant in an ongoing sequence of events violates the rules, intentionally, in order to bring about a desired new state of affairs.

However, the diversity of the community made it unlikely that any act of game mastery would be equally effective with different groups. By adding the concept of cosmopolitan communication (Pearce, 1989), we arrived at a fundamentally different orientation to contextual reconstruction. In our current view, contextual reconstruction is most likely to be successful when it is the result of collaboration, neither a single act nor a unilateral one.

Conclusion

Because CMM is, among other things, a practical theory (Cronen, 1995a), it is appropriate that this essay closes the loop in the coevolution of a tradition of practice and the discourse that guides it and makes it coherent. CMM informed the work of the PDC in a multiyear community project, and the PDC's experience in that project significantly extended CMM.

However, practical theory differs from other forms of theory and is extended in distinctive ways stemming from its nature. To extend an alethic or truth-bearing theory, for example, we would seek to make it either more general (embracing more of the world) or more rigorous (perhaps by specifying the effect of additional mediating variables). Since practical theory develops in a coevolution between traditions of practice and a grammar for discourse and practice, it is "extended" by adding useful concepts and models, developing more precise or descriptive vocabulary, learning new ways of working in difficult or new contexts, and exchanging outworn or limiting metaphors with fresh ones.

One criterion for assessing a practical theory is its ability to guide practitioners. The meaning of the term "guide" is significant. It does not refer to a "cookbook" or set of instructions; rather, a good practical theory increases the prudence or social eloquence of practitioners by enhancing their ability to discern and draw upon the resources of particular social settings in order to produce desired effects (Oliver, 1996; Pearce, 1989). If we assume that "acting naturally" is what brings us to any situation that we perceive as needing to be changed, the one sure recipe for preserving that which we want to change is to continue to act naturally. A practical theory is needed when practitioners must act sufficiently unnaturally so that they can be successful. In the Cupertino Project, we were particularly well served by CMM's insistence that communication is the primary social process. Temptations to lapse into traditional discourses of power, politics, and applied sociology were very strong, and we did well to resist them. In addition, CMM's emphasis on communication as making the events and objects of the social world was a pivotal part of our ability to reframe events and participate in a collaborative process of contextual reconstruction.

A second criterion for assessing a practical theory is its capacity to provide a grammar in which practices can be discussed coherently. This criterion is perhaps the shadow of CMM's heuristic qualities. Not only did CMM enable us to discover openings for effective action (its heuristic function), it enabled us to describe and explain those practices coherently.

Third, practical theory is appropriately assessed by the extent of its continuing coevolution between practice and grammar of discourse. This essay has described some of the major sites of the evolution in the grammar of CMM, as it evolved from application as a practical theory to a long-term, citywide public dialogue process.

As a result of this project, our understanding of "coordination" has been increased by having to come to grips with issues of power. One implication is the radical use of the question, "What are we making together?" as a way of inviting participants to step outside traditional power relations.

We have continued the development of our understanding of "forms of communication." Specifically, we have explored several traditions of dialogue and developed our own notion of "public dialogue." This notion is operationalized in our development of a three-level model of different dimensions of episodes in a multiyear project.

The concepts of logical force and of person position exploded. Their limitations were clearly seen, and we have taken the first steps toward opening these concepts for additional development. Further, the way that their limitations were revealed predisposes us to see them as "open sets" rather than expecting to find another, more comprehensive set of formulations. This development only strengthened our confidence in the basic ideas of the concepts, that actions occur within a context of rights, duties, and obligations and that these adhere to different roles we take. However, we are now much more open to finding new roles and subtle differences among roles, and we accept the necessity of a pluralistic way of describing the constraints and affordances within which we act.

Finally, the necessity we faced to do contextual reconstruction required us to integrate several concepts and to arrive with deepened understanding at the place where we began: "Persons collectively create and manage social reality" (Pearce & Cronen, 1980, p. 305). The reconstruction of contexts, and most other things worth doing, cannot be done unilaterally or in a single act. Social change, just like its apparent opposite, social order, is co-constructed in a recursive process that reconstructs us as persons, relationships, and institutions.

Author

W. Barnett Pearce (PhD, Ohio University) is a member of the faculty of the Human and Organization Development Program, the Fielding Institute. Kimberly A. Pearce (MA, San Jose State University) is professor, Department of Speech Communication, De Anza College. Both are members of the Public Dialogue Consortium and coprincipals of Pearce Associates, P.O. Box 620866, Woodside, CA 94062.

References

Branham, R. J., & Pearce, W. B. (1985). Between text and context: Toward a rhetoric of contextual reconstruction. *Quarterly Journal of Speech, 71,* 19–36.

Brown, D. (in press). Foreword. In S. Spano, *Public dialogue and participatory democracy.* Cresskill, NJ: Hampton Press.

Cronen, V. E. (1995b) Coordinated management of meaning: The consequentiality of communication and the recapturing of experience. In S. J. Sigman (Ed.), *The consequentiality of communication* (pp. 17–66). Hillsdale, NJ: Erlbaum.

Cronen, V. E., & Pearce, W. B. (1981). Logical force in interpersonal communication: A new concept of the "necessity" in social behavior. *Communication, 6,* 5–67.

Cronen, V. E., Johnson, K., & Lannamann, J. W. (1982). Paradoxes, double-binds, and reflexive loops: An alternative theoretical perspective. *Family Process, 20,* 91–112.

Cronen, V. E., & Pearce, W. B. (1985). Toward an explanation of how the Milan Method works: An invitation to a systemic epistemology and the evolution of family systems. In D. Campbell & R. Draper (Eds.), *Applications of systemic family therapy: The Milan approach* (pp. 69–86). London: Grune & Stratton.

Cronen, V. E., Pearce, W. B., & Tomm, K. (1985). A dialectical view of personal change. In K. J. Gergen & K. E. Davis (Eds.), *The social construction of the person* (pp. 203–224). New York: Springer-Verlag.

Cronen, V. E., Pearce, W. B., & Xi, C. (1989/1990). The meaning of "meaning" in CMM analysis of communication: A comparison of two traditions. *Research on Language and Social Interaction, 23,* 1–40.

Griffin, E. (2000). *A first look at communication theory* (4th ed.). Boston: McGraw-Hill.

Hammond, S. A. (1996). *The thin book of appreciative inquiry.* Plano, TX: CSS Publishing.

Harré, R. (1984). *Personal being: A theory for individual psychology.* Cambridge, MA: Harvard University Press.

Harré, R., & Grillett, G. (1994). *The discursive mind.* Newbury Park, CA: Sage.

Harré, R., & van Langehove, L. (1999). The dynamics of social episodes. In R. Harré & L. van Langenhove (Eds.), *Positioning theory* (pp. 1–13). Oxford, UK: Blackwell.

Kingston, R. J. (1999). The political importance of dialogue. *Kettering Foundation Connections, 9,* 2–5.

Krey, D. (1999). Cupertino asks, "Can we talk about diversity"? *Western City, 75,* 4–8.

Langer, S. K. (1951). *Philosophy in a new key: A study in the symbolism of reason, rite, and art* (2nd ed.). New York: New American Library.

Lappé, F. M., & Du Bois, P. M. (1994). *The quickening of America: Rebuilding our nation, remarking our lives.* San Francisco: Jossey-Bass.

McNamee, S., & Gergen, K. (1999). *Relational responsibility: Resources for sustainable dialogue.* Thousand Oaks, CA: Sage.

Narula, U., & Pearce, W. B. (1987). *Development as communication: A perspective on India.* Carbondale: Southern Illinois University Press.

Oliver, C. (1996). Systemic eloquence. *Human Systems, 7,* 247–264.

Osborne, D., & Gaebler, T. (1993). *Reinventing government: How the entrepreneurial spirit is transforming the public sector.* New York: Plume.

Pearce, W. B. (1976). The coordinated management of meaning: A rules based theory of interpersonal communication. In G. R. Miller (Ed.), *Explorations in interpersonal communication* (pp. 17–36). Beverly Hills, CA: Sage.

Pearce, W. B. (1989). *Communication and the human condition.* Carbondale: Southern Illinois University Press.

Pearce, W. B. (1993). Achieving dialogue with "the Other" in the postmodern world. In P. Gaunt (Ed.), *Beyond agendas: New directions in communications research* (pp. 59–74). Westport, CT: Greenwood Press.

Pearce, W. B. (1994). *Interpersonal communication: Making social worlds.* New York: HarperCollins.

Pearce, W. B., & Cronen, V. E. (1980). *Communication, action and meaning: The creation of social realities.* New York: Praeger.

Pearce, W. B., Johnson, D. K., & Branham, R. J. (1991). A rhetorical ambush at Reykjavik: A case study of the transformation of discourse. In M. Weiler & W. B. Pearce (Eds.), *Reagan and public discourse in America* (pp. 163–182). Tuscaloosa: University of Alabama Press.

Pearce, W. B., Littlejohn, S. W., & Alexander, A. (1987). The New Christian Right and the humanist response: Reciprocated diatribe. *Communication Quarterly, 35,* 171–192.

Pearce, W. B., & Littlejohn, S. W. (1997). *Moral conflict: When social worlds collide.* Thousand Oaks, CA: Sage.

Pearce, W. B., & Pearce, K. A. (1998). Transcendent storytelling: Abilities for systemic practitioners and their clients. *Human Systems, 9,* 167–184.

Pearce, W. B., & Pearce, K. A. (2000). Combining passions and abilities: Toward dialogic virtuosity. *Southern Communication Journal, 65,* 161–175.

Philipsen, G. (1995). The coordinated management of meaning theory of Pearce, Cronen and associates. In D. Cushman & B. Kovacic (Eds.), *Watershed research traditions in human communication theory* (pp. 13–43). Albany: State University of New York Press.

Shailor, J. C. (1994). *Empowerment in dispute mediation: A critical analysis of communication.* Westport, CT: Praeger.

Shotter, J. (1989). Social accountability and the social construction of "you." In J. Shotter & K. Gergen (Eds.), *Texts of identity* (pp. 133–151). London: Sage.

Shotter, J. (1993). *Conversational realities: Constructing life through language.* Thousand Oaks, CA: Sage

Spano, S. (in press). *Public dialogue and participatory democracy: The Cupertino Community Project.* Cresskill, NJ: Hampton.

Srivastva, S., & Cooperrider, D. (1990). *Appreciative management and leadership: The power of positive thought and action in organizations,* San Francisco: Jossey-Bass.

Weiler, M., & Pearce, W. B. (1991). Ceremonial discourse: The rhetorical ecology of the Reagan administration. In M. Weiler & W. B. Pearce (Eds.), *Reagan and public discourse in America* (pp. 11–42). Tuscaloosa: University of Alabama Press.

Wittgenstein, L. (1967). *Philosophical investigations* (3rd ed.), (G. E. M. Anscombe, Trans.). Oxford, UK: Blackwell.

Yankelovich, D. (1991). *Coming to public judgment: Making democracy work in a complex world.* Syracuse, NY: Syracuse University Press.

FOLLOW-UP QUESTIONS AND EXPLORATION PROJECTS

1. How does the structure of this article compare with the structure of the prior article? How do you account for any similarities? How do you account for any differences?

2. Visit the Public Dialogue Consortium website, *http://www.publicdialogue.org/,* and look under "About Our Projects" for the materials on the Cupertino Community project. What other examples of coordination, episodes, strategic process design, event design, and logical force can you identify? How did the process of looking for these examples affect your understanding of these terms?

3. Having visited this website, do you agree or disagree with how Pearce and Pearce presented this project in the article? Why?

4. What current issues in your local community might be useful topics for public dialogue? Has current discussion of these issues been conducted from a transmission model of communication or a CMM model of communication? How can you tell? How do you think the model of communication used matters to your community's understanding of these issues?

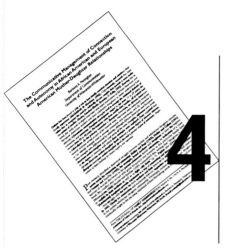

4 The Push-Me Pull-You of Connection and Independence

Issues of both ethnicity and family are highlighted in the following article by Barbara Penington. The basic question addressed in this article is how ethnicity affects family communication. The more focused question is how ethnicity affects the ways that mothers and daughters negotiate tensions between being connected and being independent.

Background of Relational Dialectics

Relational Dialectics is a theoretical approach based on the work of Russian Philosopher Mikhail Bakhtin (Baxter, 2004). Its basic premise is that any relationship involves dialogues around an inherent set of mutually exclusive goals. The tension we experience with these conflicting goals is termed a *dialectical tension*. Penington's article focuses on the dialectic of connection and autonomy. All relationships need some degree of connection between the participants to maintain the relationship. At the same time, individual autonomy is also necessary and valued. Unfortunately, more connection necessarily means less autonomy and vice versa. Prior research has identified several strategies people use to manage dialectical tensions in their relationships (Hoppe-Nagao, A. & Ting-Toomey, S., 2002). It is these strategies that Penington is examining in her study.

Article Structure

This article follows a standard structure for qualitative research: Introduction, Literature Review, Methodology, Results and Interpretation, and Conclusions. The article begins with a rationale for its focus on ethnicity and the dialectics of mother-daughter communication. It moves into an overview of the theories the author will be drawing on throughout the article, followed by the literature review. One goal in the literature review is to overview what we know about mother-daughter communication and, by doing so, demonstrate that no other study has highlighted the connection-independence dialectic in this relationship. A second goal is to demonstrate why examining ethnicity in family relationships is important. The Methodology section describes how participants were recruited, what participants were asked to do, and how the data were analyzed. The Results and Interpretation section identifies six strategies these participants used to manage tensions between connection and autonomy in their relationships. In this section, the stories of African-American and European-American mothers and daughters are presented separately within each of the six strategies. This presentation helps the author highlight the role of ethnicity in this type of relationship. The conclusion section begins by providing an overview of key conclusions the author wants to make about the role of ethnicity in mother-daughter dialectical communication. It goes on to talk about how the results of this study fit into the literature on family communication and to identify limitations in the study's findings.

Distinctive Points

This is a good example of an article that draws on a variety of different theories for its conceptual development. Obviously, connection, autonomy and dialectical tension are terms from Relational Dialectics. But notions of individualism and collectivism (Penington, p. 54) are terms referenced by such cultural theories as Anxiety-Uncertainty Management (Gudykust, 1998) and Face Negotiation theory (Oetzel et al, 2001).

Unlike Bevan (Expectancy Violation theory and sexual resistance) who used a quantitative experimental design, this article uses a "grounded approach" (p. 57) in which interview and interaction data were collected first, and then categories of analysis were developed from this data, rather than from a prior theory. Unlike quantitative research where statistics are presented to justify the study's conclusions, in qualitative research quotes from interviews or interactions are presented in the article and the author explains how each quote supports her conclusions.

References

Baxter, L. A. (2004). Relationships as dialogues. *Personal Relationships, 11,* 1–22.

Gudykunst, W. B. (1998). Applying anxiety/uncertainty management (AUM) theory to intercultural adjustment training. *International Journal of Intercultural Relations, 22,* 227–250.

Hoppe-Nagao, A., & Ting-Toomey, S. (2002). Relational dialectics and management strategies in marital couples. *Southern Communication Journal, 67,* 142–159.

Oetzel, J., Ting-Toomey, S., Masumoto, T., Yokochi, Y., Pan, X., Takai, J., & Wilcox, R. (2001). Face and facework in conflict: A cross-cultural comparison of China, Germany, Japan, and the United States. *Communication Monographs, 68,* 235–258.

Orbe, M. P. (1998). From the standpoint(s) of traditionally muted groups: explicating a co-cultural communication theoretical model. *Communication Theory, 8,* 1–26.

The Communicative Management of Connection and Autonomy in African American and European American Mother-Daughter Relationships

Barbara A. Penington
Department of Communication
University of Wisconsin-Whitewater

Culture has been found to play a role in how family members function and construct their family experience (McGoldrick & Giordano, 1996). Unfortunately, research has been rather slow to recognize the need for culturally diverse samples that provide a more inclusive picture of families (Socha, Sanchez-Hucles, Bromley, & Kelly, 1995). Bearing this in mind, this study used in-depth interviews and taped interactions of African American and European American mothers and their adolescent daughters to better understand how ethnicity differentiates communicative strategies used to manage the relational dialectic of connection and autonomy. Daughter participants ranged in age from 13 to 17 years; the mothers from 34 to 48 years. Participants came from middle class families, all of which had a father-figure. As the primary researcher is European American, an African American research assistant served as part of the research team. Interviews were inductively analyzed to (a) identify strategies used to manage connection and autonomy, and (b) determine if these strategies were differentiated by ethnicity. Although African American and European American mother-daughter dyads used many of the same strategies, differences were noted in the degree or intensity with which these strategies were employed. Data suggested that African American mother-daughter dyads favored a greater degree of closeness whereas European American mother-daughter dyads favored a greater degree of autonomy. Implications of these findings for future inquiry are reported.

Past research identified a dialectical struggle between mother and adolescent daughter simultaneous needs for connection and autonomy. Noller and Bagi (1985), Nolier and Callan (1991) and Youniss and Smollar (1985), for example, found mothers and daughters to have the highest amount of mutual disclosure in the parent-adolescent family subsystem, an indication of a close bond. Yet, conflict also occurs with great frequency and intensity in this particular family dyad (Monteniayer, 1982). Youniss and Smollar (1985) summarized this, writing that "daughters feel free to confide in their mothers as well as to fight with them" (p. 5). Pipher also (1994) stated that, "[Adolescent] daughters provoke arguments as a way of connecting and distancing at the same time . . . they struggle with the love for their mothers and their desire to be different from their mothers" (p. 286). Clearly the connection and autonomy dialectic engenders much frustration and confusion in the mother-adolescent daughter relationship. Seemingly, mothers and adolescent daughters are continually caught in the yin-yang whirlwind of their fluctuating needs for connection and autonomy,

From THE JOURNAL OF FAMILY COMMUNICATION, Volume 4, No. 1 by B. A. Penington. Reproduced by permission of Taylor & Francis, Inc., http://www.taylorandfrancis.com

Correspondence concerning this article should be addressed in Barbara A. Penington. Department of Communication. University of Wisconsin-Whitewater, Whitewater, WI 53190. E-mail peningth@mail.uww.edu but how is this whirlwind managed? As the quality of parent-child interactions sets a course for the future of their relationship and may later influence spousal or sibling relationships (Vogl-Bauer, 2003), management of dialectical tension is an important area for scholarly investigation.

The mother-adolescent daughter relationship transcends both history and culture. Although ethnicity plays a key role in how family members communicate and ultimately construct their family experience (McGoldrick & Giordano, 1996), family scholars have been slow to recognize the need for ethnically-diverse samples (Socha et al., 1995). Research in family communication has used primarily European American middle class participants (Dilworth-Anderson, Burton, & Johnson, 1993; Socha et al., 1995). This has promoted a Euro-centric view of the family which many medical professionals, social workers, clergy, and educators have relied on when counseling mothers and adolescent daughters of different ethnic backgrounds. This is especially disturbing given the fact that immigration rates in the United States are the highest in almost 100 years (McGoldrick & Giordano, 1996) and birth rates that are dropping for Whites are increasing for racial and ethnic minorities (Sue, Arredondo, & McDavis, 1992). Thus, an additional question begs attention: Do mothers and adolescent daughters of diverse ethnic groups communicatively manage connection and autonomy in similar ways? To facilitate a preliminary understanding of this question, this study utilized interview and interactional data from African American and European American mother-adolescent daughter dyads to obtain descriptive renderings and actual conversational examples of this management process.

Theoretical Framework

Several theoretical frameworks inform this study. Symbolic interactionism (Blumer, 1969: Mead, 1934/1956) asserts that individuals attach social meanings to their worlds and then act toward others on the basis of these meanings. To ascertain how individuals construct meaning, the symbolic interactionist approach encourages the scholar to query individuals about the topic under study, allowing them to describe their experiences in depth using their own words and style. An examination of narratives gleaned in this manner can provide important insights into ethnic differences in the communicative management of connection and autonomy because it draws directly on mothers' and daughters' unique perspectives which are shaped, in part, by culture.

Developmental approaches are also necessary to facilitate our understanding of this topic as they examine the adolescent's sequential progression from parental connection and control to independence from parents and a more individual sense of identity (Santrock & Yussen, 1992). In recent years, scholars have begun to recognize, however, that "adolescents do not simply move away from parental influence into a decision-making process all their own . . . there is continued connectedness to parents as adolescents move toward and gain autonomy" (Santrock & Yussen, 1992, p. 426).

The dialectical perspective, which enables us to see the yin-yang fluctuation of relationship contradictions on a daily basis, promises to be extremely useful to our understanding of family relationships. Baxter and Montgomery (Baxter, 1988, 1990; Baxter & Montgomery, 1996; Montgomery & Baxter, 1998) have been pioneers in highlighting the utility of the dialectical framework to capture the complex and paradoxical nature of personal relationships. As Baxter (1990) explained, "a contradiction is present whenever two tendencies or forces are interdependent (the dialectical principle of unity) yet mutually negate one another (the dialectical principle of negation)" (p. 70). Baxter has identified connection and autonomy as the primary contradiction in all personal relationships. Humans have the need to be interdependent as well as independent of one another. In the mother-adolescent daughter context, dialectical thinking helps us better understand how these contradictory needs can exist and be expressed simultaneously.

Still to be considered, however, is the effect of ethnicity on connection and autonomy. According to Alba (1990), members of an ethnic group "entertain a subjective belief in their common descent because of similarities of physical type or of customs or both, or because of memories of colonization and migration" (p. 16). Cross cultural communication research models suggest that ethnic groups display value orientations which may or may not be similar. The value orientations of individualism and collectivism, first identified by Hofstede (1980, 1983), may have some utility when examining issues of connection and autonomy. According to Hofstede, those in individualistic cultures put personal needs before the needs of their in-groups. They value freedom, self-reliance, and uniqueness. Collectivistic cultures, on the other hand, perceive group needs as primary, and emphasize conformity, cooperation, and harmony. Gudykunst and Lee (2001) have suggested that awareness of this specific value orientation might serve family research well.

Another valuable framework for this study has been the Afro-centric perspective. The Afro-centric approach is "grounded in an African American frame of reference and centers upon experiences on the African continent" (Socha & Diggs, 1999, p. 12). The African American emphasis on spirituality, harmony, morality, and communalism, for example, are tendencies observed in African American families today although these values are African in nature (Boykin & Toms, 1985). Incorporation of this perspective into one's research is especially crucial if the researcher is European American so as to avoid the problem of viewing (and interpreting) Black families through White cultural lenses (Daniel & Daniel, 1999).

Literature Review

Relational Dialectics

The autonomy and connection contradiction, which Baxter (1988) argued is the primary contradiction for all close relationships, involves partners managing their needs to be independent as well as interdependent. Another dialectical contradiction relevant to this study is openness and closedness, which centers on how much of one's thoughts and feelings are revealed to one's partner. Baxter identified three general strategies, selection, separation, and integration, which relationship partners used to manage dialectical tension. In the dialectical sense, management strategies are located within the relationship as opposed to within individuals. Baxter found relationship satisfaction to correlate significantly with the strategies used to manage dialectical contradictions but not the presence of dialectical contradictions in the relationship. The strategy of selection, for example, which occurs when one pole of the dialectical contradiction is enacted to the exclusion on the other, was shown to have a negative correlation with relationship satisfaction. The use of reframing, where contrasting poles are enacted simultaneously and perceived as enhancements of each other, was found to correlate positively with relationship satisfaction.

The Mother-Adolescent Daughter Relationship

Issues of Connection and Autonomy

The notion that family members continually seek to manage issues of connection and autonomy is not entirely new. Hess and Handel's *Family Worlds* (1959) and Kantor and Lehr's (1975) *Inside the Family* represent two of the earliest examples of family research that recognized those contradictory needs within the family system. Using interviews and observational methods, Hess and Handel determined that families worked to establish a pattern of both separateness and connectedness. Kantor and Lehr's work argued a similar concept, that a primary goal of family members was the negotiation of distance and closeness. Discussions surrounding the time set for the evening meal and the expectations for family members' presence at this meal, may represent a family's attempts to manage its members' needs to be connected as well as to engage in individual pursuits outside of the family.

Although scholars have studied mothers' influence on daughters career choices and employment patterns (Macke & Morgan, 1978; Moen, Erickson, & Dempster-McClain, 1997), impact on sex role behaviors and attitudes (Newcomer & Udry, 1984), and body image and weight (Ogle & Damhorst, 2000), no previous researchers have made the communicative management of connection and autonomy issues in mother-adolescent daughter relationships the centerpiece of their work. The psychoanalytic approach utilized by Chodorow (1978) and Gilligan (1982), however, serves as helpful background. Their explanations suggest that as young women reach adolescence, they begin searching for a personal identity apart from their mothers. Fischer (1983) argued that separation from the mother by the daughter is not only salient during adolescence but is a lifelong activity. Other literature (Haygood, 1991; Miller, 1992, 1995a, 1995b) has touched on connection and autonomy issues in the mother-daughter relationship. Examining women's narratives, Miller (1992) found contradictions fairly synonymous with connection and autonomy (dependence-independence and similarities-differences), although the mother-adolescent daughter relationship was not necessarily the focus of her inquiry.

Previous studies on parent-adolescent relationships (Noller & Callan, 1991; Vangelisti, 1992; Youniss & Smollar, 1985) have also discussed the tension between autonomy and connection. Vangelisti (1992), for example, found that older adolescents' accounts of communication problems with parents emphasized issues "related to the dialectical tension between individuality and connectedness" (p. 395). Thus, although the research literature has recognized the dialectical tension of connection and autonomy as salient in mother-adolescent daughter relationships, an in-depth analysis especially regarding management strategies is lacking.

Impact of Ethnicity

As McGoldrick & Giordano (1996) suggested, "ethnicity patterns our thinking, feeling, and behavior in subtle ways that we are not even aware of" (p. ix) and impacts family communication patterns for generations to come. The importance of the extended family to African Americans today, for example, has its roots in African tradition (Sudarkasa, 1997). The family's ethnic affiliation plays a critical role in human development and survival. African Americans have largely endured a cruel history and even today combat racism, segregation, and discrimination, which no doubt impact functioning within the family.

In addition to differences in historical background and social treatment, ethnic groups may display varying value orientations such as that associated with individualism and collectivism. Helms (1990) and Asante (1973) have suggested that White individuals, as compared to other cultural groups in the United States, share a strong belief in the importance of individualism. Rotheram-Boms, Dopkins, Sabate, and Lightfoot, (1996), investigating teachers' perceptions of students, found that Black students as compared to White students displayed more group orientation and respect for authority.

Unfortunately, the majority of family focused research has continued to use exclusively European American participants (Dilworth-Anderson et al., 1993). Socha and Diggs (1999) have attempted to remedy the neglect of an ethnic focus "by examining 'race' as both an outcome of family communication as well as a factor that influences children's communication development in families" (pp. 4–5). Specifically focusing on adolescent self-esteem in African American and European American adolescents, Diggs (1999) reported that "parents (generally mothers) were overwhelmingly identified as the source of positive feelings for Black and White adolescents" with parents being identified in 83% of the responses followed by friends with 29% and "God, 25%" (p. 124). White adolescents in contrast to Black adolescents reported more frequently that friends impacted their self-feelings. In a study specifically relating to African American mothers and adolescent daughters, Cance et al. (1996) found that a key developmental task for daughters was learning how to live among White people as they developed their Black identity. To explain how African American mothers and their daughters related to each other, the three constructs of closeness, conflict, and control were developed.

Clearly, family scholarship is slowly changing in an attempt to develop a more comprehensive understanding of how families communicate. Yet, there remains much unexplored ground to cover. In response to the need for more scholarly investigation of ethnically diverse families, this study used in-depth interviews and taped interactions of seven African American and seven European American mother-adolescent daughter dyads to answer the following research questions:

RQ1.   What communicative strategies do African American and European American mothers and adolescent daughters use to manage the connection and autonomy dialectic?

RQ2. Does mother-daughter ethnicity differentiate strategies for managing the connection and autonomy dialectic?

Methodology

Design

This study was part of a larger study designed to describe the experience of and communication within the mother-adolescent daughter relationship. The purpose of this study was to look more closely at how communication strategies participants employed to manage the connection and autonomy contradiction might be differentiated by ethnicity. This study used a grounded approach where data were not placed in predetermined categories, but what became important to analyze emerged from the data itself (Maykut & Morehouse, 1994). It employed a symbolic interactionist and feminist approach where both mothers and their adolescent daughters were encouraged to articulate their own unique perspectives. Depth interviews and taped interactions were employed to capture both the universality and diversity of participants' relationships. Previous research concerning relational dialectics, including that of Baxter (1988, 1990), had taken a more quantitative and deductive approach to data. It was felt that because no previous study examined ethnicity's impact on management strategies in mother-adolescent daughter relationships, a thicker, descriptive rendering of data might be helpful to better understand from the interactants' perspective how this management was communicatively accomplished. Following Cannon, Higginbotham, and Leung's (1988) recommendation that research using ethnically diverse samples employ research teams comprised of individuals from those specific ethnic groups, a European American and African American jointly introduced participants to the study, conducted participant interviews, and conferred during data analysis. This partnership was geared toward obtaining a comprehensive portrayal of the mother-daughter experience in both cultures.

Participants

Fourteen mother-adolescent daughter dyads, seven African American and seven European American, were utilized, for a total of 28 participants. A "snowball sampling" approach was used wherein several of the earliest participants obtained through recommendations from a school librarian suggested names of their acquaintances that might also be interested in participation in the study. The participants were from middle class families and came from within a 60-mile radius of a large Midwestern city. Many participants, including all the African American participants, lived in the city itself, whereas the remaining participants lived in suburbs of the city or small towns located nearby. The daughters ranged in age from 13 to 17 years (AA mean = 14.7; EA mean = 14.8). The mothers were from 34 to 48 years (African American mean = 39.7; European American mean = 43.2). All mothers were employed, 12 mothers having full-time employment. To maintain homogeneity in family structure that allows for potentially more accurate comparisons, all participants came from families where a father-figure was present. All participants were given a pseudonym and a code number indicating mother-daughter status and ethnic group identification (AA = African American, EA = European American).

Procedures

Depth interviews. Depth interviewing allows participants to reconstruct their experiences and explore meaning (Seidman, 1991). The interviews in this study were semistructured in that they followed an interview protocol (see the Appendix), but not in such a way as to interrupt or divert the participant's reconstruction of her own experience. Specific areas probed were roles, communication patterns, and conflict within the relationship. Mothers and daughters were interviewed separately to encourage a hopefully more honest accounting of their experiences, uninfluenced by the other's presence. The European American and African American researchers jointly participated in each interview. Interviews were audiotaped and lasted from 25 min to 120 min each, with an average length of 70 min. As soon as possible after the interviews, audiotapes were transcribed. Daughters, interview transcripts averaged 13 pages, whereas mothers' averaged 18.5 pages. Interviews with all but one dyad took place within the participants' home where it was felt participants would be most comfortable. Two to six weeks following the initial information-gathering session, the European American researcher returned to participants' homes to do follow-up interviews or "member checks" where participants, after reading their transcripts, were asked to verify the accuracy of their experiences (Lincoln & Guba, 1985) as portrayed in their printed transcript. The follow-up interview gave participants an opportunity to clarify information already shared or share additional stories and insights.

Joint interaction activity. To provide another method of analyzing the mother-adolescent daughter relationship and communication therein, an audiotaped interaction between members of each mother-daughter dyad was obtained. The joint interaction activity involved the participants discussing the following three topics for approximately 5 min per topic:

1. If money were no object, what would the two of you plan for the perfect family vacation—where would you go, in what type of place would you stay, how long would you stay, what would you do, etc. Come up with as many details as you can.
2. Mothers and their daughters can be both similar to each other as well as very different. In what ways are the two of you similar? In what ways are the two of you different?
3. If you two were asked to help write a book on mothers and teenage daughters, and the editor asked you for the three BEST pieces of advice you could give to help other moms and daughters have a close relationship, what would you say?

Researchers were out of the room as participants interacted. The taped interactions were later transcribed noting length of pauses, interruptions, and simultaneous speech.

Data Analysis

The constant comparative method (Glaser & Strauss, 1967; Lincoln & Guba, 1985; Maykut & Morehouse, 1994) of data analysis was used. Data in the form of interview and interaction transcripts were read, highlighted, and organized into units of meaning or accounts. For this study, an account was defined as a participant's description of a communication strategy used within her relationship which served to manage the connection and autonomy contradiction. Previous scholars have viewed connection and autonomy in slightly different ways. For this study, three variations of the contradiction fell under the umbrella term connection and autonomy. They were as follows: connection and distance, which suggested partners' needs for psychological connection as well as autonomy; dependence and independence, which centered on the need to rely on the other as opposed to the need to be one's own person; and control and laissez-faire, which focused on the need to assert one's own agenda on the other as opposed to taking a laid-back, relaxed approach to decision making. Accounts representing management strategies were placed into categories, taking note of recurring phrases, topics, and patterns (Maykut & Morehouse, 1994). Each account was labeled with the corresponding participant's code number. These categorized accounts were compared within and across groups, combined, modified, and ultimately restructured into six primary management strategies which best appeared to capture the experience of participants. The six strategies are as follows: Role Enactment, Activities Segmentation, Conflict Management Styles, Interaction Climate, Strategic Proxemics, and Protecting and Permitting. Accounts in each category were sorted according to ethnic group noting the distinguishing patterns and characteristics associated with each group.

Results and Interpretation

The following interview excerpts illustrate the struggle mothers experienced between connection and autonomy:

Sometimes it gets to the point where you just don't want to be bothered and it's like, "Oh God, I just can't wait for you to leave this house!" But then I think, I don't want you to go; I really don't want you to go (Darcy, AA participant, talking about her 16-year-old-daughter, Chandra).

I mean, I do want her to grow and expand, but at the same time it's like, oh, there goes your little girl (Bev, EA participant, talking about her 14-year-old daughter, Hope).

Darcy, an African American mother, and Bev, who is European American, share paradoxical feelings regarding their daughters. Both express hope that their daughters will one day be independent; yet, both Darcy and Bev simultaneously desire a continued connection and closeness with them as well. Daughter participants also experienced the connection and autonomy tug-of-war. Sixteen-year-old Kate (EA), who prided herself on her independence, shared her need for mother-daughter affiliation when she stated the following:

Usually, I couldn't go 3 weeks without talking to my mom . . . she and I have like an outlet where it's like, negative charges and positive charges and we equalize. It usually ends up working out that way. I usually have to talk to her, otherwise I get really, really stressed out.

Daughters from both ethnic groups enjoyed talking about themselves as individuals, and could always relate stories of disagreement or conflict within their mother-daughter relationships. Yet, they also consistently conveyed stories in which they identified mothers as important confidents who provided them with support and encouragement.

Ethnic Differences in Management Strategies

Participants of both ethnic groups experienced the dialectical struggle between connection and autonomy needs and coped with the resulting tension in a variety of ways. This section introduces each strategy, and then provides a mother-daughter story representative of both the African American and European American perspectives.

Strategy 1: Role Enactment

Mothers and daughters enacted a variety of role pairings in response to perceived connection and autonomy needs. When mothers perceived too much dependence in their relationships, for example, they often took the role of "teacher" to their daughter's "student." Although a teacher-student relationship can be close and emphasize connection, mothers appeared to play "teacher" so as to convey important life lessons and practical skills which would foster daughters' independence. On the other hand, when daughters struggled with personal issues that they had trouble resolving on their own, mothers might enact roles that emphasized connection, such as "advisor" or "advocate." Mothers served as advocates if they perceived their daughters lacked sufficient "voice" in a situation. This was exemplified when a daughter had trouble at school and her mother became personally involved by talking directly to the daughter's teachers and school administrators.

Mothers and daughters also played the role of "friends." In this particular role pairing, participants' stories indicated that they not only "connected" through mutual activities and talk, but their autonomy was simultaneously emphasized as they related on an egalitarian level as two adult female friends might. Playing the role of "friend" resembled Baxter's "reframing" strategy, where the poles of the dialectical contradiction are seen as enhancement of each (Baxter, 1990).

African American story: Katharine and Tanya (13). Katharine and Tanya enacted all of the role pairings previewed earlier. Katharine's perception that her teacher role is vitally important to her daughter's future success and happiness, for example, is highlighted when she says, "I want her

[Tanya] to grow up to be somebody . . . be a leader, and she'll be something great one day." Self-esteem messages were especially important for African-American mothers to impart to daughters, who mothers knew would have to overcome obstacles, including racial prejudice, to accomplish great things. In addition, mothers as teachers conveyed relationship lessons. As Katherine also shared

> I try to make her [Tanya] love everybody . . . to make her not go with the crowd . . . don't treat people unequally. I try to get her to look at things from a different perspective. Treat everybody the same.

According to Cauce et al. (1996), a key challenge for African American parents is teaching their children to live among European Americans while maintaining their African American identity. The lessons Katharine felt she must impart to Tanya appear to be designed to accomplish this goal.

In addition to teacher-student, Katharine and Tanya play the roles of parental authority-obedient child. This was a common role pairing in many other African American mother-daughter dyads, often enacted when mothers perceived that daughters were vying for power in the relationship. Tanya, for example, had asked her mother if she could cut her hair and get another hole pierced in her ear. Katharine, who is afraid that her daughter wants to grow up too fast, said, "I told her 'in time' . . . I already got my mind set that I'm *not* going to let her grow up." Katharine also asserts, "You can't let her do everything she wants to do . . . *I* need to be the parent!" Tanya supported the view that what her mother says goes in her family. Tanya reported that sometimes her mother makes her buy clothes that are "not my style" and have an "older look." When we asked her if she wore those clothes or if they stayed in her closet, she answered, "I wear it." Cauce et al. (1996) suggested that African American mothers often take a strong parental role.

The parental authority-obedient child role pairing, however, is foregone when Katharine and Tanya enact the role of "best friends." The best friend role highlights connection as does the parental authority-obedient child role, but when this role pairing is enacted, the relationship has a more egalitarian flavor, and Tanya's individuality and uniqueness is also emphasized. Katharine shared with us what she often tells her daughter:

> I'm your friend. You have friends, but I'm your best friend. I try to tell her that all the time. You are going to get hurt in life and what you think isn't always what it is. But me and your daddy are your best friends.

Katharine emphasizes the importance of putting trust in your family first and she emphasized that secrets they share as friends will not be revealed to others: "We're friends and I can tell her something that I would tell an adult and I would say you can't tell nobody, it's between us, and she will hold the secret." The importance of trusting your family members as you would trust a best friend was reiterated often during the interviews of African American participants.

European American story: Janna and Kari (14). Janna and Kari, much as Katharine and Tanya, play the teacher-student role. Kari says her mother has taught her important lessons of "kindness" and "how to treat others," which are similar to the lessons that are reinforced in Tanya's relationship with her mother. Through interviews, it was clear that Janna felt she was the parental authority. Janna said, "I'm the mom and I should set the rules." On occasions, however, Kari seemed to have influence in how those rules were followed: she was not always the obedient child. For example, Janna and Kari had fought for over 3 days when Janna announced she was going to chaperone Kari's eighth-grade dance. Also, when asked to describe a recent conflict, Kari shared that her mother didn't want her to go to another movie with friends because it was "wasting money." When we asked how that conflict was handled. Kari replied

Kari: Sometimes she'll say that I can go . . . or I'll offer to pay for it myself . . . but she usually pays for it anyway.

Interviewer: So are you saying you usually are able to go then?

Kari: Um hmm.

Other European American mothers' and daughters' interactions followed this pattern. The mother, although respected as the authority in the relationship by daughters, didn't always have the "final" say. It seemed many decisions were open to negotiation. Probably the most striking difference ethnically regarding this management strategy was that European American mothers and daughters, although acting as friends, rarely labeled each other as such, and never as "best friends." When we asked Kari if she had a best friend, she replied

> I'm kind of in a group of friends, and I can really talk to them about anything . . . because I do like to tell my mom some stuff, but I can tell them anything, and they won't get mad.

Janna echoes her daughter's notion that mothers and daughters shouldn't really be best friends because it undermines the parental role. Janna asserted

> I hope we [she and Kari] will be friends, but you can't always be friends. It still has to be a mother-daughter relationship. And when we first started. I wanted just to be buddies, and you can't be buddies. It don't work that way.

European American mothers, like Janna, appeared to hold the expectation that when their daughters reached middle-school age, they would automatically gravitate toward similar-aged peers as "best" friends.

In sum, ethnic differentiation in role enactment suggests that African Americans desired a higher degree of connection, both in the roles of parental authority-obedient child and in that of best friend. European Americans, although enacting the authority-child role, did it on a less consistent basis, allowing their daughters to voice personal opinions and even "fight back." This indicated comfort with a higher degree of autonomy which also played out as European American daughters were allowed to look outside their relationships with their mothers for "best friends."

Strategy 2: Activities Segmentation

This strategy was previously identified as a means married couples used to manage the autonomy and connection contradiction (Hoppe-Nagao & Ting-Toomey, 2002): It "refers to the strategy of partitioning autonomy and connection needs according to shared activities" (Hoppe-Nagao & Ting-Toomey, 2002, p. 148). It is a strategy similar to Baxter's (1990) "separation" where partners separate the poles of a dialectical contradiction either temporally or topically. Mothers' work, school, volunteering, or engagement in activities with friends or other members of the family reinforced their autonomy in their mother-daughter relationships. Daughters' school, music, theater, and sports activities, as well as time spent with friends, served a similar function. Daughters' activities apart from their mothers were often encouraged because mothers assumed that their daughters would grow from their outside experiences.

Although separate activities were often embraced both by mothers and daughters, their times together, regardless of the activity, were usually welcomed as opportunities to develop a stronger bond. Shopping was by far what mother and daughters in both ethnic groups highlighted as their favorite mutual activity.

African American story: Veronica and Keesha (15). Veronica is an officer in a correctional institution. She works third shift and is usually going out to work as Keesha is going to bed. Keesha, as well as her mother has her own activities and interests. She is an A student, so her studies keep her busy; she is involved in speaking activities at school, and holds a job at a nearby clothing store. Veronica encourages activities that emphasize Keesha's independence; she stated

I think she gets tired of me always pushing for new experiences . . . learning different things . . . like they just went skiing and I was like, "You gotta go, you gotta go!" I'm always trying to find different activities for her to go out and try.

But just as outside opportunities to facilitate a daughter's identity development were crucial, African American mothers and daughters always made time to interact. An activity that was specifically highlighted in African American interviews was "talking." Talking was clearly viewed as a separate activity, not just a by-product of an activity, such as shopping or "eating out." When Keesha was asked what she enjoyed doing most with her mother, for example, she answered, "Just sitting around talking," and when we asked about where she and her mother had their best conversations, Keesha answered, "mostly in her room. We just lay down and talk about anything." And what did her mother Veronica enjoy most about their relationship? Veronica said, "just listening to her [Keesha] talk about anything and everything." Talk was clearly central to the relationship of this mother and daughter.

European American story: Jessica and Jory (17). Jessica is a high school art teacher. In addition to artwork being an individual pursuit, it is also an activity that Jessica shares with her daughter, Jory. As Jory stated. "If I can't do something, she [Mom] can do it because she teaches the class. I like working with her a lot, even if we don't finish the project." Jory, one of the oldest daughters in this sample, was a school athlete. Other than athletics, Jory worked and had a large circle of friends with whom she "hung out." Jory's friends were important to her, and although she liked doing things with her mother, friends took up a lot of her time. Unlike the African American dyads who emphasized "talk" as an important activity in their mother-daughter relationships, here and in most of the European American dyads, talk was an activity designated more for friends than mothers. As Jory described

When it's just us in the car . . . I like talking to her [my mom]: it does feel more like a friendship relationship, but then like when I have other people, if a friend's on the phone or another person's around, I just kind of get annoyed of her [my mom] sometimes. I still love her, but if my friend's over here, I'm going to go off with my friend.

This excerpt relates directly to the previous section in which it appeared that European American mothers and daughters did not enact the "best friend" role as frequently as in African American relationships. As Jessica, Jory's mother, stated, "I don't think of myself as being a friend [to Jory]. I look at myself as . . . somebody to guide her through life."

In sum, European American mothers and daughters, like Jessica and Jory, enjoyed doing things together, but in addition to school and community activities, the expectation was that daughters would also insist on time for friends and "talk" time would happen in that context. The emphasis on activities and talk with friends highlighted the autonomy pole of the connection and autonomy continuum in European American relationships.

Strategy 3: Conflict Management Style

Many types of conflict management tactics were represented. Some served to move dyadic partners toward increased connection and some to increased distance. Autonomy-seeking strategies were often enacted by daughters to challenge their mothers' authority. Tactics of ignoring, disobeying, and even sarcasm were employed much more by daughters than mothers. Yelling, as a conflict tactic, was used by mothers of both ethnic groups and European American daughters. Mothers, who were generally in the power position in their relationships, also used unilateral authority in the form of demands and ultimatums. These "control" tactics seemed to secure a mother's position as "superior" or in charge. Daughters generally reacted negatively to such strategies, but did not always assert themselves in retaliation. Sometimes daughters acquiesced to their mothers' viewpoints seemingly to "keep peace" or because they knew it was futile to argue. Acquiescing, however, seemed to produce some lingering resentment which might later surface in the enactment of other distancing strategies, such as a daughter staying in her room, or in the most extreme case, running away from home.

Several conflict management strategies served to reestablish connection after conflict. Apologizing, for example, was a tactic used by both African American and European American mothers and daughters. Another positive strategy for resolving conflicts was compromise. When mothers and daughters "talked it out," they not only validated each other by listening to the other's opinion, but managed to reinforce their relational connection by working through a common solution to the problem.

African American story 1: Karen and Cindi (17).   Cindi is Karen's only child. For years, according to Karen. Cindi was the "perfect" child, and they got along very well. Lately, however, Cindi has been skipping school, staying out late with the car, lying about where she is going, and several months earlier, had run away from home. In the following interaction, which was taped the night of the interviews, it is clear that Karen is trying to control the conflict as Cindi chooses to simply agree with her mother's viewpoint (K = Karen, the mother; C = Cindi, the daughter; the number in brackets indicates length of pauses in seconds):

K: How are we different not similar?

C: Um . . . different . . . um . . . a lot of the stuff has to do with lazy. You do things right away and I hold them off, [4.0] What do you think? How are we different?

K: [We're different] because I have high expectations about myself. I have high goals; it might have taken me awhile to achieve them, but I'm old; you're young. Like I said we're different cuz you're lazy. You don't care about—actually you don't care about yourself. You have no goals. Nothing. Then you sit there last night and said "I can't do it, but I don't know why." You sound like you're a person on drugs or retarded. Well, buy this—I'm done with all this. I'm done. I told you last night when I'm done. I'm done, I'm done. We're a lot different . . . it's always people mess Cindi up, it's never Cindi messed herself up. It's other people that messed you up. I messed you up. Your step dad messed you up. All these other people mess Cindi up, but does she mess up her own self? [3.0] What is the difference you see?

C: That's it.

K: What do you mean, that's it?

C: That's it as far as different.

K: You're saying we're different because you're lazy, I'm not.

C: Well, I mean, it's all those things you just said.

One might expect Cindi to retaliate in response to her mother's harsh comments. A clue to her behavior was provided in an earlier interview when Karen commented that Cindi had been socialized to be respectful, and she always was. This is characteristic, according to Rotheram-Borus et al. (1996), of African American adolescents who were found to demonstrate more respect for authority than European American adolescents.

African American story 2: Darcy and Chandra (16).   Darcy and Chandra provide another example of conflict management style. Although most African American mothers used conflict management tactics that demonstrated their authority, Darcy, a social worker, shared that she was consciously trying not to be the stereotypical "iron-fisted" African American mother. In our follow-up interview, Darcy elaborated on why she used a compromise rather than a controlling style with her daughter, Chandra:

In the time period that I came from . . . it might be stereotype, but you know, the black woman has a stereotype that she don't take nothing and she's always moving her head like this and she's got everybody in check. We came up under more of an iron fist, like I told you my mom was, whereas I think in the Caucasian race, they had more of a—I think they communicated more. Because the black woman has always had to be the strong person of her race, she's always had to be the provider; she's always had to keep the family together. She's had so many things that she had to do to survive. She didn't have the luxury to be able to gell and mold and bond and all of these soft cushy things we've been talking about, because she had to make life. As time has evolved and we've become more educated and we've reached for higher positions, and higher heights, we've come to realize that there is a big communication process that needs to happen to be able to mesh and have a good relationship with your child, and it's not all about control.

Although Darcy shares that she does not use "control" in her relationship, her interview demonstrated that her daughter, Chandra, was sometimes the person "in charge." Darcy gave an example of how she has "given in" to Chandra's requests:

I had promised to Chandra to get her nails done, okay, and this was like 2 weeks ago. I was like, "Well, when I get paid we'll get our nails done." But then I had to help my other daughter out with the car insurance, so money was really tight, and I'm like, Chandra, you know, I'm not going to get the nails done this time even though I did get paid. Right away, "Oh, you promised me!" and you know, the pouts and the long faces and it's not fair and on and on and on. But Chandra just has that way of roping her mother in, and everybody's upset, everybody's upset. Eventually I'm like, "All right let's go get our nails done. Just get your face up."

Chandra in this excerpt, uses what Hoppe-Nagar and Ting-Toomey (2002) would call "antisocial strategies" for getting her way. Other times, Chandra used humor to diffuse conflicts. According to Chandra

When we argue, or when I get mad at her or she's mad at me . . . I'll just get over it and go back and mess with her until she start laughing [laughter] and then we'll be straight again.

Although use of humor was apparent in many mother-daughter relationships, Chandra was the only African American daughter to refer to its use in managing conflict.

European American story: Jessica and Jory (17). Trends in the data from this study demonstrated support for Kizielewicz's (1988) observation that European American adolescent daughters are more verbally assertive with their mothers than are African American daughters. Although overall, European American daughters understood that their mothers were "in charge," they tended to describe conflict situations in which they "argued" with or even "yelled at" their mothers. Jessica stated that her arguments with Jory could get "pretty verbal and pretty crazy." Jory's assessment of conflict in their relationship was expressed as follows:

I argue quite a bit, and I don't know—it's I think when she [my mom] disciplines me. I don't do well with that because I don't think she should be disciplining me or anything. I don't like to take anything like that.

Later in our interview. Jory's need to assert her autonomy during conflict episodes resurfaced when she said

I always have to be right . . . if we don't have the same opinion about some things, and if it's something I actually care about, then I get mad because . . . I want her to see it like the way I see it because I know I'm right. [laughter]

What is the mother's perspective here concerning her daughter's "talking back?" Although Jessica admitted that they have had some "bad days" argument-wise, she also seemed to respect her daughter's strong sense of self. When describing Jory to us, Jessica stated that she was "very outgoing and very outspoken . . . she expressed how she feels and takes a stand and pretty much doesn't give in." Jessica's comment clearly indicated an individualistic value orientation. Yet, not all European American conflict accounts indicated that daughters "talked back" to mothers; participants from this group also shared conflicts where strategies of acquiescing, apologizing, and compromise were employed.

When examining conflict management style in mother-adolescent daughter relationships. European American daughters were more likely to assert their own opinions, even to the point of "talking back" or yelling, although they also acquiesced to their mothers' ultimatums, apologized, and compromised as well. Daughters' verbal assertiveness was seldom sounded in African American interviews and even Chandra seemed to get her way with her mother using tactics of persistence and humor.

Strategy 4: Interaction Climate

Interaction climate was previously identified as a strategy marital couples used to manage autonomy and connection issues (Hoppe-Nagao & Tiag-Toomey, 2002). It essentially deals with strategizing the amount and quality of self disclosures so that the resulting openness or closedness one has with one's partner, in turn, fosters more or less connection or autonomy. The enactment of this strategy illustrates the "knot of contradictions" concept (Comforth, 1968) first introduced in which dialectical contradictions may be intricately intertwined. In this case, one dialectical contradiction serves to help manage another. Openness in the mother-adolescent relationship was clearly a strategy used to foster connection. Closedness, on the other hand, which seemed strategically enacted by daughters, was a play to assert their autonomy. Leslie (EA-16) shared, for example, "I can tell my mother anything, but I don't tell her *everything*." Daughters' refusal to discuss topics with their mothers represented a way they could assert power in the relationship.

African American story: Denise and Angela (15). Denise and Angela described their relationship in terms of a very open interaction climate which was indicative of most African American mothers and daughters in this study. Regarding openness with her daughter, Denise shared the following:

> I don't think there is anything we haven't talked about or I don't think that we can't talk about. We talk about whatever's going on, whatever could be going on, what you like, didn't like, what happened all day. You usually don't have to ask you [I] just listen . . . I don't think Angela is afraid to say what she has to say about boys and I'm never afraid to give my opinion [laughter] but we usually don't have to cut off a conversation about boys, sex, whatever. We don't have to cut off the conversation because one or the other is in total disagreement or uncomfortable.

When we interviewed Angela, however, she contradicted her mother's comments. Although reiterating that she and her mother talk "all the time" about a wide variety of topics, Angela confided that she did not feel comfortable talking about boys with her mother. As Angela explained

> When I was in 6th grade I was like, "Oh Mom, I like this guy, he's so cute" and she'd be like, "Oh yeah, you're just in sixth grade." Now it's like I don't want to say anything because I'm afraid of what she might say—now I'm afraid of what to say to her . . . getting to this dating age thing, it's like the silent treatment. We [my mom and I] never talk about it.

Most African American mothers shared Denise's perception that because they and their daughters talked "all the time," the daughters were very open with them on all subjects. It is interesting to note, however, that other daughters, like Angela, chose to stay somewhat closed on the topic of boys.

According to national statistics, the African American teen birth rate is almost double the rate for European American teens (Illinois Department of Public Health, 2000). Most African American mothers in this study had someone in their family who had become a teen mother; they were well aware that this circumstance often forced the teen mother to abandon personal academic and career goals. To combat the threat of teen pregnancy, most African American mothers were vigilant regarding their daughters' contact with boys. It was not uncommon for African American daughters in this study to be forbidden to date or even talk to boys on the phone until they were 16. In the preceding excerpt, Angela senses her mother's reluctance to talk about boys. She feels that if she brings up the topic, her mother might set even stricter rules.

Darcy and Chandra were an exception to this pattern. Darcy shared that she had always been open with her daughters regarding all aspects of her life, so that her daughters would follow her example. As she explained

> I've always kept it [communication] open and even when it came to the point where I wanted them [daughters] to tell me when they were starting to have feelings about boys . . . or if they thought they needed birth control or something . . . I don't want to be surprised. "Just come and tell me" [I said]. And both of them came to me and said, "Mom this is what's happening, this is what I'm feeling."

Darcy's emphasis on openness and being nonjudgmental seemed to have worked to keep her connected to her daughters, especially on such an important subject.

European American story: Sandy and Kate (16). Sandy and Kate's story illustrates a few ethnic differences in interaction climate. Although they were very close through middle school years, and still have what most European Americans would call a "close" relationship. Sandy and Kate have noticed a decrease in their openness which wasn't characteristic of the African American dyads, except on the topic of boys. This winter, when Sandy, the mother, felt that their relationship was suffering because she and Kate no longer had time to talk. Sandy took it on herself to share her concerns in hopes of reestablishing their close connection:

> We had a period this winter probably where we were probably the least close we've ever been, and it was really difficult for both of us, and I finally went in to her and just said, 'You know, I don't know what's going on, but I really miss you . . . and I wanted to tell you,' and she said she'd missed me too and she just had been busy in school and with her boyfriend and this and that and the other.

In her separate interview, Kate's comments reinforced the perception that her mother had regarding the distance that had crept into the relationship. It was true that Kate was spending a lot of time at school and also with her boyfriend. But in addition, Kate's developing sense of identity and need for autonomy had sometimes made her utilize a strategy of closedness. As Kate shared

> When I was little I thought, you know, all of her [Mom's] views were correct, and now since I've started developing my own sometimes she'll talk and be very adamant about it, and I'll disagree with it, and it will really start to get on my nerves, but I don't want to say, "No I don't agree" because she also is adamant in her beliefs and she, I don't think, would be changed by or swayed by what I have to say and I don't think I'd be swayed by what she had to say, so sometimes it ends up putting like a little bit of space between us, because of being different people instead of having like the same mind.

Kate's later comments further suggested that she and her mother had different interests which were getting in the way of their previous openness:

And certain things she does just bore me to death. I mean, we used to have conversations, and now she'll talk about gardening, and I really just zone out and when I talk about my flute playing, then she'll zone out, and so we don't have as much in common as we did.

The third factor influencing Kate's recent closedness with her mother was her boyfriend:

Right now my best friend is my boyfriend. My mom doesn't know as much about the things that go on in school. She doesn't know the names of the people that I go to school with, even though I mention them several times, it sort of just goes in one ear and out the other . . . so I usually end up talking to my boyfriend a lot about that and about the problems that are going on in our family and he's very supportive and that helps a lot.

Boyfriends or girlfriends who became primary confidants of the European American daughters sometimes learned much more about a daughter than even her own mother knew. This might create the perception that the mother-daughter relationship had become more closed and distant especially when compared to the relationships of African American mothers and daughters. One commonality between daughters regardless of ethnic group, however, was that even European American daughters emphasized that the topic they would more likely share with friends than with mothers was that of "boys."

Strategy 5: Strategic Proxemics

This strategy incorporates a nonverbal dimension that is sometimes lacking in communication studies. It deals with mothers' and daughters' use of physical distance to manage autonomy and connection. When mothers and daughters wanted to connect psychologically, they moved closer physically. They found each other in bedrooms, the kitchen, or wherever they expected the other to be. Sometimes the desire for connection was so strong that closer proximity evolved into touch in the way of hugs, kisses, or snuggling. Mothers and daughters also described instances, however, when incorporating physical distance was a response to too much connection.

African American story: composite of several dyads. One of the most striking differences between African American and European American dyads came in the area of proximity. Only one of the European American dyads, but all of the African American dyads, mentioned the mother's bed as a place where they liked to relax and converse. Katherine, for example, explained that her daughter, Tanya (13), had developed a pattern of laying in her bed because their father worked long hours and got home very late at night. As she described in an earlier excerpt

She [my daughter] comes in my bed . . . and we lay there and talk. She tells me everything that's going on with the other girls . . . . We are friends and I can tell her something that I would tell an adult and I would say you can't tell nobody, it's between mother and daughter, and she will hold the secret.

Keesha (15), whose mother Veronica worked third shift as a correctional officer, mentioned that she often lays in her mother's bed with her to talk. For Keesha and Veronica, this is an excellent way for them to connect as one is sometimes waking up while the other is going to bed. Finally, because Rhonda's (AA) brother lives with them (Rhonda is a single mother), she and her daughter Deleasa (14) have to share not only a bedroom, but a bed. Rhonda discussed how their bed was the location for their "best" talks:

At night when we go to bed, and we lay down, we—because pretty much I've yelled at her during the evening, (and) I've calmed down by then. You do not let, as the Bible says, the sun set on your anger. Ok? I've pretty much calmed down and I explain to her why I yelled at her and what my fears are, and if she don't pick these things up what's gonna happen to her. And then I ask her, what is your input here? What do you feel?

It would seem that African American adolescent daughters move into their mothers' beds to foster connection. During one of my follow-up visits. I asked Darcy why the African American mother's bed as a location for conversation was so important. She answered

> To me [the mother's bedroom] is a great place to talk, I mean cuz when you're sharing heart issues, they're private, they're personal, and you're most comfortable where you're private at—your room where you can lay out and be yourself.

Although African American participants seemed to enjoy physical closeness, several daughters recognized that there were times when they needed to distance themselves from their mothers. Both Keesha (13) and Camille (14) shocked their mothers during the study's interaction activity when they shared that one important piece of advice for mothers and adolescent daughters would be to take a timeaway from one another. Keesha's and her mother, Veronica's, interaction went as follows:

K: If the two of you were asked to help write a book on mothers and teenage daughters, and the editor asked you for the three best pieces of advice you could give to help other moms and daughters have a close relationship, what would you say?

V: One would be—

K: Stay out of my way!

V: What!

K: Take a time out. Time outs from each other. From everyone else. From the world. I think that's good enough.

V: [laughs] And that would make them closer?

K: I just say, give yourself some space. By the time you cool down or something you done forgot what you did. I know that's what I usually do.

V: So how would that help a mother and daughter be close?

K: Well, I still think you each need time out. If you spend too much time together you start to get on each other's nerves.

Although Veronica didn't seem to understand, Keesha's comments were extremely perceptive. In the whirlwind yin-yang of relational dialectics, too much togetherness will most likely motivate interactants to increase the distance in the relationship.

European American story: Darlene and Leslie (16). Like the African American participants, comments of the European American mothers and daughters equated closer proximity with psychological connection. Leslie (16), for example, goes to her mother's bedroom where she knows she will find her mother every evening. As Darlene, Leslie's mother, has observed.

> She [Leslie] has a way of coming around close to me wherever I am, usually when she's feeling like she wants to connect with me . . . I might be reading for a little while or watching a couple minutes of TV in the bedroom and she'll want to talk, I enjoy that.

Darlene also practiced this strategy when she wanted to connect with her daughter:

> [I'll] just hang out and maybe watch a TV show. She's [Leslie's] sitting there watching so I'll just sit down and watch it for no other reason than she's watching it. Once-in-awhile

I'll comment on what she's watching. Like if it's *Friends* I'll say, "do you really think people act that way?" So . . . just hanging around each other, doing what the young person is doing and kibitzing about that.

"Hanging out" nearby one another served to create a common topic of interest that in turn, could connect dyadic partners by opening up their channels of communication.

European American daughters' stories also tended to reinforce the notion that mothers and daughters often needed space to manage issues of connection and autonomy. Having one's individual space or bedroom seemed especially important to European American families, where every daughter interviewed had her own room. Although Leslie finds her mother when she needs to "connect," she also uses her own room as a haven from the rest of the family. Darlene shared that if Leslie didn't want to talk or get asked to help in the kitchen, "she runs upstairs to her room and closes the door."

Although African American and European American dyads used proxemic strategies to manage connection and autonomy feelings, African American participants seemed slightly more comfortable with touch and physical closeness as evidenced in their stories regarding their relaxing and conversing in the mother's bed.

Strategy 6: Protecting and Permitting

This management strategy, like interaction climate, had a dialectical nature which, when enacted, moved mothers and daughters along the continuum of connection and autonomy depending on which pole of the strategy was enacted. Mothers, for example, often used protective tactics when they wanted to keep their daughters close and safe from harm. Clearly, daughters sometimes felt stifled, and resented their mothers' overprotective strategies, seeing them as threats to the autonomy they desired. Kate thought her mother's need to protect was comical, referring to her as a "helicopter mom," always hovering around ready to swoop down and save her from danger. Mothers in both groups took their responsibility for protecting their daughters very seriously. On the other hand, they also realized that they must give daughters the freedom to make their choices and ultimately their own mistakes.

African American story 1: Rhonda and Deleasa (14). Like most African American mothers, Rhonda is very vigilant regarding her daughter Deleasa's activities. Her perception is that the world is a cruel and dangerous place, not only in a physical sense, but in a psychological one as well. As Rhonda shared

It's bad out there, really bad . . . I feel she [Deleasa] knows why I've taught her about the things going on out in the world. There's always going to be someone who will be able to fool her and my biggest fear is that if she falls into the trap it would ruin her life in the future.

One of the traps for Rhonda, as for many African Americans, was the threat of early sexual activity. Rhonda had established strict rules for her daughter as Deleasa had shared that she could not yet date or talk to boys on the telephone. Lately, however, the Internet has posed a new danger for her adolescent daughter. Rhonda has a computer at home that Deleasa likes to use, which prompted the following comment:

I won't go online with that computer upstairs. I will not do what I want to do with it because you have these perverts out there, pedophiles stalking your children, and I know with me working and going to school, I'm not here to monitor Deleasa every second . . . Deleasa is a child—I would like to believe she won't, but I've been a kid, she's going to get curious.

But although African American mothers were adamant about the need to stay connected to daughters and have them grow up in a protective environment, they were just as vocal in their assertions that one had to allow daughters to learn from their own mistakes. As Rhonda put it

> I have had my time to mold her [Deleasa] and I told her there is a time when I should not have to be behind you—a sword in one hand and a whip in the other. You should be able to walk that road by yourself.

Other African American moms echoed the idea that you had to be somewhat permissive in addition to protective, to be sure one's daughter would develop self-confidence and self-reliance. Mary, another African American mom, put it well when she said

> Because you're a parent, you don't want them to get hurt. But sometimes the school of hard knocks has to happen. You know what I'm saying? And that's the tough love. That's the hard thing. It's like, oh, I want to protect them from life, but they got to learn it like we all did.

Rhonda (AA) expressed several times during her interview that if you teach a child important life lessons, they should have the tools needed to get along in life. Still, it was difficult to back away and allow daughters to make mistakes. As Rhonda stated

> I was so protective she [my daughter] was trying to tell me, "I can do it myself, Mama! You told me! You told me!" So I finally had to step back and see her fall. See, I didn't use to let her fall. But if you play with fire you're gonna got burned.

A method African American mothers used to protect daughters and assure that in the future they would succeed on their own was use of the imperative mode, where mothers told daughters directly and honestly what they should do, expecting immediate obedience (Daniel & Daniel, 1999). Daniel and Daniel (1999) explained that African American parents use this type of communication as it has historically protected their children from a hostile environment where one wrong action or word could get them arrested or physically hurt.

Sometimes the communication between the African American mother and daughter could be so blunt that it seemed geared to scare the daughter into taking care of herself and following the pattern of behavior her parents had instilled in her. Rhonda, for example, shared a story regarding an interaction when Deleasa was only 7 years old:

> Once my daughter Deleasa got mad at me and said, "I wish I could just die!" I said, "You wanna die, You say you wanna die?" I said. "I ain't got to kill you; there enough crazy people out there to kill you. Open the door, just go right out there so they can kill you." She looked at me at 11:00 at night like, "Oh I ain't going out there!" "But you said you wanted to die! If you wanna die, you go out there and someone will surely kill you, Child!"

Katherine, another African American mother provided this example of how she and her husband tried to teach Tanya not to jump into cars to get rides:

> Last summer we had relatives that lived two blocks down and a friend of ours came up, and her cousins came by to have some fun; they were playing ball and she [Tanya] jumped in the car to ride down the street to her cousin's house. And her dad just blew his top because you don't just jump in a car with nobody! To ride nowhere! And we used the example of the girl, here in the city, who was just riding in a car and two shots were fired and someone was killed. The next day they came back to get her. And they shot her and

killed her because she saw who had shot the person the day before. It was a perfect example why we say you don't get in anybody's car. We use a lot of things like that as examples.

Use of the imperative mode and verbal bluntness was used quite often as African American moms attempted to protect daughters as well as permit them to explore within boundaries. It seemed effective in Rhonda's case as her daughter, Deleasa, shared the following:

She [Mom] has taught me well . . . I listen to her and I understand what she has taught me, and I think she should understand that she taught me well enough, and . . . I've followed in her footsteps, and I know what's wrong and I know what's right, and I hope she can trust me that I am going to do the right thing . . . and if something comes up that has to have a choice, I'll hear her voice in my head talking in me.

Protection could come through expecting direct obedience, but also through the repetition of important lessons, that would one day become part of the daughter's frame of reference allowing her to make her own intelligent choices.

European American story: Jane and Brianne (14). European American mothers were aware that their role of protector had to be tempered with the role of permitter, but the intensity and importance of these dialectically opposed actions was not as pronounced in European American dyads. European American mothers vocalized fears for their daughters, most of which centered around them getting involved with "bad" friends and possibly drinking and drugs. As Jane stated

As she [Brianne] gets older into her teens. I know her friends are going to have more influence than I do and I'm trying to guide her into which friends to pick although I know that's not always going to work either. I don't like it, but I know it will happen.

As friends seemed to play a larger role in the lives of European American daughters than in the lives of African American daughters, this would be a legitimate concern for European American parents. One way that Jane and Brianne coped with this concern was through using a protect and permit strategy that seemed to reframe the proposed activity Brianne shared that her mother tries to protect her by gathering as much information about an event as possible. As Brianne stated

Brianne: Well, like if I wanted to go to a movie or something I don't know, it gets frustrating because she [Mom] asks like every single simple question to get every single detail—like who are you going with, when are you coming back?

Interviewer: But, do you end up going then?

Brianne: Well, sometimes, yeah, usually I do.

Although Brianne, like other daughters in this study, often resented their mother's seemingly incessant questions, it seemed to be a way to protect and permit simultaneously. It was a strategy that reinforced a sense of connection as it allowed the daughters a limited exercising of their autonomy.

Conclusions

An analysis of the data revealed several trends that can facilitate our understanding of strategies mothers and daughters use to manage issues of connection and autonomy in African American and European American mother-adolescent daughter dyads. The first trend suggests that African American mothers and daughters are more comfortable with higher levels of relational connection than are European American dyads, where autonomy seems to be highlighted. This could be observed in all of the strategies illustrated. African American mothers more often than European Americans, for example, coconstructed the role of "best friend" with daughters, emphasizing that your family members, usually your mother, should be your best friend. European American daughters, however, although enjoying their activities with "Mom," were much more likely to engage in activities with friends outside the family. This tendency reinforced the European American proclivity toward individualism in that daughters were allowed to choose their own friends with whom to spend time. A tendency toward a stronger sense of connection in African American families could also be seen in conflict strategies used. African American dyads tended to use conflict management tactics that fostered connection, either through control and acquiescing, using apologies, or sometimes compromise. This finding supported Cauce et al.'s (1996) research with Black adolescent daughters which found that their relationships with their mothers were characterized by closeness and control. In European American families, daughters were more verbally assertive, even to the point of being abrasive and yelling in response to their mothers. Again, when European American daughters were allowed to voice opinions and compete for decision-making power, an individualistic value orientation was being emphasized. Other management strategies that supported the perception that African American dyads seemed more comfortable with a heightened degree of connection came in the area of conversational openness and strategic proxemics, where African American daughters and mothers often laid together in the mother's bed talking and relaxing.

Another trend that was suggested by this data was the strong need expressed by African American mothers to protect their daughters. Protective strategics involved mothers enforcing rules, being vigilant, teaching important lessons, and use of communication style, such as the imperative mode, that had expectations for a child's immediate obedience. Daniel and Daniel (1999) explained that "the imminency of the danger in the African American child's physical, emotional, social, and cognitive growth and development requires the imperatives of a survival modality" (p. 37). Although European American mothers expressed a need to protect daughters, it was not as adamantly expressed, possibly conveying their perception that the world was not as threatening to them. This may have been because psychological threats in the form of racism and discrimination are not experienced by European Americans. Yet, just as important to African American mothers as the need to protect, was the need to allow daughters opportunities to use the skills they had been taught so that they would one day be successful and self-reliant young women.

This study has expanded our knowledge of the mother-adolescent daughter relationship and suggests that ethnicity plays a role in how the yin and yang of connection and autonomy are experienced and managed. A limitation of this study was that it was, as most descriptive studies, small and cannot be generalized. Yet, it raises issues that can be examined more extensively in future studies and provides, in participants' own words and styles, insights regarding dialectical management strategies that are often difficult to capture. That the study was cross-sectional rather than longitudinal in nature should also be addressed in the future. To truly understand the adolescent transition in the mother-daughter relationship and the experience and management of connection and autonomy issues, it should be studied over time and in relation to other life transitions.

This study was also limited in type of family examined as participants were only from middle-class families where there was a father or father-figure present. Although there is some transferability to mothers and adolescent daughters of other family types, results cannot necessarily be generalized to all mothers and adolescent daughters. Clearly, single mothers, lesbian mothers, adoptive mothers, and stepmothers, to name a few, might have differences in the ways they experience and communicatively enact their relationships with adolescent daughters. Socioeconomic classes other than the middle class should also be examined.

Because this study suggested that ethnicity impacted family communication, other ethnic groups should be included in family communication research. The United States is becoming more and more diverse; thus studies drawing from Native American, Latino, Asian American, and other cultural groups are crucial to extend our understanding and enhance our ability to serve the needs of all our country's citizens.

One word of caution should be voiced. It was not my intention to evaluate the mother-daughter dyads who participated in this study. My purpose was not to determine which ethnic group was more psychologically "healthy." In fact, keeping in mind the family systems theory concept of equifinality (von Bertalanffy, 1975), which suggests that two diverse systems can achieve similar goals through different means, we must be cautious in making a judgment regarding what degree of connection or autonomy is more beneficial in the mother-adolescent daughter relationship. Boyd-Franklin (1989) pointed out, for example, that Black families differ from White families in degree of enmeshment. Boyd-Franklin suggested that in a counseling context, a Black family may be viewed by the White therapist as being too enmeshed, as White families often do not have that degree of connection. Clearly, our question should not be which ethnic group does it better, but how do they do it at all? Understanding rather than evaluation at this juncture is the most appropriate response to the results of this study.

References

Alba, R. (1990) *Ethnic identity: The transformation of white America.* New Haven, CT: Yale University Press.

Asante, M. K. (1973): *Transracial communication.* Englewood Cliffs, NJ: Prentice Hall.

Baxter, L. A. (1988). A dialectical perspective on communication strategies in relationship development. In S. W. Duck, D. F. Hay, S. E. Hobfoll, W. Iches & B. Montgomery (Eds.). *Handbook of personal relationships* (pp. 257–273) London: Wiley.

Baxter, L. A. (1990). Dialectical contradictions in relationship development. *Journal of Social and Personal Relationships, 7,* 69–88.

Baxter, L. A. & Montgomery, B. M. (1996). *Relating: Dialogues and dialectics.* New York: Guilford.

Blumer, H. (1969). *Symbolic interactionism: Perspective and method.* Englewood Cliffs, NJ: Prentice Hall.

Boyd-Franklin, N. (1989). *Black families in therapy: A multisystems approach.* New York: Guilford.

Boykin, A. W., & Toms, F. D. (1985). Black child socialization: A conceptual framework. In H. McAdoo (Eds.): *Black children: Social, education, and parental environments* (pp. 33–51). Beverly Hills, CA: Sage.

Cannon, L., Higginbotham, E., & Leung, M. (1988). Race and class bias in qualitative research on women. *Gender & Society, 2,* 449–462.

Cauce, A. M., Hiraga, Y., Graves, D., Gonzales, N., Ryan-Finn, K., & Grove, K. (1996). African American mothers and their adolescent daughters: Closeness, conflict, and control. In B. J. Ross Leadbeater and N. Way (Eds.), *Urban girls: Resisting stereotypes, creating identities* (pp. 100–116). New York: New York University Press.

Chodorow, N. (1978). *The reproduction of mothering. Psychoanalysis and the sociology of gender.* Berkeley: University of California Press.

Comforth, M. (1968). *Materialism and dialectical method.* New York: International Publishers.

Daniel, J. L., & Daniel, J. E. (1999). African American childrearing: The context of a hot stove. In T. J. Socha & R. C. Diggs (Eds.). *Communication, race, and family: Exploring communication in Black, White and Biracial families* (pp. 25–44). Mahwah, NJ: Lawrence Erlbaum Associates, Inc.

Diggs, R. C. (1999). African American and European American adolescents' perceptions of self-esteem as influenced by parent and peer communication and support environments. In T. J. Socha & R. C. Diggs (Eds.), *Communication, race, and family: Exploring communication in Black, White and Biracial families* (pp. 105–146). Mahwah, NJ: Lawrence Erlbaum Associates, Inc.

Dilworth-Anderson, P., Burton, L. M., & Johnson, L. B. (1993). Reframing theories for understanding race, ethnicity, and families. In P. G. Boss, W. J. Doherty, R. LaRossa, W. R. Schumm, & S. K. Stinmetz (Eds.). *Sourcebook of family theories and methods: A contextual approach* (pp. 135–163). New York: Plenum.

Fischer, L. R. (1983). Transition to grandmotherhood. *International Journal of Aging and Human Development, 16,* 67–78.

Gilligan, C. (1982). *In a different voice: Psychological theory and women's development.* Cambridge, MA: Harvard University Press.

Glaser, B. G., & Strauss, A. L., (1967). *The discovery of grounded theory.* Chicago: Aldine.

Gudykunst, W. B., & Lee, C. M. (2001). An agenda for studying ethnicity and family communication. *Journal of Family Communication, 7,* 75–85.

Haygood, M. S. (1991, October). *Tangled vines: An exploration of the mother-daughter bond through oral history.* Paper presented at the meeting of the Organization for the Study of Communication, Language, and Gender. Milwaukee, WI.

Helms, J. E. (1990). Toward a model of White racial identity development. In J. Helms (Ed.), *Black and White racial identity: Theory, research, and practice* (pp. 49–66). New York: Greenwood.

Hess, R. & Handel, G. (1959). *Family worlds.* Chicago: University of Chicago Press.

Hofstede, G. (1980). *Motivation, leadership, and organizations: Do American theories apply abroad. Organizational Dynamics, 9(1),* 42–63.

Hofstede, G. (1983). National cultures in four dimensions. *International Studies of Management and Organization, 13,* 46–74.

Hoppe Nagao A., & Ting-Toomey S. (2002). Relational dialectics and management strategies in marital couples. *Southern Communication Journal, 67,* 142–159.

Illinois Department of Public Health. (2000). *African-American adolescents: Living in a high-risk population.* Retrieved April 10, 2001, from www.idph.state.il.us/public/respect/african_american_ets.htm.

Kantor, D., & Lehr, W. (1975). *Inside the family: Toward a theory of family process.* San Francisco: Jossey-Bass.

Kizielewicz, N. (1988). *A study of mothers and adolescent daughters in African American families* (Report No. CG022992). Alexandria, VA: American Association for Counseling and Human Development Foundation. (ERIC Document Reproduction Service No. ED326782)

Kluckhohn, C., & Strodbeck, F. (1961). *Variations in value orientations.* Evanston, IL: Row, Peterson.

Lincoln, Y., & Guba, B. G. (1985). *Naturalistic Inquiry.* Newbury Park, CA: Sage.

Macke, A. & Morgan, W. (1978). Maternal employment, race, and work orientation of high school girls. *Social Forces, 57,* 187–204.

Maykut, P., & Morehouse, R. (1994). *Beginning qualitative research: A philosophic and practical guide.* Washington, DC: Falmer.

McGoldrick, M., & Giordano, J. (1996). Overview: ethnicity and family therapy. In M. McGoldrick, J. Giordano, & J. Pearce (Eds.), *Ethnicity and family therapy* (pp. 1–27). New York: Guilford.

Mead, G. H. (1956). *On social psychology: Selected papers.* Chicago: University of Chicago Press. (Original work published 1934).

Miller, M. A. (1992). The mother-daughter relationship: Narrative as a path to understanding. *Women's Studies in Communication, 15,* 1–2.

Miller, M. A. (1995a, November). *Daughters, mothers, and grandmothers: An ethnography of intergenerational communication.* Paper presented at the Speech Communication Association Convention in San Antonio, Texas.

Miller, M. A. (1995b). An intergenerational case study of suicidal tradition and mother-daughter communication. *Journal of Applied Communication Research, 23(4),* 247–270.

Moen, P., Erickson, M., & Dempster-McClain, D. (1997). Their mother's daughters? The intergenerational transmission of gender attitudes in a world of changing roles *Journal of Marriage and the Family, 59,* 281–293.

Montemayer, R. (1982). The relationship between parent-adolescent conflict and the amount of time adolescents spend alone and with parents and peers. *Child Development, 53,* 1512–1519.

Montgomery, B. M. & Baxter, L. A. (1998). A guide to dialectical approaches to studying personal relationships. In B. Montgomery and L. Baxter (Eds.), *Dialectical approaches to studying personal relationships* (pp. 1–16). Mahwah, NJ: Lawrence Erlbaum Associates, Inc.

Newcomer, S. F. & Udry, J. R. (1984). Mother's influence on the sexual behavior of the teenage children. *Journal of Marriage and the Family, 46,* 477–485.

Noller, P. & Bagi, S. (1985). Parent-adolescent communication. *Journal of Adolescence, 9,* 125–144.

Noller, P., & Callan, V. (1991). *The adolescent in the family.* New York: Routledge.

Ogle, J. P. & Damhorst, M. L. (2000). Dieting among adolescent girls and their mothers. An interpretive study. *Family and Consumer Sciences Research Journal, 28,* 428–463.

Pipher, M. (1994). *Reviving Ophelia: Saving the selves of adolescent girls.* New York: Ballantine.

Rotheram-Borus, M. J., Dopkins, S., Sabate, N., & Lightfoot, M. (1996). Personal and ethnic identity, values, and self esteem among Black and Latino adolescent girls. In B. J. R. Leadbeater & N. Way (Eds.). *Urban girls: Resisting stereotypes, creating identities* (pp. 35–552). New York: New York University Press.

Santrock, J. W. & Yuseen, S. R. (1992). Child development: An introduction. Dubuque, IA: Brown.

Seidman, I. E. (1991). *Interviewing as qualitative research: A guide for researchers in education and the social sciences.* New York: Teachers College Press.

Socha, T. J., & Diggs, R. C. (1999). At the crossroads of communication, race, and family: Toward understanding Black, White, and biracial family communication. In T. J. Socha & R. C. Diggs (Eds.), *Communication, race, and family: Exploring communication in Black, White, and biracial families* (pp. 1–24). Mahwah, NJ: Lawrence Erlbaum Associates, Inc.

Socha, T. J., Sanchez-Hucles, L., Bromley, J., and Kelly, B. (1995). Invisible parents and children: Exploring African-American parent-child communication. In T. J. Socha and G. H. Stamp (Eds.). *Parents, children, and communication. Frontiers of theory and research* (pp. 127–145). Mahwah, NJ: Lawrence Erlbaum Associates, Inc.

Sudarkasa, N. (1997). African-American families and family values. In H. P. McAdoo (Ed.), *Black families* (pp. 9–40). Thousand Oaks, CA: Sage.

Sue, D. W., Arredondo, J., & McDavis, R. J. (1992). Multicultural counseling competencies and standards. A call to the profession. *Journal of Counseling and Development, 70,* 477–486.

Vangelisti, A. L. (1992). Older adolescents' perceptions of communication problems with their parents. *Journal of Adolescent Research, 7,* 382–402.

Vogl-Bauer, S. (2003). Maintaining family relationships. In D. J. Canary & M. Dainton (Eds.). *Maintaining relationships through communication: Relational, contextual and cultural variations* (pp. 31–50). Mahwah, NJ: Lawrence Erlbaum Associates, Inc.

von Bertalanffy, L. (1975). *Perspectives on general system theory: Scientific philosophical studies.* New York: Brazille.

Youniss, J. & Smollar, J. (1985). *Adolescent relations with mothers, fathers, and friends.* Chicago: University of Chicago Press.

FOLLOW-UP QUESTIONS AND EXPLORATION PROJECTS

1. How did Penington measure dialectical management strategy? How do her measurements compare to those of Bevan? What do these differences say about Penington's and Bevan's respective assumptions about knowledge and about the nature of social reality?

2. How did Penington link the quotations she presented from her study participants with the six strategies of managing dialectical tension? Did you agree with her assessments? Why or why not?

3. How does Penington's view of communication compare to that of Bevan? How does it compare to that of Pearce and Pearce? What do you think accounts for any differences? How do you think these differences make a difference?

4. Why do you think Penington ends with a caution about not interpreting one ethnic group's way of interacting as "better" than the other's? Read Mark Orbe's (1998) work on co-cultural communication theory. What would this theory suggest about Penington's research, in general, and her final caution in particular?

5 | Applied Research: Central or Peripheral?

Health issues and internet information are both topics of increasing concern that are brought together in this next article by Freeman and Spyridakis. The specific concept these authors focus on is what makes web-based health information credible in the eyes of readers. The assumption is that credible information is more likely to influence readers than information that is seen as lacking credibility. This article focuses on a practical element of Web page design: the provision of a street address for the sponsoring organization (as opposed to just an email address) and the presence of external links on the site. The author's focus on these two elements is grounded in the Elaboration Likelihood Model's approach to persuasion.

Background of Elaboration Likelihood Model

The Elaboration Likelihood Model (ELM) is a theory of persuasion developed by Petty and Cacioppo (1986). It argues that long-term attitude change occurs when people engage in *elaboration* by carefully considering the arguments presented in a piece of persuasion. Cognitive processing that occurs during elaboration is said to involve the *central-route* to persuasion. Short-term attitude change, however, can be induced by situational cues that are *peripheral* to the persuasive message. Influence occurring via such cues is called the *peripheral-route* to persuasion. The specific predictions of the theory involve specifying the conditions under which people will be more likely to engage in central-route versus peripheral-route processing.

Article Structure

This article again follows a standard research article format with Introduction and Literature Review followed by Methods, Results, and Discussion. The Introduction and Literature Review sections begin with a rationale for the article's particular focus, a definition of credibility and an overview of ELM, followed by a discussion of credibility specifically in an online context and reader characteristics that might affect evaluations of credibility. The literature review concludes with a discussion of measurements of credibility. The methods section provides information on the design of the study, participants, materials used for the sample web pages, the questionnaires used and the overall procedures of the study. The results section begins with describing qualities of the participants in relation to concepts highlighted by ELM. It continues with an analysis of participant's judgments of credibility, first in terms of quantitative data and then with a more qualitative analysis of participant comments. The discussion section begins with a focus on external validity, or the ability to generalize results of this study to people other than those who participated in the study. It continues with a discussion of the results in relation to ELM.

Distinctive Points

This article uses a Table format for summarizing literature on web-site characteristics and credibility (p. 84). This is a less common summary method, but is useful for categorizing and sorting articles on specific topics and presenting that information in an easily accessible format.

Both this article and the one by Pearce and Pearce on Public Dialogue are examples of what is called "Applied Research." In both cases, the research is directed at a real-world problem and is conducted in a setting that is as much like the "real world" as is possible. Applied research is sometimes contrasted with "Theoretical research" or "Pure research" where the goal of the study is more focused on testing or extending a theory. Traditionally, Theoretical research has been seen as more central to the goals of scholarship than Applied research and therefore has been valued more. Which do you think is more important?

References

Petty, R. E., & Cacioppo, J. T. (1986). *Communication and persuasion: Central and peripheral routes to attitude change*. New York: Springer-Verlag.

An Examination of Factors That Affect the Credibility of Online Health Information

Krisandra S. Freeman and Jan H. Spyridakis

Introduction

Every day, millions of readers search among the countless pages of online health information (Baker and colleagues 2003: Bard 2000; Cain and colleagues 2000; Fox and colleagues 2000; Fox and Fallows 2003; Fox and Rainie 2002; Horrigan and Rainie 2002; PSRA 2002; UCLA 2003). They go to the Internet because it is open and available 24 hours a day, because it provides answers to embarrassingly personal questions, and because—unlike our increasingly harried doctors—it never has to cut a visit short.

But consumers searching for accurate information online may have an arduous task. Numerous studies have shown that, while there are excellent sources of online health information, many health Web pages have incomplete, spurious, or fraudulent information (Berland and colleagues 2001; CROH 2000; Crocco and colleagues 2002; Eng and EvaluMetrix 2001; FTC 2001; Fahey and Weinberg 2003; Hellawell and colleagues 2000; Latthe 2000; Pandolfi and colleagues 2000; Suarez-Almazor and colleagues 2001; Stephenson 1998; Stone and Jumper 2001; Weisbord and colleagues 1997). Given the poor quality of information on some Web sites, one might wonder how consumers decide what information to trust. While it would be optimal if readers had the ability to accurately assess the quality of online information itself, most lack the necessary expertise and must judge the information quality by other means, such as cues to credibility.

Many healthcare organizations, such as the Health on the Net Foundation and the Internet Healthcare Coalition, have published guidelines to help readers judge the credibility of online information, that is, to determine the expertise of the providers of online health information, as well as the motives and goals, or trustworthiness, of these providers. In addition, researchers have used these guidelines, in combination with methods for online audience research to develop a conceptual framework for creating credible Web sites on medical topics (Swenson and colleagues 2002). Yet little work has been done to determine how consumers actually judge the credibility of online information.

Much of the initial research on consumers' judgments of the credibility of online information focused on e-commerce sites and transactions, such as the willingness of consumers to use their credit cards online (Gheskin Research, and Studio Archetype/Sapient 1999; Cheskin Research 2000; Fogg and colleagues 2001a, 2001b, 2002a; Friedman and colleagues 2000; GVU 1999; Jones and colleagues 2000; Olson and Olson 2000; Resnick and colleagues 2000; Winn and Beck 2002).

Recently, researchers have also begun to address the credibility of online health information, primarily through large-scale surveys (Bard 2000; Cain and colleagues 2000; Fogg and colleagues 2002b; Fox and colleagues 2000; Fox and Fallows 2003; Fox and Rainie 2002; HON 1999, 2001; Horrigan and Rainie 2002; PSRA 2002; Stanford and colleagues 2002). Although these surveys provide a valuable foundation for future research, they are limited in that they ask participants to judge imaginary Web pages as opposed to actual Web pages.

From TECHNICAL COMMUNICATION, VOL 51, ISSUE 2, MAY 2004 by K.S. Freeman and J.H. Spyridakis.

Manuscript received 30 May 2003; revised 29 November 2003; accepted 30 November 2003.

It is not surprising that the results of these surveys sometimes differ from the few studies that have presented readers with specific Web pages to evaluate (Eysenbach and Köhler 2002; Fogg and colleagues 2002b; Stanford and colleagues 2002). Researchers who have conducted both types of studies write, "We found a mismatch, as in other areas of life, between what people say is important and what they actually do" (Fogg and colleagues 2002b). These discrepancies emphasize the need for more studies, such as the one described here, in which participants judge real rather than imagined texts.

The existing studies do agree on one key point: Once on a Web page, readers primarily use the information on only that page to determine the credibility of the information. Very few read "About us" and other information about the sponsors and authors of information on the pages before using the information on a given page (Eysenbach and Köhler 2002; Fox and Rainie 2002).

Given the narrow scope on which readers base their judgments, the research presented here examined the effects of two discrete cues applicable to many Web sites: a street address of the sponsoring organization (as opposed to an e-mail address) and links to other Web sites (external links). Survey research has indicated that these cues may increase credibility (Fogg and colleagues 2001a, 2002a; Fox and Rainie 2002). However, experiments have not been done to determine how such cues actually affect readers' perceptions of real Web pages.

The decision to publish contact information and construct external links on a Web site reflects key editorial and publishing decisions. Readers searching for health information will see a wide variation in the presence (or absence) and the location of street addresses on Web sites. This variety indicates that current Web site sponsors carefully consider the amount of contact information they release. Some firms may be reluctant to post a street address due to security concerns or simply to reduce nuisance visits from dissatisfied customers or hopeful job seekers. The research described in this study reveals the complex nature of such decisions.

Decisions regarding the type and number of external links to include on a site can also be complex. Some guidelines suggest that the presence of links to other sites can increase credibility by allowing consumers to easily cross-check information among sites (Nielsen 1999). However, on an operational level, the addition of external links increases site maintenance, since links must be regularly checked and updated. In addition, sponsors of some for-profit sites may wish to keep readers on their site as long as possible to maximize readers' exposure to site sponsors and advertisers.

The goal of this study is to examine the effect of street address and external links on perceptions of credibility of a Web page. This study attempts to determine how readers process these cues by drawing on key theories in both technical communication and psychology, including the Elaboration Likelihood Model.

The experiment conducted to examine these issues stemmed from a review of relevant literature, discussed next. After the literature review, hypotheses are offered concerning the expected outcomes of the experiment presented here. Then, the methodology, results, and a discussion of the results are presented. Finally, conclusions and implications for future research are discussed.

Literature Review

We will begin with a brief definition of the term *credibility* and then describe the Elaboration Likelihood Model because it provides a framework for understanding factors that affect the credibility of online health information. Then we will review reader characteristics affecting credibility and methods used to measure credibility.

Credibility *defined*

Because credibility is a characteristic defined by reader judgments, it is not necessarily equivalent to the actual quality of information, such as its accuracy or truthfulness. Many researchers have defined credibility "not as an objective property of the source [of information], but as a receiver perception" (Gunther 1992, p. 148). Fogg and colleagues (2001a) wrote that credibility "is a perceived quality; it doesn't reside in an object, a person or a piece of information" (p. 80). Therefore, in this article, the term *credible* refers to a perception of credibility rather than a direct measure of actual quality.

Credibility is a complex concept that has been defined as "believability, trust, perceived reliability, and dozens of other concepts and combinations" (Self 1996, p. 421). Hovland and Weiss (1951), who conducted seminal research on media credibility, defined credibility as having two primary components: trustworthiness and expertise. Many factors shown to affect credibility judgments can be categorized as components of or synonyms for these two traits.

For example, the traits of honesty, accountability, objectivity, character, goodwill, and concern for the public welfare have been used as credibility measurements in some studies (Frewer and colleagues 1996, 1997; Priester and Petty 1995; Swenson, Constantinides, and Gurak 2002). All these factors can contribute to judgments of trustworthiness. Others researchers, drawing from theories in speech and interpersonal communication, have considered a third key trait, sometimes referred to as dynamism, in their credibility studies (Self 1996).

The Elaboration Likelihood Model

The Elaboration Likelihood Model (ELM) developed by Petty and Cacioppo (1986) provides a useful theoretical framework for understanding how factors such as the presence of a street address or the reputation of a Web site sponsor can affect the credibility of information on a Web page. ELM, a theory of persuasion initially developed in the discipline of psychology, postulates that readers tend to judge text credibility either on the basis of arguments within a text or through external cues such as the type of publication in which a text appears.

Petty and Cacioppo (1986) call these two "routes to persuasion" the central route and the peripheral route (p. 3). According to ELM theory, the central route involves readers making a conscious cognitive effort to carefully evaluate the arguments in a text. The peripheral route is based on cues that allow readers to make a simple judgment about the merits of an argument without having to evaluate the argument itself.

Petty and Cacioppo describe a variety of factors that can influence people's use of central processing, in which they analyze the message itself, or their use of peripheral processing, in which they depend on cues such as the reputation of a newspaper or a Web site where the information appears. Readers are more likely to use central processing when they (1) believe an argument has personal relevance, (2) are knowledgeable about a given topic, (3) are motivated, and (4) are able to process the information in a message.

When readers use central processing, they give less weight to peripheral cues. In contrast, readers depend more on peripheral cues to make judgments as their motivation or ability to process arguments decreases or when they are overwhelmed with information, as is often the case for consumers of online medical information.

Credibility of online information

After briefly discussing characteristics that affect credibility judgments and some heuristics that detail these criteria, we will define the credibility variables manipulated in the current study. Then, we will discuss reader characteristics that can affect readers' judgments of online medical information in the framework of ELM theory.

Source characteristics and credibility judgments The credibility of online health information is known to be affected by characteristics relating to several levels of source information, including (1) publishers, such as the owners or sponsors of a Web site or radio station; (2) authors or anchors, such as the writers or speakers who collect and frame information; (3) originators of information—that is, sources of information contained within the text, such as scientists or politicians quoted in news stories; and (4) communication channel or technology—that is, the means by which information is transmitted, such as television or the Internet (Sundar 1998). Table 1 lists positive characteristics described by a variety of guidelines and heuristics at the levels of publisher/sponsors and authors originators (see Freeman 2002 for discussion of the impact of other source levels on credibility judgments).

TABLE 1

Web Site Characteristics That Affect Credibility and Related Guidelines

POSITIVE CHARACTERISTICS AT THE LEVEL OF THE PUBLISHER/SPONSOR (SITE-WIDE)	GUIDELINE SOURCES
Advertising, paid links, sponsorships, e-commerce partnerships	
• Clear distinctions between editorial and advertising content	Winker and colleagues 2000; ASME 2002; HIE 2000; HON 1997; IHC 2000; NIAMSD 2000; Price 2000
• Disclosure	Winker and colleagues 2000; ASME 2002; HIE 2000; HON 1997; IHC 2002; NCI 2002
• Policies	Winker and colleagues 2000; ASME 2002; FTC 2001; HIE 2000; HON 1997; HSWG 1998; IHC 2000; NCI 2002; Price 2000; Silberg, Lundgerg, and Musacchio 1997
Certifications/seals from third parties	HIE 2000; HON 1997; IHC 2000; Price 2000; Shneiderman 2000
Contact information	BIOME 2001; HON 1997
Design	
• "Professional"	BIOME 2001; Nielsen 1999, 2000
• Clear navigation	Winker and colleagues 2000; BIOME 2001; Nielsen 1999, 2000
Editorial review process and or board	Winker and colleagues 2000; BIOME 2001; Gastel 1998; HSWG 1998; HIE 2000; IHC 2000; NCI 2002; NIAMSD 2000; Price 2000
Links	
• To credible sites	BIOME 2001; HSWG 1998; Nielsen 1999, 2000; Price 2000; Silberg and colleagues 1997
• From a credible portal	BIOME 2001; Gastel 1998; NIAMSD 2000; Price 2000
• Policy regarding	NCI 2002
Logo on all pages	ASME 2002; NCI 2002
Medical disclaimers	HSWG 1998; HIE 2000; IHC 2002; Price 2000
Privacy and security policies	Winker and colleagues 2000; ASMF 2002; HIE 2000; HON 1997; IHC 2000; NCI 2002; Nielsen 1999, 2000; Price 2000; Shneiderman 2000
Reports of past performance	Friedman and colleagues 2000; Shneiderman 2000
POSITIVE CHARACTERISTICS AT THE LEVEL OF THE AUTHOR/ARTICLE	GUIDELINE SOURCES
Sponsorship by credible organization(s)	Winker and colleagues 2000; BIOME 2001; CROH 2000; FTC 1999, 2001; Gastel 1998; HON 1997; HSWG 1998; IHC 2002; NCI 2002; NIAMSD 2000; Price 2000; Silberg and colleagues 1997
Author names	Winker and colleagues 2000; BIOME 2001; HON 1997; IHC 2002; Gastel 1998; NIAMSD 2000; Price 2000; Silberg and colleagues 1997; Spyridakis 2000
Author qualifications	Winker and colleagues 2000; BIOME 2001; Gastel 1998; HIE 2000; HON 1997; IHC 2002; NCI 2002; NIAMSD 2000; Price 2000; Silberg and colleagues, 1997
Scientific citations/references	Winker and colleagues 2000; BIOME 2001; Gastel 1998; HIE 2000; HON 1997; IHC 2000; NCI 2002; NIAMSD 2000; Price 2000; Silberg and colleagues 1997
Timeliness; dates when information created/updated posted	Winker and colleagues 2000; BIOME 2001; Gastel 1998; HIE 2000; HON 1997; HSWG 1998; IHC 2002; NCI 2002; Nielsen 2000; Price 2000; Silberg and colleagues 1997

While many guidelines agree on relevant characteristics, the positive impact of all characteristics has not been proven. For example, while several guidelines suggest the use of "seals" of approval for Web sites that follow certain guidelines and recommend that readers look for such seals, a recent survey indicates that the presence of such seals or awards does not have much impact on readers' decisions to use information from a given Web site (PSRA 2002).

However, numerous studies have shown that readers tend to trust health information published, sponsored, or authored by major health institutions or physicians. Research focusing on health information in print has shown that large medical institutions and physicians are generally viewed as credible sources of health information (Christensen and colleagues 1997; Cline and Engel 1991; Dutta-Bergman 2003; Frewer and colleagues 1996). A survey commissioned by the California Healthcare Foundation (Cain and colleagues 2000) found that the tendency to view medical institutions and physicians as highly credible carries over into cyberspace. The specific institutions that readers deem credible can vary by demographic group and individual circumstances (Balshem 1991; Bernhardt and colleagues 2002; Guttman and colleagues, 1998).

In the same way that the presence of credible sources can increase the credibility of health information Web sites, the lack of source information can decrease the credibility of a site. Of participants in surveys conducted by the Pew Internet and American Life, 42% reported turning away from a health Web site "because they couldn't determine the source of the information" (Fox and Rainie 2002, p. 8).

A wide range of site-wide factors may affect the credibility of online health information, including the quality of navigation and template design, and the presence or absence of advertisements and promotional language (Eysenbach and Köhler 2002; Fogg and colleagues 2001a, 2002a, 2002b; Fox and Rainie 2002; Zhang and colleagues 2001). Some specific features cited by survey participants and recommended by credibility heuristics convey important information about the sponsor or publisher of a site. Two such features were tested in this study—the presence of a street address and links to other sites.

The presence or absence of a street address is a discrete cue that is relevant to almost any type of Web site. The presence or absence of external links is another discrete cue that is relevant to many types of online information, with the possible exception of some types of commercial sites. Although research concerning these cues stems primarily from survey participants describing their responses to imagined Web pages, the results of such studies provide a starting point for the work we report in this article.

Posting of a street address Participants in two largescale surveys (n = 1,441; n = 1,481) reported that information that increased "real world feel," such as the presence of a "physical" address and contact phone number, increased the credibility of online information (Fogg and colleagues 2001a, 2002a). Seventy-five percent of participants in another survey stated that it was very important or somewhat important for a site to list e-mail addresses for the editor or other people responsible for site content (PSRA 2002), and comments from a large-scale study (n = 2,684) in which participants were asked to rank and comment on specific Web sites indicated that the presence of contact information, such as a street address and phone number, increased credibility (Fogg and colleagues 2002b).

The presence of a street address can serve either as a tool for central processing of information or as a cue for peripheral processing. Readers engaged in central processing may use the address to contact site publishers or article authors, or they may use the address to glean more information about the site publisher. For example, a site based in Atlanta, GA, might be presumed to have relatively easy access to the U.S. Centers for Disease Control and Prevention (CDC). In contrast, readers engaged in peripheral processing may simply note the presence of a street address as a credibility cue.

External links Survey participants have also reported that external links to a site they think is believable can increase credibility (Fogg and colleagues 2001a, 2002a). Additionally, several guidelines for the design of online information list the presence of links to credible sources of health information as a sign of credibility (see Table 1). However, not all heuristics agree on this point. The Internet Healthcare Coalition warns consumers not to be "fooled by a comprehensive list of links—any Web site can link to another and this in no way implies endorsement from either site" (Internet Healthcare Coalition 2002). Lasica (2002) maintains that "paid links" can reduce the credibility of a site or article. As the name implies, paid links are placed in exchange for a fee and so serve as a subtler form of a banner ad. Broken links can also decrease credibility by serving as evidence of poor site maintenance and some credibility guidelines warn readers away from sites with many broken links (BIOME 2001).

Like the presence of a street address, links can serve either as tools for central processing of information or as cues for peripheral processing. Readers engaged in central processing may follow links to gain additional information or to compare the arguments and information on one site with that from another while readers engaged in peripheral processing may simply note the presence of links to other sites.

Reader characteristics and credibility judgments Because credibility is a perception rather than a fixed measure of quality, factors that affect credibility can vary widely from one individual to another. These factors can include a sense of being rushed for time, which affects many persons in our culture or demographic factors such as age. Another key factor can be personal experience with serious illness. In other words, the experiences that readers bring to a text will affect their judgment of that text.

Information overload and shortage of time are factors that can affect the use of central or peripheral processing by readers from all demographic groups. According to recent studies, readers seeking health information online are often in a hurry and are usually not very systematic in their searches, factors that would encourage their reliance on peripheral processing, rather than central processing. Participants in a recent study (n = 17) spent an average of five minutes researching health questions (Eysenbach and Köhler 2002). The respondents in recent Pew surveys report starting their searches at a search engine rather than of a specialized health site or portal, and simply starting at the top of the list of search results and working their way down from there (Fox and Rainie 2002). In addition, few readers seek out information on sources of the information they read (Eysenbach and Köhler 2002: Flanagin and Metzger 2000; Fox and Rainie 2002).

Age can also affect perceptions of credibility. Several studies have found that younger people are more likely to judge online media as credible than older people (Einberg and colleagues 2002; Johnson and Kaye 1998), they are also more likely to use the Internet to acquire health information (Licciardone and colleagues 2001). In contrast, a survey commissioned by Consumer WebWatch (PSRA 2002) found that concerns about credibility of online information did not vary much by "age, race, income, or education" (p. 8).

Another factor affecting readers' judgments of credibility concerns their experience with online media. Experienced users are somewhat more likely than less-experienced users to view the Internet as a credible source of information (Flanagin and Metzger 2000). Horrigan and Rainie (2002) found that the longer persons had used the Internet, the more often they used online health information, and a UCLA research team (UCLA 2003) found that "very experienced users" (six or more years of experience with the Internet) rated the Internet as their most important source of information. Internet users tend to have higher education and income levels than people who do not use the Internet (Band 2000: Fox and colleagues 2000; Cain and colleagues 2000; Fox and Rainie 2002; GVD 1999; Horrigan and Rainie 2001; PSRA 2002). Researchers report that women are more likely to research health information online than men (Baker and colleagues 2003; Cain and colleagues 2000; Fox and Fallows 2003; Fox and Rainie 2002) and the California Healthcare Foundation reports that women aged 40–49 form one of the largest segments of "Health e-people" (Cain and colleagues 2000).

While people's experience with the Internet positively correlates with their perceptions of the credibility of online information, people's knowledge of medicine may inversely correlate with their perceptions of the credibility of medical information in mass media. According to ELM theory, people who have existing knowledge about a subject are more likely to scrutinize information about that subject and use central processing, and thus pay less attention to peripheral cues. Therefore, it would be reasonable to assume that people with knowledge of medicine, such as those who have worked in medical settings or covered medical topics for a newspaper, may scrutinize online health information more carefully than people without such knowledge.

Even if readers do not have extensive medical knowledge, many will still compare the information on a given Web page with the knowledge they already have. According to the Pew Internet and American Life Project, many readers judge information solely on the basis of whether it fits with what they have already heard (Fox and Rainie 2002). When using this strategy, readers use central processing to evaluate information and are less likely to depend on peripheral cues.

Personal experience with illness also affects how readers process health information online. Personal experience with health challenges, or with a friend or family member with health challenges, makes information about that topic personally relevant. ELM theory posits that as personal relevance of information increases, so will levels of central processing. Recent studies show that almost all readers search for information of personal relevance and many search for information of relevance to a friend or family member (Fox and Fallows 2003; Fox and Rainie 2002).

Readers' health status can also affect their involvement with online information and so their use of central or peripheral processing. About 60% of people reading health information online could be categorized as "well," 5% as "newly diagnosed," and 35% as chronically ill or caregivers of the chronically ill (Cain and colleagues 2000). The "well" searchers typically make infrequent searches for information on topics such as anti-aging, wellness, and preventative medicine and wellness (Baker and colleagues 2003; Cain and colleagues 2000; Fox and Fallows 2003, Houston and Allison 2003). The level of involvement for many of these searchers may be low. In contrast, the newly diagnosed are a transient group characterized by intense searches in the first weeks after being diagnosed with a serious condition. The level of involvement felt by these searchers is apt to be quite high, as is that of the chronically ill and their caregivers, a group that is characterized by heavy online use, including the use of online chats (Cain and colleagues 2000; Fox and Fallows 2003; Houston and Allison 2003).

Familiarity and interest in a topic can increase readers' ability to use central processing of information, as well as their motivation to do so. Prior knowledge, personal relevance, or interest in a topic are known to affect reading comprehension (Isakson and Spyridakis 1999; Raphael and colleagues 1980; Wade and Adams 1990).

These factors can work together to increase or decrease central processing. For example, a person with a chronic illness who has spent considerable time researching his or her disorder will approach new information both with preexisting knowledge and a sense of personal relevance. In turn, the interaction of processing strategy and cues in print or online documents can affect judgments of credibility.

Measuring credibility

In addition to source and reader characteristics that affect credibility judgments, the various ways in which credibility has been measured are relevant to the design of the current study. Credibility has often been measured through questionnaires using Likert-scaled responses (Austin and Dong 1994; Christensen and colleagues 1997; Cline and Engel 1991; Eastin 2001; Flannagin and Metzger 2000; Fogg and colleagues 2001a, 2001b, 2002a; Frewer and colleagues 1997; Gaziano and McGrath 1986; Hovland and Weiss 1951; Kaufman and colleagues 1999; Meyer 1998; Pennbridge and colleagues 1999; Priester and Petty 1995; Sundar 1998, 1999, 2000; West 1994). In addition to Likert-scaled questionnaires, Frewer and colleagues used thought listing and interviews, Pennbridge and colleagues solicited qualitative responses, and Gaziano and McGrath conducted focus groups and had participants rate reliability of media.

The credibility of media, authors, articles, and sponsors has been assessed through a variety of adjectives, including *credible* itself, the secondary characteristics of *trustworthiness, expertise,* and *dynamism:* and adjectives that could be characterized as tertiary components of credibility that are thus categorized under the secondary characteristics of *trustworthiness* (*believable, biased, fair, objective, sensational, truthful*); *expertise* (*accurate, complete, competent, depth of reporting*); and *dynamism* (*attraction*). Some tertiary factors could arguably fall under more than one category. For example, in his factor analysis study of reader comments, Sundar (1998, 1999, 2000) found that several characteristics (*accurate* and *believable*) loaded on two scales (*credibility* and *quality*).

Several recent credibility studies of online information have focused on the trustworthiness-expertise model of credibility first posited by Hovland and colleagues, further developed by Gaziano and McGrath (1986), and refined and validated by later researchers. One widely cited scale is the Meyer (1988) subset of the Gaziano-McGrath scale which was validated by West (1994): it consists of five components (fairness, bias, depth of reporting, accuracy, and trustworthiness).

Summary of relevant literature

This literature review reveals that while millions of pages of online health information are available, many are incomplete and contain poor quality information. Credibility, which one might hope would relate to the actual quality of information, relates to users' perception of quality and has two primary components: trustworthiness and expertise. According to the Elaboration Likelihood Model (ELM), readers who are unfamiliar with, are uninterested in, or have difficulty processing information are more likely to evaluate information quality on the basis of peripheral cues, such as the reputation of a publisher, than are readers who are familiar with, are interested in, or are able to easily process the same information.

Furthermore, many readers of online information rarely spend the time to research the credibility of the publisher or author of information in Web pages they read. By default, many readers tend to judge information on a given Web page only by the information on that page. Therefore they may gauge the credibility of information on a Web page on the basis of peripheral cues on a Web page, such as the presence or absence of a street address. Reader characteristics can also affect credibility judgments, characteristics such as medical knowledge, health status, and age.

The literature reviewed here reveals a wide range of cues that may affect readers' judgments of the credibility of online information. However, many studies of cues are based on surveys in which participants have been asked to describe their responses to an imagined Web page, not on experiments in which participants have been asked to make judgments about real Web pages.

While many cues could be assessed for their effects on credibility, many are applicable only to a certain type of site. For example, the presence or absence of advertisements applies only to commercial sites, and designations such as .gov applies only to government agencies. The study presented here focused on cues that are relevant to many types of Web sites—the presence or absence of a street address and the presence or absence of links to external sites—and assessed their effects in an experiment that relied on real Web pages. The research questions and hypotheses concerning the effect of these cues are discussed next.

Study Questions and Hypotheses

Our research study asked four questions. The first two concerned the relationship of readers' credibility judgments and their (1) familiarity with, interest in, and perceptions of the difficulty of the experimental materials, and (2) employment in a health or medical setting. The second two questions assessed the effect of two manipulated variables—street address and external links—on reader's credibility judgments.

The literature led to the following hypotheses concerning participants' credibility ratings.

- Participants' familiarity with, interest in, and perceptions of difficulty of the information in the articles will relate to the ratings.
- Participant's experience or employment in a medical setting will relate to the ratings.

- Articles that include a street address or external links will receive higher ratings than articles without a street address or links.
- Presence of both a street address and external links will increase ratings more than either variable alone.

One final hypothesis related to our expectation that credibility ratings would be similar for two different articles used in the study. As described in the methods section, two articles were used to ensure that credibility effects would not be topic-specific.

Research Methods

Study design

The study used a 2 (article topic: diabetes or hepatitis) x 2 (street address: present or absent) x 2 (external links: present or absent) between subjects factorial design.

Participants

One hundred fifty participants (102 females, 48 males) took part in this study. To increase the likelihood that participants would include readers likely to use both central processing as well as readers likely to use peripheral processing in making credibility judgments about the experimental materials, participants were recruited with a goal of obtaining a mixed sample of people with varying levels of experience in a health or medical setting and experience writing about medicine or science as a professional journalist. Because many people search for health information for friends and family members, participants were not restricted to persons who had one of the diseases described in the experimental materials.

Participants were recruited through multiple venues: the electronic newsletter *Solidarity in Seattle,* published by the Seattle office of the Screen Actors Guild; the e-bulletin of the University of Washington Department of Environmental Health; and the list-servs and e-mail lists of the University of Washington (UW) Department of Technical Communication, the University of Washington student chapter of the ACM Special Interest Group in Computer Human Interaction (SIGCHI), the Puget Sound Chapter of the National Association of Science Writers, Women in Digital Journalism, and St. John United Lutheran Church in Seattle, WA. As an incentive, all participants could enter a drawing to win one of three gift certificates ($50.00, $25.00, and $10.00 USD) to Amazon.com.

Materials for experimental conditions

Eight Web pages containing health information were created by varying: (1) article topic, (2) presence or absence of a street address, and (3) presence or absence of external links. Additional pages contained instructions and the questionnaire.

Article topics Two article topics were used to avoid the possibility that the results of this study would be unique to a particular text. Selected topics concerned relatively well-known diseases—diabetes and hepatitis A (hereafter referred to as diabetes or hepatitis). Articles about these topics were selected from the Web site of the CDC (2001, 2002) and covered basic information in a question-and-answer format about the prevention and treatment of the disease.

Differences in credibility between the two articles were minimized through the selection of text that included no references, cited no sources, and had no byline. The two articles were edited so that they were similar in length (407 words for diabetes article, 395 words for the hepatitis article); structure (Q & A): and Flesch-Kincaid reading levels (9.3 for the diabetes article, 9.0 for the hepatitis article). The quality of the articles and subsequent edits was evaluated by six graduate students in the Department of Technical Communication at the University of Washington.

The text of the articles was presented flush left in black text on a white background with the name and logo of a fictitious health organization (the National Health Organization) placed on each page in the upper left-hand corner.

Address The Web pages varied in the presence or absence of a street address with phone number. If present, the address with phone number was located just below the logo of the fictitious National Health Organization. The fictitious address was on a street in Washington, DC, in an area of the city that is home to many government offices and non-profit organizations (see Figure 5.1).

Links The Web pages varied in the presence or absence of external links to additional sources of information. Web pages with links had three links to major government research organizations or non-profit agencies concerned with the disease presented. The external links were nonfunctional; participants who clicked on these links encountered a message stating that, for the purpose of the experiment, the external link was not functional. External links were placed flush left just below the text of the article.

Instructional pages

The study had several instructional pages. The welcome page told participants that the experiment would take less than half an hour, and that they would remain anonymous and could withdraw from the experiment at any time by simply closing their browser. This page also described the prize drawing. An active link at the bottom of this page was entitled, "Continue to experiment." At the end of the experiment participants were presented with the prize drawing page that allowed them to enter the drawing or move to the final screen that thanked the participants.

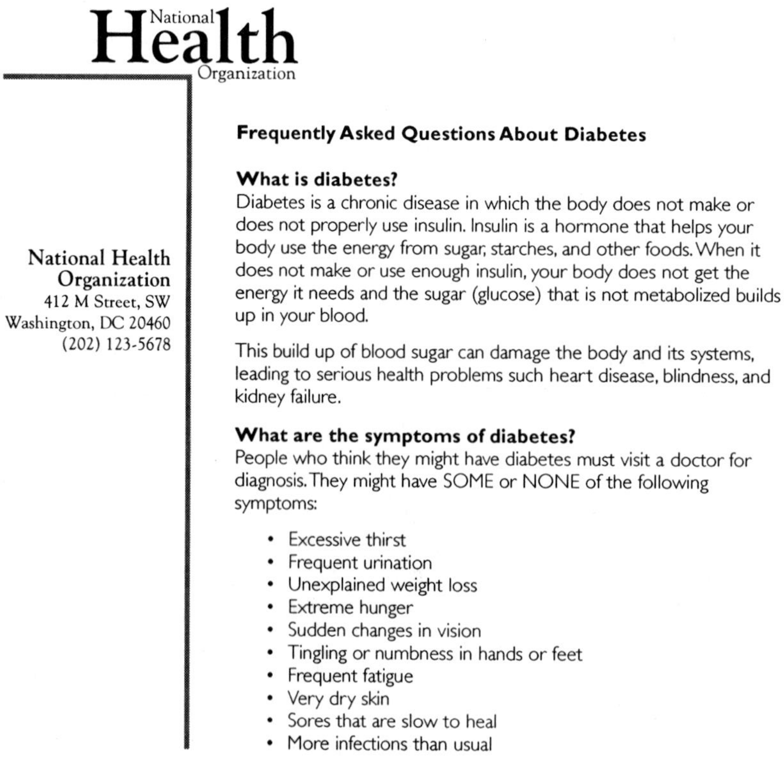

Health
National / Organization

National Health
Organization
412 M Street, SW
Washington, DC 20460
(202) 123-5678

Frequently Asked Questions About Diabetes

What is diabetes?
Diabetes is a chronic disease in which the body does not make or does not properly use insulin. Insulin is a hormone that helps your body use the energy from sugar, starches, and other foods. When it does not make or use enough insulin, your body does not get the energy it needs and the sugar (glucose) that is not metabolized builds up in your blood.

This build up of blood sugar can damage the body and its systems, leading to serious health problems such heart disease, blindness, and kidney failure.

What are the symptoms of diabetes?
People who think they might have diabetes must visit a doctor for diagnosis. They might have SOME or NONE of the following symptoms:

- Excessive thirst
- Frequent urination
- Unexplained weight loss
- Extreme hunger
- Sudden changes in vision
- Tingling or numbness in hands or feet
- Frequent fatigue
- Very dry skin
- Sores that are slow to heal
- More infections than usual

Figure 5.1. Partial screen shot of diabetes article with address present.

Questionnaire

After reading one of the randomly assigned experimental Web pages, participants were presented with a questionnaire with Likert-scaled and qualitative questions that assessed participants' credibility judgments of the articles and demographic characteristics. The questionnaire pages were developed using WebQ software (developed by the University of Washington Center for Teaching, Learning, and Technology).

Credibility and reader measures The credibility measures were based on the research described in the literature review of this article. Ten questions asked participants to indicate their level of agreement on a five-point Likert-type scale with statements about the article they had just read and about the author of the article (see Figure 5.2). The questions directly addressed credibility at three levels: credibility itself, secondary components of credibility (expertise and trustworthiness); and tertiary components of credibility (accuracy, a component of expertise; and bias, a component of trustworthiness). The scale was syntactically awkward in the case of two variables: "article is expert" and "author is accurate." However, pilot testing with a variety of phrasing possibilities suggested that consistency between the two sets of questions (about article and author) was more important than correct syntax.

Participants were asked to rate their willingness (1) to recommend the article to someone who had or was at risk for contracting the disease, or (2) to use the information in the article themselves. Participants were also asked to rate topic familiarity, interest, and difficulty.

Demographic questions Demographic questions assessed age, gender, Internet use, interest in or experience with the disease described in the article they read, and experience working in a medical setting. Questions about Internet use were adapted from GVU surveys (GVU 1999).

Open-ended, qualitative questions Open-ended, qualitative questions asked participants (1) to list some words they might use to describe the quality of the article they read and (2) to state what characteristics of a Web site would most influence their decision to use the information found on the Web site.

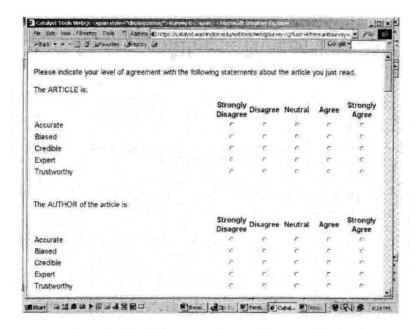

Figure 5.2. Screen shot of credibility rating questions.

Pilot testing

Materials were pilot-tested to determine whether the two articles in the no address/no link conditions would receive similar credibility ratings, and to check the functionality of the WebQ software. Unpaired/tests (n = 21) showed no significant differences between the articles in terms of credibility ratings, thus validating our assumption that the articles in their base states would have similar levels of credibility. Pilot-test participants did detect and report several technical problems in the demographic portion of the study questions. These problems were corrected.

Overall procedure

Participants accessed the online experimental Web site using the URL publicized in the electronic bulletins. They then read the general instructions for the experiment and selected the "Continue to experiment" link. At that point, one of the eight Web pages prepared for the study, randomly selected, opened in the browser. After reading the page, the participants advanced to the questionnaire, the drawing screen, and the final screen.

Data analysis

Quantitative results were analyzed in SPSS 10 and StatView 5.0.1 (a product of the SAS Institute) on a personal computer. Qualitative data from the two open-ended questions were analyzed using content analysis. Further details concerning the content analysis scheme can be found in the qualitative results section of this article. Two anonymous raters (one researcher and a colleague) rated a sample of 10 comments; since they had 95% inter-rater reliability, only one anonymous rater assessed the remaining comments.

Results

After reviewing the demographic results, we discuss the participants' ratings of familiarity with, interest in, and difficulty of the articles. We then examine quantitative measures for credibility, and discuss the qualitative results. Only results at an alpha level $< + .05$, reported as a p value, are discussed as significant; in other words, there would be only a 5% chance that the findings reported as significant are due to chance. All reported correlations are Pearson correlations as variables were either interval or were ordinal with interval-appearing scales.

Participant demographics

Participants in this study (102 females, 48 males) ranged in age from 21 to 71 (mean = 39.6; standard deviation = 12.0). They were typical of the larger population of Internet users in that they were relatively well educated (see Table 2). Further, many participants had professional experience with medical issues. Twenty percent (n = 30) had reported on medical or scientific issues as professional journalists, and one third (n = 48) had worked in a health or medical setting, for a total of 47%

TABLE 2				
Participants' Educational Levels				
EDUCATION (N = 150)				
BACHELOR'S DEGREE	MASTER'S DEGREE	DOCTORATE DEGREE	PROFESSIONAL DEGREE	OTHER
42%	32%	6%	2%	18%

of participants (n = 70) with such experience (eight participants reported experience in both categories). The number of years worked in a health or medical setting ranged from one to 35 years, with an average of 8.1 years (standard deviation = 7.9), and significantly correlated with age, $r(45) = .593, p < .01$. In other words, the more time that participants had worked in a medical setting, the older they were. This fact is revealed through the correlation r of .593 (with correlations ranging from −1 to +1) and a p of <.01 (which is considerably lower than the criterion alpha level of .05 or less).

Personal experience with article topic

Just 2% of the participants (n = 3) reported having one of the two illnesses described in the articles. About 5% of participants reported that they did not know whether they had the disease described (n = 4 for diabetes, n = 3 for hepatitis), and one third (n = 53) reported having a friend or relative with one of the two illnesses.

Internet use

Study participants were active users of the Internet to obtain general information and less frequent users of the Internet to obtain medical information. A majority of participants (74%) reported looking up general information on the Internet more than once a week (see Table 3). Only 10.7% reported looking up medical information that frequently. Half of the participants reported looking up medical information on the Internet just a few times a year. Significant correlations revealed that persons who looked up general information on the Internet were more likely to look up medical information $[r(147) = 0.370, p = 0.000]$, and older participants were significantly less likely to look up general information on the Internet $[r(146) = −0.247, p = 0.003]$.

Participants reported that they had engaged in a broad range of Internet activities and actions. Participants reported having engaged in two to eight Internet activities (such as e-mail, chat, playing interactive games), with a mean of 5.2 activities (standard deviation = 1.5). The number of Internet actions participants reported having engaged in (such as bookmarking a page or changing a browser setting) ranged from zero to five, with a mean of 3.6 actions (standard deviation = 1.6). Significant correlations showed that persons who engaged in more of the listed Internet activities were likely to participate in more of the listed Internet actions $[r(140) = 0.455, p = 0.000]$, and that the older they were, the less likely they were to engage in the listed Internet activities $[r(147) = −0.305, p = 0.000]$ or actions $[r(139) = −0.314, p = 0.000]$.

Further, participants who engaged in more of the listed Internet activities used the Internet significantly more often to look up general information $[r(147) = 0.388, p < 0.000]$ and medical information $[r(148) = 0.256, p = 0.002]$; and participants who engaged in more of the listed Internet actions used the Internet more often to look up general information $[r(139) = 0.229, p < 0.006]$.

TABLE 3				
Use of the Internet to Search For Information (% Frequency)				
NEVER	A FEW TIMES A YEAR	ABOUT ONCE A MONTH	ABOUT ONCE A WEEK	MORE THAN ONCE A WEEK
Use of the Internet to Search for General Information (n = 149)				
0.0	6.0	8.7	10.7	74.0
Use of the Internet to Search for Medical Information (n = 150)				
5.3	50.0	22.7	11.3	10.7

TABLE 4

Interest In and Perceived Difficulty of Articles (% Frequency)				
Interest in Article Read (n = 149)				
VERY UNINTERESTING	UNINTERESTING	NEUTRAL	INTERESTING	VERY INTERESTING
0.0	17.3	22.0	54.0	6.0
Perceptions of Difficulty of Article (n = 150)				
VERY DIFFICULT	DIFFICULT	NEUTRAL	EASY	VERY EASY
0.0	0.0	8.7	58.7	32.7

Participants' interest, perceptions of difficulty, and familiarity

Before analyzing the participant's perceptions of the articles, we first ran t tests to assess the effect of topic on these variables. Because the t tests were nonsignificant for interest and difficulty, the topics were collapsed for further analysis of these variables. A majority of participants rated the article they read as interesting or very interesting (60%), and easy or very easy (91.4%) (see Table 4). Participants who rated the articles as easier reported engaging in more of the listed Internet activities [$r(148) = 0.196, p = 0.016$] and Internet actions [$r(140) = 0.194, p = 0.021$].

A t test of the effect of article topic on familiarity revealed a significant difference [$t(148) = 2.216, p = 0.029$]. Participants were more familiar with the information in the diabetes article (mean = 3.61), standard deviation = 1.00) than with the information in the hepatitis article (mean = 3.23, standard deviation = 1.07). Therefore, familiarity results were examined separately by topic (see Table 5). A majority of participants rated the information in the articles as familiar or very familiar (diabetes article, 66.2%; hepatitis article, 51.9%), although more participants were unfamiliar with the hepatitis information (29.1%) than with the diabetes information (11.3%).

Participants who were familiar with the information in the articles they read were significantly less likely to be interested in the article [$r(147) = -0.199, p = 0.015$]; and more likely to look up health information online [$r(148) = 0.287, p = 0.000$].

Quantitative analysis of credibility ratings

To assess the effect of topic, address, and links on the credibility ratings, we first determined which credibility measures would be most reliable. We suspected that the primary measure (credibility) and the secondary measures (expertise and trustworthiness) would contribute the most to reliability assessments and that the tertiary measures (bias and accuracy) would contribute the least. Cronbach's alpha coefficients were used to assess the correlations among test items. The results supported our expectations.

The Cronbach's alpha for the combination of the primary and secondary credibility measures concerning article credibility was 0.87 (n = 142) and fell to 0.63 (n = 142) when the tertiary measures were added. Similarly, the Cronbach's alpha for the combination of the primary and second-

TABLE 5

Familiarity with Diabetes and Hepatitis Topics (% Frequency)				
	VERY UNFAMILIAR	UNFAMILIAR	NEUTRAL	FAMILIAR	VERY FAMILIAR
Diabetes (n = 71)	4.2	11.3	18.3	52.1	14.1
Hepatitis (n = 79)	3.8	29.1	15.2	44.3	7.6

ary credibility measures concerning author credibility was 0.90 (n = 142) and fell to 0.68 (n = 142) when the tertiary measures were added. Because a Cronbach's alpha of 0.80 is considered acceptable, we excluded the tertiary measures from further analysis.

The analyses were approached through a two-step process. The first step was to assess the effect of topic, address, and links on each of the primary credibility measures, covarying by the opposing primary measure. Hence, two three-way analyses of covariance (ANCOVAs) were run to assess the effects of topic, address, and links on article credibility. (ANCOVAs allow for the assessment of differences among experimental conditions as well as the adjustment of, or the removal of, the effect of a covariate on the dependent variable of interest.) Additional ANCOVAs were then run on some secondary measures with other covariates. The specifics of these results are discussed next, yet it is helpful to understand that the only significant results were for the effect of address.

The ANCOVA that assessed the effect of topic, links, and address on article credibility, using author credibility as a covariate, revealed a significant main effect for address ($p = 0.005$). Articles that contained physical addresses for the sponsoring organization received higher ratings (mean = 4.05) than articles without physical addresses (mean = 3.79). There were no significant main effects for topic or links, or significant interactions.

The ANCOVA that assessed the effect of topic, links, and address on author credibility, using article credibility as a covariate, showed a trend toward significance for the effect of address ($p = 0.057$). Interestingly, in this case the results were opposite of the first analyses. Articles that contained physical addresses for the sponsoring organization received lower ratings (mean = 3.55) than articles without physical addresses (mean = 3.74). There were no significant main effects for topic or links, or significant interactions.

Because the ANCOVA on author credibility was marginally significant with regard to the effect of address, we next assessed the effect of the topic, address, and links on the secondary components, using the secondary credibility components as separate covariates so that we could capture the remaining secondary component as well as other unmeasured credibility factors (such as dynamism, attractiveness, goodwill, and so forth—see Self 1996; Swenson and colleagues 2002). For example, when article expertise is removed from an analysis of article credibility, the remaining parts of article credibility concern article trustworthiness and a variety of other unmeasured credibility measures.

The ANCOVA that assessed the effect of topic, links, and address on article credibility, using article expertise and author credibility as covariates (thus focusing on trustworthiness and other unmeasured credibility factors), revealed a significant main effect for address ($p = 0.003$). Articles that contained physical addresses for the sponsoring organization received higher ratings (mean = 4.05) than articles without physical addresses (mean = 3.78). There were no significant main effects for topic or links, or significant interactions.

The ANCOVA that assessed the effect of topic, links, and address on article credibility, using article trustworthiness and author credibility as covariates (thus focusing on expertise and other unmeasured credibility factors), also revealed a significant main effect for address ($p = 0.021$). Articles that contained physical addresses for the sponsoring organization received higher ratings (mean = 4.00) than articles without physical addresses (mean = 3.82). There were no significant main effects for topic or links, or significant interactions.

The ANCOVA that assessed the effect of topic, links, and address on author credibility, using author expertise and article credibility as covariates (thus focusing on trustworthiness and other unmeasured credibility factors), also revealed a significant main effect for address ($p = 0.048$). In contrast to the earlier results on article credibility, the articles that contained physical addresses for the sponsoring organization received lower ratings (mean = 3.53) than articles without physical addresses (mean = 3.72). There were no significant main effects for topic or links, or significant interactions.

The ANCOVA that assessed the effect of topic, links, and address on author credibility, using author is trustworthiness and article credibility as covariates (thus focusing on expertise and other unmeasured credibility factors), revealed no significant effects.

In summary, the ANCOVAs identified significant effects for the effect of address on the credibility ratings. Three analyses revealed that articles were rated as significantly more credible when the

Web pages contained addresses, but one analysis revealed that authors were rated as significantly more credible when the Web pages did not contain an address.

Willingness to use/recommend article information

Analyses of variance (ANOVAs reveal whether there were statistically significant differences between experimental conditions) were run to determine the effects of topic, address, and links on participants' ratings concerning their willingness to (1) recommend that someone who had or was at risk of contracting the disease in the article (diabetes or hepatitis) read it, and (2) use the information in the article themselves. There were no significant main effects or interactions of topic, address, or links on ratings for participants' willingness to recommend or use the information in the article themselves.

Relationships of credibility ratings to other variables

Several interesting relationships were identified among the credibility ratings and other measures. There were significant inverse correlations between the number of Internet actions (such as bookmarking a page or changing a browser setting) in which participants reported engaging and three credibility variables: article credibility $[r(138) = -0.208, p = 0.014]$, article trustworthiness $[r(134) = -0.214, p = 0.011]$; and author expertise $[r(133) = -0.184, p = 0.033]$. The more facile that the participants were in terms of Internet use, the lower their ratings for article credibility and trustworthiness, and for author expertise. In addition, we discovered significantly positive correlations between article expertise and age $[r(140) = 0.197, p = 0.019]$ and author expertise and age $[r(140) = 0.178, p = 0.035]$. The older the participants, the higher their ratings on article and author expertise.

Participants' interest in the topic correlated with their willingness to use or recommend information in the articles, as well as all six credibility measures (see Table 7). Other interesting correlations concerned the ratings for using or recommending information in the articles, these two measures correlated with each other and with all six credibility measures. If participants were likely to use the information in the articles, they were likely to recommend them. Further, participants who stated that they were more likely to use or recommend the information rated the articles and authors as more credible, expert, and trustworthy (see Table 7).

TABLE 6

ANCOVA Results for Effect of Address			
	MEANS* (ST. ERROR)		
CREDIBILITY MEASURE	ADDRESS PRESENT	ADDRESS ABSENT	ANCOVAS F AND p VALUES
Article is credible (covariate: author is credible)	4.05 (0.06)	3.79 (0.06)	$F(1, 146) = 8.162, p = 0.005$
Author is credible (covariate: article is credible)	3.55 (0.07)	3.74 (0.07)	$F(1, 146) = 3.685, p = 0.057$
Article is credible (covariates: article is expert, author is credible)	4.05 (0.06)	3.78 (0.06)	$F(1, 142) = 9.347, p = 0.003$
Article is credible (covariates: article is trustworthy, author is credible)	4.00 (0.06)	3.82 (0.06)	$F(1, 142) = 5.446, p = 0.021$
Author is credible (covariates: author is expert, article is credible)	3.53 (0.07)	3.72 (0.06)	$F(1, 142) = 3.969, p = 0.048$

*Means are adjusted for covariates.

Additionally, the less difficult that the participants rated the article, the less likely they were to rate it as expert [$r(141) = -0.204$, $p = 0.0151$]. This was an inverse correlation because the Likert-type responses for ratings for difficulty and article expertise ran in opposite directions, with a rating of one equating to "very difficult," on the difficulty scale and "strongly disagree" on the scale for article expertise (equivalent to "article is very inexpert"). There were no significant correlations among the credibility variables and length of employment in a health or medical setting.

Qualitative analysis of open-ended questions

Responses to the two open-ended questions were analyzed with a content analysis scheme. The unit of analysis for the content analysis was one participant response per question, regardless of whether participants wrote only a few words or several paragraphs. Units were initially categorized as referring to the quality of the specific articles or general principles for evaluating Web sites. Comments regarding article quality were categorized on scales of positiveness, familiarity, interest, and difficulty. Other comments concerning general Web principles were categorized at the source level of the publisher sponsor, the author, or the originators of the information; or unspecified or multiple sources; or links, street address, contact information. These categories at the source level were occasionally applied to article quality comments.

Of the 140 participants' responses to the first question, which asked participants to list words they might use to describe the quality of the article read, all referred to the articles participants had read. Similarly, of the 148 responses to the second question (about characteristics of a Web site that most influence participants to use information from the site), almost all referred to factors participants use in general to evaluate Web sites, only 8 responses referred partly or wholly to the specific articles the participants read. Participants' comments reproduced here have been edited for spelling and capitalization, but not for grammar or punctuation.

Comments regarding articles read

All responses in this portion of the results refer to comments participants made regarding the articles they read.

Participant familiarity Participants' comments reflected their familiarity with the content of the articles. Three participants explicitly stated that they were unfamiliar with the information in the articles and one participant explicitly stated that she was familiar with the information. Nine other participants' comments served as strong, implicit statements of their familiarity with the material presented, primarily by characterizing the information in the article as accurate or inaccurate. For

TABLE 7

Correlations Among Various Measures (All Correlations Are Significant at $p \leq 0.01$)			
	INTEREST	RECOMMEND INFORMATION	USE INFORMATION
Interest			
Recommend article (n = 148)	0.382		
Use information (n = 148)	0.436	0.619	
Article is credible (n = 146)	0.270	0.443	0.414
Article is expert (n = 142)	0.412	0.454	0.444
Article is trustworthy (n = 142)	0.433	0.429	0.543
Author is credible (n = 146)	0.312	0.382	0.427
Author is expert (n = 141)	0.410	0.462	0.537
Author is trustworthy (n = 142)	0.340	0.380	0.487

example, one participant wrote of the article that "some of information is misleading and some is correct."

Participant interest Participants' comments also reflected their interest in the articles. Three participants referred to the articles as "interesting," and one referred to an article as uninteresting ("I have no use for this info at this time so it wasn't interesting or anything new"). One participant implicitly expressed interest by writing a lengthy comment on the article topic (hepatitis) and related issues. Five participants revealed an implicit lack of interest in the article read, with two calling it "boring" and three calling it "dull."

Perceived difficulty Participants' comments revealed their perceptions of article difficulty: 99 comments described the article as being easy or containing basic information, with 89 of these comments describing the ease of the article in positive or neutral terms, such as "basic," "introductory," or "good for uninformed general public." Ten comments described the articles as easy in negative terms, such as "dumbed down," "not enough thorough info," and "didn't contain enough info to take action." No comments described the article as difficult.

Source of information Many comments addressed issues concerning the four levels of source described in the literature review. Of the seven comments about the publisher/sponsor of the Web site, three specifically noted a lack of information about the site's sponsor or publisher and explicitly or implicitly reported this as a factor that reduced credibility. One comment noted the lack of advertising, implicitly reporting this factor as increasing credibility (the "purpose [of the site] appears to be informational rather than commercial").

Another participant revealed that she was unfamiliar with the fictitious sponsoring organization and thus relied on the accuracy of the information for judging quality: "I am not familiar with this organization, so I am neutral about judging the quality of the content. However, I am somewhat familiar with the topic, so my impression is that it is accurate." Two other comments referred to the publisher/sponsor in positive ways, specifically citing the presence of the name and logo of the fictitious source as increasing credibility: for example, "The source is the most important—This was a national health organization, unbiased, so it was o.k."

Many negative judgments occurred regarding the lack of clear source information. Three comments noted the lack of supporting information such as statistics and scientific references. Three comments mentioned the lack of information about the author of the articles as a negative factor: for example, "Who is the author? Where did this info come from?" Further negativity was seen in one comment that mentioned a general lack of source information. Six comments explicitly linked the lack of source information to reduced credibility; the following are examples:

No author information. No publication information. It is hard to trust it.

The fact that there were no references provided for some of the statements makes me question the authority of many statements, so I can't give high marks for accuracy or trustworthiness.

I don't remember any source being given in the article, including who produced it, which would be hugely important to me in determining whether it is credible or not.

Two participants, including one who explicitly mentioned trustworthiness, discussed the need to corroborate information from one Web site with that from others: "I found the article easy and pretty straightforward, however, you cannot believe what you read from one source, you need to corroborate the data from trustworthy sites."

Street address and links Although no participants mentioned the presence or absence of a street address, two mentioned the presence or absence of links. One participant, who read an article with links, apparently felt that the links were insufficient in providing guidance: "[the article] had little in-depth organization and little direction provided to the reader other than URLs for other organizations." Another participant, who read an article without links, noted that the lack of links decreased credibility: "No sources, links, or visuals made it seem dull and less than expert."

Other information One participant pointed out an error in the hepatitis article. The hepatitis article cites an inaccurate boiling point for water—a statement that was taken directly from the Web site of the CDC (2001). The error was not detected in pilot testing.

Comments regarding general evaluation strategies

All 148 responses refer to characteristics that participants stated would influence their decisions to use information from a Web site. Unless otherwise noted, the factors analyzed have a positive impact on participants' willingness to use a site.

Source of information Ninety-eight comments mentioned source at some level as an important consideration in participants decisions to use information from a site. Some comments made multiple mentions of source, for a total of 125 mentions of source. Specifically, 59 comments mentioned the publisher or sponsor of a site as an important consideration in participants decisions to use information from a site. Credible sources listed by the participants included hospitals, universities, government agencies, and well-known non-profit organizations. One participant wrote, "I want to see writers or quotes from faculty and staff at Johns Hopkins or Mayo Clinic or other respected research academic facilities." Another wrote: "For instance www.newsweek.com would be a 'sorta' credible site but www.americanmedicalassociation.com would be more credible and the CDC site would be my preferred choice." Some participants also wrote that they would use sites suggested by their physicians or other health professionals.

Negative factors related to source at the publisher/sponsor level included advertisements, ".com" designations, and nonauthoritative personal sites. One participant wrote, "I would be more likely to believe information from the American Diabetes Association than I would from Joe Diabetic's Web site" (The American Diabetes Association was one of the links on the page this participant read.)

Source at the level of author was mentioned in 22 comments as a factor in participants' evaluations of medical information online. Comments included "written by health professionals." Source at the level of originators of information, such as scientific references, was mentioned in 24 comments. For example, one participant referred to "well-known physicians quoted on the Web site." Finally, 20 comments mentioned the importance of source at a general or unspecific level as opposed to specifically referring to source at the level of publishers/sponsor, author, or originator of information.

Street address and links Although no participants mentioned the presence or absence of a street address, 17 comments mentioned the presence of external links as a positive factor in participants' evaluation of a Web site. Comments included: "links for further info," "scientific references and links," and "links to supporting organizations." In some cases, the reference to links was qualified with participants specifying that a particular type of link would be viewed as a positive factor. Qualifying comments included: "credible links are provided for further information" and "external links jump to other high-quality sites."

Contact information Two comments mentioned unspecified types of contact information as a positive factor in participants' evaluation of a Web site with medical information. One participant wrote, "credible sources with full contact info."

Other factors Of the 148 comments on Web site characteristics influencing use of a Web site, 26 addressed design elements that affect participants' evaluation of Web sites. Factors that participants described as positive included: "easy to navigate," "easy to scan," "modular information with graphics," "page e-mailable," "page e-printable," "professional design," "rapid loading time," and "usability." Negative factors included: "annoying moving graphics," "glaring pop-up ads or problems with links," and "unnecessary graphics." Participants' negative comments also stated: "A junky site has less credibility" and "I probably wouldn't trust medical information that was presented in Comic Sans [a typeface]."

Some additional factors included institutional accreditation, information quality, and perceptions of source bias. One participant mentioned third-party accreditation as a positive factor in her evaluation of a health information Web site. The comment referred to "credibility indicators, such as the AMA seal." Other participants mentioned issues related to information accuracy and lack of errors, and factors related to writing and editing, such as clear, logical organization of information, as factors that would tend to increase their willingness to use information from a Web site. One participant explained her bias rating: "Also, FYI, I say that the author is very biased because I believe we are all biased—it's not bad, just reality."

Discussion

We first examine results regarding reader characteristics as they relate to external validity and participants use of central or peripheral processing. Then we discuss credibility ratings related to specific reader characteristics and credibility measures in general, followed by a brief statement concerning limitations of the implementation of the study variables.

Reader characteristics and external validity

Regarding age, level of education, and gender, the participants in this study were representative of the Internet population as a whole, especially people who use the Internet to search for medical information. Like the population of user of online medical information interviewed by other researchers (Baker and colleagues 2003; Cain and colleagues 2000; Fox and Fallows 2003; Fox and Rainie 2002), a majority (68%) of the participants in this study were female. The gender and average age of participants (mean = 39.6) matched the demographic profile of one of the largest categories of "Health e-people," women aged 40–49 (Cain and colleagues 2000).

Participants were also typical in their frequency of use of medical information online: like the majority of participants in previous studies (Baker and colleagues 2003; Cain and colleagues 2000; Fox and Fallows 2003; Bouston and Allison 2003), participants searched for medical information infrequently, just a few times a year. In addition, the finding that the older the participants, the less likely they were to use the Internet to look up general information and to engage in Internet actions and activities is consistent with the findings of other studies (Licciardone and colleagues 2001).

Regarding professional experience in a health or medical setting, or with health or medical information, participants were less representative of the general Internet population in that nearly half of the study participants had worked in a health or medical setting, or had covered medical or scientific issues as a professional journalist. Therefore, it would be reasonable to assume that participants had a relatively high level of medical knowledge compared with the general population of Internet users.

Furthermore, because 82% had at least a four-year college degree, it would be reasonable to assume that participants would have had an easy time understanding the study directions and questions, including the credibility scales used in the study.

Reader characteristics and use of central or peripheral processing

The effects of reader demographics on credibility ratings can be evaluated in the framework of ELM theory and what it suggests about the use of central vs. peripheral processing to judge credibility. ELM theory posits that personal or general interest in, familiarity with, and perceptions of reading ease of a topic can increase motivation and the ability to use central processing to evaluate information about that topic.

Concerning topic interest, 60% of the participants reported being interested or very interested in the articles that they read. While the survey question regarding interest did not distinguish between types of interest, such as general, professional, and personal, several of the demographic questions implicitly addressed issues related to personal and professional interest (the participants having the disease or having a friend or relative with the disease, or experience as a professional journalist or in a health or medical setting). About one third of participants had personal experience with the disease they read about, or had a friend or relative who had personal experience with this disease. It could be assumed that personal experience of some participants could translate into personal interest, and that fact could increase their motivation to use central processing to evaluate the articles they read.

Participants with experience in a health or medical setting, or with reporting about medical or scientific issues as a professional journalist (nearly half the participants in this study), could be presumed to have a professional interest in the articles, a fact that might increase their tendency to use central processing. Professional concern regarding the accuracy of medical information might provide these participants with motivation to evaluate the articles using central processing. In addition, participants with professional experience in health, medicine, or science were likely to be better able to interpret the articles than the rest of the participants, increasing the likelihood that they would use central processing.

The general medical experience of the participants, as well as their personal interest, was reflected in the overall participants' familiarity with the topics in the articles they read; 66.2% rated the information in the diabetes article as familiar or very familiar, and 51.9% rated the information in the hepatitis article as familiar or very familiar. These participants would have had more ability and possibly more motivation to use central processing to evaluate the articles they read, compared with readers who were not familiar with the information in the articles.

Results also showed that while readers' interest in a topic can contribute to their familiarity, readers' familiarity with a topic does not always cause them be interested in a specific text. A significant inverse correlation showed that participants who were familiar with the information in the articles were less likely to find it interesting. This relationship may reflect the fact that the articles were written at a basic level more likely to appeal to people with little knowledge of or familiarity with the topics than to people with greater topic knowledge or familiarity.

Regarding the difficulty of the articles, quantitative and qualitative results showed that a large majority of participants rated the articles as easy or very easy. Therefore, the majority of participants had the ability to use central processing to evaluate the articles.

The significant inverse correlations between Internet experience, as operationalized by experience with the listed Internet actions and activities, and ratings for article difficulty may be associated with the findings that participants who engaged in more Internet activities were also more likely to look up medical and general information, and participants who engaged in more Internet actions were more likely to look up general information online. This searching activity may have provided these participants with background knowledge or other experience that caused them to perceive the articles as easier.

Factors that may have decreased participants' ability or motivation to use central processing and to scrutinize the information might have included a desire to complete the study quickly and the knowledge that the Web pages were part of an academic study.

Reader characteristics and credibility ratings

Reader characteristics of age, interest in the information, perceptions of text difficulty, experience in medical settings, and Internet experience related to many of the participants' credibility ratings. Age positively correlated with ratings for article expertise and author expertise; in other words, the older the participants, the higher the ratings, and the younger the participants, the lower the ratings. These findings contrast with other studies that have shown an inverse correlation between age and credibility ratings for the Internet as a channel of information (Finberg and colleagues; Johnson and Kaye 1998; PSRA 2002). Since participants in this study were, by definition, users of the

Internet, this finding may speak more to the relationship between the age of the participants and their judgments of the credibility of online medical information than to their judgments of the credibility of online information in general.

Interest in the articles positively correlated with all six of the credibility ratings. In other words, participants who were more interested in the articles rated them more highly on these credibility criteria. However, the inverse correlation between participants' interest in and familiarity with the articles indicates that at least some interested participants may have lacked the ability to critically evaluate the articles. Therefore, they may have rated the articles more highly than participants who had greater medical knowledge.

There was a significant inverse correlation between ratings for article difficulty and article expertise. In other words, participants tended to equate ease with lack of expertise. These quantitative findings were reinforced by some of the qualitative comments that referred to the articles as "dumbed down," "lightweight," and "shallow." This result reinforces the findings of a recent Pew Internet and American Life Project survey (Fox and Rainie 2002) where participants "suggested that high-level writing may inspire trust in a site" (p. 24).

The lack of significant correlations between participants' familiarity with the information in the articles and credibility ratings may indicate that other reader characteristics, such as interest, may be stronger predictors of credibility ratings. Another possibility is that varying levels of interest among participants who were familiar with the information in the articles confounded any significant relationships between familiarity and the credibility ratings.

Participants' Internet experience, as gauged by their reported participation in the listed Internet actions, also correlated with credibility ratings. The greater participants' experience with the listed Internet actions, the lower their ratings for article credibility, article trustworthiness, and author expertise. These correlations may be associated with the finding that participants who reported engaging in more Internet activities reported that they were also more likely to look up general information online. Therefore, they may have had greater experience encountering poor quality or deceptive information on the Internet than readers with less Internet experience. These encounters may have decreased their tendency to view online information, including online medical information, as credible, trustworthy, or expert.

Credibility measures

Participants gave articles with an address significantly higher ratings for article credibility and significantly lower ratings for author credibility than they gave articles without addresses. Although the presence or absence of an address affected quantitative results, participants made almost no mention of physical or street addresses in their qualitative comments. The presence of a physical address apparently triggered participants to evaluate article and author credibility in different ways. The presence of address relates to source credibility at the level of the site publisher—and when participants answered credibility questions about the article itself, they were apparently thinking about credibility at the publisher level.

It may very well be that readers engaged in peripheral processing and simply noted the presence of a street address as a cue toward credibility. In contrast, when they answered questions about author credibility, they were considering a different level of source (and were perhaps contrasting the author and publisher levels). Participants may then have engaged in central processing, which in turn made them more critical, as they apparently took the address cue as a negative cue regarding author credibility.

There is also qualitative evidence that the presence of an address served as a peripheral cue for evaluating the articles. In other words, the topic of contact information provided by an address did not seem to be a focus of attention or conscious thought, that is, of central processing. No participants mentioned a street address in their comments about the article read or their general strategies for evaluating Web sites and only two participants mentioned contact information (of an unspecified nature) as a factor in their general strategies for evaluating Web sites.

While the presence or absence of links did not significantly affect credibility ratings, there is qualitative evidence that links factor into participants' credibility judgments. Nineteen participants mentioned links in the qualitative comments, even though no questions we asked could have cued such comments. In addition, participants discussed specific types of links that would positively affect their decision to use information on a Web site ("credible," "high-quality"). Therefore it appears that external links were an object of conscious thought and evaluation, and so may have been processed by some participants through the central route. As a result, links may serve as more complex cues of credibility than the presence or absence of an address, and may be more affected by reader characteristics.

Qualitative results from this study regarding the importance of aspects of information sources and Web site design in evaluating health information online were congruent with previous studies. Source was the factor mentioned most frequently by participants as a factor in their decision to use health information on a Web site. Two thirds of the participants discussed how positive and negative characteristics of the sources of information at some level—publisher/sponsor, author, originator of information, or unspecified—affected their opinion of health information. After aspects of source, aspects of Web site design (such as the use of graphics and illustrations) were mentioned most frequently by participants as factors affecting their evaluation of online information.

Study variables

A few limitations concerning the implementation of the address and link variables merit further discussion. The organization name and address used in the experimental materials were fictional, factors that could have decreased credibility ratings by readers who were aware that the "National Health Organization" did not exist. One participant reported, "I am not familiar with this organization, so I am neutral about judging the quality of the content." However, at least one participant found the organization title and logo to be reassuring. "This was a national health organization, unbiased, so it was O.K."

In addition, the external links were not functional, a factor that could have affected credibility ratings by limiting the ability for further analysis by readers using central processing to evaluate the articles and links. The mere fact that the links were not functional, though not broken, could have also decreased credibility ratings.

Conclusion

The results of this study confirm previous credibility research in several areas, as well as breaking new ground in other areas. This study confirmed the strong relationship between readers' evaluations of sources of information at various levels—publisher/sponsor, author, and originator of information—and their evaluation of the information provided by or attributed to that source.

Results also demonstrated that ELM theory provides a useful framework for studying the credibility of online information because ELM theory posits that readers' personal experiences and circumstances determine whether they use central or peripheral processing to evaluate a specific Web page. The characteristics of participants in this study appeared to affect the processes they used to evaluate the articles they read, and so also affected their credibility ratings of those articles.

Study results revealed several areas where readers personal experiences affect their evaluations of the credibility of online information. Readers may judge online medical information less critically if it interests them. They may equate difficulty with expertise when evaluating medical information online. In addition, readers with greater internet experience may be more critical in their credibility judgments than those with less experience.

The findings indicate that the presence of a street address serves as a basic cue of credibility for a broad range of Internet users with varying prior knowledge, and that readers may process the presence of a street address as a cue to trigger either peripheral or central processing, which in turn can affect their credibility judgments. In this study, it appears that when readers used peripheral processing, they perceived a street address as a feature that increased credibility, yet when readers used central processing, they perceived a street address as a feature that decreased credibility. Because this study used a fictitious address from an area of Washington, DC, that is home to many federal agencies, it is unclear whether the mere presence of a street address, or rather the presence of a *credible* street address, affected credibility ratings.

The fact that the presence of an address significantly affected credibility ratings among a population not likely to rely on such cues, especially cues related to an unknown organization, demonstrates that a street address can serve as powerful cue of credibility. It would be reasonable to assume that the presence of a street address might have greater impact among participants with less medical knowledge or less ability to process the information in the articles. This cue might also have more impact if readers were processing less familiar information or text that they perceived to be difficult.

It is interesting that, while addresses clearly affected credibility ratings, participants did not discuss them in their comments about the article read or their general strategies in evaluating Web pages. Still, participants' comments did indicate that many are aware of links and that some carefully evaluate the credibility of individual links. Readers may be more likely to consider the type of links in an article, rather than the mere presence or absence of links, when making credibility judgments. The contrasting results for quantitative ratings vs. qualitative comments speak to the need to elicit both kinds of data when investigating credibility effects.

Although this study was restricted to online medical information, it is extremely likely that these results would apply to many types of Web pages. Publishers, editors, and authors should carefully consider adding a street address to their Web pages, realizing that in some cases it will increase credibility and in other cases it may decrease credibility. While further research should clarify these differences, Web publishers would be well advised to pilot test pages with street addresses to see how they affect readers. Further, Web publishers would also be advised to pilot test external links to determine their impact on the credibility of Web pages.

Directions for Future Research

The results of this study suggest several areas for future research. Future research should compare the effects of several types of addresses, perhaps a Washington, DC address, like the one used in this study, with an address from an area less well known and less likely to be associated with government or medical agencies. It would also be instructive to test specific address components to determine whether a "contact us" link on a Web page had the same impact as a street address on a Web page, and to determine the relative impacts of street address, e-mail address, phone number, and other contact information, such as the names of editors or publishers.

The results of this study also indicate directions for research into the potential impact of external links as cues to credibility. Future research could focus on the factors that may affect the credibility of external links—such as whether the page being linked to is part of a commercial, non-profit, or government site. Once factors that affect the credibility of links have been better determined, it would be instructive to test the effects of high- and low-credibility links on overall credibility ratings of a Web page.

Future research should also assess other Web design issues known to affect credibility judgments. The broad issue of design could be parsed into many factors, such as usability, accessibility, and use of graphics, and the effects of these factors on credibility.

Study results regarding relationships among reader characteristics and credibility ratings also indicate directions for further research. It would be instructive to confirm whether some readers truly equate difficulty with expertise, and if so, how the use of difficult text to increase credibility among some readers can be reconciled with the need for clear information accessible to readers at a wide range of literacy levels. Further examination of the effects of reader interest vs. reader familiarity on credibility ratings could provide valuable insight into the ways that expert and non-expert readers evaluate online medical information.

Findings linking Internet experience with lower credibility ratings also invite further exploration. Internet experience could be operationalized in a number of ways, such as time spent searching for medical information or personalization of browser settings, factors that could impact credibility judgments independently or in concert. It may also prove important to distinguish among readers by their health status. The credibility cues used by people who are healthy may differ from those used by people who are chronically ill or the caregivers of chronically ill people.

The practical benefits of research into credibility cues online may be matched by their contributions to the understanding of a new medium. It will be fascinating to look back in 20, 30, or 50 years to see whether the credibility cues used by readers have changed, and if so, how their evolution reflects that of the Internet as a whole.

Acknowledgments

Support for this study came from the National Institute of Environmental Health Sciences, National Institutes of Health, Grants ES10738 and ES07033.

References

American Society of Magazine Editors (ASME), 2002. *Guidelines for editors and publishers: Best practices for digital media.* 11th ed. New York, NY: American Society of Magazine Editors. http://www.asme.magazine.org/guidelines/new media.html

Austin, E. W., and Qingwen Dong. 1994. Source v. content effects of judgments of news credibility. *Journalism quarterly* 71:973–983.

Baker, L., T. H. Wagner, S. Singer, and M. K. Bundorf. 2003. Use of the Internet and e-mail for health care information. *Journal of the American Medical Association* 289:2400–2406.

Balshem, M. 1991. Cancer, control, and causality: Talking about cancer in a working-class community. *American ethnologist* 18:152–172.

Bard, M. R. 2000. *The future of e-health.* New York, NY: Cyber Dialogue, Inc. www.cyberdialogue.com

Berland, G. K., M. N. Elliott, L. S. Morales, J. I. Algazy, R. L. Kravitz, M. S. Broder, D. E. Kanouse, J. A. Munoz, J. A. Puyol, M. Lara, K. E. Watkins, H. Yang, and E. A. McGlynn. 2001. Health information on the Internet: Accessibility, quality, and readability in English and Spanish. *Journal of the American Medical Association* 285:2612–2621.

Bernhardt, J. M., R. A. W. Lariscy, R. L. Parrott, K. J. Silk, and E. M. Felter. 2002. Perceived barriers to Internet-based health communication on human genetics. *Journal of health communication* 7:325–340.

BIOME. 2001. How to evaluate an Internet-based information source. Nottingham, UK: University of Nottingham. http://biome.ac.uk/guidelines/oval/howto.html

Cain, M. M., J. Sarasohn-Kahn, and J. C. Wayne. 2000. *Health e-People: The online consumer experience.* Menlo Park, CA: Institute for the Future. http://www.chcf.org/topics/view.cfm?itemID = 12540

Centers for Disease Control and Prevention (CDC). 2001. *Viral hepatitis A fact sheet.* Atlanta, GA: Centers for Disease Control and Prevention. http://www.cdc.gov/ncidod/diseases/hepatitis/a/fact.htm

——. 2002. *Diabetes: Disabling, deadly, and on the rise, at a glance 2002.* Atlanta, GA: Centers for Disease Control and Prevention. http://www.cdc.gov/diabetes/pubs/glance.htm

Cheskin Research. 2000. *Trust in the wired Americas.* Redwood Shores, CA: Cheskin Research. www.cheskin.com

——, and Studio Archetype/Sapient. 1999. *eCommerce trust study.* Redwood Shores, CA: Cheskin Research. www.cheskin.com

Christensen, T. P., F. J. Ascione, and R. P. Bagozzi. 1997. Understanding how elderly patients process drug information: A test of a theory of information processing. *Pharmaceutical research* 14:1589–1596.

Cline, R. J., and J. L. Engel. 1991. College student's perceptions of sources of information about AIDS. *Journal of American college health* 40(2):55–63.

Consumer Reports on Health (CROH). 2000. How to research a medical topic. *Consumer Reports on health,* October, 7–9.

Crocco, A. G., M. Villasis-Keever, and A. R. Jadad. 2002. Analysis of cases of harm associated with use of health information on the Internet. *Journal of the American Medical Association* 287:2869–2871.

Dutta-Bergman, M. 2003. Trusted online sources of health information: Differences in demographics, health beliefs, and health-information orientation. *Journal of medical Internet research* 5 (3): e21. http://jmir.org/2003/3/e21

Eastin, M. S. 2001. Credibility assessments of online health information: The effects of source expertise and knowledge of content. *Journal of computer mediated-communication* 6 (4). http://www.ascusc.org/jcmc/vol6/issue4/eastin.html

Eng, T. R., and Evalulmetrix LLC. 2001. The eHealth landscape: A terrain map of emerging information and communication technologies in health and health care. Princeton, NJ. Robert Wood Johnson Foundation. http://www.rwjf.org/publicationsPdfs/eHealth.pdf

Eysenbach, G., and C. Köhler. 2002. How do consumers search for and appraise health information on the World Wide Web? Qualitative study using focus groups: usability tests, and in-depth interviews. *British medical journal* 324:573–577.

Fahey, D. K., and J. Weinberg. 2003. LASIK complications and the Internet: Is the public being misled? *Journal of medical Internet research* 5 (1): e2.

Federal Trade Commission (FTC). 2001. "Operation Cure.All" wages new battle in ongoing war against Internet health fraud [press release]. Washington, DC: Federal Trade Commission. http://www.ftc.gov/opa/2001/06/cureall.htm

Finberg, H. I., M. L. Stone, and D. Lynch. 2002. *Digital journalism credibility study: Online News Association.* http://www.journalists.org

Flanagin, A. J., and M. J. Metzger. 2000. Perceptions of Internet information credibility. *Journalism and mass communication quarterly* 77:515–540.

Fogg, B. J., T. Kameda, J. Boyd, J. Marshall, R. Sethi, M. Sockol, and T. Trowbridge. 2002a. *Stanford-Makovsky Web credibility study 2002: Investing what makes Web sites credible today.* Palo Alto, CA: Stanford Persuasive Technology Laboratory, Stanford University. http://www.webcredibility.org/

———, L. Marable, J. Stanford, and E. R. Tauber. 2002b. How do people evaluate a Web site's credibility? Results from a large study. Yonkers, NY: Consumer WebWatch. http://www.consumerwebwatch.org/news/report3_credibilityresearch/stanfordPTL_abstract.htm

———, J. Marshall, T. Kameda, J. Solomon, A. Rangnekar, J. Boyd, and B. Brown. 2001a. What makes Web sites credible? A report on a large qualitative study. In *Proceedings of the Conference on Human Factors in Computing Systems.* New York, NY: ACM Press, pp. 61–68.

———, J. Marshall, L. Othman, Alex Osipovich, C. Varma, N. Fang, J. Paul, A. Rangnekar, J. Shon, P. Swani, and M. Treinen. 2001b. Web credibility research: A method for online experiments and early study results. In *Proceedings of the Conference on Human Factors in Computing Systems* [extended abstracts]. New York, NY: ACM Press, p. 295.

Fox, S. L., and D. Fallows. 2003. *Internet health resources: Health searches and email have become commonplace, but there is room for improvement in searches and overall Internet access?* Washington, DC: The Pew Internet and American Life Project. http://www.pewinternet.org/reports/toc.asp?Report=95

———, L. Rainie, J. Horrigan, A. Lenhart, T. Spooner, and C. Carter. 2000. *Trust and privacy online: Why Americans want to re-write the rules.* Washington, DC: The Pew Internet & American Life Project. http://www.pewinternet.org/reports/toc.asp?Report=19

———, and L. Rainie. 2002. *Vital decisions: How Internet users decide what information to trust when they or their loved ones are sick.* Washington, DC: The Pew Internet & American Life Project. http://www.pewinternet.org/reports/toc.asp?Report=59

Freeman, K. 2002. *An examination of factors that affect the credibility of health information on the Internet.* Master's thesis, University of Washington.

Frewer, L. J., C. Howard, D. Hedderley, and R. Shepherd. 1996. What determines trust in information about food-related risks? Underlying psychological constructs. *Risk analysis* 16:473–486.

———. 1997. The elaboration likelihood model and communication about food risks. *Risk analysis* 17:759–770.

Friedman, B., P. H. Kahn, and D. C. Howe. 2000. Trust online. *Communications of the ACM* 43 (12): 34–40

Gastel, B. 1998. *Health writer's handbook.* Ames, IA: Iowa State University Press.

Gaziano, C., and K. McGrath. 1986. Measuring the concept of credibility. *Journalism quarterly* 63:451–462.

Graphic, Visualization, and Usability Center (GVU). 1999. 10th WWW user survey. Atlanta, GA: Georgia Institute of Technology. http://www.gvu.gatech.edu/user_surveys/survey-1998-10/

Gunther, A. C. 1992. Biased press or biased public? Attitudes toward media coverage of social groups. *Public opinion quarterly* 56:147–167.

Guttman, N., D. Boccher-Lattimore, and C. T. Salmon. 1998. Credibility of information from official sources on HIV/AIDS transmission. *Public health reports* 113:465–471.

Health Internet Ethics (HIE). 2000. Health Internet ethics: Ethical principles for offering health services to consumers. http://www.hiethics.com/Principles/index.asp

Health on the Net Foundation (HON). 1997. *HON code of conduct for medical and health Web sites.* Geneva, Switzerland: Health on the Net Foundation. http://www.hon.ch/HONcode/Conduct.html

———. 1999. *Fifth HON survey on the evolution of Internet usage for health purposes.* Geneva, Switzerland: Health on the Net Foundation. http://www.hon.ch/Survey/ResultsSummary_oct_nov99.html

———. 2001. *Evolution of Internet use for health purposes.* Geneva, Switzerland: Health on the Net Foundation. http://www.hon.ch/Survey/FebMar2001/survey.html

Health Summit Working Group (HSWG). 1998. *Criteria for assessing the quality of health information on the Internet.* McLean, VA: Health Information Technology Systems, Mitretek Systems. http://hitiweb.mitretek.org/hswg/default.asp

Hellawell, G. O., K. J. Turner, K. J. Le Monnier, and S. F. Brewster. 2000. Urology and the Internet: An evaluation of Internet use by urology patients and of information available on urological topics. *BJU International* 86:191–194.

Horrigan, J. B., and L. Rainie. 2002. *Getting serious online.* Washington, D.C.: Pew Internet & American Life Project. http://www.pewinternet.org/reports/toc.asp?Report=55

Houston, T. K., and J. J. Allison. 2003. Users of Internet health information: Differences by health status. *Journal of medical Internet research* 5 (4): e7.

Hovland, C. I., and W. Weiss. 1951. The influence of source credibility on communication effectiveness. *Public opinion quarterly* 15:635–650.

Internet Healthcare Coalition (IHC). 2000. eHealth code of ethics. Newtown, PA: Internet Healthcare Coalition. http://www.ihealthcoalition.org/ethics/ehcode.html

———. 2002. Tips for health consumers: Finding quality health information on the Internet. Newtown, PA: Internet Healthcare Coalition. http://www.ihealthcoalition.org/content/tips.html

Isakson, C. S., and J. H. Spyridakis. 1999. The influence of semantics and syntax on what readers remember. *Technical communication* 46:366–381.

Johnson, T. J., and B. K. Kaye. 1998. Cruising is believing? Comparing Internet and traditional sources on media credibility measures. *Journalism and mass communication quarterly* 75:325–340.

Jones, S., M. Wilkens, P. Morris, and M. Masera. 2000. Trust requirements in e-business. *Communications of the ACM* 43 (12): 81–87.

Kaulman, D. G., M. F. Stasson, and J. W. Hart. 1999. Are the tabloids always wrong or is that just what we think? Need for cognition and perceptions of articles in print media: *Journal of applied social psychology* 29:1984–1997.

Lasica, J. D. 2002. Online news: Credibility Gap Ahead? *Online journalism review.* April 17. http://www.ojr.org/ojr/lasica/1019079841.php

Latthe, P. M. 2000. Quality of medical information about menorrhagia on the Worldwide Web. *British journal of obstetrics and gynaecology* 107:39–43.

Licciardone, J. C., P. Smith-Barbaro, and S. T. Coleridge. 2001. Use of the Internet as a resource for consumer health information: Results of the second osteopathic survey of health care in America (OSTEOSURV-II). *Journal of medical Internet research* 3 (4): e31.

Meyer, P. 1988. Defining and measuring credibility of newspapers: Developing an index. *Journalism quarterly* 65:567–574.

National Cancer Institute (NCI). 2002. How to evaluate health information on the Internet: Questions and answers. http://cis.nci.nih.gov/fact/2_10.htm

National Institute of Arthritis and Musculoskeletal and Skin Diseases (NIAMSD). 2000. How to find medical information. Bethesda, MD: National Institutes of Health.

Nielsen, J. 2000. *Designing Web usability.* Indianapolis, IN: New Riders.

Nielsen, J. 1999. Trust or bust: Communicating trustworthiness in Web design. *Nielsen's Alertbox.* March 7. http://www.useit.com/alertbox/990307.html

Olson, J. S., and G. M. Olson. 2000. i2i trust in e-commerce. *Communications of the ACM* 43 (12): 41–44.

Pandolfi, C., P. Impicciatore, and B. Bonati. 2000. Parents on the Web: Risks for quality management of cough in children. *Pediatrics* 105 (1): e1.

Pennbridge, J., R. Moya, and L. Rodrigues. 1999. Questionnaire survey of California consumers' use and rating of sources of health care information including the Internet. *Western journal of medicine* 171:302–306.

Petty, R. E., and J. T. Cacioppo. 1986. *Communication and persuasion: Central and peripheral routes to attitude change.* New York, NY: Springer-Verlag.

Price, J. 2000. *The complete idiot's guide to online medical resources.* Indianapolis, IN: QUE, division of Macmillan.

Priester, J. R., and R. E. Petty. 1995. Source attributions and persuasion: Perceived honesty as a determinant of source honesty. *Personality and social psychology bulletin* 21: 637–654.

Princeton Survey Research Associates (PSRA). 2002. *A matter of trust: What users want from Web sites.* Yonkers, NY: Consumer WebWatch. http://www.consumerwebwatch.org/news/1_abstract.htm

Raphael, T. E., A. C. Myers, P. Freebody, W. C. Tirre, and M. Fritz. 1980. Contrasting the effects of some text variables on comprehension and ratings of comprehensibility. Technical Report No. 190. Urbana, IL: Cambridge, MA: Illinois University, Center for the Study of Reading; Bolt, Beranek and Newman, Inc.

Resnick, P., R. Zeckhauser, E. Friedman, and K. Kuwabara. 2000. Reputation systems. *Communications of the ACM* 43 (12): 45–48.

Self, C. C. 1996. Credibility. In *An integrated approach to communication theory and research,* eds. M. B. Salwen and D. W. Stacks. Mahwah; NJ: Lawrence Erlbaum Associates.

Shneiderman, B. 2000. Designing trust into user experiences. *Communications of the ACM* 57 (12): 57–59.

Silberg, W. M., G. D. Lundberg, and R. A. Musacchio. 1997. Assessing, controlling and assuring the quality of medical information on the Internet. *Journal of the American Medical Association* 277:1244–1245.

Spyridakis, J. H. 2000. Guidelines for authoring comprehensible Web pages and evaluating their success. *Technical communication* 47:359–382.

Stanford, J., E. R. Tauber, B. J. Fogg, and L. Marable. 2002. Experts vs. online consumers: A comparative credibility study of health and finance Web sites: Consumer WebWatch. http://www.consumerwebwatch.org/news/report3_credibilityresearch/slicedbread_abstract.htm

Stephenson, J. 1998. Patient pretenders weave tangled "Web" of deceit. *Journal of the American Medical Association* 280:1297.

Stone, T. W., and J. M. Jumper. 2001. Information about age-related macular degeneration on the Internet. *Southern medical journal* 94:22–25.

Suarez-Almazor, M. E., C. J. Kendall, and M. Dorgan. 2001. Surfing the net—Information on the World Wide Web for persons with arthritis: Patient empowerment or patient deceit? *Journal of rheumatology* 28:1–2.

Sundar, S. S. 1998. Effect of source attribution on perception of online news stories. *Journalism and mass communication quarterly* 75:55–68.

———. 1999. Exploring receivers' criteria for perception of print and online news. *Journalism and mass communication quarterly* 76:373–386.

———. 2000. Multimedia effects on processing and perception of online news: A study of picture, audio, and video downloads. *Journalism and mass communication quarterly* 77:480–499.

Swenson, J., H. Constantinides, and L. Gurak. 2002. Audience-drive Web design: An application to medical Web sites. *Technical communication* 49:341–352.

University of California, Los Angeles (UCLA). 2003. *Surveying the Digital Future: UCLA Center for Communication Policy.* http://www.ccp.ucla.edu/pages/internet-report.asp

Wade, S. E., and R. B. Adams. 1990. Effects of importance and interest on recall of biographical text. *Journal of reading behavior* 22:331–351.

Weisbord, S. D., J. B. Soule, and P. L. Kimmel. 1997. Poison on line: Acute renal failure caused by oil of wormwood purchased through the Internet. *New England journal of medicine* 337:825–827.

West, M. D. 1994. Validating a scale for the measurement of credibility: A covariance structure modeling approach. *Journalism quarterly* 71 (1): 159–168.

Winker, M. A., A. Flanagin, B. Chi-Lum, J. White, K. Andrews, R. L. Kennett, C. D. DeAngelis, and R. A. Musacchio. 2000. Guidelines for medical and health information on the Internet. *Journal of the American Medical Association* 283:1600–1606.

Winn, W., and K. Beck. 2002. The persuasive power of design elements on an e-commerce Web site. *Technical communication* 49:17–35.

Zhang, P., G. M. von Dran, P. Blake, and V. Pipithsuksunt. 2001. Important design features in different web site domains. *e-service journal* 1:77–91.

KRISANDRA S. FREEMAN, MS, ELS, is a public information specialist at the University of Washington Center for Ecogenetics and Environmental Health. Prior to coming to the University of Washington, she was a newspaper reporter magazine editor and full-time freelance writer, specializing in medical and technical topics. Her articles have appeared in *Encarta encyclopedia* and abcnews.com and have won awards from STC and the National Association of Government Communicators. Contact information: freeman@u.washington.edu

JAN H. SPYRIDAKIS, a professor in the Department of Technical Communication at the University of Washington, teaches courses on style in writing, research methodology, and international and advanced technical communication. Her research focuses on the effect of document and screen design variables on comprehension and usability, and on the refinement of research methods. She is a fellow of STC. Contact information: jansp@u.washington.edu

FOLLOW-UP QUESTIONS AND EXPLORATION PROJECTS

1. The Theoretical versus Applied research distinction is more of a continuum than a set of discrete categories. That said, the articles by Bevan and by Penington would fall more at the Theoretical end of the continuum and the articles by Freeman and Spyridakis and by Pearce and Pearce would fall more at the Applied end of the continuum. Looking at this set of four articles what conclusions can you draw about how Theoretical and Applied research is similar and different? Which type of research appeals to you more? Why?

2. Which concepts from ELM did Freeman and Spyridakis choose to measure? Why did they choose these concepts and not others? What effect did these choices have on what they found?

3. Given this study do you think ELM is a theory that applies to internet communication? Why or why not? What does your analysis suggest about how you see internet communication comparing to other forms of communication?

4. If you think of this journal article as a piece of persuasion, how would the concepts of ELM explain your reaction to this article? Did you use central-route or peripheral-route processing? Would ELM's predictions about the articles relevance to you and your ability and motivation to understand it be correct in identifying which route you used?

6 Structuration Theory: Communication and Social Rules at Work

Several of the theories considered in the chapters of this book claim that communication is the means by which we better understand and make sense of the world around us. For example, Coordinated Management of Meaning theory suggests that through our communication and interactions with other people, we create social reality. When people communicate they influence their social environment, while at the same time their social environment influences their communication. Whether we are making decisions about which college to attend, participating as a new member of a fraternity or sorority, or starting a new romantic relationship, we use communication to help us understand our roles and the rules associated with each one of these interactions. Also, through communication we create structures or rules of interaction which influence our relational roles. Structuration Theory offers an explanation of how our conscious and unconscious actions influence others and ultimately construct reality.

Background of Structuration Theory

Structuration Theory is based primarily on the work of British philosopher Anthony Giddens who suggested that social structures, such as organizations, are created through conscious human interaction, which is what makes this theory unique (1984). Traditional perspectives on social interaction proposed that societal structures are created primarily through unconscious acts, where people involved in the interaction have little control over how social structures are communicated and formed. While Giddens accepted to some degree that social interaction and the creation of societal structure is unconscious, he theorized that humans are active in the creation of societal structures based upon past experiences and mutually understood societal norms (Giddens, 1984). People know how to interact and make decisions about their interactions based on goals and motivations.

Communication scholars have used structuration as a theoretical approach, especially in organizational and small group studies where they have looked at topics including decision-making, work-family policies, organizational change, culture, and technological development (Witmer, 1997). Researchers use structuration as a way to demonstrate active communication in the development of rules and resources, which lead to the construction of reality and meaning.

Article Structure

This article (Kirby and Krone, 2002) uses structuration as a way to understand how people in organizations make sense of work and family policies. The article uses a qualitative structure for the Results and Interpretation section, in which propositions are made and supported by interview segments. These demonstrate the active nature of human participants in their decisions to use or not to use work and family organizational initiatives like maternity and paternity leave. The article demonstrates how active discourse by participants creates the structure, or rules and resources, for understanding the proper use or misuse of organizational work and family policies.

Distinctive Points

This article considers several important points from a structuration perspective. First, regarding work and family policy, the article considers how structuration relates to practical organizational problems. Second, the article demonstrates that in organizations many sense-making structures are established depending on the communication and interpretation of organizational and personal rules and resources. Third, this research demonstrates that structure emerges differently at various organizational levels because different rules and resources are available to workers, depending on where they fall on the organization's hierarchy. Fourth, the article shows that the perceptions of work-family benefits were both actively enabled and constrained by the participants in the organization, and that policies were interpreted differently by workers than they were intended by the organization.

References

Giddens, A. (1984). *The constitution of society: Outline of the theory of structuration.* Cambridge, MA: Polity Press.

Kirby, E.L. & Krone, K.J. (2002). "The policy exists but you can't really use it": Communication and the structuration of work-family policies. *Journal of Applied Communication Research, 30,* 50–77.

Witmer, D.F. (1997). Communication and recovery: Structuration as an ontological approach to organizational culture. *Communication Monographs, 64,* 325–349.

"The Policy Exists But You Can't Really Use It": Communication and the Structuration of Work-Family Policies

Erika L. Kirby and Kathleen J. Krone

ABSTRACT *Although work-family benefits are increasingly important organizational policies, limited research addresses the impact of communication on benefit utilization. However, communication is significant because the perceived appropriateness of work-family benefits emerges through interaction. For example, when coworkers complain about "picking up the slack" for those using family leave, their discourse may impact future decisions of other workers regarding whether they utilize the work-family benefits available to them. We apply Giddens' (1984) Structuration Theory to examine organizational members' discursive responses to conditions (and contradictions) present in utilizing work-family benefits in a governmental organization. We argue the daily discursive practices of individuals can either reinforce or undermine formally stated work-family initiatives, and in turn discuss the implications of this "structuration" of policy.*

KEY WORDS: *Work-Family Policies, Structuration, Coworker Communication, Work-Family Communication.*

> *No one talked to me directly and said, "Gee, I resent the fact that you were on maternity leave," but I know that people felt that way.*

> *People don't understand that when I had six weeks off [for maternity leave], I needed six weeks off. I didn't sit there and play cards, you know what I mean, go shopping every day.*

> *I have heard situations within the agency where men have asked for paternity leave and not gotten receptive feedback. Either not gotten it approved at all, or certainly not what they had asked for.*

> *Someone wanted paternity leave, and everybody laughed. I mean, they thought that was funny.*

> *I wanted to take two weeks [of paternity leave] and the supervisor was saying, "No, I don't think, you know, that's probably not a very good idea."*

From JOURNAL OF APPLIED COMMUNICATION RESEARCH, 30, 1, February 2002 by Erika L. Kirby and Kathleen J. Krone. Copyright © 2002 by Taylor & Francis Ltd., http://www.tandf.co.uk/journals. Reprinted by permission.

Erika L. Kirby, (Ph.D., University of Nebraska-Lincoln, 2000) is an Assistant Professor in the Department of Communication Studies at Creighton University. This article is based on her dissertation directed by the second author, Kathleen J. Krone (Ph.D., University of Texas, 1985), who is an Associate Professor in the Department of Communication Studies at the University of Nebraska-Lincoln. We would like to thank the members of the organization for sharing their experiences, as well as Dan O'Hair and the anonymous reviewers for their constructive comments. Correspondence regarding this manuscript may be directed to Erika Kirby, Department of Communication Studies, Creighton University, 2500 California Plaza, Omaha, NE 68178 or ekirby@creighton.edu.

These observations from organizational members regarding parental leave surrounding child-birth illustrate an important yet often overlooked aspect of organizational policies: the fact that a policy exists on paper does *not* mean it is always accepted as legitimate or followed as written. Although organizational policies are a form of structure, they are produced and reproduced through processes of interpretation and interaction. Consequently, interpersonal, organizational, and public discourse surrounding organizational policies impact the structuring of the policies and, ultimately, policy implementation in that written policies may differ from policies "in-use." Individuals experience and implement organizational policies in environments that may discursively reinforce or contradict these policies; therefore, in this study we examined the communicative nature of policy implementation.

Communication and Work-Family Policy Implementation

Specifically, we explored the discourse of organizational members regarding the implementation and utilization of work-family policies. In organizations, three major types of work-family policies have been created to assist employees in "balancing" their work and family lives, including flexible work options, family-leave policies, and dependent-care benefits[1] (Morgan & Milliken, 1992). We argue that taking a communicative perspective allows for an examination of how such work-family benefits are enacted through discourse and interactions about the policy because the intent of work-family policies does not come into fruition until they are put into action. Work-family benefits provide a rich context to study policy for several reasons. First, "work-family balance" became a hot career issue starting in the 1990s (Lobel, 1991), and over the past decade, work-family benefits have been a growing trend in terms of personnel policies (Mitchell, 1997; Osterman, 1995). Yet widespread organizational culture change toward work and family is not *automatically* achieved by implementing family-friendly policies in the workplace (Lewis, 1997). This becomes important because research indicates that a supportive work-family culture is significantly related to benefit utilization and work attitudes, such as organizational commitment, intention to leave the organization, and less work-to-family conflict—beyond the mere availability of work-family benefits (Thompson, Beauvais, & Lyness, 1999).

Since work-family policies are relatively new to organizations, there is still some dissent as to whether these policies are even appropriate given traditional separations of work and home (Kanter, 1977). To some organizational members, the idea of assisting employees with their personal lives is contested terrain, because it allows "non-work" issues (i.e., childcare, eldercare, spousal care) to have a clear impact on the working environment. For example, maternity leave to birth a child, recover and provide newborn care essentially removes that working mother from the office for six weeks. However, the workload for the organization does not change, and so her responsibilities are covered by temporary workers, part-time staff, or coworkers. When such leave is also extended to new fathers, the physical component of birthing and recovery is removed. Instead, he would care for the newborn and perhaps the mother—but he still might miss work for six weeks under some family leave policies, and again, his workload must be covered, which in turn impacts the working environment and other employees who must fulfill his responsibilities.

As a result, organizational members may struggle with getting all the work done when individuals are absent for family reasons; even family leaves of shorter than six weeks can increase the workload for others, as can flexible working arrangements such as part-time work. A situation emerges where although work-family policies may be in place, organizational members do not really want others to utilize these benefits because it may increase their own responsibilities. Thus, even in "family-friendly" organizations, managers may send "negative signals indicating that the use of flexible, family-friendly benefits is a problem for them and for the company as a whole" (Rapoport & Bailyn, 1996, p. 19). Research has demonstrated that work-family policies are ineffective if supervisors do not openly support them (Cramer & Pearce, 1990; Thomas & Ganster, 1995). Consequently, a growing body of research has disclosed that formal policies do not always equate with corresponding practices; employees may not be consistently informed of their benefits or be pressured not to use them (Kamerman & Kahn, 1987; Raabe & Gessner, 1988; Rapoport & Bailyn, 1996).

Saltzman (1997) refers to work-family policies as a "paradox of the American workplace" in that career repercussions exist for individuals who utilize them; companies who have them in place "expect their most ambitious and devoted workers to forgo such options" (p. 1). The Ford Foundation study of Corning, Xerox, and Tandem Computers found employees who utilized work-family benefits suffered career consequences, although they were typically more efficient and productive than their colleagues were (Rapoport & Bailyn, 1996). Since employees may fear such consequences in using work-family benefits, many companies find a lower-than-expected number of employees take advantage of such benefits even though they have the need (Jenner, 1994; Rapoport & Bailyn, 1996; Solomon, 1994). Gender has a significant and substantive influence on family leave-taking behaviors (Sandberg, 1999); women are more likely than men to take leave (Kim, 1998). Men seem to be penalized in terms of perceived commitment and reward recommendations when they take advantage of family leave (Allen & Russell, 1999). Consequently, benefits are "underutilized" by men, single workers, and career-oriented mothers (Bailyn, Fletcher, & Kolb, 1997). As Lee (1991) suggests, this creates a situation where policies "live or die" by the ways they are applied to individual employees by individual managers.

However, this existing research still does not consider how *communication* between and among supervisors and subordinates impacts whether or not individuals utilize work-family benefits, or how work-family policies are produced and reproduced through interaction. This is a significant oversight, because communication from organizational members creates cultural norms as to the appropriateness of work-family benefit utilization. An exception is the work of Kirby (2000) who examined supervisory communication surrounding the implementation of work-family policies. In this related study of Regulatory Alliance,[2] discourse indicated supervisors were being told to simultaneously push harder to meet deadlines while remaining sensitive to work-family issues. Amidst such contradictions, the supervisors sometimes sent mixed messages about the policies; thus, while supervisors communicated to their employees that work-family benefits were open to them, at times they did not *really* want people to utilize their benefits so the work would get done. Some of these mixed messages were communicated in direct verbal and written forms, such as emphasizing deadlines over leave. In addition, there were more indirect forms of mixed messages, such as the role modeling of individuals who worked twelve or more hours a day to the detriment of time with their families (Kirby, 2000).

As a result of these mixed messages, employees were not always sure whether supervisors supported the work-family policies and, consequently, whether it was acceptable to utilize the programs. Even though the employees felt their supervisors sent mixed messages about work and family, their discourse did not suggest that supervisors intentionally set out to sabotage the organization's work-family agenda. Instead, the employees saw their supervisors as supportive—even though they still had concerns about taking leave and using other work-family benefits. This can partially be explained through the mixed messages they received; when Regulators were exposed to many of these contradictory messages over time, work emerged as taking precedence over family—without supervisors ever directly addressing the topic (Kirby, 2000). This study illustrates the centrality of communication processes in shaping the implementation and utilization of benefits beyond the individual personalities or agendas of supervisors. However, even though this research is centered in communication, it still echoes prior research in using supervisors as the fulcrum for examining work-family policy implementation. Even when other sources of influence are considered, the typical sources are spouses, friends, and employers (i.e., Lee & Duxbury, 1998). In overlooking the potential impact of coworkers on the process of work-family benefit utilization, existing research ignores an important source of organizational discourse.

Coworker Communication and Work-Family Policy Implementation

As Nippert-Eng (1996) illustrates, if organizational norms concerning work-family issues and policies are "silent, vague, or negotiable, *the work group is where they are most likely interpreted . . .* work groups let us know if we actually have flexible working hours and places" (p. 188, emphasis added). There is growing literature on how work-family policies may generate resentment rather than support from employees who have no need for them (Gilbert, 1994). Issues of equity emerge, where individuals without families are feeling burdened by work-family policies because of the increased workloads they are facing (Gilbert, 1994; Kirkpatrick, 1997; Rapoport & Bailyn, 1996). In particular, many perceive a child care bias in family friendly policies (Medjuck, Keefe, & Fancey, 1998). In fact, a national organization called the "Childfree Network" has been founded to create camaraderie and support among employees without children to advocate for equal treatment, calling work-family policies discriminatory (Kirkpatrick, 1997). It follows that co-workers often differ in the support they provide to their peers who want to use work-family programs. Just as managers may be reluctant to grant flexibility, co-workers may fear having to take on more work as a result of individuals taking advantage of policies such as family leave (Rees Edwards, 1997). Hence, they might not be supportive of individuals who want to use work-family benefits and communicate about the policies in a negative manner.

Of course, coworkers may discuss the process of utilizing the benefits for informational purposes as well. For example, negotiation of maternity leave "does not occur in a social vacuum . . . workgroup members will discuss the process and outcomes with the leavetaker as well as with one another" (Miller, Jablin, Casey, Lamphear-Van Horn, & Ethington, 1996, p. 302). Accordingly, the communicative interactions concerning using maternity leave (or other work-family programs), and the resulting arrangements, affect future interactions and arrangements with other workers. The outcomes of the current negotiation may enable or constrain future negotiations. A central assumption in this inquiry is that micro-communication practices surrounding work, family, and work-family policies have the ability to influence macro-issues, such as organizational policies and even dominant ideologies in the organization concerning work and family. At the same time, more macro-level constructs, such as societal and organizational discourse surrounding work, family and work-family policies, have the ability to impact micro-level interpersonal interactions. Specifically, we are interested in how discursive practices of coworkers reinforce or undermine work-family policy implementation and utilization. This leads to the first research question: What do coworkers say when they talk about work-family policies?

Structuration and Work-Family Policy Implementation

To this point, a two-fold rationale has been offered for this study; (a) the need to explore the role of communication in policy implementation and (b) the need to explore coworker discourse in the process of policy implementation. A final impetus for this study is the need to theoretically ground research on work-family issues and policies. Currently, much of the work-family research creates models to examine mechanisms linking work and family; a primary thrust concerns quantitative outcome variables that measure the amount of "work-family conflict" (Greenhaus & Beutell, 1985) experienced by individuals, as well as its antecedents and consequences (Edwards & Rothbard, 2000). In contrast, in this study we attempt to ground knowledge of work-family issues and work-family policy in a theoretical base beyond the construct of work-family conflict.

Since we argue that talk about work, family, and work-family policies impacts policy implementation, a theoretical framework is needed to substantiate this claim. Several theories address how the process of communication impacts individual perceptions of that person, place or thing in the future. For example, one approach based in social-information processing examines individual differences in perceptions of a task based not only on having direct experience with the task, but also on how coworkers and supervisors talk about the task (Salancik & Pfeffer, 1978). Although this offers a useful explanation, this research is primarily centered in interpersonal communication. In contrast, a primary assumption of this study is that interactions of individuals concerning work-family policies are shaped and constrained by the material working conditions they face, as well as discourse, policy, and ideology about work and family at the organizational and societal levels. At the same time, these interactions among individuals can either reinforce or undermine these larger social systems.

In order to conceptualize discourse across these levels of analysis, we employ Giddens' (1984) Structuration Theory as the ontology for this communication research (Banks & Riley, 1993). In using Structuration Theory to explore work-family policy, we liken this research to the metaphor of organizations as discourse, concentrating on structure and process (Putnam, Phillips, & Chapman,

1997). Our thinking is guided by Poole and DeSanctis (1990, 1992), who examine concrete ways that "talk about" Group Decision Support System (GDSS) technology impacts the use of technology (also see DeSanctis & Poole, 1994). In this study, we adopt a similar view toward the potential impact of "talk about" work-family policies, looking instead at how discourse (that may reflect organizational and societal expectations) generates and sustains the system of how work-family policies are interpreted and implemented in an organization (Poole, Seibold, & McPhee, 1996).

As an example of this perspective, presume that a new father has taken six weeks off for paternity leave. In this process, he has (a) probably increased the workload for others, (b) violated organizational norms (only about three percent of fathers actually take this much leave), and (c) questioned macrosocietal expectations that he is the breadwinner while the mother is the primary caregiver. A disgruntled co-worker, in turn, can use discourse across these levels in complaining about the arrangement (i.e., "I have to do his work," "I can't believe he took that much leave *here;* that's career suicide," "Why should he be staying home? That's the mother's job!"). Co-workers who hear these comments may take this discourse into consideration if and when they are faced with the same circumstances—and may not feel it is appropriate to take six weeks off. Of course, the opposite could happen as well, and if the father is discursively championed for taking six weeks at home with his newborn child, other men in the organization may be encouraged to do the same. The discourse may create rules and resources for addressing work-family issues within the organizational system; these "recipes" for acting are called structures (Giddens, 1984; Poole, Seibold & McPhee, 1996).

This reflects structuration, where the reproduction of social systems lies in the routinized, day-to-day interactions of agents in their use of rules and resources; "In and through their activities agents reproduce the conditions that make these activities possible" (Giddens, 1984, p. 2). The way organizational members talk about work-family programs helps to construct reality as to the "meaning" of such programs in the organization, which in turn shapes the attitudes and behaviors of organizational members. Through the variety of social processes that occur in interaction, people create their own "structures-in-use" (Poole & DeSanctis, 1992). Individuals have the ability to "appropriate" structures in terms of how they use, adapt, and reproduce them (Barley, 1986; DeSanctis & Poole, 1994; Lewis & Seibold, 1993; Poole & DeSanctis, 1990, 1992). Thus, discourse surrounding work-family policies may serve to reinforce or undermine the policies as written. This leads to the second research question: How does coworker discourse structure work-family policies?

Method

As noted, in this study we are concerned with discourse surrounding work-family policies. Specifically, in this study we asked organizational members to talk about their experiences concerning how work, family, and work-family policies are treated in the organization. Lindlof (1995) summarizes this orientation as "if we want to know how something is done and what it means, we have to know how it is talked about" (p. 234).

Research Respondents and Context

Regulatory Alliance is a governmental body that supervises and examines national banks to confirm that they are following legal requirements. This study details the experiences of Regulators from the Midwestern District of the organization. The primary focus was on the "Metro" field office, which encompasses individuals from three cities (duty stations) in a two-state area. In the study, we were interested in studying groups of coworkers and their respective supervisors to understand both sides of work-family policy construction and implementation, and so participants were purposefully selected to fit this criterion. In the Metro field office, a potential subject pool of 38 individuals existed, and of these individuals, 25 were men (19 were married) and 13 were women (all were married). Of these, the first author interviewed 35 Regulators either in a focus group, an individual interview, or both. Included among these 35 participants were two Assistant Deputy Comptrollers (ADCs), who are essentially the supervisors in the Metro field office.

In addition, we also wanted a generalized perspective as to how work-family policies are viewed by those who work with the policies on an ongoing basis. To this end, the first author interviewed the ADCs from all the Midwestern District field offices (including Metro); there were 11 male participants (all were married) and four female participants (three were married). Members of the Employee Relations Committee (ERC) were also interviewed. The ERC includes employees from all the field offices within the District, and handles work-life and other employee concerns; participants included three males (all were married) and four females (three were married). In total, 56 individuals from the Midwestern District of Regulatory Alliance participated in the study. Of these individuals, 15 were at the management level of ADCs, 36 were bank examiners, and five were in administrative staff positions.

The nature of their job requires the bank examiners (Regulators) to travel in order to complete bank examinations. Examiners often leave on Monday morning and do not return to their families until Thursday or Friday night, and at the Metro field office, examiners traveled about 30% of the time. Typically, a crew of four to five Regulators traveled to bank locations. Each crew functioned as a self-directed work team and under this structure, the actions of one person readily impacted others. For example, if an examiner did not travel, someone else needed to pick up the slack. This interdependence within each crew at times created tensions when individuals wanted to use work-family benefits, especially in the time surrounding data collection as the agency was understaffed.

In terms of existing work-family benefits, Regulatory Alliance has family leave, flexible scheduling and dependent care benefits in place. The potential types of leave include: (a) annual leave, which is earned time off for personal use; (b) sick leave, which is earned time off for medical appointments and unscheduled absences due to personal illness, injury, pregnancy, childbirth, or adoption and may include limited sick leave under the Federal Employees Family Friendly Leave Act (FEFFLA) to provide care for family members; (c) family and medical leave taken under the Family Medical Leave Act of 1993, which may be paid or unpaid depending upon whether annual/sick leave time is available; and (d) leave without pay (LWOP). At Regulatory Alliance, unless an individual is on extended leave, there are no replacements hired to cover his or her responsibilities.

Concerning flexible scheduling, the organization uses compressed weeks, particularly in the form of "flex-Fridays," where individuals work nine out of every ten days and get every other Friday off. Another compressed work program, the "4–10," allows individuals to work ten hours a day for four days when they are in overnight travel status. In addition, the Regulators have the options of part-time work, job-sharing, and work-at-home. When an individual chooses to work part-time, his or her responsibilities are reduced accordingly; however, as with leave, the organization does not hire additional workers to cover the employee's prior responsibilities; instead these are distributed among the current workforce. The dependent care benefits of the Regulators include referral services for locating childcare and eldercare, and financial assistance through pretax payroll deductions. Regulators primarily access information about these benefits through the company website and a written "Employee Benefits Summary." As some Regulators noted, the typical protocol for communicating about work-family benefits is that when an initiative comes up, they receive a system-wide message or "newsblast" on e-mail or an electronic bulletin board, and then must take the initiative to follow up if they are interested. Given this context for work-family discourse, we detail procedures used for data collection and analysis.

Procedures

Data collection. The experiences of Regulators regarding work-family policies were gathered in three ways, including reviewing documented material, facilitating focus group interviews, and conducting extended individual interviews. We started the research process with organizational documents, because these leave a paper trail "indicating what an organization produces and how it certifies certain kinds of activities . . . codifies procedures or policies . . . and tracks its own activities" (Lindlof, 1995, p. 208). Thus, formal documents on work-family/work-life programs were examined for publicly stated work-family efforts in order to examine organizational rhetoric as well as to provide ideas about important questions to pursue through interviews (Patton, 1990).

In the next stage of research, focus groups were utilized to "explain how people regard an experience, idea, or event" (Kreuger, 1994, p. 8). Using an open-ended interview protocol to guide discussion, the first author conducted and tape-recorded four focus group interviews with peer-groups of Regulators from the Metro field office about their experiences with work-family policies. The first two focus groups included two groups of employees from the primary duty station in sex-segregated groups of men and women; the rationale for these groupings was that since work-family policies are often stereotyped as being "benefits for women," men and women might have differing perceptions that they might be reluctant to share outside of a same sex group. The second set of focus groups included groups of examiners from the duty stations in other cities, and the first author traveled to these locations. The final two focus groups took place at the Midwestern District headquarters. The first group included ADCs from all the district field offices, and the second was comprised of the Employee Relations Committee. In total, six focus groups were conducted that ranged in length from 70 to 90 minutes.

Individual interviews were then completed as a follow-up to the focus groups. Building on feedback received in focus groups, the original interview protocol was broadened and revised. All individual interviews were conducted within the primary duty station to explore work-family policy communication between groups of coworkers and their ADC. Using the protocol as a guide for discussion, the first author conducted individual interviews that were tape-recorded for later transcription. Interviews were conducted until participant responses became repetitive to information in prior interviews (Patton, 1990); in total, 16 individuals were interviewed anywhere from 30 to 75 minutes.

Data analysis. After processing organizational documents and conducting focus group and individual interviews, the data was transcribed verbatim; in combination, the focus group and interview data resulted in 529 pages of single-spaced dialogue. This data was analyzed using a process of "reduction" and "interpretation" (Marshall & Rossman, 1989). The transcriptions were first entered into QSR NUD*IST (Qualitative Solutions and Research Non-numerical Unstructured Data * Indexing Searching and Theorizing). The NUD*IST program was used primarily as a tool to assist in organizing, searching, and sorting the coded data. To clarify themes that emerged in talk about work-family policies, the transcripts generated through NUD*IST were analyzed for recurring patterns in the discourse using constant comparative analysis (Glaser & Strauss, 1967; Strauss & Corbin, 1998).

The first iteration involved reading through the printed transcriptions, and composing six potential themes regarding Regulator discourse about work-family policies that seemed consistent across both focus group and interview responses.[4] The first theme encompassed talk about inequities for individuals who did not have the opportunity to use the policies. In addition, Regulators talked about inequities in how work-family policies were applied based on three demographic characteristics: (a) whether the employee had children (theme two), (b) whether the employee was male or female (theme three), and (c) whether the employee was part-time or full-time (theme four). Regulator discourse also grouped around a fifth theme of how policies can be "used" or "abused." The sixth and final theme concerned peer pressure that surrounded work-family policy utilization. The transcriptions were coded first on paper and then in NUD*IST using these six themes and print reports were generated for each.

In the second stage, the first author went through another iteration of the process, reducing the six original themes to two major themes that characterized the discourse (Creswell, 1994). The first major theme, talk about preferential treatment, integrated the four original sub-themes surrounding perceptions of inequities, and in this process themes two and three (regarding family status and gender) were combined. The second major theme, talk about work-family policy utilization, included the sub-themes of policy "use" versus "abuse" and the resulting peer pressure that Regulators discussed. Through these themes, we attempted to capture the sense of organizational members' meanings regarding the treatment of work-family policies in their organization.

Results and Interpretations

Everybody's perception is different, but I think at times I probably perceive differences in maybe what's expected out of male versus female or single versus married, or kids versus no kids. (female examiner)

Our first research question asked what coworkers say when they talk about work-family policies. Although some spoke of the merits of these programs, the overarching issue examiners communicated in terms of work-family programs was the perception that such programs granted preferential treatment. A contradiction the Regulators confronted concerning work-family programs was that the work did not go away when someone was granted leave or part-time work, so they needed to assist in completing the work. This created feelings (and discourse) of resentment toward those who utilized work-family benefits. Our second research question asked how coworker discourse structures work-family policies. Coworkers created a rule of determining "use versus abuse" of work-family benefits that contributed to a system of peer pressure where many Regulators felt pressured not to utilize the benefits that were available to them.

"That Just Doesn't Seem Quite Fair": Talk about Preferential Treatment

In the discourse about work-family policies at Regulatory Alliance, the examiners continually compared themselves to each other in terms of benefits they were and were not able to use. Since the Regulators were a composite of single and married individuals with and without children, there was obvious variability in how many people actually utilized work-family programs, and beyond this, in how frequently individuals used these benefits. These variations were reflected in the discourse; perceived inequities emerged according to whether individuals could use the policies in the first place, and if they did, how these were applied based on whether the employee had children or not, was a male or a female, and had part-time or full-time status.

"It is always the buzz": Talk about inequities in work-family policies. As illustrated, perceived inequities emerged in the discourse of individuals who did not make use of the policies. One female examiner "kind of look[s] at them and go[es], 'You know, that just doesn't quite seem fair that just because that person has young children, they get to take an extra 10–15 days a year.'" For another:

I think that there definitely are perceptions of inequity. Definitely. And in how much benefits some people receive from what the [Regulators] touts as family-life things that are so great. It's like, "Well, yeah, that's great, but that's not doing anything for me." And I don't know what more they would do for people without children, what they could do. But there's still the perception that they're really helping them but they're not helping us. (female examiner)

The discourse of several Regulators reflected perceptions that the use of policies by others created more work for them to accomplish. As a male ERC member commented, "That has worked out very well for them. Unfortunately it has increased the workload for us." A male examiner echoed that "sometimes when I take off two or three hours to go to a kids' basketball game . . . in a way you kind of feel guilty about that, because you have been on the other end of things and you know it kind of ticked you off." In this discourse, examiners also exhibited a common concern regarding how much they traveled in reference to their peers—they resented others whom they perceived traveled less than they did. One female examiner saw "people . . . that barely travel and . . . those of us that travel 100 nights a year. So, if things were more consistent there, I think it would be easier to take." As a male ADC had observed, when "people didn't travel nearly as much [as others], it doesn't take too long and the rest of the crew starts to grumble."

Thus, examiners compared how long they were working and how much they were traveling to other examiners. In this process of comparison, the typical result was a perception of "you get more time off work than I do, because I don't have a need or reason to utilize these things because [of] the fact that I am not married and I don't have children" (male examiner). One female examiner characterized this perception as an underlying resentment; others would "not necessarily confront you on it . . . [but] it is always the buzz." Most of this "buzz" was circulated by the single examiners, because the "number of times that a single person has a use of it [work-family leave] is not going to be significant" (female examiner). Instead, single examiners "see all these days that somebody got to take off in the year because their child was supposedly sick . . . it's like, 'Okay, they've had all these benefits for however many years' and it doesn't benefit the rest of us" (female examiner). In fact, this has apparently been a point of conversation several times among Regulators who did not utilize the policies.

> All the single people in the office used to talk and say we all understood and what a great program it is, but really, I mean, what are we getting in return for that . . . we felt that we needed to be compensated somehow . . . because maybe we will never be able to have kids or something, so we will go through our whole careers never using a benefit like that. (female examiner)

A male examiner agreed that "it would be nice if there would be something to counterbalance that as a benefit to me." As a result, one male examiner "think[s] there's probably a little resentment . . . if you have a child at home sick, I think maybe there's a little more resentment that 'This person has to stay home with their kids where I have to pick up their work.'" But another male examiner "think[s] maybe the biggest problem we have is that those perceptions . . . are allowed to fester within small groups of people." A female support staff member has heard both sides of this discourse of comparison, and in her view, it is "just human nature. 'She's got a bigger bow than I've got. She's got a prettier dress than I have' . . . the inequities are pretty vague." In summary, although the same benefits were offered on paper to all employees, the discourse regarding perceived inequities indicated that not all employees felt these benefits were really open to them. Instead, benefits were discursively constructed as being targeted at parents, especially female parents.

"We are discriminated against sometimes": Talk about family circumstances. Regulator discourse illustrated differentials in perceived treatment between individuals who were single and those who were married—with and without children. The ERC members reported this was a major concern among Regulators; in fact, "The most consistent work life [issues] are travel and perceived inequities for people who have kids" (female ERC member). Basically, single examiners perceived *they* traveled more because they did not have a spouse or family. One complained how "it's easier to put [us] out on the road than it is somebody that has kids. It's like, 'Oh. Well, they don't need to be home. They don't have children'" (female examiner). To another female examiner:

> It just seems to me that those with the children don't travel as much, and those who don't have children and who aren't married seem to travel a lot more. And that's based on the discussions I hear . . . it does seem that the comments I hear are, "Well gee, how come I always end up getting the exams that are in Timbuktu and so-and-so who's married and has some little kids at home is always in town or has a nice easy commute." I don't think that is fair. I think we're hired for the exact same job, and our job descriptions are the same, and there's nothing that says because you're not married, you can do all the on-the-road assignments. (female examiner)

A female ERC member has heard some of this negative discourse; as she illustrated, "From the peer standpoint, the comments that you get from them. People with no kids, the perception is the people with, the single folks are the ones that are feeling it a little bit more versus people with families." As illustrated, Regulator discourse indicated perceptions that married people might travel less, and that parents received still more preferential treatment in terms of work-family benefits and reduced travel. But *female* parents seemed to be the brunt of most of the resentment regarding preferential treatment.

Regulator discourse illustrated a perception that female examiners with children were really the ones who benefited from work-family policies—even in comparison to married men with children. The perceived differences were most apparent in the situation of parental leave for the birth of a child—maternity versus paternity leave. There were a few women who perceived some resentment of maternity leave. As a female examiner explained, "No one talked to me directly and said, 'Gee I resent the fact that you were on maternity leave,' but I know that people felt that way." However, even amidst such perceived resentment, no female examiners expressed ever being questioned as to whether as women they "needed" to have maternity leave. On the other hand, men did not have similar biologically based reasons for leave-taking, and as noted in the opening quotes, paternity leave seemed to be left open for scrutiny. As a male ADC commented, "Parental leave . . . is still seen as very different for the women as compared to men." Since the reasons that men would want to take parental leave did not seem to be understood in the organization, few men took advantage of this benefit.

Furthermore, examiners perceived that when returning to work from parental leave, women *still* seemed to be awarded more leniency and understanding. As a female ADC noted, "In order to be fair, you have to have a standard policy, but the mothers find it harder in some cases than the fathers do." For example, one male ADC remembered making special arrangements for a mother with young babies: "I probably made an adjustment, and I think there were a couple of people who resented the fact that she had, maybe, a more favorable schedule." Based on similar situations, perceptions existed among examiners that new mothers "have got it a little bit easier" than new fathers in terms of travel and getting preferential assignments. As one female examiner noted, "If we've got a big complicated bank coming up, I can pretty well guarantee it's not going to be a new mother in charge of it . . . there are accommodations made, work schedule-wise, travel-wise." But at the same time, new fathers "may have had two hours of sleep the night before and yet soon after the birth they're expected to go into work the next day and perform like nothing ever happened" (female examiner).

In addition to these perceptions of preferential treatment toward mothers versus fathers in infancy, Regulator discourse indicated that even when children are older, it was still presumed to be the mother's job to take leave for family responsibilities and the father's job to stay at work as the provider. As a result, "there's probably more understanding that if you stay home a day because a child is sick . . . I think maybe there's more understanding if you're a woman than if it's a guy" (female examiner). Thus, "taking time off as a male is much more difficult than as a female parent" (male examiner). In addition, working part-time was perceived to be more difficult for men than women.

"They are treated more favorably": Talk about part-time examiners. Like female parents, part-time workers were perceived to have it "easier"—and the fact that all part-timers in the district were female ultimately implied differential treatment based on gender.

> A very high percentage, very close to 100 . . . have been, mostly women with children and a new baby that we have made an accommodation of a part time schedule for . . . if we are not careful, we will become the talk that the programs we have are really only for the new parents. Or at least a parent . . . I have heard it . . . I am not sure of the depth of it. If it is rampant that single people are talking, but I think it is an issue. (female ADC)

A male ADC reiterated that going part-time would probably be easier for women than men. As he described, "If I am a female and I've got kids that I want to stay home with a couple of days a week and you try to sell that to the rest of the crew they would say that's a valid reason." But he felt if a man went part-time, the "question would be, 'Well, why is he only working part-time?' as opposed to if it's a mother there's kind of like a reason." A male examiner agreed that "realistically, I think it's much more difficult for probably the male to go part-time . . . I think it just kind of goes against the norm." This perception that part-time was just a program for women could be problematic. A female ERC member illustrated that "if the only really good [reason] is women having children, that fosters that resentment . . . 'She wants to go part-time and I am going to have to pick up more work' and then you get that backlash."

Based on this perception that part-time is only for women, there was an underlying resentment or "backlash" toward part-timers at Regulators. This led to situations where "maybe people in the office talk about them [part-timers] a little bit more, about them not being as dedicated or so forth" (male examiner). A male ERC member emphasized that "somebody goes part time, [and] from full travel like everybody else to zero travel . . . that means somebody else has to pick up that slack . . . I am likely to be resentful toward that." A female support staff member expanded that part-timers had "the best of both worlds. They work like three days a week, exams are worked totally around them . . . [but] I think there is a lot of resentment . . . Very much so." This resentment translated to a "negative connotation that you're part-time. I'm very aware of that . . . 'I don't have to do as much work as what some others do' . . . I know that there's that type of talk out there" (female part-time examiner). As an illustration of this type of talk, men "will say things to the effect that, 'Well I wish I could go part-time. Then I wouldn't have to travel as much, or I'd get the assignments that were close to home. I would commute.' That sort of thing" (male examiner). In light of these negative perceptions, one female part-time examiner felt she "pay[s] a price being a part-timer."

Such coworker discourse regarding part-timers had actual material consequences. The ADCs illustrated when individuals perceived resentment about their use of the program, they tended to overcompensate by working more than their allotted hours. Consequently, not many individuals requested part-time status because "most people that have been part time end up working full time" (female examiner). In summary, the part-time program and part-time workers were discussed in a negative manner, especially in terms of being a "woman's benefit." Part-timers and women with children (and to some extent, men with children) were constructed by examiners as receiving "preferential treatment" in terms of the policies that were open to them and their easier travel schedules.

As illustrated, when certain individuals or groups seemed to be continually benefiting from work-family policies, tones of resentment emerged. At times, this caused the Regulators to communicate about work-family benefits and the individuals who utilized them in a negative manner; subgroups of "married versus single," "full-time versus part-time," "parents versus nonparents," and "men versus women" were created. Of these groups, resentment seemed to repeatedly occur in the case of married examiners with children and female examiners with children in particular, especially those who were part-time examiners. The Regulators illustrated a key problem that emerges with work-family initiatives, in that employees assumed the benefits applied only to a few people for part of their work lives—primarily women with young children (Bailyn et al., 1997).

This reflects the growing literature on how work-family policies may impact issues of equity and generate resentment because individuals without families are feeling burdened by family-friendly policies (Gilbert, 1994; Kirkpatrick, 1997; Rapoport & Bailyn, 1996). For example, the single examiners in the study talked about "banding together" to share their perceptions of inequity, which translated to feelings of resentment toward those who were using the policies. Such feelings surfaced when examiners negatively communicated about work-family policies. As a result, part-timers experienced a "negative connotation" for using the program, and examiners who needed leave for family reasons were occasionally talked about with disfavor. A structurational framework implies that such talk may actually impact work-family benefit utilization, and we explore this possibility through the second major theme.

"It Kind of Ticked Me Off": Talk about Work-Family Policy Utilization

The discourse surrounding how work-family benefits were utilized exists at two levels. Since many Regulators did not feel the policies really applied to them, there seemed to be scrutiny of individuals who did use the policies and whether or not they really had a good "reason." In making these determinations, examiners constructed a notion of "use versus abuse" of work-family benefits. In light of this scrutiny, some individuals were less likely to use the work-family benefits that were available to them. Thus, as a result of the structure of "use versus abuse" and perceptions of preferential treatment, peer pressure existed not to use the benefits.

"That person is always gone": Talk about use versus abuse of policies. Regulator discourse articulated an underlying assumption concerning "use versus abuse" of work-family policies, where it was acceptable for individuals to utilize the work-life benefits available to them as long as other examiners did not perceive the benefits were being abused. As a male examiner explained, "If you know somebody that's out of the office frequently, then maybe the topic will pop up. 'Well, maybe they're abusing their benefits.'" A female examiner noted how

> You see some examiners that are just routinely always gone . . . [and] it impacts my exam when I have a lot of people taking all this time off. And I think it probably is mostly legitimate, but there's still times I sit there and think, "Gee, it seems like that person is always gone and never works their full day and the boss doesn't seem too concerned about it. How can that happen for that person but not for the next?" . . . There's just sometimes you look at that and say, "It seems like some people get more benefit from that than others."

Although another female examiner thought "everyone is pretty good about, you know, if their child is sick that's what they're using it for and they're not lying about it and going shopping or anything," certain policies were regarded as having potential for abuse, especially the 4–10 policy. This was a sore spot in terms of policy because it was not available to everyone, and "a couple of people that are utilizing that, well, they're taking advantage of it" (male examiner). The discourse from examiners also illustrated that some actually did take this idea of "use versus abuse" into consideration when using the policies. To one male examiner, "We know everybody so well that nobody can afford to abuse it because you have peer pressure or whatever, so I don't think anybody has abused it." The potential for abuse was often related to time; as one examiner noted, he did not "feel uncomfortable asking for that time off, as long as it's not a long period of time" (male examiner). Another male examiner actually used the word "abuse" in articulating his own circumstances:

> I haven't used much [FMLA] for kids. I mean I stay home with the kids when they're sick, but I try not to abuse it. I haven't felt anything that was overt . . . I've used the [benefits] that I'm aware of that I think have some merit and benefit me, and I haven't felt like I've abused anything.

Essentially, "use versus abuse" structured interaction and served as a control mechanism over individuals who wanted to utilize work-family benefits. As an example, if a female examiner worked at home, "She's afraid that guys are going to say . . . 'If you're a woman with kids, you get to do this and that. Man, I could never do that' . . . That's the control mechanism" (male ADC). The notion of use versus abuse had more concrete consequences in actual interactions between co-workers, where they exerted "peer pressure" over each other concerning the appropriateness of work-family requests.

"The crew will reward or punish you": Talk about peer pressure. Given the discourses of preferential treatment and "use versus abuse" expressed by coworkers about work-family benefits, individuals had mixed feelings about whether they should utilize the programs. One male examiner did not "think there's any negativism attached to using any of them." However, many more examiners did see negative perceptions attached to utilizing work-family benefits. A male ADC perceived "considerable peer pressure that keeps people from taking advantage of those." As described, within the Regulators a team structure existed where the examiners worked as a crew. This created a unique situation where supervisory influence did not seem to be the primary factor driving policy utilization. Instead, individuals seemed to feel more pressure not to utilize work-family benefits from their *coworkers* than from their ADCs. One male ADC commented that "most of the people here know and think I'm kind of easy about those things. And I don't think very many people fear that I'm going to downgrade them or penalize them." A female ERC member expressed how she has "gotten more conflicts from peers than managers. The managers have been supportive . . . but the comments from the peers is oh, you are pregnant, you are going to have the easy world [and] the in town assignments."

Echoing this perception, a female examiner who had utilized work-family benefits explained, "The bosses have never made me feel guilty. I have had other people at work make me feel guilty." A male ADC conceptualized such behavior in the context of peer pressure because the "four or five person crew is totally dependent upon one another to get the work done . . . they just don't want to do it [ask for leave] unless they absolutely have to."

> There's an enormous amount of peer pressure that happens, and so you're out there with four other people and you, if you don't pull your weight, it's not ever going to get back to the ADC that you're not working. They will, the people who are on that crew, will reward you or punish you because you're either contributing or not contributing to the team. Because if you're not contributing, they have to pull your slack for you and it makes it painful for them, so there's an awful lot of pressure that's put on you to make sure that they conform to this standard of working hard . . . you get to know people and there's also an awful lot of peer pressure. (male ADC)

One male ADC felt this system "normally keeps those requests reasonable, because they have that sense of awareness of what impact it is going to have on others." Another ADC agreed that "a lot of people are pretty apprehensive about asking for anything special that would require the other examiners to travel more . . . if it is me at his detriment, then I am not probably going to ask for it." A male examiner echoed these perceptions in regard to leave: "I could take it if I wanted to but I know that it will make me farther behind and be putting a burden on everyone else to get work done." Beyond the crew structure, fear was also a component of this peer pressure. A female ADC explained that "some people keep close track on who is going and who is not, who got that and who didn't get that. They can tend to rile people up a little bit." A male ADC agreed:

> There's a fair amount of peer pressure . . . Let's say that [Regulator name] decided she was going to work at home half the time or a third of the time or occasionally when she's scheduled to be in the office. I think [Regulator name] is afraid, not that I'm going to be on her case, but that somebody else will say, "Well, where's [Regulator name] . . . I'll bet she isn't working. I'll bet she's shopping or something like that." I think there's a considerable peer pressure that keeps people from taking advantage of those, not as much from the managers . . . I think they fear each other. And I think that goes particularly between some of the men and women.

In fact, several ADCs heard stories where examiners actually consulted each other prior to making a work-family benefit request to management. Thus, "they talked among each other first . . . I think a lot of these things are worked out informally before they come to us" (female ADC). A male ADC agreed that "you don't know how many of those requests they have run up the flag pole and nobody salutes and they just don't do it." This peer pressure created a situation where coworkers did not want to be seen as getting special treatment. Thus, a female examiner who had recently had a baby came to her ADC "horrified that people were going to think that she was getting preferential treatment in staying in town longer, when in fact it was mere coincidence. She didn't want anybody to think she was asking for special accommodations" (female ADC).

Consequently, when examiners needed to utilize work-family benefits, there were many factors they took into account when approaching their coworkers. First, they knew that some coworkers were more supportive of these policies than others, and so they often talked to individuals who had used the policies before. Even though it was often unspoken, examiners in the study recognized the underlying resentment toward some of these policies, and this created a fear of coworker reactions. As a result, they sometimes "tested the waters" to see how coworkers might react if they needed to use a certain program. This fear of coworker reactions sometimes created situations where individuals were reluctant to utilize the work-family benefits that were available to them. As a female examiner explained, "They may feel like they'll be criticized if they do some certain program, like maybe they feel if they go part-time that people will look negatively on them for that . . . that can have an impact on them." A female examiner articulated some of the fears, where "sometimes I feel like people look at me, 'Oh my God, she's leaving early.' And I just feel guilty . . . it makes a big deal to me if people are saying 'I don't think [Regulator name]'s putting in her time.'" This fear also created situations where individuals who did utilize work-family policies tended to overcompensate, as illustrated by part-timers who worked more than the allotted hours.

Ultimately, the way coworkers responded seemed to depend on whether or not examiners were perceived to be "using" or "abusing" the work-life programs available to them. Thus, examiners addressed dilemmas regarding the use of policies by creating informal norms of what constituted "use" versus "abuse." Overall, the examiners did not want to push their luck by using too many work-family benefits, because this would impact how peers viewed them. As a result, a system of peer pressure seemed to impact policy utilization even more than supervisory attitudes; in this team culture, coworkers served as a system of control over the utilization of work-family policies. The Regulators have discursively created meanings surrounding work-family programs that in turn structured work-family policy implementation. The locus of control shifted from ADCs to the examiners themselves, who watched each other as "peer managers" more closely than managers (Barker, 1993). However, this is not to say that all examiners in the study were equally subject to such "control mechanisms." Some employees did not seem to succumb as easily to the perceptions of others; one examiner "earned the leave and was going to use it. That's just my priority" (female examiner).

Yet despite some of the polarized discourse summarized in these results, there were some glimpses of a "coming together." Several examiners emphasized that even though there may be perceived differential treatment at times, individuals should not be so resentful because "their time is coming" (female examiner).

> They are going to have needs later on, whether you are married or not, whether you have kids or not, somebody is going to have needs eventually. They are going to need support and as long as they know that is there, I think a lot of people can live with that. (male ADC)

Even when some examiners were complaining about programs or individuals, they still thought they might eventually use the policies themselves. A male examiner explained, "If they're not using it now they can see themselves using it in two to three years or five to seven years or somewhere down the road." Although one female examiner complained about the current conditions, she did not "want to give the impression that I'm knocking the program because I think it's great. I know I will use that when I have children and I will love it." Another female examiner summarized that "they'll all have kids eventually and they'll realize what a wonderful benefit that is. But by that time, it'll be too late. They'll all have been so mad all those years for no reason."

Discussion

To explore these results in more depth, we revisit our original areas of inquiry. While the previous discourse addresses our question as to what Regulators say when they talk about work-family policies, it is also of theoretical and practical consequence to explore what was not said/what was absent from participant discourse about work-family policies. Furthermore, participant talk about work-family policy utilization begins to illustrate how coworker discourse structures work-family policies, and in this discussion we explicitly address these processes in relation to structuration theory. In particular, we look at macro-level structures Regulators seemed to be appropriating through discourse in micro-level interactions, even though they did not specifically articulate these. Following this discussion, we suggest directions for future research on work-family communication, outline limitations, and offer implications for both theory and practice.

Revisiting the RQs: Coworker Discourse and the Structuration of Work-Family Policies

As illustrated, predominant in the discourse of what coworkers said about work-family policies was that the programs created conditions of inequity and preferential treatment. In thinking about how structures, or "recipes for action" emerged in this context, examiners resented when others seemed to travel less or work fewer hours due to work-family circumstances. These Regulators, in turn, used agency to allocate resources to "control" others—mainly in the form of using discourse that was supportive or unsupportive of coworkers who utilized work-family benefits. When coworkers were not supportive of those who utilized work-family policies and talked badly about either the individuals or the policies (or both), this sent a message to others who were considering the same benefits and created a system of peer pressure not to utilize work-family programs.

We argue that in this structurational process, there were macro-level structures from the wider social system being appropriated in this process (Poole, Seibold, & McPhee, 1996); organizational and societal discourse and expectations did seem to influence the meanings Regulators held for work-family programs. Examining *what was not said* about work-family policies and their utilization serves as a framework for exposing these structures. Regarding the perceptions of inequity, the examiners who expressed resentment did not reconcile the fact that they really do not have the same responsibilities for dependent care their coworkers do. Amongst examiners without child or elder care responsibilities, there was no talk about the "second shift" (Hochschild, 1989) that coworkers would be performing when they left work. Instead, their use of family leave or a part-time schedule seemed to be perceived as "time away" from *real* work. This reflects societal norms that reward work performed in the public sphere while marginalizing work performed in the private sphere (Auerbach, 1988; Gilbert, 1994) and the related assumption that commitment is lessened for workers in caregiving roles (Bruce & Reed, 1994). Since these benefits effectively remove the employees from the "public sphere," for some these benefits seemed to reward employees for having children. As a married female examiner with children noted:

> They think that we're getting all these benefits that they're not getting . . . the leave for fam-ily that they don't take. Also, the occasional sick day that your kids have . . . so I think they look at it like we're getting all these benefits that they're not getting . . . Does that make them happier if I'm on annual leave rather than if I'm on sick leave [under FEFFLA]? Well, that doesn't make any sense. Why should that matter to them except that then they think I'm getting an extra day off. Well, they've never been home with a sick kid. You know, that's not a fun day . . . It's so unnecessary. There's no reason we need to compare.

This Regulator did not feel that other examiners understood that she was not utilizing the poli-cies in order to get out of work and do something more fun. In fact, no examiners reflected a collec-tivist orientation by saying they were glad the benefits were available to their coworkers to help them balance work and family; instead, the response was more likely that "I had to cover so-and-so's work so he could spend time with his family." This discourse was accompanied by the unspoken (and sometimes spoken) sentiment that this difference in work efforts might not be reflected in the per-formance appraisal process. This reflects an individualistic orientation that is consistent with work-ers in the system of American capitalism (Fricke, 2000).

The emphasis Regulators placed on covering the work of others who take family leave reveals another "silence" in the discourse. Although work-family programs and benefits were constructed broadly, Regulators almost always narrowed the focus to parental leave and part-time work, even though flexible work schedules and dependent care benefits existed as well. There did seem to be a perception that if people took annual leave, it was nothing that deserved resentment because all Regulators earned similar amounts of annual leave. Furthermore, while the organization operated on compressed weeks and offered pretax benefits for dependent care, no one complained about these policies as discriminatory. The inequities emerged when sick leave was used for family, or the Fam-ily Medical Leave Act was utilized.

Looking at the notion of meritocracy (where individual hard work is rewarded with individual merit and rewards) as a structure being appropriated to interpret work-family policies assists in illuminating these characteristics of the discourse. For example, everyone received the benefit of compressed weeks, and so although it was a "work-family" type of benefit, it was not perceived as exclusive because all employees were rewarded with this work schedule. But when work-family policies were employed, some examiners experienced violations of the principle of meritocracy because they perceived that individuals who had dependent care responsibilities were "rewarded" by getting additional time off from work. At the same time, their hard work and efforts to be a loyal employee by staying at work were "rewarded" by needing to work harder to cover the workload of examiners who were absent on work-family leave or a part-time schedule. Work-family policies were therefore perceived as rewarding employees with dependents by allowing them to do less "real work" in the organization, which then impacted the workload of those without dependents. Thus, when Regulators believe in meritocracy and related individual rewards, the utilization of work-family policies contradicted this structure; therefore, their discourse reflects inequities they perceive as inconsistent with meritocratic principles.

But what was missing from this discourse was any recognition of what individuals may be giving up in utilizing work-family programs. As illustrated, women who utilized the policies felt resentment from coworkers, and even the men were cognizant of needing to balance "use" versus "abuse" so as not to be seen (and treated) as a less committed worker. It could become a matter of trade-offs, where examiners "gave up" some facets of coworker relationships in order to preserve family relationships. Furthermore, some benefits had material consequences; part-time employees at Regulators received a proportionate decrease in salary, and had to subsidize more of their insurance and other benefits (also see Skinner, 1999). Yet this was never mentioned by anyone except part-timers and their managers; fellow examiners seemed largely oblivious to the trade-offs that were made, despite their access to the published policies. In fact, this was an underlying current throughout the discourse, in that work-family policies were seen as peripheral until they were perceived as infringing on others.

In addition, it appears the system of sex-role stereotypes in our society was appropriated in the structuration of work-family policies. Among these examiners, an underlying expectation existed (and was somewhat articulated) that it was the responsibility of the female examiners to take a primary caregiving role. This "recipe for action" based on sex-role stereotypes was appropriated in the structuration of work-family benefits. As a result, when women were granted leave for family, their coworkers were often more understanding than they would be to men; however, the women in the study still suffered consequences in terms of being perceived as less dedicated to the organization (Perlow, 1997). While maternity leave was never questioned (even though it may have been resented), the need for paternity leave of more than a short endurance *was questioned* in the organization. Since men were assumed to be the breadwinners, when they wanted to utilize programs such as parental leave, other Regulators "thought that was funny."

In summary, what was said (and unsaid) in examiner discourse illustrated that both "micro" structures, such as coworker interactions, and "macro" level structures, such as traditional separations between public and private, gendered expectations, and orientations of individualism and meritocracy, impacted the system of how work-family benefits were constructed. These structures both enabled and constrained Regulators in determining whether or not to utilize work-family benefits. In particular, examining coworker interactions as structures illustrated the amount of influence peers had in this system. The power of coworker discourse goes beyond traditional conceptions of the structure of power interests in organizations. A typical instinct, as illustrated in the literature, is to place all the power for influencing work-family program utilization in the hands of supervisors. But in the team structure at Regulators, coworkers seemed to have as much influence as the ADCs. ADCs obviously had more "power" to allocate material resources in the form of allowing (or not allowing) individuals to utilize work-family policies in given circumstances. However, both ADCs and coworkers allocated the resource of social support, and since examiners spent their days with each other rather than ADCs, meeting the expectations of their coworkers was often of primary concern. Consequently, when examiners feared the consequences from coworkers in using work-family benefits, there was not a widespread use of work-family policies.

Future Directions for Research

A primary direction toward which this study leads is the need to seriously consider the role of coworkers and their discourse in the process of policy implementation. Since modern organizations are moving more toward self-directed teams, the implication that coworkers have an impact on policy use is significant. These findings suggest that in this team culture, coworkers are beginning to serve as a system of control over the utilization of work-family policies. This definitely warrants future research. How do coworkers communicate what is and is not acceptable concerning not only policy utilization, but broader behaviors (i.e., Barker, 1993)? How do they influence and control the actions of others through their *discourse?*

In addition, this study implies a direction for future research outside the realm of work and family. The discourse (in the context of work-family programs) continually illustrated the tension between the policy as written by Human Resources and the policy as implemented and utilized. We do not believe this is a unique phenomenon; a bountiful area for future research is to examine how managers and coworkers appropriate organizational policies such as those generated by Human Resources. How are policies appropriated faithfully and ironically? What is the role of communication in this process? All of these directions emphasize the centrality of communication processes in shaping organizational outcomes, which is a central strength of this study. However, there are potential limitations as well.

Limitations of the Study

The implications of this research must be contextualized in light of its limitations. The organizational context itself might be viewed as a limitation. The Regulators operated in the public sector, and as a branch of the federal government they were subject to clear federal policies, which granted equal access and rights to employees, while holding the organization accountable for enforcing them. It follows that the same study of a private sector organization, such as a bank, that has even fewer policies and/or less accountability for enacting these programs, could have very different results, which limits the generalizability of the findings. Another drawback of the research is that although it taps into how Regulators talk about work, family, and work-family policies, it does so through the method of interviewing. In terms of the efficiency of data gathering, this was the preferable method because work and family issues are not a predominant focus of Regulator discussions. However, it would be interesting to follow the conversations of participants in "real time" to see how these interactions operate and serve to structure how individuals perceive work and family in the organization. Yet we believe these limitations are minimized in light of the implications of this study.

Implications and Conclusions

Structuration increases knowledge of work-family policy implementation by providing a lens to view how discourse, at multiple levels of analysis, structures policies as they are constructed and reconstructed on an ongoing basis. These policies are structured not only by intentional efforts, but are produced and reproduced through unintentional consequences as well. At Regulatory Alliance, the work-family policies were designed at least in part to help examiners "balance" their work and family lives. But even though Regulators saw value in the policies, a primary reason they did not use them was due to intentional and unintentional forms of communication from other organizational members that sent messages about work-family policies. Specifically, coworker discourse and communication processes have shaped their perceptions of what is valued by their "team members" in the organization, and the policies did not always mesh with these values. Exploring the discourse of organizational members reveals how communication influenced the implementation and utilization of work-family policies.

Furthermore, a structurational perspective illustrated how micro-level interactions rooted in policy can have macro-level implications. For example, the way work-family policies were talked about in the organization reflected (and reproduced) broader conceptions of the "proper role" of men and women—not only in the workplace but society as a whole. Since women were encouraged to take maternity leave and spend time with their children, but men were discouraged from paternity and parental leave, this sends a message about gender stereotypes that extends beyond the confines of the organization. This relationship can also be examined from the reverse perspective, lending insight into how cultural conceptions of men and women as parents and workers are communicated in micro-level interactions, and the implications when generalized stereotypes and public discourse constrain individual and organizational conceptions of work and family. But perhaps the strongest contribution to theory is that policy as written is not always policy as practiced; policy implementation and utilization is instead a communicative and structurational process. Consequently, future studies of policy may also benefit from the theoretical frame of structuration (Giddens, 1984).

As a further theoretical implication of this study, institutional theory suggests the increased attention being given to issues of work and family creates pressure for organizations to respond (Goodstein, 1994). Once leaders in an industry begin to implement work-family policies, competitive forces drive other companies in those industries to follow (Morgan & Milliken, 1992) because work-family initiatives at one company are made known to employees and managers in other companies (Goodstein, 1994). Gonyea and Googins (1992) note that "as corporate work-family programs have moved from the curious to the mainstream, they have also moved from the lifestyle pages to the business section of the newspapers" (p. 210). Through this perspective, the adoption of childcare, eldercare, and workplace flexibility benefits is a tangible accommodation to institutional pressures; it signals to important constituents that an organization is responsive (Goodstein, 1994, 1995). As Kingston (1990) observes, the responsive workplace may come to symbolize the "good" workplace. Thus, organizations often respond to work-family pressures in order to enhance external legitimacy as well as satisfy internal constituencies (Milliken, Dutton, & Beyer, 1990).

However, when policies are implemented primarily because of institutional pressures, they basically position the organization in reference to other similar organizations. Simply instituting policies does not address the "inner workings" of the organization; as illustrated, if work-family are just "added on" to the existing culture (Rapoport & Bailyn, 1996), coworkers and supervisors may not see the full merits of the policies, and they may remain underutilized. This seems to be the case at Regulatory Alliance—the Regulators expressed mixed feelings about the policies themselves as well as their utilization. Consequently, in some ways the policies seemed to be serving institutional rather than human purposes; while they look good on paper, they may not be fully understood, which may lead to mixed messages and impact benefit utilization, so the human needs are never served. This leads to practical implications concerning how to alter these dynamics.

We have established that putting a policy on paper does not ensure it will be embraced or followed as written. In order to create a supportive climate for work-family policies, attention must be given to structures that might facilitate their implementation and utilization. In previous research, the primary structure of interest has been managerial discourse; however, we were interested in how coworkers constructed the programs through their ongoing discourse. As illustrated, the existence and use of work-family benefits can divide employees and create perceptions of preferential treatment that stimulate negative discourse about work-family policies.

In addition, these perceptions may create more "hidden" conflict in the organization, where individuals are not confronted about their use of policies but "it is always the buzz" (female examiner). A male examiner noted a "problem we have is that those perceptions are allowed to fester within small groups of people . . . they say this is unfair, but yet . . . I don't think they brought those issues to their supervisors." If supervisors, organizational leaders, and Human Resource professionals are aware of the subtle yet pervasive role that communication plays in the process of work-family benefit utilization, perhaps they can address these issues and the resulting potential for conflict in a proactive and productive manner. This is important, because if individuals are feeling work-family conflict, yet do not utilize policies to help alleviate this stress, it can create problems both at work and at home.

So what suggestions would we offer to enact positive changes on the discourse of work-family policies? Rodgers (1992) outlines features of organizational environments where work-family initiatives have been successful and "fully integrated" into corporate culture, rather than simply being adopted to increase external legitimacy. Once work-family policies are formally instituted, support for the implementation of such policies is clearly communicated from the top of the organization, and expectations for the programs are communicated to employees. Managers are trained not only to understand the reasons for the policies, but they have also been trained in specific skills they will need to implement flexibility. Finally, success stories of implementing programs are disseminated throughout the organization (Rodgers, 1992). Embedded in these features are several potentials for improving the current environment at Regulators.

At the organizational level, Regulatory Alliance should start by more clearly communicating support for work-family policy implementation from the top. The current practice of providing factual information via the website only serves to illustrate that a policy is on paper—it does not guarantee that the policy will be embraced in practice. As part of this communication, Human Resources departments should focus on communicating that these programs are not just "women's benefits" or only for those with children. The use of success stories in localized discourse as well as in formal company newsletters (Friedman & Johnson, 1991; Rodgers, 1992) may help mitigate the negative perceptions of work-family policies. For example, profiling examples of men working part-time, providing elder-care, taking paternity leave (etc.), might frame the policies more broadly than the current discourse has allowed by effectively questioning the public/private dichotomy and sex-role stereotypes that are now being appropriated in talk about work-family policies.

In reducing negativism among coworkers, a key factor that seems to be missing is organizational communication about the reasoning behind these policies to *employees* (rather than just managers), as well as communicating expectations of what the programs entail. When corporate work-family initiatives are considered as a whole, "the evidence points to positive effects of organizational support on productivity, absenteeism, turnover, tardiness, stability and loyalty, employee morale, and recruitment and retention of quality employees" (Zedeck and Mosier, 1990, p. 245). Perhaps some of these advantages should be communicated to workers; training sessions could illustrate the positive aspects of work-family programs (such as increased commitment and retention), while providing a realistic overview of their limitations. In the larger scheme, employees may prefer taking over a day of work for someone on work-family leave than training a new person for two weeks because a colleague who was dissatisfied with his or her work-family balance resigned. But if employees do not have the full context, it can be hard to see how work-family benefits are of any assistance to those who do not have dependents.

Still, no matter how much knowledge employees have about the merits of work-family policies, if they are being burdened with someone else's work, and operate from individualistic and meritocratic structures, they are bound to be frustrated. If Regulatory Alliance does not currently have access to material resources (i.e. temporary workers, part-time staff) to take on excess workloads, then perhaps communicative resources at the interpersonal level can be utilized to reduce examiner frustrations. For instance, if an examiner has to complete the work of a colleague gone on family leave, but she feels rewarded for these extra efforts through informal means or praise, perhaps that could mitigate some resentment. Supervisors (and coworkers) can communicate in rewarding ways even if more material resources are not available.

In addition, managers should set up an open communication environment where employees feel free to share their perceptions of inequity, so these do not "fester" in small groups. For example, if someone complained about the nice schedule a part-time examiner is receiving, and the supervisor reminds him or her about their proportionate reduction in salary and benefits, perhaps this would diffuse some resentment and reduce some of the negative discourse. Of course, the same goes for coworkers; to begin, those who use the policies might want to stick up for themselves and point out the tradeoffs involved. To improve the discourse across groups, another possibility is to "open up" negotiations of work-family policies to the coworkers who will experience increased workloads by covering for the leavetaker.

Thus, after an individual approaches his or her supervisor about taking family leave (see Miller et al., 1996), meetings could also be scheduled between coworkers, with or without the presence of the supervisor. For example, they might arrange a trade-off where the coworker who takes on the extra work of the leavetaker is then "repaid the favor," perhaps the leavetaker could cover his or her coworker's responsibilities to allow vacation time upon returning. Regardless of the final agreement, the process of group negotiation could help determine what facets of the leavetaker's workload need to be done in his or her absence, which may also help diffuse resentment and negative discourse. This additional step would broaden policy negotiation so that all invested parties have at least some involvement in the process. In short, while discourse can create a system where work-family benefits are not utilized, perhaps discourse can also change this same system.

Yet we realize communication can not solve all the problems embedded in the system of work-family policies and their utilization. Organizations must make more than "half-hearted" attempts at implementation to have lasting changes. Thus, to really encourage individuals to take family leave and not worry about the consequences from coworkers and supervisors, temporary or contingent workers should eventually be brought in to replace leavetakers in their absence. Alternatively, additional compensation could be offered to permanent employees who agree to take on extra work for those who are on family leave. Such actions would position the organization in a way that gives more than just lip-service to issues of work and family; this takes more organizational commitment than just putting a policy on paper. We do not foresee that any of these changes can necessarily be immediate, but hope that incremental changes over time will improve the climate for work-family issues and policies in this and other organizations.

To conclude, these observations as to how coworkers shaped work-family policy through communication were observed in a branch of the federal government in the financial field, an industry with significant institutional pressures to offer work-family benefits. In other words, this organization is a "best case scenario" of sorts. Yet even in these circumstances, a climate was created in which employees hesitated to request or utilize the available policies. We assume the difficulties associated with work-family programs and their implementation and utilization would be more prominent in less ideal circumstances. Consequently, we hope this study prompts similar research that conceptualizes work, family, and work-family policy through the lens of communication in order to begin illustrating process as an addition to existing causal models and linking mechanisms of work and family.

Endnotes

1. Flexible work options, also called alternate work arrangements, may include: (a) flextime, (b) permanent and temporary part-time work, (c) job sharing, (d) flexplace or telecommuting, and (e) flexible use of vacation time and personal days (Morgan & Milliken, 1992; Rodgers, 1992; Swiss, 1998). Typical forms of family leave include maternity leave, parental and paternity leaves, adoptive leave, and leave for elder care or other family emergencies (Morgan & Milliken, 1992). These forms of leave vary widely among organizations concerning their length and compensation, if paid leave is an option (Raabe & Gessner, 1988). Finally, dependent care benefits exist in the form of financial assistance, information and referral services, and childcare and eldercare services (Magid & Fleming, 1987; Morgan & Milliken, 1992; Zedeck & Mosier, 1990). With all types of work-family initiatives, the scope of the policies and programs can be organization-wide, or only applicable to certain departments or employees; a process some researchers call "modified" adoption (Raabe & Gessner, 1988). In addition, informal, unwritten policies can be created and applied to individual employees, whereas formal written policies pertain to large groups of employees (MacDermid, Williams, & Marks, 1994; Raabe & Gessner, 1988).
2. This study was generated out of a larger project describing and analyzing work-family ideologies, work-family communication and work-family policy implementation in the organization of "Regulatory Alliance" (pseudonym). Although the present study uses the same interviews that formed the basis of a previous article (Kirby, 2000), it draws on different data and extends the analysis beyond supervisory discourse.
3. As part of the larger project, the data collection and interpretation was completed by the first author under the advisement of the second author.
4. As part of the larger project, there were more than six themes in the data; however, in regards to the research questions in this report, only six themes emerged.

References

Allen, T. D., & Russell, J. A. (1999). Parental leave of absence: Some not so family-friendly implications. *Journal of Applied Social Psychology, 29,* 166–191.

Auerbach, J. D. (1988). *In the business of child care: Employer initiative and working women.* New York: Praeger.

Bailyn, L., Fletcher, J. K., & Kolb, D. (1997). Unexpected connections: Considering employees' personal lives can revitalize your business. *Sloan Management Review, 38,* 11–19.

Banks, S. P., & Riley, P. (1993). Structuration theory as an ontology for communication research. In S. A. Deetz (Ed.), *Communication yearbook 16* (pp. 167–196). Newbury Park, CA: Sage.

Barker, J. R. (1993). Tightening the iron cage: Concertive control in self-managing teams. *Administrative Science Quarterly, 38,* 408–437.

Barley, S. R. (1986). Technology as an occasion for structuring: Evidence from observations of CT scanners and the social order of radiology departments. *Administrative Science Quarterly, 31,* 61–103.

Bruce, W., & Reed, C. (1994). Preparing supervisors for the future work force: The dual income couple and the work-family dichotomy. *Public Administration Review, 54,* 36–43.

Cramer, K., & Pearce, J. (1990). Work and family policies become productivity tools. *Management Review, 79,* 42–44.

Creswell, J. W. (1994). *Research design: Qualitative & quantitative approaches.* Thousand Oaks, CA: Sage.

DeSanctis, G., & Poole, M. S. (1994). Capturing the complexity in advanced technology use: Adaptive structuration theory. *Organization Science, 5,* 121–147.

Edwards, J. R., & Rothbard, N. P. (2000). Mechanisms linking work and family: Clarifying the relationship between work and family constructs. *Academy of Management Review, 25,* 178–199.

Fricke, T. (2000). Cultural dilemmas in changing work and family life in the United States. In E. Appelbaum (Ed.), *Balancing acts: Easing the burden & improving the options for working families* (pp. 37–47). Washington, D.C.: Economic Policy Institute.

Friedman, D. E., & Johnson, A. A. (1991). *Strategies for promoting a work-family agenda.* New York: The Conference Board.

Giddens, A. (1984). *The constitution of society: Outline of the theory of structuration.* Cambridge, MA: Polity Press.

Gilbert, L. A. (1994). Current perspectives on dual-career families. *Current Directions in Psychological Science, 3,* 101–105.

Glaser, B., & Strauss, A. L. (1967). *The discovery of grounded theory: Strategies for qualitative research.* Chicago: Aldine.

Gonyea, J. G., & Googins, B. K. (1992). Linking the worlds of work and family: Beyond the productivity trap. *Human Resource Management, 31,* 209–226.

Goodstein, J. D. (1994). Institutional pressures and strategic responsiveness: Employer involvement in work-family issues. *Academy of Management Journal, 37,* 350–382.

Goodstein, J. D. (1995). Employer involvement in eldercare: An organizational adaptation perspective. *Academy of Management Journal, 38,* 1657–1671.

Greenhaus, J. H., & Beutell, N. J. (1985). Sources of conflict between work and family roles. *Academy of Management Review, 10,* 76–88.

Jenner, L. (1994). Work-family programs: Looking beyond written policies. *HR Focus, 71*(1), 19–20.

Kamerman, S. B., & Kahn, A. J. (1987). *The responsive workplace.* New York: Columbia University Press.

Kanter, R. M. (1977). *Work and family in the U.S.: A critical review and agenda for research and policy.* Newbury Park, CA: Sage.

Kim, S. (1998). Toward understanding family leave policy in public organizations: Family leave use and conceptual framework for the family leave implementation process. *Public Productivity and Management Review, 22,* 71–87.

Kingston, P. W. (1990). Illusions and ignorance about the family-responsive workplace. *Journal of Family Issues, 11,* 438–454.

Kirby, E. L. (2000). Should I do as you say or do as you do?: Mixed messages about work and family. *The Electronic Journal of Communication/La Revue de Electronique de Communication, 10* [Online]. Available: http://www.cios.org/www/ejcmain.htm.

Kirkpatrick, D. (1997). Child-free employees see another side of the equation. *The Wall Street Journal Interactive* [Online]. Available: http://www.wsj.com/public/current/articles/SB859238936898216000 .html.

Kreuger, R. A. (1994). *Focus groups: A practical guide for applied research* (2nd ed.). Thousand Oaks, CA: Sage.

Lee, C. (1991). Balancing work and family. *Training, 28*(9), 23–28.

Lee, C. M., & Duxbury, L. (1998). Employed parents' support from partners, employers, and friends. *Journal of Social Psychology, 138,* 303–322.

Lewis, L. K., & Seibold, D. R. (1993). Innovation modification during intraorganizational adoption. *Academy of Management Review, 18,* 322–354.

Lewis, S. (1997). "Family friendly" employment policies: A route to changing organizational culture or playing about at the margins? *Gender and Work Organization, 4,* 13–23.

Lindlof, T. R. (1995). *Qualitative communication research methods.* Thousand Oaks, CA: Sage.

Lobel, S. A. (1991). Allocation of investment in work and family roles: Alternative theories and implications for research. *Academy of Management Review, 16,* 1–15.

MacDermid, S. M., Williams, M., & Marks, S. (1994). Is small beautiful? Work family tension, work conditions, and organizational size. *Family Relations, 43,* 159–167.

Magid, R. Y., & Fleming, N. E. (1987). *When mothers and fathers work: Creative strategies for balancing career and family,* New York: American Management Association.

Marshall, C., & Rossman, G. B. (1989). *Designing qualitative research.* Newbury Park, CA: Sage.

Medjuck, S., Keefe, J. M., & Fancey, P. J. (1998). Available but not accessible: An examination of the use of workplace policies for caregivers of elderly kin. *Journal of Family Issues, 19,* 274–299.

Miller, V. D., Jablin, F. M., Casey, M. K., Lamphear-Van Horn, M., & Ethington, C. (1996). The maternity leave as a role negotiation process. *Journal of Managerial Issues, 8,* 286–309.

Milliken, F., Dutton, J., & Beyer, J. (1990). Understanding the organizational adaptation to change: The case of work-family issues. *Human Resource Planning, 13,* 91–107.

Mitchell, O. S. (1997). Work and family benefits. In F. D. Blau, & R. G. Ehrenberg (Eds.), *Gender and family issues in the workplace* (pp. 268–276). New York: Russell Sage Foundation.

Morgan, H., & Milliken, F. J. (1992). Keys to action: Understanding differences in organizations' responsiveness to work-and-family issues. *Human Resource Management, 31,* 227–248.

Nippert-Eng, C. E. (1996). *Home and work: Negotiating boundaries through everyday life.* Chicago: University of Chicago Press.

Osterman, P. (1995). Work/family programs and the employment relationship. *Administrative Science Quarterly, 40,* 681–700.

Patton, M. Q. (1990). *Qualitative evaluation and research methods.* Newbury Park, CA: Sage.

Perlow, L. A. (1997). *Finding time: How corporations, individuals and families can benefit from new work practices.* Ithaca, NY: ILR Press.

Poole, M. S., & DeSanctis, G. (1990). Understanding the use of group decision support systems: The theory of adaptive structuration. In J. Fulk & C. Steinfield (Eds.), *Organizations and communication technology* (pp. 173–193). Newbury Park, CA: Sage.

Poole, M. S., & DeSanctis, G. (1992). Microlevel structuration in computer-supported group decision-making. *Human Communication Research, 19,* 5–49.

Poole, M. S., Seibold, D. R., & McPhee, R. D. (1996). The structuration of group decisions. In R. Y. Hirokawa & M. S. Poole (Eds.), *Communication and group decision-making* (2nd ed., pp. 114–146). Newbury Park, CA: Sage.

Putnam, L. L., Phillips, N., & Chapman, P. (1996). Metaphors of communication and organization. In S. R. Clegg, C. Hardy, & W. R. Nord (Eds.). *Handbook of organization studies* (pp. 375–408). Thousand Oaks, CA: Sage.

Raabe, P., & Gessner, J. (1988). Employer family-supportive policies: Diverse variations on a theme. *Family Relations, 37,* 196–202.

Rapoport, R., & Bailyn, L. (1996). *Relinking life and work: Toward a better future.* New York: The Ford Foundation.

Rees Edwards, M. R. (1997). *The problems employed mothers face: A call for communication research.* Paper presented at the annual meeting of the National Communication Association, Chicago, Illinois.

Rodgers, C. S. (1992). The flexible workplace: What have we learned? *Human Resource Management, 31,* 83–199.

Salancik, G. R., & Pfeffer, J. (1978). A social information processing approach to job attitudes and task design. *Administrative Science Quarterly, 23,* 224–253.

Saltzman, A. (1997, May 12). Companies in a family way. *U.S. News and World Report* [Online]. Available: http://www.usnews.com/usnews/issue/970512/12comp.html.

Sandberg, J. C. (1999). The effects of family obligations and workplace resources in men's and women's use of family leaves. In T. L. Parcel (Ed.), *Research in the sociology of work: Work and family.* Stamford, CT: JAI Press.

Skinner, D. (1999). The reality of equal opportunities: The expectations and experiences of part-time staff and their managers. *Personnel Review, 28,* 425–438.

Solomon, C. M. (1994). Work/family's failing grade: Why today's initiatives aren't enough. *Personnel Journal, 73,* 72–87.

Strauss, A., & Corbin, J. (1998). Grounded theory methodology: An overview. In N. K. Denzin & Y. S. Lincoln (Eds.), *Strategies of qualitative inquiry* (pp. 158–183). Thousand Oaks, CA: Sage.

Swiss, D. J. (1998). Good worker or good parent: The conflict between policy and practice. In M. G. Mackavey & R. L. Levin (Eds.), *Shared purpose: Working together to build strong families and high-performance companies* (pp. 87–104). New York: AMACOM.

Thomas, L. T., & Ganster, D. C. (1995). Impact of family-supportive work variables on work-family conflict and strain: A control perspective. *Journal of Applied Psychology, 80,* 6–15.

Thompson, C. A., Beauvais, L. L., & Lyness, K. S. (1999). When work-family benefits are not enough: The influence of work-family culture on benefit utilization, organizational attachment, and work-family conflict. *Journal of Vocational Behavior, 54,* 392–415.

Zedeck, S., & Mosier, K. L. (1990). Work in the family and employing organization. *American Psychologist, 45,* 240–251.

Received August 2, 2000
Accepted April 11, 2001

FOLLOW-UP QUESTIONS AND EXPLORATION PROJECTS

1. Structuration Theory suggests that social interaction is an active and conscious process. Compare this article with the article about organizational culture. How do they compare in terms of their perceptions on the consciousness of social interaction. How might Structuration Theory suggest the meaning behind organizational symbols is created and maintained?

2. Find three organizational policies in an organization with which you are currently involved. What is your perception on the way these policies have been structured by the interactions of employees and employers? Are the interpretive structures created by the worker, similar to the intention of the policies?

3. From your perspective, is the creation of societal structures an active (conscious) or passive (unconscious) process? Why?

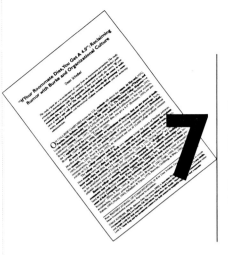

7 Organizational Culture: Unique Symbols of Shared Purpose

Culture consists of unique characteristics of a collection of people that help us understand what the group holds as important, and how they live and make sense of their surroundings. Culture develops as people communicate and make sense of past experiences. From these interactions, values and assumptions are influenced and patterns of group behavior develop. We gain insight into the values, assumptions, and behaviors of a culture by considering the way that groups communicate, act out (Burke, 1966) and interpret (Bantz, 1993) culture. Culture is symbolic and is indicated through physical artifacts like statues, money, or clothing, but also through the communication and interpretation of words, language, and stories.

Although we tend think about culture as a descriptor of a region or nation, it is also used to consider organizations. Symbols represent the culture of organizations in which we are involved. For example, at a university, buildings, school logos, stories, legends, jargon, and jokes are descriptors that identify the culture of the school, a culture distinct from that of other schools, even in the same state or city. The communication and interpretation of organizational symbols helps us gain insight into the values, assumptions, and behaviors of the organization and its members. The notion of communication helping us cope with and make sense of organizational culture is the theme of the following article.

Background of Organizational Culture

Like other theories discussed in this book, organizational culture originated during a time of great interest in traditional social-scientific research. In fact, researchers initially considered organizational culture from a somewhat objective and variable perspective. The quantitative study of organizational culture was awkward, and left little flexibility for the influence of communication and interaction on culture. In the early 1980s communication researchers began looking at organizational culture from an interpretive perspective. The perspective suggested that organizational culture was an emergent phenomenon that materialized through communication about organizational symbols. From this emergent viewpoint, researchers began to consider how organizational culture differed from organization to organization based on a communicated understanding of organizational symbols.

Article Structure

The article considers organizational rumors as a symbol that helps members cope with and make sense of uncertainty in a university setting. Specifically, it looks at how students use the rumor "If your roommate dies, you get a 4.0" to make sense of the challenges of university life and especially achieving the somewhat elusive 4.0 grade point average (Scheibel, 1999). The article discusses rumor as a symbolic form of communication. Burke's (1966) perspectives on symbol-using to interpret meaning together with Bantz's (1993) interpretive view of organizational culture are used as a theoretical framework for conceptualizing rumor as a part of the organizational culture of American universities and colleges.

Distinctive Points

By considering rumors as a communicative symbol for understanding organizational culture, this article demonstrates that organizational culture is a communication-based entity that emerges through a process of interaction. Burkean principles of symbolic action allow for the interpretation of organizational symbols to differ from person to person and organization to organization, creating distinct organizational cultures, yet be understood in different ways because the people and circumstances around which symbols exist differ. By considering rumor as a communicative symbol, the article also shows the importance of organizational stories as an abstract cultural artifact used for making sense of or explaining certain aspects of everyday organizational life.

References

Bantz, C.R. (1993). *Understanding organizations: Interpreting organizational communication cultures.* Columbia, SC: University of South Carolina Press.

Burke, K. (1966). *Language as symbolic action.* Berkeley, CA: University of California Press.

Scheibel, D. (1999). "If your roommate dies, you get a 4.0": Reclaiming rumor with Burke and Organizational Culture. *Western Journal of Communication, 63,* 168–192.

"If Your Roommate Dies, You Get A 4.0": Reclaiming Rumor with Burke and Organizational Culture

Dean Scheibel

The study argues for a reconsideration of rumor from an interpretive perspective. The study articulates a theoretical perspective that combines organizational culture with Burke's guilt-purification-redemption cycle. The perspective is then used to study the rumor, "If your roommate dies, you get a 4.0." The study concludes that students use the rumor to make sense of and to cope with problematic aspects of their university-life pertaining to room-mates, academic pressures, and hierarchical relations between students and the university administration.

ON COLLEGE CAMPUSES across the U.S., students talk about the rumor. At Harvard, NYU, Purdue, Yale, Indiana, Stanford, Tulane, the University of Michigan, University of Virginia, and Loyola Marymount University they can read this rumor in *U., The National College Magazine*[1]—a publication claiming a circulation of 2,250,000 and an audience of 6,600,000 (see Braddom, 1995; Brunvand, 1989; Urbano, 1997). Indeed, in one story that seemed addressed to first year students, the *U* explicitly stated the rumor: "If your roommate dies, you get a 4.0" (Braddom, 1995; see also Brunvand, 1989[2]; McGrath, 1996; Urbano, 1997).

As much as colleges and universities are institutions of learning, they are also places of death. Murders and suicides occur with some frequency, and some receive prominent news coverage. Such, for example, was the case with the murder-suicide of two young women at Harvard (Butterfield, 1995; Mehren, 1995; Press & Rosenberg, 1995). According to one university psychologist (personal communication, M. Doyle, 7 July 1997), an estimated one out of 10,000 college students commits suicide on U.S. college campuses each year.

The college experience is cyclical. Each new semester brings the return of familiar patterns: New students enter and often are assigned to room with other new students; sometimes the students know each other, but often they do not. Each semester also brings midterms, finals, and term papers, and despite their repetition, such events are crises for the students, in that such events are "break[s] in the established routine of [college] life" (Shibutani, 1966, p. 172). During these crises, an almost palpable tension arises and coping activities such as "cramming" and "all-nighters" are resurrected.

Entering college is stressful, meeting academic standards may be difficult, and dealing with roommates may be unpleasant. Research suggests that problematic roommate relationships are related to lower grade point averages (Pace, 1970; Waldo, 1984); in fact, "many students feel that, because of their [assigned] roommate, the institution is responsible for their inadequate academic performance" (Elton & Bate, 1966, p. 77). In sum, entrance into college marks a point of transition, socialization, academic pressure, and stress (see Brunvand, 1981; Degh, 1969; Jorgensen-Earp & Staton, 1993; Nudd, 1965; Palladino & Tryon, 1978; Rosecan, Goldberg, & Wise, 1992; Scherer &

From WESTERN JOURNAL OF COMMUNICATION, 63 © by Dean Scheibel. Copyright © 1992 by Western States Communication Association. Reprinted by permission.

DEAN SCHEIBEL (Ph.D., Arizona State University, 1991) is Associate Professor of Communication at Loyola Marymount University, Los Angeles, CA. The author wishes to thank Laura McGrath, Mike Farkash, Christy Mullis, and Joseph Ayala for their respective contributions. The author also thanks *Western Journal of Communication* editor Leah R. Vande Berg and the anonymous reviewers for their numerous insightful suggestions and comments.

Wygant, 1982). No wonder, then, that the "roommate's death" rumor which explicitly links roommates and grades with the university's administration pervades many college campuses.

Rumor as Communication

Rumor is a collective, communicatively constituted cultural phenomenon composed of the "interrelated activities of individuals who constitute a public" (Shibutani, 1966, p. 121). Rumors, thus, are contextually produced and reproduced within particular situations. Specifically, rumors emerge during times of collective crisis; that is, during "any break in the established routine of life" (Shibutani, 1966, p. 172). In this sense, rumors are produced and reproduced in relation to important topics in ambiguous situations (see Allport & Postman, 1947; Shibutani, 1966).

Rumors create situations in which people come together, communicate, and collectively fight or reduce anxiety (Allport & Postman, 1947; Shibutani, 1966). Anxiety may be relieved through rumors that provide a "camouflaged means of expressing . . . feelings" (Shibutani, 1966, p. 88). Rumors also serve to express, project, evade, or displace "guilt" (Allport & Postman, 1947) and to achieve "catharsis" through "scapegoating" (Allport & Postman, 1947; Kapferer, 1990; Shibutani, 1966).

Rumor has a history of interest to organizational communication scholars as well as social psychologists, psychologists, and sociologists (see Allport & Postman, 1947; Conrad, 1985; Davis, 1953a, 1953b, 1969; Shibutani, 1966; Stohl & Redding, 1987). Seminal studies (Davis, 1953a, 1953b) using ECCO analysis (i.e., Episodic Communication Channels in Organizations) examined rumor as informal communication, and focused on the serial transmission of messages. Such studies provided information on communication networks, including method of communication, accuracy of transmission, pattern of rumor transmission, and organizational level and function of sender and receiver (Davis, 1978; Stohl & Redding, 1987). However, research on rumor[3] has been largely neglected in recent decades by communication scholars generally and by organizational communication scholars in particular (Weinberg & Eich, 1977).

This study demonstrates that integrating Burke's dramatistic guilt-purification-redemption cycle and Bantz's (1993) interpretive approach to organizational culture provides an efficacious vocabulary for analyzing rumors (such as the "If your roommate dies, you get a 4.0" rumor) in organizations.

Burke's Dramatism and Organizational Culture

Burke's (1989) idea that "language is primarily a species of action" points to an appreciation of human action as the use of symbols (p. 53). Through the action of "symbol-using," people name things, define situations, and interpret meanings (Burke, 1966, p. 3). Essential to dramatism, Burke's (1966) theory of human action, is the idea that through symbol-using, people produce all manner of *hierarchies.* Within organizational cultures, these hierarchical productions constitute organizational meanings and organizational expectations; they reflect graded rankings within cultural orders, and, thus, they unify and divide. The various divisions within the university organizational hierarchy (e.g., "first year students" and "juniors") simultaneously unify (both are part of the student body) and divide (e.g., there are social distinctions between "administrators" and "students" in terms of decision making on faculty tenure), and make classes of people that are "subtly mysterious to each other" (Burke, 1969, p. 115). Further, the subdivisions of social orders create not only cultures, but "cultures within cultures, since [an organization] can be subdivided into groups with divergent standards and interests" (Burke, 1931, p. 161).

According to Burke (1984a), hierarchies create the conditions for the guilt-purification-redemption cycle. They do so, first, because participation in hierarchies creates the conditions for "hierarchic psychosis" or *guilt.* For Burke (1984a) guilt is "inevitable in social relations" (p. 279). Such guilt, Rueckert (1982) explains, is equivalent to forms of "uneasiness" or "tensions" (p. 131).

The removal or *symbolic purification* of this unease, or guilt, is made possible through language. For Burke (1969), the symbolic purification of guilt is achieved through victimage or symbolic *kill-*

ing.[4] Such killing may take the form of *scapegoating* others or *mortification* of self (Burke, 1952). Through these symbolic killings, a collective "stylistic cleansing" or *catharsis* is achieved, which is followed by *redemption,* in which guilt is alleviated (Burke, 1984a, p. 285). The idea of redemption, Rueckert (1982) explains, is "a moment of stasis, the still moment following the fusion and release of a symbol-induced catharsis" (p. 137).

Bantz's (1993) interpretive approach to organizational culture is explicitly linked to dramatism. According to Bantz, communicative interaction is "best seen dramatistically and is related to the concept of performance" (p. 36). As the following discussion suggests, the interpretation of various elements within Bantz's approach (e.g., stories, fantasies, roles, motives) all imply a resonance between Burke's dramatism and Bantz's (1993) interpretive approach to organizational culture.

Bantz's (1993) perspective views organizational culture as constituted through the "creation, maintenance, and transformation of meanings and expectations" (p. 19). Bantz's interpretive perspective studies organizations as socially constructed realities which are constituted primarily through organizational members' messages. Thus, the interpretation of organizational culture is accomplished primarily through the analysis of organizational members' messages.

Organizational messages (including those co-created between the organizational member and the researcher) are "traces" of communicative social interaction (Bantz, 1993). A scholar using Bantz's perspective first analyzes these messages in terms of vocabulary, themes, temporality,[5] and architecture.[6] Next, the researcher examines these organization messages as symbolic forms that include stories, metaphors, and fantasies. These symbolic forms have received considerable attention from organizational culture researchers (see Bormann, Pratt, & Putnam, 1978; Brown, 1990).

Based on these analyses, the researcher then creates interpretations of *organizational meanings* through the analysis of central and/or recurrent constructs (e.g., "students"), and relations among constructs (e.g., "students," "administration" and "grades") in the organizational messages. These organizational meanings next are examined for the *organizational expectations,* the "taken-for-granted" patterns of members' coordinated behavior," they reveal (Bantz, 1993, p. 135). Organizational expectations include norms, roles, agendas, styles, and motives. The resulting interpretation of organizational culture, then, provides an understanding of the patterns of organizational meanings and expectations created and enacted through organizational members' communication practices.

Several insights into organizational rumor emerge from combining the central analytical concepts of these two scholars. Burke's guilt-purification-redemption cycle has a pronounced resonance with the symbolic form of rumor. Thus, a Burkeian-infused approach to organizational culture can provide a more nuanced reading of the meanings and functions of performances of organizational rumors as symbolic forms. Further, Burke's dramatistic focus on human action and symbolic performance provides an explicitly *critical*-interpretive vocabulary that augments the analysis of organizational activities, particularly clashes between organizational subcultures.

Concomitantly, Bantz's (1993) meaning-centered approach adds to Burke's rhetorical frame and focuses on identifying motives and a vocabulary for organizational performances of interest to organizational scholars (i.e., norms, roles, agendas, motives, styles). In so doing, Bantz's (1993) perspective complements Burke's dramatistic framework and provides a useful tool with which organizational scholars can examine organizational messages as symbolic performances.

This article illustrates the efficacy of combining these two analytical perspectives by examining the college rumor "If your roommate dies, you get a 4.0." In doing so, the current study shows how this combination of approaches can reveal how a particular rumor, and student narratives about that rumor, create subcultural meanings and expectations. It also provides insights into how some organizational members—college students—use rumor to cope with the problematic and emotional exigencies of organizational (college) life.

A Multi-level Dramatistic Analysis of Organizational Rumor

Interpreting both the content of the "roommate's death" rumor and students' narratives about the rumor provides a more nuanced understanding of the meanings of the rumor than just analyzing one rumor alone (see Dundes, 1966; Mullen, 1972). A thorough interpretive analysis of the meanings of an organizational rumor such as the "roommate's death" rumor for organizational members involves at least three levels or domains of analysis (Kapferer, 1990). Level one involves analyzing and interpreting the rumor's type (Knapp, 1944; Nkpa, 1977). A second level of analysis involves interpreting the dramatistic and cultural meanings and expectations that are communicatively created, maintained, and transformed through the performance of the rumor (Bantz, 1993; Burke, 1966). Such second level interpretations are primarily concerned with the meanings and functions of the rumor within the organization in which the rumor circulates (Kapferer, 1990, p. 158). The third level entails a dramatistic interpretation of the rumor for "hidden messages" that may not be readily apparent in either the explicit subject matter/content of the rumor or student narratives about the rumor (Burke, 1984a; Kapferer, 1990, p. 145). This level of interpretation incorporates analysis of the "place, country, or culture in which [the rumor] circulates as well as the rumor's particular public" (Kapferer, 1990, p. 145). In this sense, the interpretation has significant implications for understanding a particular organizational culture; that is, rumors "can reveal much about the culture where [the rumor] flourishe[s], and about the nature of truth in that culture" (Rosnow & Fine, 1976, p. 17).

The current study asked the following research questions: (1) What variations of the rumor are exhibited in students' narratives? (2) How is the rumor used by students' to make sense of problematic situations? (3) In what ways does the content of student narratives about the rumor create and reflect students' cultural meanings and expectations about college, grades and roommates? (4) How does the content of students narratives about the rumor reflect ideas of collective guilt, purification, and redemption?

I collected data primarily through unstructured interviewing over a two-year period (Spradley, 1979). Of the eight audiotaped and transcribed interviews, I conducted two and Laura McGrath conducted six additional interviews during the course of completing her undergraduate thesis (McGrath, 1996). During this two-year period I also collected data from America Online and other Internet sources[7] by periodically checking discussion groups and postings dealing with urban legends. These data were analyzed using Bantz's (1993) procedure for interpreting organizational culture[8] and the Burkeian dramatistic constructs of hierarchy, guilt, mystery, perfection, scapegoating, and mortification. [Throughout the analysis of the rumor the central, recurring constructs from which interpretations of organizational meanings and expectations were created are underlined]. Several students reviewed the analysis as a "member check" of the interpretations (Lincoln & Guba, 1985).

The Rumor as Cultural Orientation

It is common for first year college students—particularly those living in dormitories—to hear the "roommate's death" rumor. Often, new students have not heard the rumor prior to their arrival at the university. In this sense, new students' introduction to the rumor marks a point of *orientation* (see Blankenship, Murphy, & Rosenwasser, 1974; Burke, 1984b), or perhaps, re-orientation, to college life. For these new students the question of "accepting" or "rejecting" the rumor may be problematic, as the following narrative illustrates:

Well, my first two years here at Loyola—my freshman and sophomore years—I lived in the dorms, in Whalen Hall, and usually one wing or one floor gets to be closeknit, and so everybody kind of hangs out together. And I don't know specifically when it came up, but I'm sure it just, somebody just mentioned it and I [said] *"What?!"* And basically they just said, "Yeah. Didn't you know that? If your roommate dies, they'll just give a 4.0 and you don't have to worry about the rest of the semester." And I [said], "Really?" It just provided all kinds of sick thoughts, especially during times of stress. When you're all stressed out, like during finals week, and you feel like killing your roommate. (Transcript 2, Lines 1–17)

The narrator of this account of first exposure to the rumor here frames learning about the rumor within a particular cultural context; that is, the rumor is brought to the student's attention through a collective, a group of dormitory residents who have developed a "closeknit" relationship. The narrative reflects the initial sense of "amazement" (Shibutani, 1966, p. 77) that may accompany first hearing the rumor (i.e., *"What?!"*, "Really?"). In one sense, the new student's introduction to the rumor serves as a form of cultural initiation (Pacanowsky & O'Donnell-Trujillo, 1983). In another sense, the initial amazement expressed in the narrative reflects a change in orientation. That is, the rumor provides a new frame of interpretation, one that recognizes, ironically, the "sick" or grotesque nature of the rumor.

The narrative also clearly suggests relationships among several important elements of the students' (college) organizational world, including stress, finals, and roommate interactions. The "stress" attributed to taking exams is a reoccurring aspect of student culture. More specifically, the understanding that there are *"times* of stress" such as "finals week" during which other students also feel—to a greater or lesser degree—"stressed" suggests that stress may be considered an "emotional disposition" shared by substantial portions of students (Shibutani, 1966, p. 88). Further, "finals week" is one recurring anxiety-producing situation in which the rumor creates a focus for anxious students. Task-occasions such as final exam "study groups" become contexts for collectively reproducing the rumor, and provide a way for students to collectively address their common anxiety.

Most significantly, students' finals week stress is related to their anxiety about receiving *grades*. Grades are the hierarchic, pre-existing orders of academic achievement that provide students with measures of perfection about what they should and should not, did and did not, achieve in their intellectual life. Consequently guilt is inevitable, and students' anxieties over having failed to achieve perfection in the past, and/or the possibility of failing to do so once again create the context that informs students' "roommate's death" rumor performances, as well as the motives for purging that guilt and achieving catharsis.

A Plausible Rumor

For the initiated college student, disagreements about the truthfulness of the "roommate's death" rumor organize collective discussion. Such is evinced in the following narrative:

> Almost every time it was brought up, somebody would say, "It's not true. It's not true." And then whoever had brought it up would have to argue their point: "Of course it's true." 'Cause they'd brought it up in the first place. And they have the brother's or sister's cousin that they knew at Cornell that it happened to. And so there'd be just a little small argument whether or not it was true . . . and then you'd just go on with the discussion about wherever you were at, about how tough the paper you were writing was. (Transcript 1, Lines 296–312)

Such occasions are cultural performances. The significance of such performances points to organizational members as not only making choices about the actions they engage in, but also centralizes the "theatricality in organizational life," by noting the interactional, contextual, and episodic character of collective rumor construction (Pacanowsky & O'Donnell-Trujillo, 1983). The student narrative portrays these performances as having a somewhat clear beginning, which occurs when the rumor "was brought up." Furthermore, the student narrative suggests the structural boundaries of the performance; that is, the student narrative suggests that the individuals engaged in the episode have a sense of the episode's conclusion ("then you'd just go on with the discussion about wherever you were at. . .").

This student narrative suggests that addressing the "truth" of the "roommate's death" rumor is a reoccurring issue that is addressed "almost every time [the rumor] was brought up." As this narrative demonstrates, the performance of the rumor addresses the verifiability of the rumor and indicates the nature of the cultural expectations and meanings brought to the discussion (Bantz, 1993).

First, there is a norm that there will be an argument over "whether or not it [i.e., the roommate's death rumor] was true." A second norm revealed in this narrative is that the individuals who bring up the rumor should "argue their point." Third, the narrative explicitly defines the presentation of abbreviated "arguments" as the style of such episodes (Bantz, 1993). Finally, the narrative reveals that the construct of personal knowledge may serve as evidence for the rumor's verifiability (e.g., knowing someone who knew someone at another college where the policy existed).

The narrative also demonstrates that this rumor continually is being reconstructed, and that the issue of plausibility becomes a focus for collective problem-solving. Students' definition of the rumor as plausible leads to its repetition ("every time it was brought up"). These repeated social reconstructions suggest a "repetition compulsion" that is consistent with the principle of perfection, or the entelechial motive (Burke, 1966, pp. 17–19). As further analysis reveals, the compulsion toward repetition implicates a " 'perfecting' of victimage" that creates the conditions for students' catharsis (Burke, 1984a, p. 286).

Students' judgments about the plausibility of the rumor occur in a context informed by knowledge that "acts of kindness" *do* occur; for example, teachers routinely do give students "leeway" (Urbano, 1997) in the event of hurtful occurrences (e.g., "my grandmother died"). Thus, there is enough precedent to make a case for the consideration that the rumor might be true.

However, evidence of plausibility is not limited to assertions of personal experience; in fact, although claims of personal experience may be the only evidence available, such is not the most preferred type of evidence (Brunvand, 1989). Rather, students attempt to verify the truthfulness of the rumor by locating sources considered "official" (i.e., acknowledged by the university). Consider the following excerpt from an Internet conversation between two students:

> Okay, so it's not in an OFFICIAL Handbook, but I don't see why it is so hard for everyone to believe that it could be true! Living with someone for a whole year (or more) makes you very close to them, and if that person died, I know I wouldn't be able to concentrate on anything for a while. (Internet chatroom; emphasis in original)

As this student comment indicates, the search for "OFFICIAL" sources, such as university handbooks, typically fails to uncover any such sources. However, students have developed plausible reasons for their inability to verify the rumor through "official" sources.

The narrative above reflects very different perspectives relevant to the rumor's plausibility—that is, some individuals, like this narrator, seem quite willing to believe the rumor, whereas others (e.g., the addressee of the narrator's comments) seem less inclined to believe that the rumor is "true." Nevertheless, the narrative does reveal one of the basic assumptions of the rumor: Being "roommates"—even randomly assigned roommates, in the case of incoming first-year students—is a situation in which roommates can develop a "very close" relationship. Not surprisingly, then, the death of one's roommate might impair the surviving roommate's ability of "concentrate on anything," particularly schoolwork. Concomitantly, however, even "very close" roommate relationships do not preclude periodic tension, as indicated in the earlier narrative, in which a first year student acknowledged times of stress, "like during finals week, and you feel like killing your roommate." Further, the architecture of dorm rooms makes being "very close" a physical reality, even if the roommates' relationship is not emotionally close.

One Problem of Guilt: Variability in the Roommate's Death

One way in which performances of the rumor varies is in terms of the cause of the roommate's death: One version favors *murder* whereas another favors *suicide*. However, both forms of the rumor reflect a guilt-purification-redemption cycle. Similar to students' experience of guilt concerning the hierarchy of grades, students also experience guilt because their social relations with roommates either are problematic or can be represented as problematic in performances of the rumor. In both cases, students' experience of guilt creates the conditions for purgation, catharsis, and symbolic redemption (Burke, 1984a).

As reflected in student performances of the rumor narrative, murdering one's roommate allows for some tension-relieving play with other students, for example, through hypothetical "plotting about how to kill her roommate" and get away with it (McGrath, 1996, p. 46). However, suggesting the idea of murdering one's roommate is not socially acceptable unless it is performed under certain circumstances, as indicated in the narratives above, in which the style clearly is understood as "jok[ing]" or "play" (Bantz, 1993; McGrath, 1996, p. 63). Such cultural assumptions are reflected in the performance of the rumor itself; that is, murder is never mentioned. Indeed, the forms of rumor—"If you *kill* your roommate . . .," or "If you *murder* your roommate. . ."—are *never* stated. One possible explanation for this is because the rumor is completely incompatable with the cultural assumption "Thou shalt not kill." So, rather than explicitly specifying murder, the rumor typically is stated as, "If your roommate *dies*. . . ," which allows for all manner of deaths, including accidental deaths (Brunvand, 1989; Urbano, 1997).

In contrast to murderous rumors, rumors specifying suicide apparently are considered less problematic since, as the student narrative below indicates, if one's roommate commits suicide, the surviving roommate is, arguably, *not* responsible. However, even in this form of the rumor, as the following example illustrates, the narrator of the "roommate's death" rumor still may feel "really bad" (i.e., guilty) about thinking that one's roommate's death is a "cool idea":

> [The rumor] was just kind of a cool idea to play around with. *That sounds really bad doesn't it?* Everyone who met [my roommate] thought she might [commit suicide]; I was just projecting the inevitable benefits. It's like when you buy a lottery ticket and think about all of things you'll buy. . . . A lot of people talked about it, joked about it, it was just so incredible, it was just kind of amazing that anyone could be so lucky. I spent a lot of time thinking about it . . . Pretty much every time I saw her. (McGrath, 1996, p. 63; emphasis added)

Here the narrator tries to distance herself from her apparent guilt at having characterized the possible suicide of her roommate as a "cool idea to play around with." More specifically, she rationalizes talking about this form of rumor in terms of her roommate by stating that others ("everyone who met my roommate") judged the roommate as potentially suicidal. Additionally, the narrator minimizes ("I just") her own role. Further, the narrator's retreat into economic metaphors suggests a desire to escape guilt for performing the rumor by making the rumor seem rational. The idea that such "benefits" (a 4.0) may be a form of "compensation" (for the loss of someone close) is then elaborated on, in a less rational form. That is, the roommate—who is characterized as a potential suicide—is likened to a "lottery ticket" which may be redeemed with the roommate's suicide (i.e., the surviving roommate implicitly *wins* with the roommate's suicide). Both metaphors are symbolic justifications that "purify" the surviving roommate.

The form of the "roommate's death" rumor that specifies suicide may be viewed as the "perfection" of the rumor form,[9] for it provides the warrant that ultimately justifies the giving of perfect grades to the surviving roommate (Burke, 1931, 1984a). As one student explains,

> I think we always accepted it as . . . . just being a fact that you'd be so traumatized, and that you would have spent all semester working, or what have [you], and you're so traumatized that you're going to fail all your classes. And the university's gonna know this, and so, you kind of just accept it as being, *still*, kind of the truth. (Transcript 1, Lines 56–64; emphasis in original)

In contrast with the entertainment function of the rumor that is available when one contemplates symbolically killing one's roommate (e.g., figuring out ways to kill your roommate), the actual possibility of suicide *legitimates* the idea that the surviving roommate has been emotionally "traumatized," has "suffered," or has experienced an emotional crisis (McGrath, 1996, p. 48). Less apparent is that the narrator sets up the university as the source which can provide the remedy (i.e., grades) for "traumatized" students, by virtue of the university's knowledge of the situation ("the university's gonna know this"). In so doing, the university's "sympathetic witnessing of a tragedy" serves to justify the motive of curing (Burke, 1984b, p. 363), and implicitly makes the university responsible for providing the cure.

From a Burkeian perspective, the "roommate's death" rumor's content and students' narratives about it reveal how scapegoating and mortification serve to purify students' guilt about performing this organizational rumor. In symbolically murdering the roommate, narrators are straightforwardly scapegoating the roommate who has been a source of aggravation for the surviving roommate; the victim is chosen because she or he is the "most blamable (the villainy principle)" (Burke, 1959, p. 361). For example, the expression, "I would get rid of this bitch" (McGrath, 1996, p. 46) scapegoats through the lowering of the roommate; that is, the roommate is symbolically transformed into a non-human species, in that a "bitch" is also a "dog." Thus, the egalitarian status of equals is altered, and the surviving roommate is hierarchically raised.

Scapegoating also occurs when narrators express the desire that their roommates will commit suicide. However, such expressions as "I wished she would just kill herself and get me a 4.0," (McGrath, 1996, p. 73) suggest the paradoxical idea that the narrator of the rumor does not want to face the negative sanction of overtly symbolically killing the roommate, and yet is doing just that through "wishing" for the roommate's suicide.[10]

Finally, the scapegoating of the roommate and the purification of the narrator is completed through references to bodily processes; more specifically, purification is achieved through narrators' purgative images of bodily processes. As Burke (1959) explains, "when catharsis attains its full poetic statement . . . its terminology may also be expected to re-enact some or other of these bodily analogues" (p. 355). Thus, one student states, "[Students] wanted to talk about [the rumor]; they wanted to talk shit about their roommate" (McGrath, 1996, p. 71). Here the student purifies the "pollution" of "*discord*" by the symbolic elimination of "shit" onto the roommate (Rueckert, 1982, p. 222).

The roommate's death through suicide allows the surviving roommate to claim that s/he has legitimately "suffered" or has been "traumatized," whereas having symbolically "murdered" one's roommate obviates the ability to claim that one has suffered; although such a claim may be advanced to the extent that roommates have become "very close." In rumor performances in which the roommate has been murdered, the narrator implicitly uses a strategy of mortification to achieve redemption (Burke, 1959). The quality of that trauma, of losing someone close to you in such a manner, the narratives explain, would be so profound that "you're going to fail all your classes." Thus, the surviving roommate would be twice victimized—once by the "traumatic" death of the roommate and again by the subsequent failure of classes. In the "deliberate clamping of limitations upon the self" through these twin tragedies we can discern an appeal to *depth* (Burke, 1952, p. 372; 1969, p. 301). Both feelings and grades are symbolically *sunken;* these images, in turn, provide the motive for *ascension,* both in emotion and in grade. Thus, redemption is achieved in that the surviving roommate is subject to "pity" which "has in itself a cathartic element" (Burke, 1959, p. 356).

These narratives suggest that the variability in the "If your roommate dies, you get a 4.0" rumor allows for scapegoating (through murder of the roommate) and mortification (through suffering or trauma to the surviving roommate). On the other hand, hoping that one's roommate commits suicide is somewhat ambiguous, in that it implies that the surviving roommate wouldn't "really" suffer. However, to the extent that the rumor is taken to be plausible if not altogether true, the hope-for-suicide version might be viewed as the "perfection" of the rumor, in the sense that it superficially conforms to the cultural axiom (i.e., "thou shalt not kill") and also to the expectation that people should feel badly when someone "very close" to them dies.

"The Fantasy of an Easy 4.0"

The consequence of the roommate's death is that the surviving roommate supposedly receives perfect grades (i.e., "a 4.0"). As the following narrative suggests, collective discussions of the rumor serve a wish-fulfilling function during times of collective stress and anxiety:

It was like wishful thinking, y'know, "What if you wouldn't have to work at all this semester?" It was a stress reliever, I think. Just one those things where you were totally stressed out. You had so much to do. You didn't think you could get it done. So you just wanted to think of a quick way out. And that [the rumor] was the quickest way anybody could think of [laughs]. Nobody wants to *really* work their freshman year. They just want to get through it. (Transcript 2, Lines 126–136)

The central construct in this narrative is the idea of taking college classes as "work." In the narrative, "work" is viewed as a source of "stress," something to escape from ("a quick way out"), and a quantifiable activity ("so much to do"). There is a confluence of stress-producing influences in the narrative above. The first-year student, on one hand, is overburdened with work, and anxious about his or her ability to "get it [school work] done." The end of the semester with the stress of producing good performances on final exams and term papers, has arrived. The student feels pressure to "make the grade," both in terms of the new career as college student and also in terms of the grades *as* grades.

The "roommate's death" rumor's content, and the students' narratives about the rumor, express cultural meanings and expectations about the hierarchic *perfection* of "grades," not only in the scholastic sense, but also as recognition of the division of classes people within the university. In this latter sense, the student narratives about the rumor also reflect organizational cultural meanings and expectations concerning the "mystery" between students and the university administration (Burke, 1984a, p. 277).

Part of the "roommate's death" rumor's resonance is its near-universal appeal to college students. Although the problem of "your" roommate isn't a relevant issue for all students, the cyclical problem of "making grades" is a universal concern. This dual focus, the relief the rumor provides from two potential problems (roommates and grades) by cleverly interrelating the two areas, is recognized explicitly in this student narrative.

I think it would just be the fantasy of having the roommate out of their life, [that] would be the key, in the people who hated their roommates. And the other one, it would be the fantasy of an easy 4.0. (Transcript 1 Lines, 188–193)

A Burkeian perspective suggests that the notion of "grades"[11] is infinitely hierarchic; in fact, the very form of the letter "A" is essentially pyramidal,[12] and thus is exemplary in terms of symbolizing the hierarchic perfection of grades. Similarly, "4.0" may be viewed as a more bureacratized hierarchic perfection of grading, in the sense that the *"substitution"* of numbers for letters allow for the numerical calculation of many grades (emphasis in original, Burke, 1966, p. 343; see also Rueckert, 1982, p. 95). Furthermore, such calculations are essentially administrative in origin, in the sense that teachers turn in individual "letter" grades which then are transformed into cumulative numbers.

The significance of this substitution is twofold. First, the "roommate's death" rumor reflects the conditions for mystification by implicitly invoking the administration, which is the agency responsible for granting perfect grades ("a 4.0"). As a result, the antecedent condition in the rumor ("If your roommate dies") also now is implicitly linked with the administration. Thus, the rumor has achieved a certain perfection of form in that the university administration is implicitly embedded within the rumor without actually being mentioned. That is, the "roommate's death" rumor's form is the symbolic creation of a class of symbol-users (students), who, moved by the principle of perfection, create a symbolic form that is perfected, in the sense that the rumor implies the administration without explicitly mentioning the administration.

The narrative above reflects that the rumor is the extension of students' "fantasy of an easy 4.0"; that is, perfect grades ("4.0") without having to *work* ("easy") for the grades. In the rumor "If your roommate dies, you get a 4.0," the phrase "get a 4.0" may be easily transformed into "get an A for nothing," which embodies the "fantasy of an *easy* 4.0," in the sense that the surviving roommate receives the 4.0 by *not* working. Such an interpretation is consistent with the meaning of the word "get," which in its broadest application means "to come into possession of, with or without effort, or volition" (Guralnik, 1980, p. 588). In this sense, the word "nothing" duplicates the lack of effort (the ease) of "getting."

The "fantasy of an easy 4.0," that is, the fantasy of achieving "perfect" grades, is a form of "occupational psychosis" (Burke, 1984a, p. 37). For many students, grades are an essentially economic metaphor in which school work is an "exchange of performance for grades" (Doyle, 1983, p. 181, cited in Evans & Engelberg, 1988, p. 45). Students' failure to achieve perfect grades serves as a motive for purging that guilt. Narrative performances of the rumor both scapegoat the dead roommate and mortify the surviving roommate. In so doing, catharsis and redemption are realized.

The Mystification of "the Administration"

Students' narratives about the rumor recognize that it is the university administration that grants "perfect grades." Such narratives reflect both the strangeness between students and the administration that is characteristic of hierarchy and mystery, and how the hierarchically-inspired guilt is purged through discursive redemptive strategies that address administrative motives.

Within universities, the division of labor and power creates hierarchical stratification between students and the university administration. In turn, the "hierarchical order creates a reciprocal mystery between those at the bottom [i.e., students] and those at the top [i.e., administrators]" (Tompkins, et al., 1977, p. 137; see also Goodall, Wilson, & Waagen, 1986). In students' narratives about the rumor, the mystification of the administration serves to affirm subcultural meanings while reproducing the hierarchically-inspired "social divisiveness" (Burke, 1969, p. 108). Mystification is a symbolic action that enacts the purgative cycle of guilt-purification-redemption.

Although rumor performances overwhelmingly agree that the surviving roommate "*gets* a 4.0," these performances remain vague in terms of exactly how the student "gets" the "4.0"; that is, in terms of who or what agency gives the 4.0 grade. While student narratives about the rumor are quite clear that it is the "administration" or "the university" that gives the "4.0," the inherent ambiguity surrounding the issue of the giving of the "4.0" is such that it too becomes a focus for organizational members' theorizing and sense-making. Such theorizing includes (a) students' sensemaking of the rumor in terms of its "official" status in relation to the administration, and (b) students' characterizations about the administration's motives for giving the "4.0."

[Un]official status of rumor. One issue related the giving of the 4.0 concerns students' deliberations about why the rumor is *not* stated as a formal administrative policy. As this student narrative explains.

> I don't think anybody really looked for it. And if somebody said that they did, I'd think that we would think that, "it's too sensitive of an issue." Something like that. Where, it was like a gift kind of thing. You wouldn't, *shouldn't* be expecting it. Because it is kind of a morbid thought to put in any kind of student guidelines. . . I guess everybody considered it an unwritten rule, plus a rumor. (Transcript 2, Lines 78–87; emphasis in original)

In attempting to explain why the rumor is not in official documents ("student guidelines"), the narrative creates a "plausible extrapolation" for why students are unable to locate official verification of the rumor's official status (Shibutani, 1966, p. 76). As this student explains, the content of the rumor is deemed as "too sensitive of an issue." The construct of sensitivity not only provides the warrant for students' acceptance ("everybody considered it") of the rumor as an "unwritten rule," but it also attributes two motives for the administration's actions [in not officially stating the rumor as policy]: *governance* of and *service* to students.[13]

Additionally, the narrative's suggestions that students should not be "expecting [the 4.0]" implies the hypothesized violation of a norm about how someone should behave under such "sensitive" circumstances. That is, one's organizational performance style should reflect a somberness that is appreciative of the gravity of death, rather than a forward-looking expectation of entitlement (Bantz, 1993).

Administrative motives. The following student narrative affirms the administration's service and governance motives as explanations of why the rumor does not appear in official sources:

> The theory as to why it wasn't in the [hand]book was because the administration *didn't* want it known. So, it was a big top secret. . . It was like, they didn't want the word out because then people would start killing their roommates. So that was the policy of the school. But it wasn't a formal policy. So, you'd discuss how. . . you'd read the book—it wasn't there—so you tried to figure out how to prove that it existed, even though it wasn't written anywhere. . . "Of *course* it's not in the book! What are you, an idiot? If it was in the book, there would be deaths *everywhere.* It's not in the book. But if it *happens* [i.e., your roommate dies], they'll come to you." (Transcript 1, Lines 200–225; emphasis in original)

The hyperbolic character of this narrative is illustrated thematically by referring both to the policy itself as a "big top secret" and to the reason it is kept secret. The reason given for the absence of "formal" policy is to prevent the wholesale slaughter of students ("there would be deaths *everywhere*"). In fact, the narrative's conclusion suggests a dramatic—almost clandestine—meeting between the administration and the surviving roommate ("they'll come to you"). The exaggerated language and scenario ("deaths *everywhere*") in this narrative suggests a performance ethos consistent with "joking" and other performances of organizational sociability (Pacanowsky & O'Donnell-Trujillo, 1983). Nonetheless, both of these narratives imply administrative motives (Bantz, 1993) that are consistent with the "cultural axiom" that educational institutions generally act with appropriate regard for the well-being of students (Shibutani, 1966). Specifically, the narrator's attributions of administration motives are justified through the suggestion that the consequences of having an official policy "in the book" would lead to a situation in which "people would start killing their roommates." Further, the reasonableness of such a position is heightened in the narrative by the naming of a discussion participant as "an idiot." Thus, the narrator affirms that the administration has a good reason (the potential culpability of students acting improperly under stress) for keeping the rumor an "unwritten rule."

Beyond affirming the hypothesized administrative motive (altercentric concern for student members of the university organization) for the "unofficial" existence of the policy reflected in the rumor, students' narratives about the rumor also include attributions of university motives for giving the surviving roommate a "4.0": compensation, compassion, and covering their ass.

The compensation motive. The idea of receiving grades as "compensation" for one's roommate's death is related to but different from students' understanding that the "4.0" is "like a gift kind of thing" (Transcript 2, Line 81). While both entail the economic metaphor, as the example below illustrates, "compensation" suggests being owed or entitled to something, whereas receiving a gift does not:

> The basic thing was your roommate dies, you get *compensated,* and we didn't know where that *compensation* was going to come from, but the thought that it was there was essential to our belief as freshmen. (McGrath, 1996, p. 57; emphasis added)

"Compensation" suggests that the 4.0 is "given as an equivalent" to the surviving roommate's suffering (Guralnik, 1980, p. 289). The narrator's claim that "we didn't know where that compensation was going to come from" is a bit difficult to interpret; on one hand, it seems reasonable to suggest that the narrator is referring to the fact that the university (the administrative arm of which "gives out" student grades) is *not* explicitly mentioned in the stereotypical forms that the rumor takes. Additionally, students—especially first-year students—are often unclear about the labyrinthian nature of academic administration; thus, the narrator also may be suggesting a lack of knowledge about *which* specific office or individual would be in charge of decisions regarding grades in the event that one's roommate died.

However, the fact that the university is not explicitly mentioned may also heighten the mystery and nature of students' involvement in the receipt of the perfect 4.0, and thereby, enhance the students' involvement in performances of the rumor. As Kapferer (1990) explains, in rumors "anonymous characters also create the kind of audience involvement that is indispensable to a rumor's success" (p. 130). That is, the anonymous character of the administration deepens its elusiveness and heightens the strangeness of the rumor itself, which "must in part be perceived through the fog of the social mystery" (Burke, 1984a, p. 278).

Conversely, the student's narrative also invokes a *hierarchical mystification* which in turn superficially creates an ethos of innocence ("we didn't know") while masking the narrator's possible disingenuousness. The narrator's use of an architectural metaphor ("we didn't know *where* that compensation was going to come from") explicitly "stress[es] the element of Mystery arising from the social hierarchy" (Burke, 1984a, p. 277). Further, the portrayal of the collective ("we") as *not* knowing ("didn't know") implicitly invokes the *negative,* thus implying a hierarchy of people who *would* know, with the "we" occupying a "low" place on the social hierarchy of those possessing such knowledge. Thus, students' lack of knowledge becomes a source of *guilt,* which is removed through the self-victimage of *mortification* along two trajectories: students have suffered *and* students lack knowledge.

The compassion motive. Some students' narratives also portray the university as being motivated by compassion toward the student who has had to deal with the death of his or her roommate. The idea that the student "did suffer" or had become emotionally "traumatized" (Transcript 1, Lines 55, 60, 197) provides a plausible reason for why the university would give the surviving roommate a 4.0. Consider the following excerpt from an Internet discussion of the "roommate's death" rumor:

> I really think that most schools would want to do something *to help* at a time like that . . . I can't see them saying, "Oh that's really tragic, but it's time to get back to work!" And, yes, this is just my opinion, but I would expect a little *compassion* from the administration. If you guys really need PROOF in order to believe it, why don't you try killing your roommate to see what happens? (Internet; emphasis added)

The narrative suggests the hypothesized beneficence of the university. That is, the 4.0 is placed within the context of the organizational norm that the university attempts "to help" students. To support this motive attribution, the narrator juxtaposes it with an improbable hypothetical interaction in which the university cynically denies the survivor's trauma and thus blunts the legitimacy of the student's mortification ("Oh that's really tragic, but it's time to get back to work"). Thus, there is a sense in this narrative that the administration is being scapegoated by those who doubt the rumor's plausibility, despite the narrator's claim that he or she "can't see them saying" something cynical. Moreover, the narrator's characterization of "most" schools' probable charity ("would want to do something to help") creates a hierarchy of schools-that-would-help. Such an organizational context implicates the violation of a hypothesized moral imperative: "The administration" should act in accordance with the charitable norms that guide other schools.

The defense motive. Finally, the administration's possible motive of defense (*covering their ass*) also is phrased in economic terms:

> The fact that [the student] had obviously had to deal with some sort of emotional crisis and that the school doesn't want to be responsible for that and the person shouldn't have to be responsible for that. It's just the school's easy way of saying, "Okay, let's just forget about this, just keep paying us our tuition dollars and enroll until you graduate". . . .Just because potential lawsuits or something like that. Somebody always has an angle, you know. So it's just their [the school's] way of *covering their ass* and making everybody happy

all around. . . . The school has weird policies and shit and I wouldn't doubt this one at all. There's weird shit going on at that school. (McGrath, 1996, pp. 67–68; emphasis added)

The naming of the rumor as a "weird policy" mystifies the administration in the sense that "weird" implies a strangeness that is "suggestive of ghosts, evil spirits, or other supernatural things" (Guralnik, 1980, p. 1613).

The narrative also suggests that the rumor serves as a way for "the school" to finesse the question of "responsibility" and potential "law-suits." Thus, the rumor is interpreted as "the school's easy way" of maintaining the *status quo* ("Okay, let's just forget about this, just keep paying us our tuition dollars and enroll until you graduate"). At a somewhat superficial level, the narrator is scapegoating "the school"; that is, the roommate's death is trivialized ("let's just forget about this") and subordinated to the the school's alleged economic motive ("just keep paying us our tuition dollars and enroll"). Further, the narrator distances herself from this scapegoating by characterizing the administration's position as "just the school's easy way of saying. . . ." That is, the rumor is put forward as possessing a hardened, callous communicative style ("easy way of saying") that is lacking in mercy or pity in a tragic occasion.

The attribution of multiple motives in this student narrative serves as a cathartic function through its use of "bodily imagery." According to Burke (1959), "when catharsis attains its full poetic statement (as it must if it is to be thorough), its terminology may also be expected to re-enact some or other of these bodily analogues" (p. 355; see also, Burke, 1969, pp. 308–310). The use of bodily imagery is inherently *purgative* and *cleansing*. That is, the symbolic purging of the hierarchically-inspired guilt is transcended when bodily images are "expressed and 'redeemed'" (Burke, 1969, p. 309).[14]

The narrative expresses the idea that the giving of a "4.0" is a strategic way for the administration to "cover their ass" in the event that a student commits suicide. Implicated in the narrative is the notion that hierarchic mystery between students and the administration reproduces social relations that create guilt. The "roommate's death" rumor gives the power of redeeming the situation to the administration; this creates unequal power relations, and thus, becomes an impetus for scapegoating the administration. The portrayal of the school as being in the untenable position of having to "cover their ass" speaks to the idea of "hierarchal embarrassment" inherent in unequal social relations (Burke, 1984a, p. 278). That is, the depiction of the administration as having to "cover their ass" implies that something has been *inadvertently* disclosed and that the administration's motive of self-serving protection is not appropriate. Thus, the administration is not really "guilty," but rather just "*embarrassed*" or em-BARE-ASSED. Finally, hierarchical social distance between students and the administration is lessened through scapegoating: The student "denies the reality of [the administration's] virtue, while at the same time. . .upholding] his [or her] own lowly standards" (Duncan, 1985, p. 198).

Instances of bodily imagery in student narratives take various forms. Narrators may reference the body itself, but they also more explicitly may reference bodily processes. For example, in the following narrative, scatological language is used to scapegoat "the university" in an ironic style (Bantz, 1993):

It was kind of like, the university actually *gave a shit about us* enough to—I can't believe it's not true, I feel so betrayed—but, they actually realized that there are hardships that desire recognition. (McGrath, 1996, p. 71; emphasis added)

The narrator's personal aside ("I can't believe it's not true, I feel so betrayed") reveals a strategic mortification through linguistic *reversal* in attitude, in the sense that the narrator's belief in the rumor's existence *had* been interpreted as a display of the culturally appropriate administrative acts of "governance" and "condolence"; that is, the university had realized that there are some hardships [i.e., the roommate's death] that deserve recognition. However, the narrator's repeated use of the word "actually" evokes a poignant tone and implies pity (Guralnik, 1980, p. 1100). Thus, the narrative ultimately suggests that the rumor is actually consistent with the narrator's attribution of the administration's admirable motives of understanding ("they realized"); that is, the university "actually" *did* "give a shit about us."

However, the colloquial use of "shit" in conjunction with the narrator's use of "actually" which connotes surprise also distances the students from the administration. That is, the narrator's statement that "they actually gave a shit about us" implies a historical relationship in which the administration "actually" has not "given a shit" about students. Such an interpretation suggests not a denial of the appropriateness of the act of condolence, but rather, a sense that such an act was an abberation from normal student expectations about administrative motives. In this interpretation, the administration is being depicted slyly as being too prideful to care about students. Burke (1959) explicitly states that "though anything can be an object of pride, pride in its simplicity would be excremental," and "insofar as pride incites to anger and vengeance (also 'excremental') it may provoke a kind of counter-pride" (p. 356). Thus, the narrator turns the "shit" *against* the university, the too-prideful administration is scapegoated, and the narrator achieves catharsis and is thus redeemed.

Discussion

The rumor addresses two problematic aspects of student life: roommates and grades. Both are sources of hierarchic imperfection, and as such, are sources of guilt. The genius of the rumor is that the implicit scapegoating achieved through the death of the roommate simultaneously creates the conditions of mortification for the surviving roommate, who has "suffered" or has been "traumatized," and enables the surviving roommate to transcend guilt and achieve redemption by receiving the perfect grade, "a 4.0." Less apparent in the rumor itself, but evidenced in students' narratives, is the mystification and scapegoating of the university administration.

The juxtaposition of Burke's theory about the guilt-purification-redemption cycle in *rhetorical* performances and Bantz's descriptive framework for interpreting organizational cultural performances enhances our understanding of the ways organizational rumors function. Students' narratives reveal their interpretations of the patterns of meanings and behavioral expectations that inform the performance of the rumor in this (university) organization. A scholarly interpretation of this organizational culture is enriched greatly through the combination of Burke's guilt-purification-redemption cycle, which both contextualizes students' narrative performances and accesses students' "hidden" subcultural organization, with Bantz's interpretive framework. Indeed, because Burke's dramatistic approach recognizes the hierarchic, mystery-laden nature of organizational culture (in the current study, the "strangeness" between students and the university administration), its theoretical vocabulary enables us to see how the performances of the "roommate's death" rumor, a subcultural symbolic form, creates, maintains, and transforms cultural meanings and expectations concerning the hierarchic disjunctions between the university administration and the students. Collectively, the combination of these two frameworks allows for a more nuanced interpretation of organizational rumor than each framework might achieve separately.

In the students' performances of the rumor, variations in the manner of death of the roommate serve different functions. In the rumor in which the manner of death is not specified, the nebulous manner of death allows students to "play" with the idea of killing their respective roommates who may be sources of tension. In another version of the rumor, the roommate's suicide creates the perfect scenario in which the surviving roommate "suffers" and deserves compensation. Both versions serve to purge hierarchic guilt through victimage of the roommate (scapegoating) or the self (mortification).

Students' narratives about the "roommate's death" rumor reveal various organizational meanings and organizational expectations. Often narrative performances are contextualized during "times of stress" such as "finals week," which may exascerbate tensions between roommates. Such contexts, when coupled with the ambiguous "truth" of the rumor, create opportunities for the reproduction of collective sensemaking. Collective performances have an "episodic" quality and follow particular expectations (Bantz, 1993). The role of the rumor's initiator carries an obligation to present evidence; a preferred form of which is "personal knowledge," which is presented in a brief argument style. In particular, students' performance create plausible extrapolations that seek to demonstrate the rumor's truth, such as explaining why the rumor cannot be found in "official" sources, like student handbooks.

Students' narratives about the rumor specify "the administration" as the agent responsible for granting the rumor's "4.0." Such narratives reflect the "mystery" that arises from the social distinctions in the academic hierarchy (Burke, 1969). These narratives attribute a variety of motives to the university administration. In narratives dealing with the "unofficial status" of the rumor, students' narratives attempt to create a plausible extrapolation through the attribution of motives that include governance and service. Additionally, students' narratives also attempt to scapegoat the administration by attributing motives that are inconsistent with the welfare of students. In so doing, the students' narratives also use a strategy of mortification. In using these strategies of scapegoating and mortification, students' narratives serve a cathartic function, including the strategic use of "bodily images" that are analogies for excess pride, and pity (Burke, 1959, 1969).

Implications of the Study

The current study has several implications for studying rumors in other organizations. First, it demonstrates the resonance between dramatism and Bantz's interpretive framework and suggests this combined method would be a useful one for studying other rumors in various organizational contexts. Second, the examination of this "sick" rumor suggests that the assessment of the "health" of organizations might be approached through the study of organizational rumors. The content and performance of rumors might be indications of problematic aspects of organizational life (e.g., reoccurring periods of stress, mystification of managers). Prevalent and persistent rumors may be indications of widely held collective anxieties or tensions. The widespread, persistent nature of the rumor "If your roommate dies, you get a 4.0" speaks to the anxiety of students at many universities; however, the continual collective sense-making serves to fight the anxiety. Thus, the continuation of the rumor might be interpreted as an indication of "health."

A rumor's *type* also may have implications for the "health" of an organization. Thus, a wish-fulfilling rumor or rumors derived from anxieties and fears, such as the rumor in the current study, may be less problematic than "wedge-driving" rumors that express aggression or hatred (see Knapp, 1944). Future research might explore the use of the current study's interpretive framework to examine different types of rumor within organizations. The prevalence of particular types of rumors could be revealing in terms of subcultural clashes.

Finally, the "health" of organizations might be examined in terms of the *management* of rumor. For example, one response to the rumor "If your roommate dies, you get a 4.0" has been to *deny* that the rumor is "true" (see Kapferer, 1990). However, a cultural approach to the management of rumor could examine the strategies by which members of various subcultures within an organization manage the rumor. Alternatively, studies might examine the strategies for "managing" different types of rumors.

Notes

1. This magazine was supplied by Joseph Ayala, a former Loyola Marymount University student.
2. Brunvand (1989) discusses "the suicide rule" as an "urban legend" and notes variability in terms of the roommate's death.
3. Rumor research focuses on topics including wars (e.g. Knapp, 1944), race riots (e.g., Knopf, 1975), public opinion (e.g., Peterson & Gist, 1951), commerce (e.g., Koenig, 1985), and organizations (e.g., Davis, 1953a, 1969).
4. The current study is similar in orientation to Goodall, Wilson, and Waagen's (1986) study of performance appraisal interviews. The authors focus on a mystery-inspired hierarchy, that eventuates in the symbolic "kill."
5. Bantz (1993) uses the term "temporality" to analyze the pacing, flow, and frequency of messages.
6. Bantz (1993) uses the term "architecture" to analyze the structuring of space in documents, including the architecture of buildings and the order of arguments in messages.

7. Mike Farkash and Christy Mullis were instrumental in accessing the "Legs Urbano" feature area on urban legends, as well as a related bulletin board on *America Online*. My ignorance of proper ways to cite data collected from the Internet resulted in errors resulting in not noting the "address" or "path." When the journal editor requested that I obtain the addresses, I was unable to find the data (possibly because it ceased to exist on the Internet) as well as the address. However, I did locate three related Internet locations on 16 October 1998 ("College Legends," 1998; Taff, 1998; "Urban Legends Reference Pages," 1998).

8. Bantz (1993) uses the term "organizational communication culture" as a way to signal "the centrality of communicative processes in constituting the culture that is an organization" (p. 32).

9. The stereotypical form (Shibutani, 1966) of the rumor is generally "progressive," and specifically "syllogistic," in that the rumor takes the "if-then" formation (Burke, 1931). In overlaying content onto form, note that the "if" (antecedent) concerns roommates, while the "then" (consequent) implicates the action to be taken by the administration. The "syllogistic progression" guides "the arrows of our desire [to be] turned in a certain direction" (Burke, 1931, p. 124).

10. Knapp's (1944) taxonomy of rumors delineates three types of rumor, each of which "expresses" and "gratifies" the emotional needs of the collective: (a) the "pipe dream" or "wish rumor," which expresses hope; (b) the "bogie rumor," which is derived from anxieties and fears; and (c) "wedge-driving" or "aggression rumors," that are motivated from aggression or hatred. The expressions of wish-fulfillment and hostility constitute two forms of Knapp's (1944) taxonomy of rumors, and thus suggest that this rumor is an example of a *hybrid* form of rumor (Ngka, 1977).

11. Burke (1984b) discusses the theological history of the "'graded series' of sins" as a form of "moral arithmetic" (p. 221).

12. Burke (1966) uses the pyramid image in reference to "terministic pyramids" in the discussion of "entitlement." The pyramid is also used to discuss the hierarchic motive's "range of mountings" (Burke, 1969, p. 308). Discussions of hierarchy implicate the entire guilt-purification-redemption cycle (Burke, 1984a).

13. The administration is prohibited against violating motives of *governance* and *service* (Burke, 1984b, p. 358), as would be the case by presenting students with "morbid thought[s]," which connote the unhealthy, the diseased, and the gruesome (Guralnik, 1980, p. 925). Thus, morbid thoughts are symbolically related to death, which is the "dialectical opposite" of life (Burke, 1952, p. 370). To include such thoughts in "student guidelines" is inappropriate in that such guidelines represent appropriate conduct for student *life*.

14. Burke's (1959) discussion of catharsis—drawing on Aristotle's *Poetics*—and the use of bodily imagery extends well beyond the current study's scope. That is, the "body" refers to not only the human body, but also the "'world's body' (the natural scene), and the body politic, which includes the 'whole range of personal and social relations'" (p. 338). The current study draws on the realms of the human body and the body politic. More specifically, Burke (1959) discusses the purging of the emotions *pity, fear,* and *pride*. Bodily images and bodily processes are used as symbolic analogies that are expressed, and which are part of the process of catharsis.

References

Allport, G. W., & Postman, L. (1947). *The psychology of rumor.* New York: Henry Holt.

Bantz, C. R. (1993). *Understanding organizations: Interpreting organizational communication cultures.* Columbia, SC: University of South Carolina Press.

Blankenship, J., Murphy, E., & Rosenwasser, M. (1974). Pivotal terms in the early works of Kenneth Burke. *Philosophy and Rhetoric, 7,* 1–24.

Bormann, E. G., Pratt, J., & Putnam, L. (1978). Power, authority, and sex: Male response to female leadership. *Communication Monographs, 45,* 119–155.

Braddom, K. (1995). Meet your new roomie!: Will you be soul mates or rue mates? *U., The National College Magazine,* 7.

Brown, M. H. (1990). Defining stories in organizations: Characteristics and functions. In J. A. Anderson (Ed.) *Communication yearbook 13* (pp. 162–190). Newbury Park, CA: Sage.

Brunvand, J. H. (1989). *Curses! broiled again!: The hottest urban legends going.* New York: Norton.

Brunvand, J. H. (1981). *The vanishing hitchhiker: American urban legends and their meaning.* New York: Norton.

Burke, K. (1989). *On symbols and society.* (J. R. Gusfield, Ed.). Chicago: University of Chicago Press.

Burke, K. (1984a). *Permanence and change* (3rd. ed.). Berkeley: University of California Press.

Burke, K. (1984b). *Attitudes toward history* (3rd ed.). Berkeley: University of California Press.

Burke, K. (1969). *A rhetoric of motives.* Berkeley: University of California Press.

Burke, K. (1966). *Language as symbolic action.* Berkeley: University of California Press.

Burke, K. (1959). On catharsis, or resolution. *The Kenyon Review, 21,* 337–375.

Burke, K. (1952). Thanatopsis for critics: A brief thesaurus of deaths and dyings. *Essays in Criticism, 2,* 369–375.

Burke, K. (1931). *Counter-statement.* Berkeley: University of California Press.

Butterfield, F. (1995, May 29). Harvard student stabs roommate to death. *New York Times,* 6.

College legends. (1998, October 16). http://www.whatnext.com/articles/urbanlegend/ul-college.html.

Conrad, C. (1985). Chrysanthemums and swords: A reading of contemporary organizational communication theory and research. *Southern Speech Communication Journal, 50,* 189–200.

Davis, K. (1953a). A method of studying communication patterns in organizations. *Personnel Psychology, 6,* 301–312.

Davis, K. (1953b). Management communication and the grapevine. *Harvard Business Review, 31*(5), 43–49.

Davis, K. (1969, April). Grapevine communication among lower and middle managers. *Personnel Journal,* 269–272.

Davis, K. (1978). Methods for studying informal communication. *Journal of Communication, 28,* 112–116.

Degh, L. (1969). "The Roommate's Death" and related dormitory stories in formation. *Indiana Folklore, 2,* 55–74.

Doyle, W. (1983). Academic work. *Review of Educational Research, 53,* 159–199.

Duncan, H. D. (1985). *Communication and social order.* New Brunswick, NJ: Transaction.

Dundes, A. (1966). Metafolklore and oral literary criticism. *The Monist, 50,* 505–516.

Elton, C. F., & Bate, W. S. (1966). The effect of housing policy on grade-point average. *Journal of College Student Personnel, 7,* 73–77.

Evans, E. D., & Engelberg, R. A. (1988). Student perceptions of school grading. *Journal of Research and Development in Education, 21,* 45–54.

Goodall, Jr., H. L., Wilson, G. L., & Waagen, C. L. (1986). The performance appraisal interview: An interpretive reassessment. *Quarterly Journal of Speech, 72,* 74–87.

Guralnik, D. B. (Ed.). (1980). *Webster's new world dictionary* (2nd college ed.). New York: Simon and Schuster.

Jorgensen-Earp, C. R., & Staton, A. Q. (1993). Student metaphors for the college freshman experience. *Communication Education, 42,* 123–141.

Kapferer, J. (1990). *Rumors: Uses, interpretations, and images.* New Brunswick: Transaction.

Knapp, R. H. (1944). A psychology of rumor. *Public Opinion Quarterly, 8,* 22–37.

Knopf, T. (1975). *Rumors, race and riots.* New Brunswick, NJ: Transaction Books.

Koenig, F. (1985). *Rumor in the marketplace: The social psychology of commercial hearsay.* Dover, MA: Auburn House.

Lincoln, Y. S., & Guba, E. G. (1985). *Naturalistic inquiry.* Beverly Hills: Sage.

McGrath, L. (1996). *Symbolic convergence within the roommate suicide death myth.* Unpublished undergraduate thesis, Loyola Marymount University, Los Angeles, California.

Mehren, E. (1995, May 29). Two premed students die, 3rd woman hurt in Harvard murder-suicide. *Los Angeles Times,* p. A15.

Mullen, P. B. (1972). Modern legend and rumor theory. *Journal of the Folklore Institute, 9,* 94–109.

Nkpa, N. K. (1977). Rumors of mass poisoning in Biafra. *Public Opinion Quarterly, 41,* 332–346.

Nudd, T. R. (1965). Satisfied and dissatisfied college roommates. *Journal of College Student Personnel, 6,* 161–164.

Pacanowksy, M. E., & O'Donnell-Trujillo, N. (1983). Organizational communication as cultural performance. *Communication Monographs, 50,* 126–147.

Pace, T. (1970). Roommate dissatisfaction in residence halls. *Journal of College Student Personnel, 11,* 144–147.

Palladino, J. J., & Tryon, G. S. (1978). Have the problems of entering freshmen changed? *Journal of College Student Personnel, 19,* 313–316.

Peterson, W. A., & Gist, N. P. (1951). Rumor and public opinion. *American Journal of Sociology, 57,* 159–167.

Press, A., & Rosenberg, D. (1995, June 12). Death at an early age. *Newsweek,* 69.

Rosecan, A. S., Goldberg, R. L., & Wise, T. N. (1992). Psychiatrically hospitalized college students: A pilot study. *Journal of American College Health, 41,* 11–15.

Rosnow, R. L., & Fine, G. A. (1976). *Rumor and gossip: The social psychology of hearsay.* New York: Elsevier.

Rueckert, W. H. (1982). *Kenneth Burke and the drama of human relations* (2nd ed.). Berkeley: University of California Press.

Scherer, C., & Wygant, N. S. (1982). Sound beginnings support freshmen transition into university life. *Journal of College Student Personnel, 23,* 378–383.

Shibutani, T. (1966). *Improvised news: A sociological study of rumor.* Indianapolis: Bobbs-Merrill.

Spradley, J. P. (1979). *The ethnographic interview.* New York: Holt, Rinehart & Winston.

Stohl, C., & Redding, W. C. (1987). Messages and message exchange processes. In F. M. Jablin, L. L. Putnam, K. H. Roberts, and L. W. Porter (Eds.) *Handbook of organizational communication* (pp. 451–502). Beverly Hills: Sage.

Taff, J. (1998, October 16). College myth about roommate death permeates campuses. *The Minnesota Daily* [online]. http://www.daily.umn.edu.daily/1998/08/17/news/dead/

Tompkins, P. K., Fisher, J. Y., Infante, D. A., & Tompkins, E. L. (1977). Kenneth Burke and the inherent characteristics of formal organizations: A field study. *Speech Monographs, 42,* 135–142.

Urban legends reference pages: College (Grade Expectations). (1998, October 16). http://snopes.simplenet.com/college/regulate/asuicide.htm

Urbano, L. (1997, June 17). Urban legends [bulletin board]. America Online.

Waldo, M. (1984). Roommate communication as related to students' personal and social adjustment. *Journal of College Student Personnel, 25,* 39–44.

Weinberg, S. B., & Eich, R. K. (1978). Fighting fire with fire: Establishment of a rumor control center. *Communication Quarterly, 26*(3), 26–31.

FOLLOW-UP QUESTIONS AND EXPLORATION OF POINTS

1. How does organizational culture theory relate to other theories of interpersonal and intergroup communication? How is it similar and how does it differ?

2. Consider an organization in which you are currently involved. What symbols exist that demonstrate the culture of your organization? Which of these symbols tend to be more communicative in nature? Do similar symbols exist in other organizations, yet differ in interpretation?

3. In this article, rumor helped people make sense of uncertain situations and become an important part of an academic organizational culture. How do different forms of communication help you and your fellow organizational members cope with organizational uncertainty? How are these forms of communication a part of the culture of your organization?

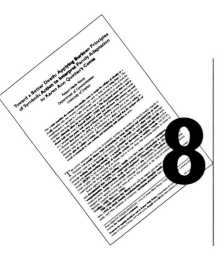

8 Drama of Life, Death, and Personhood

The cases of Karen Ann Quinlan and, more recently, Terri Schiavo, tragically attracted national attention to ethical dilemmas regarding health care. In part because neither Karen nor Terri were able to speak for themselves, they each became the center of family, medical, and legal dramas about their care and, ultimately, their personhood. The following article (Kenny, 2001), illustrates one way in which an abstract theory of communication, Dramatism, can be used to understand real, even tragic, circumstances.

Background of Dramatism

Although Dramatism, as a theory, is also associated with the work of sociologist Erving Goffman (1959), the version of the theory used in Kenny's article is that of scholar Kenneth Burke. "By common consent Kenneth Burke ranks as the foremost rhetorician in the twentieth century" (Golden, Berquist, & Coleman, 1976, pg. 235). He was a prolific writer and his ideas have had widespread influence. It is impossible to summarize his ideas in this brief format, so we will content ourselves with providing an overview of a very small sampling of Burke's concepts. Burke was concerned with understanding an author's or a speaker's motives (Crable, 2000). For Burke, the concept of "motives" refers to completed action (Golden et al, 1976). The form of action that Burke's ideas are most commonly used to understand is symbolic action, or language (Fox, 2002). For Burke, the completion of linguistic action (or its motive) was frequently "identification," or perceived similarity between speaker and audience. The dramatistic pentad of act, scene, agent, agency and purpose is probably Burke's most recognizable analytical tool for understanding motives and identification (Crable, 2000).

> In a rounded statement about motives, you must have some word that names the *act* (names that took place, in thought or deed), and another that names the *scene* (the background of the act, the situation in which it occurred); also, you must indicate what person or kind of person (*agent*) performed the act, what means or instruments he used (*agency*), and the *purpose*. (Burke, 1950, pg. xv)

By analyzing the part of the Quinlan's communication drama, Kenny is able to highlight ways in which Karen Quinlan's family shifted their understanding of the role she played in their family's script.

Article Structure

Journal articles presenting rhetorical analysis follow a different structure than quantitative and qualitative research articles. One of the biggest differences you will notice between Kenny's article and others we have examined is that it does not have either a Methods section or a Results section. Instead, the article is divided into three basic sections. The beginning of the article through to the first major heading is the introduction. In this section, Kenny justifies his focus on the case of Karen Ann Quinlan as a way of understanding meaning-making in relation to illness. The second part of the article, forming the bulk of the paper, begins with the heading "Dramatic Collapse: Case of Karen Quinlan" (p. 164) and ends with the Conclusion heading (p. 175). This part of the article has three sub-sections. In the first (headed "Medical Emergency as Disruption of Routine," p. 164), Kenny identifies the central claim of the paper; "this change in the way that Karen is viewed [from person to body] is a rite of passage that the Quinlan family in particular undergoes" (p. 165). He also introduces Dramatism as the theoretical framework he will use for his analysis and justifies its relevance. In the second sub-section (pp. 166–170), Kenny uses Dramatistic concepts to examine the language used to name Karen's circumstances and behavior. In the final sub-section (pp. 170–175) he looks at how those language practices functioned to change the way Karen is viewed, especially by her family. In the Conclusion, Kenny summarizes his analysis and discusses how it is relevant to health care practitioners.

Distinctive Points

One of the differences between rhetorical scholarship and qualitative or quantitative research is in where the data used for analysis comes from. Rhetorical scholarship usually uses texts that are already in existence, such as speeches, songs, advertisements, or, in this case, books. In addition, it is most common for rhetorical analysis to focus on persuasive texts rather than other forms of communication. Qualitative and quantitative research usually, though not always, involves collecting the examples of communication (data) that are analyzed. This research tends to be more focused on present behavior/communication than on texts produced in the past. It also encompasses not only persuasion but many other kinds of communication as well.

Kenny's article is somewhat unusual in that he applies rhetorical analysis to health communication: a topic usually studied with qualitative or quantitative research (although Weldon, 2001, also uses Burkian analysis in a health-related context). Although Burke defines rhetoric as both using and studying persuasion (1950), Kenny argues that Dramatism can be used as a "theory of interpersonal action" (pg. 363). This paper, then, serves as an illustration of how Dramatism might function to understand interpersonal as well as rhetorical texts.

References

Burke, K. (1950). *A rhetoric of motives.* New York: Prentice-Hall, Inc.

Crable, B. (2000). Burke's perspective on perspectives: Grounding dramatism in the representative anecdote. *Quarterly Journal of Speech, 86,* 318–333.

Fox, C. (2002). Beyond the "Tyranny of the Real": Revisiting Burke's pentad as research method for professional communication. *Technical Communication Quarterly, 11,* 365–388.

Goffman, E. (1959). *The presentation of self in everyday life.* Garden City, NY: Doubleday.

Golden, J. L., Berquist, G. F., & Coleman, W. E. (1976). *The rhetoric of western thought, 2nd edition.* Dubuque, IA: Kendall/Hunt Publishing Company.

Kenny, R. W. (2001). Toward a better death: Applying Burkean principles of symbolic action to interpret family adaptation to Karen Ann Quinlan's coma. *Health Communication, 13,* 363–385.

Weldon, R. A. (2001). The rhetorical construction of the predatorial virus: A Burkian Analysis of nonfiction accounts of the ebola virus. *Qualitative Health Research, 11,* 5–25.

Toward a Better Death: Applying Burkean Principles of Symbolic Action to Interpret Family Adaptation to Karen Ann Quinlan's Coma

Robert Wade Kenny
Department of Communication
University of Dayton

This article considers the manner that families come to accept the collapse of identity in a family member who has entered a medical crisis with no hope of returning from it. The transformation is regarded as a "right of passage" and is characterized in terms of both the conditions that bring about resistance to the passage as well as the sorts of symbolic activities that ultimately allow the transformation to occur. The theoretical source that is used to discuss both these issues is Kenneth Burke's (1969) theory of Dramatism, regarded herein as a template that guides both interpersonal action and experience. The primary text used to illustrate these points is the story of Karen Ann Quinlan, a young woman who fell into persistent vegetative state in 1975, as told by her parents. A general goal of this article is to illustrate some of the characteristics of Dramatism as a theory of interpersonal action, especially after the collapse of routine. More particularly, it is hoped that the analysis will aid health professionals in sense making and interacting with families in crisis.

This article examines the function of symbolic activity in the midst of a family health tragedy to illustrate how people whose sense of meaning has been disrupted and scattered by an unexpected event come to a consensus of meaning, not only through talk and other forms of strategic message making, but also through the symbolic potential of actions and objects not typically associated with message-making strategies. It is hoped that the discussion will attune health care professionals (HCPs) to the broader range of symbolic activity that arises as families, friends, and HCPs come to grips with the meaning of an illness, and to accept what that meaning implies, in terms of consequences for them and for the patient.

Some aspects of meaning making in health crisis have been extensively investigated, and it is well documented that HCPs who competently present relevant information to patients enhance "comprehension, understanding, recall, and compliance" (Thompson, 2000, p. 26). To the extent communication occurs between people, however, it is also necessary for medical practitioners to enhance their capacity to recognize the meanings of symbolic activity produced by patients and their families. Limited attention has been given to this premise in the area of treatment termination (Erstling, 1985; Germino, 1998).

This article assumes that illness is not only an organic process but also a rite of passage (Joralemon, 1999) in which identity transformation occurs alongside family and patient counseling, treatment, and even cessation of treatment. Joralemon presumed that a familiarity with this process of

From HEALTH COMMUNICATION, 13(4), by Robert Wade Kenny. Copyright © 2001 by Lawrence Erlbaum Associates, Inc. Reprinted by permission.

Requests for reprints should be sent to Robert Wade Kenny, Department of Communication, 300 College Park, University of Dayton, Dayton, OH 45469-2376. E-mail: kenny@rider.stjoe.udayton.edu passage and its watershed moments would enhance a HCP's ability to experience a medical crisis alongside the family of the patient.

It would be naive to claim that HCPs necessarily require this sort of information, for they might easily have deeper insights into such issues, as a result of the significant exposure they have to the sort of phenomenon that are described in this article. However, it is talk about such phenomenon, and not exposure alone, that gives HCPs the ability to make sense of their experiences. This article is intended to contribute to such a conversation. It arises from the belief that familiarity is by itself a poor prophylactic against the depression, anxiety, and frustration that is associated with involvement in medically unresponsive cases—it holds that the quality of analysis brought to such situations can significantly enhance the HCP's ability to emotionally and practically function in such environments, without alienating him or her from the experience to accomplish that result.

The tragedy to be examined is the painful narrative of suffering and loss told by Joe and Julia Quinlan. Their daughter, Karen, entered a quasi-comatose condition characterized by limited and spastic neuromuscular activity and referred to as *persistent vegetative state*. As Karen's family went through the agonizing process of accepting her condition and dealing with it, she became a major public figure, used by others to exemplify a growing concern over the issue of protracted, technological continuance of life, which has been referred to elsewhere as a rhetorical icon (Kenny, 2000b).[1]

Consequently, she was a cover story for both *Time* (The Right to Live—Or Die, 1975) and *Newsweek* (Clark et al., 1975), and her case is now a primary reference in the extant euthanasia literature, still regularly discussed in journals of medicine and law (Angell, 1993, 1996; Frader, 1996; Kinky, Korein, Panigrahy, Pikkes, & Goode, 1994; Stevens, 1996), and regularly cited in cases heard by the Supreme Court (*Cruzan v. Director*, 1990; *Vacco v. Quill*, 1997). Karen Quinlan entered the hospital as a person and she left as a body, even though there was no significant change in her physical condition during that time. The process by which her family came to accept this transformation can be regarded as a rite of passage, and by examining it in this article, I hope to illustrate the logic and grammar of such rites of passage for family members.

Dramatic Collapse: Case of Karen Quinlan

Medical Emergency as Disruption of Routine

At 2:00 a.m., April 15, 1975, Joseph and Julia Quinlan received a call from Newton Memorial hospital. Their daughter, Karen, was unconscious and in serious condition. Earlier, after light drinking at Falconer's tavern, she seemed incoherent and had been taken home. Her condition deteriorated rapidly, and shortly after friends placed her on her bed, she stopped breathing. Rushed to the hospital and placed on a resuscitator, it was but hours before Julia Quinlan watched doctors give her daughter a tracheotomy and connect her to a respirator, which regularly buzzed alarms when she choked:

> The first time that happened, Karen raised way up in the bed and her arms flew out and her eyes popped open, and she looked like she was in so much pain I was scared out of my mind. (Quinlan, Quinlan, & Battelle, 1977, p. 20)

Other than these spasms, however, Karen remained unconscious for several days. Then she opened her eyes:

> But she didn't recognize us. She was staring right through us. A nurse placed her open hand a few feet from Karen's face, and slowly moved it forward until it almost touched her nose, and Karen blinked. But when the hand moved to one side, Karen's eyes didn't follow it. . . . In a way, that was the most disheartening development of all, watching her eyes look into space, or move all around the room, as though she were looking and looking for something—and finally forcing ourselves to recognize that she couldn't see. (Quinlan et al., 1977, pp. 23–24)

Thus begins the remarkable story of the Quinlan family tragedy. It speaks of Karen as a young girl under emergency medical care and subject to the sort of attention that medical practitioners, family, and friends bring to such situations. However, she will not maintain her status as a person in need of heroic treatment, nor will she retain her identity as a daughter caught up in a whirlwind medical emergency. A point will come when family, physicians, and friends will state that Karen is no longer present in the body that is cared for at the hospital. They will do this regardless of the fact that some sorts of evidence can be gathered to say otherwise. This change in the way that Karen is viewed is a rite of passage that the Quinlan family in particular undergoes, and the following pages chronicle some of its major moments.

Whereas the following events are interpreted as they are presented, it is necessary to briefly address the theoretical framework used. That model is Burkean Dramatism (1969), for which we can get a ready feeling if we imagine the Quinlan family as characters in a play. If that were the case, Karen would be an actress who used certain equipment, appeared in certain scenes, performed certain actions, and had certain goals. Burkean Dramatism is based on the premise that real-life experience has much of this dramatistic quality to it and argues that people relate to each other and are dependent on each other, in much the way that stage actors are codependent to act out a script. Thus, Mary-Ellen, Karen's sister (coagent), might enter (action) Karen's room (scene) to talk about (action) whether Karen also wants to go to a rock concert (purpose), because Karen owns the car (agency) they would use to drive (action) there. Even so trivial an event contains the acts, scenes, agents, agencies, and purposes that are the elements of Kenneth Burke's Dramatism (he called those elements the *pentad*).

Certainly, Karen's personhood is more than the sum total of all dramatic descriptions that could be given of her, but it would be hard to say exactly what that extra is. Burke (1969) did not mean to argue that life is a hollow facade, rather that we tend to speak dramatically and live dramatically because life must have some sort of template for us to engage in it successfully with each other. Burke (1969) tried to convince us that Dramatism is the template unwittingly used.

Dramatism allows us some sense of what occurs to a family when someone is abruptly removed from it, for the consequence is much like what happens when an actor goes missing from a play. Under that circumstance, it is not uncommon for the play to completely fold, and this is why there is an understudy in theater drama—directors know that the play can only go on if all the characters are there to take their places. A similar phenomenon occurs in life, so that people are unable to position their own acts, scenes, agents, agencies, and purposes unless their coagents are able to take their places alongside them. An operating room, for example, requires a team including surgeons, nurses, orderlies, and anesthetists; and it would be quite a challenge to perform the same event should any of these characters go missing. Moreover, later, when the surgical team leaves the hospital, each member will traverse to a personal life that also is composed of characters whose presence is required to make that particular drama possible.

The existential drama is also profoundly distinct from theater, however, because the drama of life is not contained inside another drama in which we might rest to endure. If a stage play fails because a person is not present to play his or her role, the other members of the troupe can simply step down from the stage and back into their lives while they wait for another acting opportunity. If a life drama breaks, however, there is nowhere to step out, to await a new opportunity, or to make sense of the event. The profundity of this issue only reaches us when we realize that stage actors leave the stage physically but at the same time leave it psychically. It would be a great actor who could completely enter a stage role and a disturbed one who could not then get out of it. Actors on the stage of life do not have the luxury of a parenthetical psychic life that characters on stage do. For the person in real-life drama, there is no way out, physically or psychically. Therefore, although we may benefit from recognizing the dramatic dimensions of abrupt changes in family dynamics, we can also benefit by recognizing that there is something else much more powerful that is lost when a person goes, something that may be impossible for us to fully grasp when it happens in someone else's family, and that we might only look reasonably on with reverence and empathy.

Few changes in the script of reality can alter things more radically than a life threatening medical emergency. Therefore, it is not surprising that Karen's admission to the hospital had a remarkable impact on the Quinlan family. Most of their everyday and familiar patterns were disrupted as they attempted to include this medical emergency into the lived story of their lives. There is a general social script for enduring the hospitalization of a loved one, which includes hospital visits, consultations with doctors, arguments with insurance companies, and the like. However, in the Quinlan case, it gradually becomes clear that something other than a medical emergency is occurring, and the family begins to face an even more radical and unusual situation. As that happens, significant communicative efforts and communicative failures begin to occur, and there are two primary reasons: (a) Family members suffer from a general inability to face the transformation that has occurred in Karen and are emotionally unwilling to face the changes that will now have to occur in them, and (b) the script that organizes family actions around a coma is vague at best, particularly in cases like Karen's, in which the body of the person remains animated. With this in mind, as this article proceeds, I achieve two goals: (a) I suggest a manner of thinking about family resistance to identity transformation, one which gives less claim to the classic interpretation of this resistance as denial, by focusing on what it means to be with others, and (b) I describe symbolic activities that occur as the family is guided toward the adaptation that they originally cannot accept.

Change in the Medical Event as Change in Patient Identity from a Medical Emergency to a Medical Condition

Regardless, whether people identify Karen as a patient in crisis or a body past living, they are making epistemic claims. Such contradictory claims can be made because it is typical of language to be both *constituting* (name making) and *dialectical* (name contesting). Burke (1969) called such claims *constitutions,* and he identified two types: (a) *descriptive* constitutions, which name things, and (b), *declared* constitutions, which proclaim responsibilities.[2] In that regard, it is worth noting that the proclamation of either type of constitution implies at the same time the application of its partner. Therefore, in this case, (a) if Karen is a patient in crisis (descriptive constitution), then we must apply the best emergency care (declared constitution), but (b) if she is a body past living (descriptive constitution), then we must bring an end to extraordinary measures (declared constitution).

Of course, Karen could be one or the other, depending on how you look at it, and this exemplifies what Burke (1969) meant by the "ambiguity of substance" (p. 75), a quality of experience that always allows epistemic claims to be contested. In Karen's case, one cannot be certain whether she remains a person or has moved on to be a body—she has that sort of ambiguous identity that is not unfamiliar to medical practitioners. It is because of this ambiguity, however, that an argument can emerge as to which Karen "is." Once that has been determined as a descriptive constitution or substance, then families and physicians will implicitly have come to terms with what should be done as their declared constitution or motive. In that light, Burke's (1969) words are highly instructive, for he said, "men induce themselves and others to act by devices that deduce, 'let us' from 'we must' . . . and 'we must' from 'it *is*'—for only by assertions as to how things are can we finally substantiate a judgment" (p. 337). For Burke (1969), "Questions of motivation come to a head in questions of substantiation and transubstantiation" (p. 320), and consequently, "'Substance' and 'motivation' are convertible terms" (p. 376).

Constituting is not, however, random—the act, such as a diagnostic act, is an attempt to adequately represent the circumstances that have appeared, in terms of what is and what must be done. Karen's coma, as an "embodied resistance," has erupted from the recalcitrant (Burke, 1984b, p. 255) Earth—it is a physically undeniable condition that transforms the order of things, whether she or anyone else would have it that way, and it must be named adequately to be handled. As things develop, for example, the physician will say that Karen is a coma victim, and this will inform his relationship to her. Others who have known Karen in much different ways, however, will be less willing to acknowledge that identity and more preoccupied with her former role as a partner in their lives. For the physician, Karen's coma initiates a medical drama that calls out the players in a hospital environment. For the family, the coma brings an abrupt collapse to a drama that was previously stable, familiar, and even certain—the intersections between Karen's life and the lives of all these others have been radically shifted because of a condition that must be faced. Therefore, it is ironic and significant that her medical condition provides the greater part of her dramatic identity for the HCP even as it removes much of her dramatic identity for all who knew her before the accident.

Karen's family, friends, and physicians first hold that she has entered the hospital as a person in crisis. For her to maintain this status, however, medicine must be able to intercede on her behalf and guide her back to the relationships that existed prior to the accident. In that light, Heidegger (1962) described a theory of care that suggests that people will live in the presence of "absent" others, both awaiting them and tending to their lives while they await. That awaiting is predicated, however, on a return and a tendency to resist the fateful change that circumstances have brought to light. Burke (1984a) called this resistance "cultural lag" (p. 40), and we see some demonstration of it occurring in Karen's family. We will also see the way that an inadequate constitution fails to endure, and thus, how it is that people change; for as the Quinlans attempt to maintain their view of Karen as a person in crisis, their capacity to relate to her and their capacity to relate to others diminishes. As they and others face medicine's inability to bring her back, there develops a transformation so that her case is no longer a medical emergency, but a medical condition. At the same time, she loses her identity as a person-patient and becomes a body kept alive, with no one in it.

At first, the tendency for people to resist this transformation in Karen was profound. Karen's sister, for example, recalls that Karen, "blinked once, and she looked right at me, and I was sure she recognized me. I will always think she recognized me" (Quinlan et al., 1977, p. 25), whereas her brother was so deeply embodied[3] in Karen that he "dances an attitude" (Burke, 1967b, p. 9):

> John had come in after Mary-Ellen's visit, and when he saw Karen, his color drained away as though someone had slapped him across the face with whitewash. He was physically ill. He rushed out of the room. (Quinlan et al., 1977, p. 19)

The Quinlans document numerous examples of this surreal quality in their narrative, so that a reader senses how much more readily they would believe in a medical miracle than accept the reality of the existential loss that is before them. As forthcoming quotes show, even months after the tragedy struck, Joe Quinlan would be less amazed if he walked into the hospital and found his daughter brushing her hair than he was every day that he found her still in a coma. To a family member, the death of a loved one might make no more sense than the suspension of the laws of gravity or distance, because human experience has no line that clearly separates such material realities from the existential environment (lives) in which we experience them—in day-to-day living, one is written on top of the other. Consequently, existential objects, such as people (intentionally speaking beings), can seem more real to us than physical objects, like stones—and this makes perfect sense in that the way we first come to know the stone as an abstract object is through its presentation to us alongside the constituting acts of others.

In a forthcoming article (Kenny, in press), I argue that fiction is particularly distinguished from reality in that story-worlds allow the structural principles of narrative to overshadow the laws of physics, so that in fiction the best predictor of what will happen to a character is not the natural imposition of the obstacles that are placed before him or her, but rather it is the righteousness of his character and the structure of the dramatic progression. This can be demonstrated simply by turning off the TV 4 min before the end of any movie and telling your friend watching that the main character did fall from the bridge and die. She will not believe it, because she implicitly recognizes that natural law is discounted or controlled in fiction, to correspond with a sense of the right, or the true. If Burke's (1969) claim that we live our lives dramatistically is accurate, however, then there would also be in lived experience a regular tendency to act as if life, like fiction, were guided or protected by the guarantees that protect the characters of fiction. Such a conviction can leave loved ones in a state of profound disbelief when tragedy strikes, because they cannot accept that natural law alone can impose such tyranny on their worlds, causing events and ruling their outcomes—they are disposed, by virtue of the way people script drama onto the natural world, to fixate on the story-like progression of their lives as the criteria that should override and control any physical crisis they experience.

More generally, dramatic interpersonal reality is the condition in which material reality comes to be recognized and experienced. Even a moment's reflection will provide evidence that the speech of others enters us in a manner that no entity ever can—in fact, entities only enter us as things, when they are given to us through the language of others, a language that is oriented around characterizing the drama that is lived. This speech of others (symbolicity in general, that is to say) is the fundamental reality that engages our psychic life, even if the material reality that lies beneath it holds us hostage and accountable throughout the entire experience.

Karen is, thus, a part of her family, not merely in the sense that she is there alongside them. Rather, in the drama of their lives she is in them—in their past, present, and future. Her exit from the drama of their lives is an existential amputation, with a residual as persistent and enduring as the phantom limb. This is why ontological drama, literal drama, cannot be bracketed, and this is its horror. It is interesting to note that Burke (1970) provided a perfect example when he described in a poem the death of his wife: There he writes that he has outlived both her and himself; that her death, in a sense, killed him (p. 127).

Constantly scripted into being through each other's discursive eyes, our coinvolvements also habituate, as we rely on each other both to recognize and to become ourselves. Therefore, the horror that the Quinlan family encountered when Karen's eyes look about yet see nothing is that, in terms of the being of their worlds, the space that was her, through which they became and recognized their selves has been vacated. In that sense, the dissolution of the other is a dissolution of the self, a phenomenon that produces irrational, yet very understandable, reactions from loved ones.

Neither was the enigmatic pain that Karen experienced a trivial element in the floundering of the family. Of particular notice is the nonstrategic nature of Karen's moans, grimaces, and contortions, for they violate our understanding of what it means to be in pain. Thomas Ssasz (1957) distinguished between two types of pain: "one, a signal informing the ego of a danger to the body, and the other, a message requesting help from another person" (p. 88). Typical to the *aporia* that is Quinlan, her case challenges both the characterizations Ssasz used. In particular, there is no communicative meaning of pain, as Ssasz identified it—her pain is not, "a command addressed to a particular person, from whom assistance may be expected, to come and to help" (p. 89). Nevertheless, we experience it as *suffering in the other, where for me it is unpardonable and solicits me"* (O'Connor, 1987, p. 232). Consider, for example, what happened after cuff deflation—an hourly procedure that involves letting air out of a balloon inserted below the trachea. This was the only time that Karen could make sounds

> for about five minutes' time, and the nurses would say, "Why don't you talk to Karen now? She's deflated . . . ." At the beginning there was always hope that she might be able to talk back, in case she heard us. But now, when she's deflated, the only sound that came from Karen's mouth was a series of loud groans. As though she were in terrible pain. She would just roll her head back and groan. (Quinlan et al., 1977, p. 139)

Nevertheless, even this suffering is in the form of an aporia, for doctors denied it offered evidence of a persisting and tortured agent in the daughter's body (Quinlan et al., 1977, p. 82).

If we recall the earlier discussion of Burke's (1969) notion of constituting, we can see that the descriptive substance that the doctor gives to the daughter's sounds is distinct from the parents'. This difference in perspective is a critical aspect of Kenneth Burke's (1969) thought and also forms a crucial part of medical decision making in general. Bearing in mind Burke's (1969) claim that " 'substance' and 'motivation' are convertible terms" (p. 376), we can attune to the fact that the hospital had one identity and plan of action for Karen, whereas the family was developing another, expressed in the text by the mother who says she, "would always wish (Doctor) Morse would come in while she (Karen) was groaning. I just wanted him to hear it . . . . I thought then he would agree with us, that this misery had to be ended" (Quinlan et al., 1977, p. 139). Consequently, the disagreement is verbally localized around two descriptive constitutions that compete against each other (what the sound meant), but ultimately amounts to a difference in declared constitutions and intended actions (what should be done for Karen).

When people see things the same way, they tend to join forces or bond (particularly in relation to their plans). Burke (1969) called this phenomenon *consubstantiality,* and he reminded us that "a concern with substance is a concern with the problems of consubstantiality" (p. 338). In fact, it is a concern with what we may call *disubstantiality* as well, following him; for we want to suggest the equally important notion that when people do not see a thing in the same way they tend to break apart or not see themselves as a unit. When Karen makes these noises, then, we can say that the parents as a unit experience the sounds as substantially the same thing (a daughter's agony), whereas the attending physician is at a distance (di-stance) and hears the sounds as substantially something else (a body's reflex). We can diagram the difference as follows (see Figure 8.1).

The diagram shows that Joe and Julia are transparent to each other much in the manner Scheler (1973) described when he said, "Two parents stand beside the dead body of a beloved child. They feel in common the 'same' sorrow, the 'same' anguish. It is not that A feels this sorrow and B feels it also, and moreover that they both know they are feeling it. No, it is a *feeling in common*" (pp. 12–13).[4] The Quinlans in this sense are a singular entity, made into one by this feeling for Karen. Dr. Morse does not see Karen in that way, though, and is therefore not on the Quinlan team. Of course, this does not mean Dr. Morse is left out in the cold, for there are other hospital personnel who see Karen in the way he does and consequently he is able to keep his perspective while still being a member of some community, although not the Quinlan community. Should the entire world usher into the Quinlan triangle, however, Dr. Morse would find it harder to hold his view. On the other hand, consider the implications if Dr. Morse were to travel to the hospital, informing all his coworkers that he could hear the agonizing cries of the Quinlan's daughter, or better still his daughter. Most likely, he would suffer status and identity loss from them because the capacity to see things distinctly from the way the parents see them is both that which keeps him out of the Quinlan unit and at the same time within his own.

Burke's (1969) concept of consubstantiality thus reminds us that a group of factors are present whenever a person ascribes to particular epistemic claims, suggesting that a group of factors plays a part in any person's claim to know a thing: (a) the range of possible meaningful descriptions for the phenomenon being identified (e.g., Karen's sounds could not be called "tables"), (b) the accuracy and adequacy of the identification (e.g., no one suggested the groans were expressions of boredom), (c) the intention and ability to handle the thing named in a certain way, and (d) the need to take a stance from within a community to stay a part of that community.

One reason that Dr. Morse constitutes the sounds in a different way is that Karen has never been substantially a "person" in the drama of his life—she has been substantially a patient. This discrepancy, which was characterized earlier as ironic, is a general condition for some part of medicine as an anonymous institution of care, and thus amounts to a sort of necessary evil. In some ways it may be asking too much of physicians and HCPs to form personal relations with patients, for a "human" attachment means that the patient's risk is also the physician's—a choice that would leave any HCP on an emotional tightrope every day of his or her professional life. It is perhaps one of those

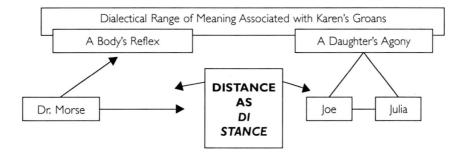

Figure 8.1. Consubstantial and Disubstantial perspectives toward Karen's groans.

moral commitments that each one must make autonomously. Nevertheless, it bears mentioning that there might often be a communicative chasm and even resistance between the HCP and the family, simply because one talks of a person, and the other a patient.

It is interesting to note that when people are on opposite teams, they tend to look at each other, whereas people on the same team tend to look instead at the third thing, which binds them transparently, so that they are closest to each other when they disregard each other's presence and orient instead toward the substantial phenomenon that they see in the same way. This is an interesting aspect of interpersonal communication that is implicit in Burke's (1969) notion of consubstantiality: One that offers some direction to HCPs in terms of how to establish relations with family members. It also provides some guidance for us as we reflect on the family's trauma in relation to Karen's illness, for although they have been previously bound to her transparently by virtue of their collective focus on the substantial reality of their family and their world, they now experience a radical rupture in that reality because the unity of existence, which is described by the consubstantial bond, has been disrupted by a break in one of the mechanisms that makes it possible—the other person.

As mentioned earlier, Karen did not live only in her body. She also lived in her family. Therefore, although this suffering is not interior to the daughter, it is of the daughter. Consequently, even though she is gone from the others in some fundamental manner, her continuing presence as a suffering body and person, who is present in them, creates a need for a new constitution that will produce actions to relieve this suffering.

Symbolic Activity in Transformation

Even Heidegger (1962) had not imagined a "change-over of an entity from Dasein's kind of Being (or life) to no-longer-Dasein" (p. 281), which did not involve "funeral rites, interment, and the cult of graves" (p. 281). Karen did not die and could not be rightfully placed within the dramatic script that is associated with a deceased loved one. Her condition, even less familiar than death, marks the degree to which families find themselves within each other because of the historic drama of their relationship. Like any parent who looks at a dead child and expects him or her to wake up at any moment, the Quinlans look at Karen; yet, they have even more reason for faith in the impossible, because Karen's body is still active, and it is not easy to deny the presence of a person in a human body that moves. The medical record states, for example, that on May 7, Karen "opens eyes when called loudly by name" (Quinlan et al., 1977, p. 84), and on May 14, is "crying with tears when mother is speaking to her" (p. 85). Therefore, she is present as an enigma with no ready status as a self, and consequently leaves her others with no ready motivational vocabulary to live into and through her. Burke (1967a) informed us that "the names for typical, recurrent social situations are not developed out of 'disinterested curiosity,' but because the names imply a command (what to expect, what to look out for)" (p. 294). The Quinlan tragedy had no name, nor did Karen; consequently, Burke (1967a) would draw our attention to the new name needed for Karen, a name which might not only explain what happened, but one which would also direct what would happen, by initiating a new drama that would allow the family to resume a meaningful relationship with their daughter and their lives.

Constituting has already been discussed and mentioned as a fundamental mechanism for organizing social action. Until this point, however, we have examined it solely in terms of the use of language to specifically name things. Now we shall examine how symbolic activity in general amounts to an articulation of substance, and how the people involved in Karen's life used that activity to transform Karen from a person into a body. This will involve both how she was articulated differently within pentadic ratios and how others enacted a new relationship with her that articulated her transformation of identity by analogic extension. We see how family members went through an ontological and an epistemological shift as they committed to a certain dramatistic constellation, one in which the various pentadic elements were shaped with the particular ratios that generated actions and discourse of themselves. Such dramatistic structuring that occurs in the interpersonal realm as a sort of "coming to grips" or "coming into being" is nothing less than the rhetoric of existence. It will render a new world emergent—one in which the possibility for judgment is present. It should not be understood as a reasoning process brought on through reflection, however—better to say that a drama is being shaped for us and by us, even when we do not realize we are doing so. For a community of rhetorical scholars, therefore, one of the significant aspects of this case is that it shows how an ontological recalibration precedes and even contains the epistemological transformations that are associated with it.

It will become the case, then, that Karen will gradually be experienced as one who has passed into no longer being, so that the mother can say before the case has been heard in court, "she isn't really living anymore" (The Right to Live—Or Die, 1975, p. 40), a discursive attempt to articulate deanimated substance—to move Karen from her primary pentadic identity as actor to a new dominant identity as agency.

The way that individuals restructure their lifeworld with Karen can be considered in terms of Kenneth Burke's (1969) dramatistic principles, and in that sense one could say that they will set the stage for the termination of Karen's life support, for "when the curtain rises to disclose a given stage-set, this stage-set contains, simultaneously, implicitly, all that the narrative is to draw out as a sequence explicitly" (p. 7). Others will change in their actions toward Karen. Her body will be placed in new scenes. New people (agents) will be involved with her. The equipment (agency) that is used in her life will change. The purposes others have in relation to her will change. These are the primary elements of the dramatistic model. As practical shifts are made in them, there will be an implicit transformation in the identity of Karen. Eventually, it will be understood that she is no longer living.

Choosing to remove someone from life support, however, calls for a radical transformation in that person's pentadic identity, one that features a ratio that does not contradict "several centuries of individualism" (Burke, 1969, p. 265). Consequently, it would be hard to face that sort of transformation in only a moment, by virtue of a statement. There have already been, however, necessary actions that symbolize the diminishment of the daughter's agent status, for example, when the nurses "tied her to the bed so that, if she should wake up suddenly, she couldn't thrash around and hurt herself" (Quinlan et al., 1977, p. 23), a practical action that symbolically constitutes the girl as agency (a thing to be handled) rather than agent (a person with rights). At the same time, the purpose of the action shows how Karen herself is still being considered. Therefore, the example illustrates how Karen's coma has generated innovative discursive and semiotic practices on two fronts:

1. There have been attempts to constitute Karen as agency, to handle her in an equipmental way; and the very nature of the embodied resistance that compels her to be handled, and spoken about, as equipment has contributed to that semiotic, by virtue of analogic extension.
2. Attempts have been made to handle her in a manner that affirms her status as human agent, if only to affirm the humanity of the caretakers performing those gestures.

Now, a new strategy will arise as a means of making the transition into a nonenigmatic world. Attempts will be made to situate Karen's agency status in the people who are left behind, while minimizing any agent presence within the hospitalized body.

We can see the tension of this transition in the treatment of Karen's once beloved but now tangled long hair (agency), for Karen's mother lets the nurses cut it, trimming it "a bit at a time, until it was quite short, curling in little damp wisps around her face (Quinlan et al., 1977, p. 88). The haircut figures within the motivational framework that treats Karen as equipment (agency) in the equipmental world of the hospital. In addition, because it is an action, it is symbolic and thus tends to call the tune on future motivational vectors, by suggesting that handling Karen as equipment is allowed. Nevertheless, this agency status for the daughter is not one to which the mother is totally willing to surrender at this point, so that for example she brought the nurses a bottle of "Herbal Essence, the shampoo she used, and told them that the most important thing to her would be that her hair is kept clean" (p. 88). By engaging in such actions, the mother symbolically affirms the agency status of the body, while characterizing her own memory of Karen as the locus of the daughter as agent. Soon, this will become an explicit discursive project in which the family acts as the "medium" for the daughter's spirit—an interesting inversion by which they make themselves the agency and her the agent—a critical tactic when the Quinlans reach court.

On the discursive front, the family pastor announces that, "In terms of what I had been taught in my training, from a moral, theological point of view, this was a classic case of a hopeless life being prolonged unnecessarily through the use of extraordinary means" (Quinlan et al., 1977, p. 90)—a characterization that maps well onto Burke's (1969) notion of constitutional enactment, for he told us to attend to the "constitution beneath the constitution" (p. 387), which grounds both what we say and how we experience things in "theological, metaphysical, or naturalistic terminology's" (p. 388).[5] The Quinlan pastor is using the moralistic and theological constitution beneath the constitution of personhood to shift Karen's status in the drama of the Quinlan family from coagent to nonagent, and to move the family toward a drama of termination and interment. A similar move is made on the metaphysical and medical front, when the doctors make it clear "that Karen's chances of returning to a state of consciousness were non-existent" (Quinlan et al., 1977, p. 96).

Nevertheless, the symbolic constitution of Karen as a nonperson, as something that must be handled or what Burke (1969) called agency, is a subtle and dangerous venture on the part of those who make the effort. Family members in particular were compelled to announce Karen's agency status in a manner that preserved their coagent relationship with her, to claim they were vicariously performing her act, in requesting termination of treatment. There is always a risk of self-demonizing in any effort to depose another from her identity. Should the mother be too abrupt in characterizing her daughter as dead, those she seeks to influence might eventually believe her, but during her argument, or even after it, they might question her appropriateness as executor of Karen's wishes, which nevertheless does happen to the Quinlans when they lose guardianship of their daughter as part of the first court ruling.

Therefore, constituting Karen's agent status as a present spirit acting in the world through agencies (e.g., her friends, her family, and notes she had written) is a critical means for deflecting certain forms of accountability and blame that might arise in pushing forward to a termination. Consequently, Tommy Flynn said, "If Karen could see herself like this, it would be like the worst thing in the world for her" (Quinlan et al., 1977, p. 29). Julia said she "remember[s] the things she [Karen] said about not wanting to be kept alive, the way Bill Birch was and Nanette's father were" (p. 89). The family pastor recalls the mother saying that "Karen would never want this" (p. 90) within the first month. Various members of the family dug out poems written by Karen, which talk about how she would like to go "back over the rainbow," (p. 73) or "rest in the eternal womb a while" (p. 328). In fact, the mother is so powerfully mobilized to mediate Karen's agent status that she writes a poem as if she were Karen, and speaking through Karen's voice in this way, asks to be removed from the "machine" so that she might sleep in peace for eternity (pp. 170–171).

In these ways, those involved sought to evade a personal choosing by generating through discourse an alternative drama, with a present Karen able to give directions concerning what should be done, and thereby transforming themselves into "persons used as instrumentalities in carrying out the primary intentions of others" (Burke, 1969, p. 229). Imagining that Karen is acting at a distance, through them they positioned themselves as agency to the agent status of a Karen they constituted through reflection and discourse.

As this project continues, the mother sits the other daughter down for tea and reveals her decision (action) to remove Karen from life support equipment, what Farrell (1993) regarded as *premeditated rhetoric* introduced into a conversational event. The daughter will be influenced by this conversation, but she will also be affected by the way that actions are speaking into her world, and her response to the nurse's removal of Karen's restraints illustrates this, for she understood the act to mean "they were saying it's all over—she's not ever going to come out of it" (Quinlan et al., 1977, p. 94). The father, however, has not turned that page and still considers Karen as a person, so that the mother "warned the children to be careful. 'We must never talk about how we feel, in front of Dad,' she said. 'He still hasn't accepted this. He is in another world'" (p. 90).

For the father, the drama of Karen's life is still a future to be lived, and the stage he sets is oriented around a day when he will see her "racing out of the hospital" (Quinlan et al., 1977, p. 97). To him, the scene of "St. Clare's hospital had become a prison, and he knew that one day she would leave it" (p. 97). Joe acted with Karen as he had acted with her in the drama of her life, so much so that "he would stand and talk to Karen as though she could hear him, as though she would wake up any time" (p. 90). His relationship to Karen retained its characteristics as a past, present, and future ontological drama, with Karen an actor in their shared world. Therefore, he would still see her "going up to her room, and I could visualize her leaping off that fourth step and swinging herself down into the kitchen with that loud whoop of hers" (p. 98). With this attitude in place, he attended to her differently from others, visiting the hospital morning, noon, and night, waiting for her to return to the Karen that she was. These actions, as symbolic actions, were world constituting. They challenged the dominant model of reality that was already being constituted about the embodied resistance of Karen's enduring coma—they were symbolically an argument against the position of the others. Consequently, the doctors literally told him to stop visiting (action) because his experience of her as a person was confounding the nurses:

> Well listen, Joe, how do you think it makes us feel when you come here all the time. The nurses see you coming from the window upstairs every single morning, at lunchtime, and then again at night and then back with your wife. It makes us feel terrible. (Quinlan et al., 1977, p. 98)

Both the doctor's demand that Joe stop visiting and the mother's statement that her husband was in "another world" illustrate Burke's (1969) notion of consubstantiality as a key for co-living, because Joe is separated symbolically or literally from them while he continues to experience his daughter as an ongoing person, temporarily off course. In addition, though the mother says, "We had to play his game. We were afraid of what would happen to him if we didn't" (Quinlan et al., 1977, p. 100). Joe's game is already coming to a close, for the actions of doctors, nurses, and family are constantly shrinking the lived world where Karen resides as an agent, over which they have been caretakers, until it is impossible for Joe's motivational apparatus to move effectively and credibly within it. If we refer to the multiple ways that consubstantiality impacts our sense of substance, we can see that Joe may be able to satisfy his own needs by relating to Karen as he does, but the closure of everyone else around another interpretation of what she is, generates a body of activity that confounds his efforts to keep this perspective. Earlier, I mentioned that his "di-stance" in terms of what he thinks Karen is, also distances him from his family and his physician. Therefore, by virtue of this characteristic of consubstantiality, he is distant from the others in terms of a relationship with them. Now, as a second feature of consubstantiality, the experience that others have of Karen causes them to create an environment for her that makes it impossible for Joe's relationship with her to function effectively. His view of her is now, because of the way others are treating her, no longer adequate to the situation. Their actions have become a language with consequences, a language that produces an order of things that not only can be understood, but also bumped into. Soon, it will be as if Joe is a small child trying to return to the bedroom of a house that his parents have already sold.

At this point, Joe's dramatic experience of Karen's ongoing life goes supernova, so to speak:

> I thought if I could get Karen off the respirator . . . maybe I could find a physiotherapy facility. I could rent a motor home and the whole family could go out to Arizona . . . . If she could get special therapy, maybe she could even walk, with leg braces. I could fix a bed for her in the motor home . . . and . . . maybe with a special saddle, Karen could even ride a horse . . . . We could ride through the hills together all day—or as long as she felt up to it. I went to a Trailer Sales place . . . and asked about the price. (Quinlan et al., 1977, p. 101)

This is Joe's last and most sensational effort to structure a drama of Karen that lives beyond the possibilities implicated by the coma, certainly outside the world making that others are producing. The distance between him and the others was so profound that the mother says of his actions in general, "It was unreal. I thought . . . I would go out of my mind" (Quinlan et al., 1977, p. 100). Joe goes into action to carry out his plan, including weaning Karen from the respirator (p. 105) during her "wake cycles," the agitated periods when Karen's eyes were open and moving. The plan failed, however, and the pressure from others to treat Karen in line with their view increased. For him, a critical moment in the symbolically laden action of the event occurred when Karen was placed in the background area of the intensive care unit (ICU), away from primary activity (alteration of scene) but not given a private room. He felt, "It was as though they were saying, 'We cannot do anything more for her now, except merely sustain her'" (p. 107). This movement is an example of Burke's (1969, pp. 403–406) notion of identification, which he characterized as strategies of merger and division to articulate a substance.[6] Clearly, Karen is divided from the central area of the ICU and merged with its periphery. (Even more significantly, social workers were looking for a long-term facility at which Karen might be moved, an action that would divide her from the hospital scene and merge her with a chronic care scene.) When Joe resisted the ICU move, Dr. Morse said, "Now you're being extremely selfish, Mr. Quinlan. Do you really think it's fair that we keep your daughter here in intensive care under the circumstances, when we need those beds for emergency care and not for chronic cases like Karen's?" (Quinlan et al., 1977, p. 110). This illustration of Farrell's (1993) *disturbance rhetoric* in a conversation causes Joe Quinlan to "beat a hasty retreat, to withdraw as gracefully as circumstances allow" (p. 245). However, Joe's withdrawal from his immediate request is less significant than the withdrawal he is making from the drama of Karen as a person, which the hospital has affected as well, simply as a result of the surfeit of symbolism that arises when personnel perform their actions. In addition, considered in terms of the substance and motive dialectic, we see how the motives of medical personnel generate a substantial Karen, even as those motives embody a practice that creates a physical realm that pushes off the stage, or into a holding bin, anyone who is not comotivated, hence consubstantial.

This is when Joe comes to see Karen as no longer Dasein, as reflected in his refusal to envision her in ongoing drama, realizing that "Even if she woke up, she would not be able to swim or drive her car or do anything that she loves . . . . Arizona is impossible because they won't take her off the machine" (Quinlan et al., 1977, p. 111). Consequently, the phenomenal codrama that Joe maintained with Karen, even after the onset of her coma, collapses and is supplanted before he comes to agree with family and doctors in a judgment about his daughter. When he tells the wife he wishes to look at a family plot, and then mentions that he would like to talk to Father Tom (a declared constitution or motive, which implies the descriptive constitution that Karen is no longer alive), the mother "walked over to her husband and reached her arms around his waist—causing him almost to spill the cup of coffee he now carefully slid onto the breakfast table behind him—and she put her head on his shoulder and began to cry" (p. 112). If we refer to the diagram of consubstantiality, we can see how Julia's spontaneous reaction to Joe's statement completes the triangular structure of the consubstantial process, such that the merger in the perception of Karen is coincident with the transparent merger of the perceivers, which her hugging action symbolizes. In addition, if we operate on a simple principle of inversion here, we can speculate that the couple had been emotionally distant during the period that they saw things differently, and certainly Julia's claim that he was in another world and that it was making her lose her mind suggest that such a distance did exist. Therefore, just as Joe's unique view of Karen distanced him in line with the laws of consubstantiality, so did that distance motivate him to change his view.

Joe felt overwhelmed, for he realized that the choice was his own, "And that, to me, was an awful responsibility" (Quinlan et al., 1977, p. 112). However, when Joe is told by the priest that the decision was actually made by God, "You're just agreeing with God's decision, that's all" (p. 113), Joe recognized that he was accepting rather than choosing, and this tranquilizes him. In Burkean (1969) parlance, we would say that his motive and substance for Karen at this point is grounded in a God as an ultimate motive (p. 43) and in that manner he manages to transcend guilt, which is given over to the crucifixion, so to speak (p. 265).

Coscripting this reality of Karen as no longer Dasein involves investments from all directions. Mary-Ellen announces that she hated the respirator because it caused her sister so much pain and seemed "to be more alive than Karen" (Quinlan et al., 1977, p. 114). Here we see how Karen's movement from Dasein to no longer Dasein articulates a radical dramatistic change, dialectically shifting the pentadic properties of things, so that the respirator loses its status as a helping agency of the hospital and family to become a harming agent, and one which is demonized. This is an interesting rhetorical move, which the mother also makes, describing the respirator as a mechanical mind, "making hissing and gurgling noises as it endlessly pumped air down into a hole in Karen's throat" (p. 88). The shift in the status of the respirator as a direct result of the shift in the family's view of Karen is one which HCPs should note, for the image they generate in the eyes of the family may also be coincident with the stage of process through this rite of passage, and a change in the family's perspective of the patient could result in a change in the perception of the HCP as well, even though the HCP continues to act exactly the same. The movement of the respirator toward the status of demonic agent is a critical stage in the transposition—one which converts the drama from a postmodern and incommensurable torment–torture, into a fairy tale in which the princess (Karen's spirit) can only be freed if the demon (respirator) is "killed." This is the model the Quinlan's take to court, when seeking permission to pull the respirator's plug.

In addition to the change in the agency status of the respirator, Joe rescripts his past in a manner consubstantial with other players, so that he can now say of his past self that others, "were afraid I was losing touch with reality" (Quinlan et al., 1977, p. 113). Reality has a decidedly political cast here, and we are reminded of Burke's (1967c) claim that, "Identity itself is a mystification" (p. 308).

Scene changes equally occur, as the Quinlans begin to enter law offices, courts, and nursing homes. Clearly, purposes now also change as the family mobilizes to allow Karen's body to reach its end. In addition, coterminously, there is a radical transformation in Joe's experience of Karen's suffering:

> And that night when we went back to the hospital, Karen was quieter than she had been in the morning. Her fever had gone down, and she was not thrashing about. Like us, she seemed at peace. (Quinlan et al., 1977, p. 114)

Conclusions

The suffering of the Quinlan family and the difficulty they had facing the reality of what happened to Karen point to the difference between an HCP's interpretation of a medical phenomenon and a family member's experience of it. To physicians and other HCPs who first encounter patients under these circumstances, radical medical conditions are real because they happen to bodies that are composed of certain organs that perform certain functions. For them, a change in the medical identity in a patient means a change of location for a patient, and a change of treatment. To the families, however, such extreme medical conditions are unreal because they remove what they feel to be the most genuine part of the patient, the person with whom they live and who is ultimately a part of them and their lives. Therefore, a radical change in the identity of the patient does not occur easily in families, and coping with people compelled to accept such changes requires tremendous empathy and patience. Gradually, through language and symbolic action in general, families and friends somehow and eventually stumble through this process, which can be facilitated but perhaps never efficiently controlled through insight and understanding on the part of HCPs. However, it must be recognized that the interpersonal disruption that occurs as a result of such losses might never be routinized with the goal of efficiency that marks the practice of large-scale, corporate medicine.

The other side of the story of such medical tragedies is the story of the HCP who encounters such shocked and bewildered families. It would be a mistake to assume that the HCP is satisfied when he or she achieves the institutional goals that are associated with dealing with such families. Rather, it is precisely where institutional goals of efficiency and routine direct or pressure the HCP to react in ways that do not align with family needs that HCPs face one of their most anxiety provoking challenges, for such a moment is one that forces HCPs to recognize the space that exists between their role as a representative of the institution that employs them and their role as a member of the human race. Consequently, one should not overlook the fact that HCPs encounter families in the midst of a broken lifeworld, from the center of their stable, albeit bizarre, lifeworld (a lifeworld in which such tragic events are experienced alongside other activities and responsibilities that range from the exhilarating to the boring) and that this unique circumstance juxtaposes, for the HCP, emotional situations that span much of the human spectrum, at the same time and even within the same corridor. In many medical settings, it may be impossible to organize experiences that are emotionally consistent and stable for HCPs, and it is important to recognize that this limit is part of the very nature of the medical institution as well as its practices.

In fact, the actual dramatic transformation of the Quinlans cannot be measured by the decision to treat Karen as a body no longer alive. That decision was a minor element in the overall drama that transformed all their choices, which made the parents lifelong leaders of the right to die movement, well-known authors, founders and active participants in the Karen Ann Quinlan Center of Hope hospice, which has helped 2,000 terminally ill patients spend their last days in their homes. Even the daughter, Mary-Ellen was radically changed, switching to special education rather than the basic music education that she had been trained for, because "I can't do that now, Mom. I've seen too much suffering" (Quinlan, 1993, p. 67). As recently as 1996, Joe Quinlan, now dead, submitted a brief to the Supreme Court during their deliberations on the issue of physician assisted suicide. What started as a rupture in the drama of the Quinlan family eventually became the center of their family drama, placing them in the *terra nuevo* through which they guided others.

The next stage of this historic story of dramatistic impoverishment occurs when the family attempts to make good its decision, through the hospital and the courts. Just as they were faced with a radical aporia in dealing with Karen as an individual, so too were the hospital, and ultimately the state faced with an aporia in terms of relating to her in any everyday sense. At the same time, the process by which Karen's father obtains the right to remove her from the respirator opens a discursive space that people from all over the world entered to consider the aporia emergent from technology and prolonged life and to think out a way of routine coping with that, which until then had never been routine. A characterization of this process was well described by Burke (1969) and provided the bridge for understanding the linkage between public argument and private practice, showing us how a public that is lax in its willingness to participate in formal public judgment is nevertheless vigorously involved in the study of public discourse for the sake of personal action. This article provides the ground for consideration of those issues, in a forthcoming manuscript.

A story, such as the story of the Quinlans, serves to remind us that

Always the Eternal Enigma is there, right on the edges of our metropolitan bickerings, stretching outward to interstellar infinity and inward to the depths of the mind. And in this staggering disproportion between man and noman, there is no place for human boasts of grandeur, or for forgetting that men build their cultures by huddling, nervously loquacious, at the edge of an abyss. (Burke, 1984b, p. 272)

The Quinlan family, as a group obligated to enter a rite of passage, parsed a Burkean drama without any knowledge of dramatism, even in a circumstance that threatened the foundations of their lives. Nevertheless, they would not have been able to continue their loquacious efforts before their enigmatic daughter who hovered over the abyss of existence without engaging in discursive practices that make of lived experience something that is also reasoned. It is hoped that their story, as well as this analysis, provides a manner of seeing similar medical circumstances when they arise.

Notes

1. In the article referenced (Kenny, 2000b), I show how the contemporary public figure's rhetorical platform is subverted by a plethora of other voices that manufacture, in their speaking, images and identities that are distinct, sometimes even at odds, with what the rhetor represents. The concept was originally developed for considering Karen Quinlan who, because she had lost her speech before entering the public sphere, exemplified the notion of a public figure who serves to gather discourse, rather than produce it. That work has taken longer to appear in print, but is currently in press with this journal (Kenny, in press).
2. In this regard, see Kenny (2000a).
3. Embodiment is a crucial issue in Burke (1996), one that focuses on the intimate relation between the function of (internal) physiological systems and the (external) interpersonal environment. See Burke (1996) as well as Kenny & Bentz (1997).

4. The capacity for this feeling in common, however, is determined by a *being* in common, which is to say that the parents, to the extent they live the same family drama are already invisible to each other because they are each other, just as they are Karen (a primary thesis of this article). We see a similar phenomenon always present in the activities of the human body, for example, in the way a person's legs are invisible to him or her is intimately involved in using or being them by walking.

5. See also Kenny (2000a).

6. It is my practice to refer to identification as characterized in the *Grammer* by the processes of merger and division rather than identification and division, although Burke (1952, 1969) employed such use in the *Rhetoric*. I believe that the relation between identification and substance can only be made clear if one honors the fact that substance is articulated both by virtue of mergers and divisions and that identification, as attributions of substance is but partial without full attention to the dialectical merger or division pair.

References

Angell, M. (1993). The legacy of Karen Ann Quinlan. *Trends in Health Care, Law, and Ethics, 8*(1), 17–19.

Angell, M. (1996). After Quinlan: The dilemma of the persistent vegetative state. *New England Journal of Medicine, 330,* 1524–1525.

Clark, M., Agrest, S., Gosnell, M., Shapiro, D., McGee, H., & Shiels, M. (1975, November 3). A right to die? *Newsweek, 86,* 58–69.

Burke, K. (1952). *A rhetoric of motives.* New York: Prentice-Hall.

Burke, K. (1966). *Mind, body, and the unconscious. Language as symbolic action.* Berkeley: University of California Press.

Burke, K. (1967a). *Literature as equipment for living. The philosophy of literary form.* Los Angeles: University of California Press.

Burke, K. (1967b). *The philosophy of literary form.* Los Angeles: University of California Press.

Burke, K. (1967c). *Twelve propositions. The philosophy of literary form.* Los Angeles: University of California Press.

Burke, K. (1969). *A grammar of motives.* Berkeley: University of California Press.

Burke, K. (1970). Two poems of abandonment. *New Republic, 162,* 27.

Burke, K. (1984a). *Attitudes toward history.* Berkeley: University of California Press.

Burke, K. (1984b). *Permanence and change.* Berkeley: University of California Press.

Cruzan v. Director, Missouri Department of Health, 497 U.S. 291 (1990). In R. M. Baird & S. E. Rosenbaum (Eds.), *Euthanasia: The moral issues.* Buffalo, NY: Prometheus.

Erstling, S. S. (1985). The shared burden: When physicians and families decide to forego life-sustaining treatment. *Journal of Family Practice, 20,* 393–399.

Farrell, T. (1993). *The norms of rhetorical culture.* New Haven, CT: Yale University Press.

Frader, J. (1996). Commentary: The Quinlan case revisited. *Journal of Health Politics, Policy and Law, 21,* 367–372.

Germino, B. B. (1998). When a chronic illness becomes terminal. *ANNA Journal, 25,* 579–582.

Heidegger, M. (1962). *Being and time.* New York: Harper & Row.

Joraelmon, D. (1999). *Exploring medical anthropology.* Toronto: Prentice Hall.

Kenny, R. W. (2000a). The constitutional dialectic. *Quarterly Journal of Speech, 86,* 455–464.

Kenny, R. W. (2000b). The rhetoric of Kevorkian's battle. *Quarterly Journal of Speech, 86,* 386–401.

Kenny, R. W. (in press). The death of loving: Maternal identity as moral constraint in a narrative testimonial advocating physician assisted suicide. *Journal of Health Communication.*

Kenny, W., & Bentz, V. (1997). "Body-as-world": Kenneth Burke's answer to the postmodernist charges against sociology. *Sociological Theory, 15,* 81–96.

Kinky, H., Korein, J., Panigrahy, A., Dikkes, P., & Goode, R. (1994). Neuro-pathological findings in the brain of Karen Ann Quinlan. *New England Journal of Medicine, 330,* 1469–1475.

O'Connor, N. (1987). Who suffers? In R. Bernasconi & S. Critchley (Eds.), *Re-reading Levinas* (pp. 229–233). Bloomington: Indiana University Press.

Quinlan, J. (1993). From the families . . . . *Trends in Health Care, Law, and Ethics, 8*(1), 65–68.

Quinlan, J., Quinlan, J., & Battelle, P. (1977). *Karen Ann: The Quinlans tell their story.* New York: Doubleday.

Scheler, M. (1973). *The nature of sympathy.* Hamden, CT: Archon.

Ssasz, T. (1957). *Pain and pleasure: A study of bodily feelings.* London: Tavistock.

Stevens, T. (1996). The Quinlan case revisited: A history of the cultural practices of medicine and law. *Journal of Health Politics, Policy, and Law, 21,* 347–366.

Thompson, T. L. (2000). The nature and language of illness explanations. In B. B. Whaley (Ed.), *Explaining illness: Research, theory, and strategies* (pp. 3–39). Mahwah, NJ: Lawrence Erlbaum Associates, Inc.

The Right to Live—Or Die. (1975, October 27). *Time, 106,* 40.

Vacco, Attorney General of New York v. Quill, 521 U.S. 793 (1997). Physician assisted suicide: Expanding the debate. New York: Routledge.

FOLLOW-UP QUESTIONS AND EXPLORATION PROJECTS

1. Identify a more recent case than that of Karen Quinlan in which there was public discourse about life support issues for a person in a permanent vegetative state. One example would be the case of Terri Schiavo, but you may be more familiar with yet another example. To what extent would the analysis Kenny uses in this article apply in this other case? What does it say about Kenny's conclusions that they apply or don't apply in other, apparently similar, circumstances?

2. Compare Kenny's approach to a health-related subject with that taken by Freeman & Spyridkis (2004). What is similar and different in the structure of the two articles? How are the claims and the ways they are supported similar and different? How do you see these authors' use of different theories (Dramatism and Elaboration Likelihood Model) affecting their work?

3. Given the articles by Kenny and by Freeman & Spyridkis (2004), which do you like better? Why? What does your answer say about your interests and your theoretical preferences?

4. Having read Kenny's article, write your own definition of the following concepts from Dramatism: Identification, consubstantiality, and the five elements of the pentad. Find another example of rhetoric and apply these concepts to it. What does your analysis tell you? How did your understanding of these concepts change as you used them in this case.

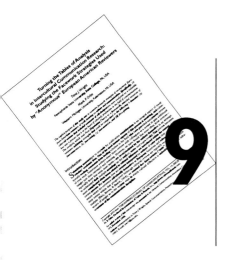

9 Faces of Knowledge

We include the following article by Wright and Orbe (2003) not only because it is an interesting application of Face Negotiation theory, but also because it addresses the issues of how journal articles get published. Once an author finishes writing an article he or she submits it to a journal to be considered for publication. Many scholarly journals use a "blind-review" process (also called "peer-review") to decide which articles to publish. This process is one of the key things distinguishing "scholarly" journals from other forms of publication. In the "blind-review" process, information identifying the author is removed from the manuscript and it is sent to other scholars, frequently those with some expertise in the field, for review. These scholars evaluate the quality of the manuscript and provide feedback to the author. This feedback can range from very positive to very negative. Based on this feedback, a decision is made to (a) publish the article, (b) return it to the author to be revised and resubmitted, or (c) not publish the article. This is an important process for you to be aware of as consumers of research.

Background of Face Negotiation Theory

The version of Face Negotiation theory used in this article was developed by Ting-Toomey (1988) based in prior work done by sociologist Erving Goffman (1959) and by linguists Penelope Brown and Steven Levinson (1987). There is some variation across these approaches in the terminology used and the precise definition of the term *face*. In Ting-Toomey's version, the concept of *face* refers to a universal concern with *self-face* referring to our own image, *other-face* referring to issues related to the other person's image, and *mutual-face* referring to the face of the relationship or both parties, together (Oetzel & Ting-Toomey, 2003). When face-related images are damaged or have the potential for damage, conditions of *face-threat* occur. According to this theory, we respond to face-threat with communication strategies designed to address the threat and restore face-related images. These strategies are called *facework* or *face negotiation strategies*.

Wright and Orbe draw on Face Negotiation theory in their analysis of "blind-review" letters because such letters offer evaluations, both positive and negative, of an author's work. Such evaluations are relevant to face concerns because they, presumably, affect an author's sense of competence as a writer and scholar. Such evaluations may also affect the reviewer's self-image as a rigorous scholar and/or as a just human being, thus impacting on the reviewer's face as well. To the extent that reviewers are aware of these face-threats, we would expect them to use communication strategically to address them.

Article Structure

This article follows the format which you should begin, by now, to recognize as standard for research articles (Introduction/Literature Review, Methods, Results, Discussion) though authors don't always use these headings. For example, rather than using the Literature Review heading, Wright and Orbe highlight the theoretical terms: Face Work, Face Threat, and Face Negotiation. In addition, because existing texts are being used for analysis, the Methods section describes how texts were selected and then discusses the processes used for analysis. The Results section is titled Thematic/Critical Analysis to better reflect the type of analysis and interpretation presented in this section.

Distinctive Points

One of the issues raised by Critical approaches to scholarship (i.e., Harding, 1991) is that knowledge is produced in and influenced by a particular cultural and political context. One feature of our current socio-political context is that individuals of European-American descent tend to be privileged over individuals of color (Johnson, 2001). As a result, Euro-American cultural practices and values are more widely reflected in the literature than those of other cultural groups (a point raised earlier by Penington (2004), this volume). Wright and Orbe ground their work in the Critical premise that knowledge is not value-free, but add to this idea the notion that interpersonal processes are also at work in the knowledge production process. Not only do privilege-based cultural issues affect what gets studied and published, but interpersonal face-concerns affect the process as well. This is a very different view of knowledge than the view that it is a set of "objective facts" about the "real world."

References

Brown, P., & Levinson, S. (1987). *Politeness: Some universals in language usage.* Cambridge, UK: Cambridge University Press.

Goffman, E. (1959). *The presentation of self in everyday life.* Garden City, NY: Doubleday.

Harding, S. (1991). *Whose science? Whose knowledge? Thinking from women's lives.* Ithaca, NY: Cornell University Press.

Johnson, A. G. (2001). *Privilege, power, and difference.* Boston: McGraw Hill.

Oetzel, J. G., & Ting-Toomey, S. (2003). Face concerns in interpersonal conflict: A cross-cultural empirical test of the face negotiation theory. *Communication Research, 30,* 599–624.

Ting-Toomey, S. (1988). Intercultural conflict styles: A face-negotiation theory. In Y. Y. Kim and W. Gudykunst (Eds.) *Theories in intercultural communication* (pp. 213–235). Newbury Park, CA: Sage.

Turning the Tables of Analysis in Intercultural Communication Research: Studying the Facework Strategies Used by "Anonymous" European American Reviewers

Trina J. Wright

Pennsylvania State University, State College, PA, USA

Mark P. Orbe

Western Michigan University, Kalamazoo, MI, USA

The explicit purpose of this study was to examine facework strategies of anonymous European American reviewers of work focusing on culture and communication. Specifically, 10 editorial reviews that included comments of self-designations were analyzed as a valuable lens into a process that is at the heart of scholarly production in the field of communication. The analysis, which used Face Negotiation Theory as a framework, revealed instances of reviewers exhibiting strategies that could be categorized in the following 4 domains: (a) face-restoration, (b) face-saving, (c) face-assertion, and (d) face-giving.

Introduction

Submitting manuscripts to journals for publication consideration is an integral aspect of many scholars' academic lives. One of the most intense aspects of this process is receiving, and subsequently reading, comments from leading scholars in the field who have provided anonymous reviews of your work. Sometimes authors share these reviews with colleagues as a means to gain additional insight into their relevance and meaning. However, we have found that most often these reviews—especially those that seem most harsh—are (over)analyzed by the authors themselves in an attempt to understand their multiple meanings (at the surface, meta- and supra-levels). This process becomes more complicated when issues related to cultural difference are introduced within the context of the review process. For instance, how are reviews interpreted by authors of color when they receive comments where the reviewers self-identify themselves as European American and subsequently situate their review within that perspective? Although editorial reviews are typically exempt from public analysis (Blair, Brown, & Baxter, 1994), we contend that these reviews ("texts") provide a valuable source of insight as to the various ways in which cultural difference is embedded within the infrastructures of the communication discipline.

An earlier version of this manuscript was presented at the National Communication Association Convention, New York, NY, November 1998.

Address correspondence to Trina J. Wright, Speech Communication, Pennsylvania State University, State College, PA 16802. E-mail: tjw10@psu.edu.

To his end, this article highlights the value of collaborative research that focuses on issues of race/culture, power, and communication that are inherent within the "blind review process" used to make editorial decisions in our field. Specifically, we analyze the "anonymous" reviews of 10 different European American scholars who have critiqued communication and culture research submitted to various publication outlets (all authored by Mark P. Orbe). Other examples of qualitative work that have used anonymous reviews as texts for analyses exist (see, e.g., Allen, Orbe, & Olivas, 1989; Blair et al., 1994; Medhurst, 1989; Peters & Ceci, 1982). Although scholarly reviews have traditionally been exempt from public scrutiny, we contend that this form of inquiry is valuable in that it allows researchers to access one process that is integral to the ways in which a scholarly community functions. Like Blair et al., we use "reviews as explicit objects of analysis . . . [and] bring them into the public conversation of scholarly discourse" (p. 387). Although we continue in a tradition set by these existing studies, the work reported on here is unique in that it draws from Face Negotiation Theory as a guide for analysis. In this regard, our analysis was informed by the following research question: "How is face negotiation evident in the "anonymous" reviews of European American scholars responding to work that focuses on culture and communication?"

Facework

Face refers to a projected social image in a diverse range of communicative situations. More specifically, face is a "claimed sense of self-respect in an interactive situation" (Ting-Toomey, 1994, p. 1). It is associated with the amount of respect, pride, dignity, shame, and embarrassment issues in a communication process. Most individuals in a society have the desire to be respected by others and to appear credible and competent in front of others. In contrast, few individuals want to appear weak and incompetent. Thus, when an individual's face is being threatened in any given situation she or he will have the need to save her or his face.

Historically, scholars have studied facework in a number of interpersonal and organizational contexts. These include embarrassing interpersonal situations (Cupach & Metts, 1990, 1991; Imahori & Cupach, 1994; Cupach & Imahori, 1993; Metts & Cupach, 1989), persuasion attempts (Ifert & Roloff, 1997; Leichty & Applegate, 1991), intercultural negotiation (Cai & Donohue, 1997), friendships (Trees & Manusov, 1998; Wright, 1996), and supervisor/subordinate communication (Wagoner & Waldron, 1999). Different contexts notwithstanding, what these studies have in common is that each involves a communication interaction where a person has her or his face threatened. Although no study has been identified that looks specifically at the context of scholarly reviews, we contend that similar dynamics are present making the use of Face Negotiation Theory a valuable framework for this analysis. Face Negotiation Theory manifests in the reviewing process through reviewers who want to project a credible image to the journal editor. Those who serve as a reviewer are considered to have prestigious roles in the field. As such, they have a strong need to protect their face/image in front of other scholars. Prior work has specifically explored contexts where messages included criticism or potentially "bad news" (Trees & Manusov, 1998; Wagoner & Waldron, 1999). These particular studies, among others grounded in Face Negotiation Theory, serve as the conceptual framework for our analysis.

In its most basic form, Face Negotiation Theory (Ting-Toomey, 1988) posits four assumptions that are central to this study. First, members of all individualistic and collectivistic cultures value the concept of "face." Second, members from individualistic cultures tend to emphasize an image of "I" identity in face negotiation and collectivistic members emphasize a "we" identity in face negotiation. Third, the "I" identity facework maintains a face negotiation process based on a competitive process, and the "we" identity facework maintains a collaborative approach to face negotiation. Finally, the "I" identity face orientation focuses more on self-face preserving and other-face threat strategies, and the "we" identity face orientation emphasizes mutual face-saving strategies (Ting-Toomey, 1988). In addition to this work, our analysis also draws from further work on face-threat and face-saving.

Face-Threat

Face-threat refers to one's assessment of a negative attack on his/her perceived positive public image (Lim, 1994). Cupach and Metts (1994) asserted that face-threats usually occur when one's desired perceived image in a particular situation is challenged. According to Tracy (1990), it is practically impossible for an individual to avoid face-threatening situations. Tracy posited that almost any interaction can be seen as having the potential to be face-threatening. In addition, Cupach and Metts asserted that "even the most skillful and well-intended communicator sometimes finds him or herself in the position of having spoken an inappropriate comment or having felt diminished by receiving a complaint or criticism from someone else" (p. 4).

Brown and Levinson (1987) stated that there are two distinct ways that one's face may be threatened. There are two types of universal face needs: positive and negative (Brown & Levinson, 1987). *Positive face* refers to "the desire to be liked and respected by the significant people in our lives" (Cupach & Metts, 1994, p. 5). Therefore, messages received from others that hold value or appreciation for us help support positive face. When one's "fellowship" or "abilities" are devalued or questioned our positive face is threatened (Cupach & Metts, 1994). *Negative face* refers to "the desire to be free from constraint and imposition" (Cupach & Metts, 1994, p. 5). Messages that respect autonomy help enforce negative face, whereas messages that conflict with one's desire are threatening to negative face. Cupach and Metts (1994) stated that it is Brown and Levinson's (1987) theory that uncovers the dilemma of people trying to meet both positive and negative face needs for themselves as well as others.

More specifically, according to Lim and Bowers (1991), there are three basic types of universal face that can be threatened: autonomy, fellowship, and competence. Lim (1994) defined *autonomy face* as a "persons' image that they are in control of their own fate, that is they have the virtues of a full-fledged, mature, and responsible adult" (p. 211). In addition, this type of face includes values such as "independent" and "self-sufficient" to name a few. Autonomy face is connected with one's view of independence, where they believe they control their own actions and are therefore reliable for such consequences (Lim, 1994). *Fellowship face* is the "persons' image that they are worthy companions [colleagues]" (p. 211). This face type incorporates the essential "social aspect" of a person, for example, how "desirable," "cooperative," or "friendly" she or he is. *Competence face* is the "image that one is a person of ability" (p. 211). This face type involves concern for past accomplishments and reputations that are used to judge the success of future capabilities in maintaining face (Lim, 1994). In their study, Lim and Bowers (1991) extended the Brown and Levinson's (1987) model of politeness to explain the forms of interaction in three various types of facework: solidarity, approbation, and tact. The researchers apply three social factors to their study—relational intimacy, power difference and the right to perform a given act in a given situation. Lim and Bowers reported that facework entails more than attending to the other's autonomy face or fellowship face. They stated that when people have the need to criticize others, they also make strides to satisfy the other's competence face or their want for respect.

Face-Negotiation

Face-Negotiation strategies are impacted by the attention the speaker gives to her or his face that is endangered (Tracy, 1990). The attention can be self-focused, mutual-focused, or other-focused (Ting-Toomey, 1988). This includes self-face, mutual-face, and other-face. According to Cocroft and Ting-Toomey (1994), *self-face* refers to paying attention to self-interest image more so than the other-interest image. Therefore, the individual is more likely to use a strategy to save a self-projected image that is for her or his own benefit without concern for the other's face. In contrast to self-face, *other-face* concern would refer to an individual using a strategy that would restore the other party's face before concern for her or his own face image. *Mutual-face* refers to the relational-oriented process whereby the individual attempts to restore her or his face in addition to the other's face or self-image. Ting-Toomey's theory (1988) posited that members in all cultural/ethnic groups display a concern to use self-face or other-face (or both) protective strategies. However, the theory also assumes that the dimension of self-interest face and mutual-interest face are influenced by cultural, ethnic, personality, and situational factors.

Understanding different face-negotiation strategies used with the review process will help us to better understand the communication phenomenon more effectively. Specifically, Ting-Toomey (1988) described four specific face-negotiation strategies: (a) face-restoration, (b) face-saving, (c) face-assertion, and (d) face-giving. *Face-restoration,* the strategy most used within individualistic cultures, involves communication that works to ensure self-freedom and space. This type of face-negotiation protects the self from others' infringement and autonomy. *Face-saving,* on the other hand, signals respect of others' need for freedom and space. Its primary focus is on other-face (not self-face). *Face-assertion* focuses on self-face, especially in terms of defending and supporting one's need for inclusion. Finally, *face-giving* strategies are reflected in communication that defends and supports the other person's need for inclusion. Ting-Toomey described this strategy as one most common in collectivistic cultures. Face-restoration, face-saving, face-assertion, and face-giving manifests themselves in the review process. For example, a reviewer submitting a late review may decide to give a more intense critique of an article to maintain good status with the editor.

Methods

To gain insight into the facework of European American reviewers of culture and communication research, we gathered 10 editorial reviews from manuscripts submitted by Mark P. Orbe. These reviews were in response to eight different manuscripts that had a specific focus on race/culture and power. Received over a span of 7 years (1992–1999), the texts represented comments from reviewers associated with five communication journals *(Communication Studies, Communication Quarterly, Critical Studies in Mass Communication, Management Communication Quarterly,* and *Southern Communication Journal)* and one publisher (Sage). Within each of the 10 editorial reviews selected, the "anonymous" reviewer (7 men, 3 women) identified him/herself as White or European American. In short, the texts for our analysis ranged from 1–5 pages (single-spaced) and represented a valuable lens into a process that is at the heart of scholarly production in our field (Blair et al., 1994).

Analytical Framework

As described earlier, the texts for this analysis consisted of written responses from anonymous reviewers of scholarship that focused on communication and culture. Specifically, we used McCracken's (1988) guidelines to discover emerging themes with the texts. According to McCracken, analysis should follow several steps: (a) initial sorting out of important from unimportant data; (b) examination of the slices of data for logical relationships and contradictions; (c) re-reading of transcripts to confirm or disconfirm emerging relationships and beginning recognition of general properties of the data; (d) identification of general themes and sorting of the themes in a hierarchical fashion, while discarding those that prove useless in the organization; and (e) review of the emergent themes for each of the interviews and determination of how these can be synthesized into themes.

The collaborative nature of our analysis proved an important aspect of this research inquiry. This was especially important given that Mark P. Orbe was analyzing reviews directed at his own work. In this regard, a collaborative analysis provided both insider and outsider perspectives to the texts. It also allowed us to bring our diverse perspectives into the analysis and develop over time. For example, upon reading the small sample of written responses in their entirety, specific sections of the responses that are related to the meaning of face-negotiation were highlighted. The highlighted sections were then put into themes to identify their meaning. These pieces of data were re-read by the researchers to develop a coherent thematic analysis process and to ensure thematic clarity. Thematic labels, thematic definitions, and thematic examples were cross-checked between the two researchers. In this regard, particular interpretations of what constituted which type of face-negotiation strategy were re-evaluated in the context of collective vantage points.

Three criteria—repetition, recurrence, and forcefulness—helped shape this process (Owen, 1984). *Repetition criterion* refers to the repetition of key words and phrases and words that are "special" or significant in describing a certain experience or feeling. *Recurrence criterion* examines the meanings that were threaded throughout the text, even if the reviewers use different wording to represent the same meaning. The *forcefulness criterion* enables the researcher to understand the importance or uniqueness of certain words or phrases. Forcefulness is traditionally displayed through the use of vocal inflection, volume, of the written messages. Within our analysis, examples of forcefulness were seen in the use of bold or underline text, using all capital letters, or other forms of accentuation (i.e., adding "*******" around certain comments).

Thematic/Critical Analysis

Our collaborative analysis of "anonymous" European Americans' comments on culture and communication research revealed the various ways in which face was negotiated. To structure our analysis, we constructed this section of the article around four distinct variations of negotiating face (face-restoration, face-saving, face-assertion, and face-giving). Within each point of analysis, we will use other aspects of face negotiation (e.g., positive face threats, mutual face concern, remediation strategies) to capture the complexity that is inherent in the process of "anonymous" reviews where culture and cultural difference are enacted as salient issues.

Face-restoration. As illustrated throughout this section, no particular type of face-work stood out as the "norm" for reviewers' comments. However, given their focus on protecting self-face (Ting-Toomey, 1988) and highlighting needs for autonomy (Lim & Bowers, 1991), comments reflecting face-restoration appear to take on a hypervisibility for authors. In other words, face-restoration comments are typically ones that authors spend the most time reflecting on. The following excerpt illustrates such a comment:

It is difficult to review this article without saying first that it appears that the author has other works, including a book, in press detailing the various aspects of [this] theory. I say this in light of the fact that the author has made little attempt to disguise his identity—works "in progress" or "in press" are a dead give-away. I have no idea whether or not this is a strategic move on the author's part; however, I do come away with the impression that as a reader I am expected to overlook the many holes in this manuscript simply because the theory is explained in much greater depth and to other reviewers' satisfaction elsewhere.

These comments represent an insightful point of analysis in terms of how face-restoration functions in the anonymous review process. First, the reviewer's focus is on preserving his own freedom and autonomy (self-face). This can be seen specifically in terms of the reviewers' perception that the author attempted to infringe on his "right" to criticize work that other reviewers found valuable. Second, the comments work as a positive face threat (Cupach & Metts, 1994) to the author's standards of ethics because he is accused of attempting to manipulate the review process to his advantage.

Another set of comments (that were in response to a different manuscript) also mirror similar dynamics where autonomous self-face and positive face threat (in this case, concerning competency issues) are enacted with little concern for other-face.

I was delighted to read this essay, especially given my philosophical biases. But I was also a bit shocked . . . What the author says about [methodology] indicates that he/she has received some decent training in the ways of this method. Apparently, however, the author's training has not included some rigorous lessons in the history of a certain tradition of communication and rhetorical scholarship . . . This essay should never have been submitted to the Journal. . . It's somewhat embarrassing.

The previous examples of face-restoration focused on needs to protect self-face (Cocroft & Ting-Toomey, 1994). However, other comments appeared to protect self-face but also give some attention to other-face as well. For instance, consider the following set of comments from a different submission:

> Here is where your claims finally become so personal as to require author identification of race, class, and gender. You are claiming that what we ALL should SEE is a racial representation issue; I think it is fairer to conclude that is what YOU see. At least own your experiences. I can empathize a lot easier if I figure you gain insight via personal identification, and it doesn't require me to [go] along with what you see.

This set of reviewer comments, like the earlier excerpts, highlights a need to maintain autonomy in terms of an interpretative analysis of racialized media images. In essence, his request for the author to identify his or her cultural standpoint is done so that the reviewer can understand the interpretative analysis as an alternative one (and subsequently allowing the validity of a European American male perspective). The comments, therefore, do contain some attention to other-face and signals some level of respect/tolerance (Ting-Toomey, 1988). In this regard, they include aspects of mutual face concern reflective of both face-restoration and face-saving strategies.

Face-saving. Several of the sets of reviewers' comments contained clear attempts to signal respect for the author's ideas, one key aspect of face-saving. In fact, a pattern emerged whereby reviewers prefaced their comments with attempts to recognize the value of the submission. Some face-saving comments were minimal and ineffective given the larger context of their comments (e.g., the reviewer who "was delighted to read the essay" but later described it as "somewhat embarrassing" and something that "should never have been submitted"). However, others initiated a face negotiation strategy informed by a clear sensitivity (Ifert & Roloff, 1997) to the author throughout the review. In other words, the reviewers comments were situated in a perspective whereby the author's work was simultaneously respected and critiqued.

> In the following comments I try to point up what I see as both the strengths and perhaps some of the weaknesses of the paper. In many cases, I ask questions and pursue lines of thinking as a sort of dialogue with the authors . . . in fact, this paper has been very stimulating for me. I hope these comments are useful as you revise this piece for publication, which I would strongly encourage you to do.

One review in particular captured the role that face-saving plays in the process of gaining feedback for one's scholarship. The reviewer, a European American woman, provided a comprehensive set of comments (4 full pages, single-spaced) including strong remarks on both the strengths and weaknesses of the manuscript. However, the spirit of her review featured a mutual face concern (Cocroft & Ting-Toomey, 1994) and a clear attempt to ensure that the author's face was not endangered (Tracy, 1990).

> Your conclusion looks good. Your points about these issues as ongoing inquiry are right on mark—my comments above are designed to add more to your framework rather than detract from what you have already done. I believe that you can do more at this point because of the references to your data and to extant literature. Making additional connections with prior research and developing your ideas more fully can help you develop this manuscript from an okay manuscript to an article that really contributes something fresh to our understandings of [this] theory and provides a springboard for future research by yourself and others. In no way do I want you to think that I did not enjoy your manuscript or appreciate the intricacies of the area in which you are working. My comments are meant to push you further. I appreciate it when a reviewer not only gives me a new insight

into my research and thinking but also provides direction through sources. I wish you good luck.

Instead of face-restoration strategies that featured comments focused on self-needs, comments reflecting attempts at face-saving included a consciousness toward other-needs. In many ways, several of the reviews were offered in a collaborative/cooperative spirit whereby mutual face need and concern (Ting-Toomey, 1988) were maintained.

Face-assertion. As noted in the literature review, face-assertion strategies focus on defending and supporting one's need for inclusion. In the case of analyzing the comments of European American reviewers within the blind review process, examples of face-assertion appeared in a couple of different contexts. First, some European American reviewers used face-assertion statements to defend their "right" to critique scholarship that sought to represent the lived experiences of other cultural group members. As illustrated by the set of comments below, these strategies featured a rationale as to the value of European American reviewers' perspectives within the review process of research that works to engage the privileged positioning in society.

I am an Anglophone male. Though I have had very extensive, very considerable, very extended contact with those of other cultures and ethnicities, the critical stance of this book labels me an outsider. I say this in the interest of bracketing any assumptions, since an essentialistic world view such as that presented in the text could deny any particular insight into the problematics addressed by this text . . . I wouldn't, myself, "fiat" the white, male dominator to act as a "foil" against which to unite all Others.

Further along in his critique, this same reviewer urged the author to "engage the white, male co-cultural interactant as part of [the] theory." This comment reflected a pattern of response from European American reviewers as explicated next.

The second set of examples of face-assertion strategies featured comments that focused on including European American male experiences within research specifically (and explicitly) aimed at focusing on the lived experiences of marginalized groups (from their particular cultural standpoints). Consistent across three different journal article review processes, reviewers self-identified themselves as "White males" and asked the author to consider them as well. For instance, one of these reviewers wrote:

As I read your rationale and your excerpts, I began to wonder to what degree the feelings and conversational strategies described by your co-researchers were a function of power differences rather than (or in addition to) being a function of not being a member of the "dominant" culture. For example, on p. 14 I wondered whether young, white male employees at lower level of hierarchical organizations also may have to "work to have their voices heard, only to be ignored by others." Again, on p. 21 I wondered whether young white males might feel pressured to engage in "extensive preparation" when communicating with organizational superiors. As a young, white male, I certainly would feel this way if I were called on to interact regularly with my university president, or even my dean (whether the individual was a male or female).

On one level, this reviewer's recognition of how communication often is situated within power imbalances is noteworthy. However, such face-assertion strategies, ones which focused on self-face and inclusion issues (Ting-Toomey, 1988), negated the very core of the fundamental premises that the research was based. These comments emulate an interesting point of analysis in that the European American reviewers' attempts to align themselves with marginalized group members might indicate an unconscious denial of their privilege as dominant group members. In other words, their comments work to diminish the role that larger social power dynamics have within the workings of everyday interactions in particular situations (e.g., in the workplace).

Face-giving. The final way that Ting-Toomey (1988) described that face is negotiated is through face-giving, communication that defends and supports the other person's need for inclusion. Within the European American reviewer comments analyzed, several face-giving strategies were evident. As you can see within the example below, some of these focused on the importance of including culture and communication research in certain publication outlets.

> It is very important that you have chosen MCQ as your desired platform for this work. This is precisely the kind of work we need to publish. So much work on co-cultural, particularly marginalized groups is published in fora that find as their audience scholars who are members of such groups—important as it is that these fora exist, much of it "preaches to the choir." MCQ's traditional readership is largely dominant cultural members (read, white people). Although I like to think that communication scholars are a culturally sensitive group, my experience (and yours as well, I wager) is that there is a full-force culture of exclusion in the discipline. Simply put, Eurocentric thinking is entrenched. You need to provide twice as much theoretic strength to gain half the foothold we need for this kind of theory (a familiar cliche to co-cultural members). Cultural bias in the mind of the reader is strong. To get through that, we need to provide extra-strong evidence of the type that convinces that kind of reader. Only then will the "mainstream" be able to recognize the importance and richness of the co-cultural experience and influence.

These comments were from a European American woman and prefaced a review that acknowledged the value of the submission but requested the author to strengthen aspects of the article (with "extra-strong evidence") in order to have the greatest effect with journal's audience. In this regard, this example of face-giving reflected a mutual face concern (Ting-Toomey, 1988) where the reviewer aligned herself with the author in his/her attempts to publish nontraditional research. In some sense, her comments regarding the "full-force culture of exclusion in the discipline" comprise an apology of sorts (Imahori & Cupach, 1994).

The concluding comments from a European American male reviewer (for the same submission) reveal a similar pattern that emerged when analyzing face-giving strategies: Reviewers argued for inclusion of the author's work in "mainstream" journal publications but did so by legitimizing the work through how it related to European Americans. Consider the comments below, giving particular attention to how publication for the article is legitimized through the contribution it can make to general [European American] organizational communication scholarship.

> Your framework reveals commonalities across diverse standpoints. Why? Because adopting a communication orientation is truly a universal process for all co-cultures, dominant as well as token. This process, however, is more readily apprehended by examining the lived experiences of underrepresented members because they deal with these decisions of orientation at a more conscious level AND on a much more regular-permanent basis. I am not forced to confront my racial status on a daily basis, an African American male in a predominately white organization is. The African American male, therefore, has more resources (personal narratives) to draw upon when asked, "So, how do you attempt to fit in?" My answer to that question might be, "I never really have thought about it." That wouldn't be the answer of the African American male in the cubicle next to mine. In the end, I believe that you have begun to develop a framework that explains the process of adopting a communication orientation in organizational settings and that the truly unique contribution you make is that this process can be accessed most effectively (perhaps only) through the experiences of the traditional outsiders within. In essence, you are making a strong case for examining and understanding diversity because understanding diversity in an organization allows all of us (marginalized or dominant cultural members) to understand our experiences a bit better.

This set of comments was from a second round of reviews from the reviewer who initially recommended that the article be rejected (this was the same reviewer who suggested that the author had used "in press" articles to sway the reviewers' opinion of the submission). On one hand, the comments illustrate a strategy of face-giving in that the reviewer is arguing for the acceptance of the piece and it's inclusion in a [dominant] mainstream journal. Given his initial review, these comments might be interpreted as a remediation strategy—one which is used to repair damage caused by unfavorable behavior (Imahori & Curpach, 1994). Simultaneously, however, he is doing so only because he recognizes the value of the work in terms of dominant group experiences (self-face concern). In short, he was involved in face-giving, not face-saving, which would have argued for including the piece because of the ways in which it contributed exclusively to scholarship focusing of the experiences of traditionally marginalized group members (face concern/autonomy).

Discussion

We initiated this project as an attempt to explore the use of Face Negotiation Theory in understanding the comments of anonymous reviewers. We chose to focus specifically on European American reviewers of culture and communication research because of the perceived intensity of some of their comments. Initially, we consciously chose to use the term blind in our article title to draw its possible double meaning. "Mainstream" journals in the field of communication use a blind review process whereby authors are asked to mask their identities and reviewers are encouraged to remain anonymous. [Interestingly, other significant journals in our field—most notably *The Howard Journal of Communications* and *Women's Studies in Communication*—give reviewers the option of identifying themselves or not.] However, in terms of research on cultural group members, "blind" was also used to illustrate how a social position of privilege (Whiteness) prompted reviews that were oblivious to the complexities of how people of color in the United States communicate. Our cursory assumption was that some of the reviewers' comments reflected that "they just didn't get it" (Orbe, 1998)—meaning that European American scholars could not fully understand the life experiences of people of color in the United States and this was evident in some of their comments that seem accusatory, attacking, and/or off-target. However, although a few negative face comments stand out, they only do so because they take on a hypervisibility for authors. On closer analysis, these examples of face assertion (positive face threats) represent only a small (albeit significant) portion of all of the face negotiation strategies used by "anonymous" reviewers.

Some might suggest that identifying oneself racially within the context of a scholarly review is, in itself, a type of face negotiation strategy. In fact, this was the assumption that was implicit in our initial interests in conducting this line of research. Although we still believe that such anonymous (yet not so anonymous) self-identifiers within the review process constitute face-work, we have found that they are representative of a number of ways in which face negotiation occurs. Simply identifying oneself as European American in reviews of intercultural communication research provides a context for feedback, however, it does not represent any one type of face negotiation strategy. In fact, one of the most valuable insights that emerged from this collaborative research was the recognition that "anonymous" European American reviewers enacted various types of face negotiation strategies in their comments. Given existing literature of the impact of culture on conflict strategies (Ting-Toomey, 1988), one might predict that the predominant strategy for European American reviewers would be face-restoration. However, given our analysis, this was certainly not the use. We found comparable examples of all four primary face-negotiation strategies across all 10 reviews. Interestingly, each review contained comments that reflected at least two different face strategies; several actually had examples of each strategy. In addition, although we found that some European American reviewers focused on maintaining self-face (in terms of highlighting their role/right as a gatekeeper to what was going to be published), most adopted a style that represented mutual face concern.

Thus, upon a more systemic analysis of European American reviewers, we found it difficult to draw any specific conclusion as to their ability to comprehend the complexities of how traditionally marginalized group members negotiate their "outsider-within" social positions. Clearly, our use of

Face Negotiation Theory indicated that some reviewers' comments were situated in a racialized standpoint that made it difficult to see the value of research on "Others"; in this regard, they did operate from a cultural blindness of sorts. However, this was explicitly not the case across the board. The comments of several European American reviewers—including both those of support and critique—reflected a sense of understanding that transcended perceptions of an assumed racial division. Therefore, the assumption that European American reviewers can never evaluate research on culture and communication with the same level of expertise and sensitivity that people of color do has proven faulty. In fact, we suggest that sensitivity to others (e.g., Ifert & Roloff, 1997) within the review process may be correlated with a decreased likelihood of face-restoration and face-assertion. In short, the findings generated within this collaborative research endeavor appear insightful on a number of fronts. However, they need to be contextualized within an identification of the inherent limitations of our work, as well as how they represent a mere starting point for future research.

Limitations and Implications for Future Research

Several significant limitations of our analysis lie within its narrow focus, something that was largely the result of the accessibility to a convenient set of texts. First, our analysis was limited to that of 10 self-identified European American reviewers who chose to self-identify themselves in terms of their race. Given the racial composition of our journal editorial boards, it stands to reason that a significant number of other reviewers were also European American (although they did not make this explicitly clear within their comments). Second, although these reviewers were responding to work originating from various diverse projects, it was all authored by the same person and situated within limited paradigms (interpretative/radical humanist).

A related concern is related to the fact that the author of this work was involved in the analytic process. So several questions remain: Would similar or different patterns be found within a larger number of European American reviewers' comments? Would an analysis by other intercultural scholars with familiarity in face-work scholarship result in similar interpretations of the reviewers' comments? Are our findings indicative of a cultural standpoint and face negotiation strategy? Or are they specific to a personality trait that fosters assertiveness (in terms of self-identification), reaction to work in culture and communication within specific paradigms, or other factors? For instance, Cai and Donahue (1997) concluded that contextual factors within an interaction have the strongest influence (more so than cultural identity or personality) on the overall use of facework. Is this the case with face-negotiation within the anonymous review process? If so, what other factors are most salient?

Consider the work of Leichty and Applegate (1991) who examined (among other variables) how speaker power influenced face-negotiation. In essence, they found that speakers with little power typically provided greater face support and allowed for greater autonomy. Future research might explore these findings in the context of reviewer's face-negotiation strategies. Specifically, one might hypothesize that those reviewers with less power in the academy (e.g., assistant professors without tenure) use more face-saving and face-giving strategies than their more powerful counterparts (e.g., tenured full professors). Given the work by Cai and Donohue (1997), however, power might simply be one factor—alongside others like sensitivity (Ifert & Roloff, 1997)—to be studied. Clearly, our analysis holds significant heuristic value for various lines of research that broaden the narrow focus that we adopted.

A second limitation relates to our interpretations of reviewers' comments. One of the strengths of this article can be seen within the ways in which our analysis reflects a collaborative effort to bring multiple perspectives (e.g., race/ethnicity, gender, age, geographical region, academic rank, etc.) into qualitative research. However, we cannot be sure that the European American reviewers themselves would describe their comments in similar ways. One avenue to rectify this limitation is to invite these very "anonymous" reviewers into the research process. Although this may appear as difficult given the current procedures that govern the review process, examples of such dialogue do exist and appear especially productive (see Allen et al., 1999). Another interesting "turn of the tables" could involve analyses that extend to how authors use different strategies to cope with the loss of face (Edelman, 1994). In other words, how do authors react to threats to their positive face within their comments to the editor and reviewers (e.g., during the revise and resubmit process)? Additionally, how do reviewers perceive author's comments: As attempts to regain face or threaten the positive face of the reviewers themselves (face-retaliation)? In-depth textual analyses of the "paper trail" that typically accompanies the review process (including author's cover letters, anonymous reviews, editor's letters, author's responses, etc.) might provide valuable insight into these questions. We especially are excited about this line of inquiry given that it represents a cyclical "turning of the tables"—one in which incorporates the facework of all parties involved within the review process (not simply the reviewers).

As demonstrated by Blair et al. (1994) and others, engaging anonymous reviews as explicit objects of analysis constitutes a valuable lens into understanding how such a process reflects the values of a discipline. Within our analysis, we have initiated a line of inquiry that seeks to reveal how cultural difference is negotiated within the "anonymous" review process. As the field of communication attempts to acknowledge—and possibly embrace—the role that culture plays within an increasingly diverse society, collaborative research projects that seek to reveal the inextricable relationship between culture and communication within various contexts will serve invaluable. We hope that this article illustrates the value and necessity of engaging all communication processes—including those at the heart of our discipline that traditionally have gone uninterrogated—with equal intensity and thoroughness.

References

Allen, B. J., Orbe, M., & Olivas, M. R. (1999). The complexity of our tears: Dis/enchantment and (in)difference in the academy. *Communication Theory, 9,* 402–429.

Blair, C., Brown, J. R., & Baxter, L. A. (1994). Disciplining the feminine. *Quarterly Journal of Speech, 80,* 383–409.

Brown, P., & Levinson, S. (1987). *Politeness: Some universals in language usage.* Cambridge, England: Cambridge University Press.

Cai, D. A., & Donohue, W. A. (1997). Determinants of facework in intercultural negotiation. *Asian Journal of Communication, 7*(1), 85–110.

Cocroft, B. K., & Ting-Toomey, S. (1994). Facework in Japan and the United States. *International Journal of Intercultural Relations, 18,* 469–509.

Cupach, W. R., & Imahori, T. (1993). Managing social predicaments created by others: A comparison of Japanese and American facework. *Western Journal of Communication, 57,* 431–444.

Cupach, W. R., & Metts, S. (1993). Remedial processes in embarrassing predicaments. In J. A. Anderson (Ed.), *Communication Yearbook* (Vol. 13, pp. 323–352). Newbury Park, CA: Sage.

Cupach, W. R., & Metts, S. (1991). The effects of predicaments and embarrasability on remedial responses to embarrassing situations. *Communications Quarterly, 40*(2), 149–161.

Cupach, W. R., & Metts, S. (1994). *Facework.* Thousand Oaks, CA: Sage.

Edelman, R. J. (1994). Embarrassment and blushing: Factors influencing face-saving strategies. In S. Ting-Toomey (Ed.), *The challenge of facework* (pp. 231–267). Albany: State University of New York Press: Sage.

Ifert, D. E., & Roloff, M. E. (1997). Overcoming expressed obstacles to compliance: The role of sensitivity to the expressions of others and ability to modify self-presentation. *Communication Quarterly, 45,* 55–67.

Imahori, T. T., & Cupach, W. R. (1994). A cross-cultural comparison of the interpretation and management of face: U.S. American and Japanese response to embarrassing situations. *International Journal of Intercultural Relations, 18,* 193–219.

Leichty, G., & Applegate, J. L. (1991). Social cognitive and situational influences on the use of face-saving persuasive strategies. *Human Communication Research, 17,* 451–484.

Lim, T. S. (1994). Facework and interpersonal relationships. In S. Ting-Toomey (Ed.), *The challenge of facework* (pp. 209–229). Albany, NY: State University of New York Press.

Lim, T. S., & Bowers, J. W. (1991). Facework: Solidarity, approbation, and tact. *Human Communication Research, 17,* 415–450.

McCracken, G. (1988). *The long interview.* Newbury Park, CA: Sage.

Medhurst, M. J. (1989). Public address and significant scholarship: Four challenges to the rhetorical renaissance. In M. C. Left & F. J. Kauffeld (Eds.), *Texts in conflict: Critical dialogues on significant episodes in American political rhetoric* (pp. 29–42). Davis, CA: Hermagoras Press.

Metts, S., & Cupach, W. R. (1989). Situational influence on the use of remedial strategies in embarrassing predicaments. *Communication Monographs, 56,* 151–162.

Orbe, M. (1998, November). *African Americans in corporate America: Everyday lived experiences as points of negotiation.* Paper presented at the annual meeting of the National Communication Association convention, New York.

Owen, W. (1984). Interpretive themes in relational communication. *Quarterly Journal of Speech, 70,* 274–287.

Peters, D. P., & Ceci, S. J. (1982). Peer review practices of psychological journals: The fate of published articles, submitted again. *The Behavior & Brain Sciences, 5,* 187–255.

Ting-Toomey, S. (1988). Intercultural conflict styles: A face negotiation theory. In Y. Kim & W. Gudykunst (Eds.), *Theories in intercultural communication* (pp. 213–235). Newbury Park, CA: Sage.

Ting-Toomey, S. (1994). (Ed.) *The challenge of facework* (pp. 1–15). Albany: State University of New York Press.

Tracy, K. (1990). The many faces of facework. In H. Giles & W. P. Robinson (Eds.), *Handbook of language and social psychology* (pp. 209–226). New York: Wiley.

Trees, A. R., & Manusov, V. (1998). Managing face concerns in criticism: Integrating nonverbal behaviors as a dimension of politeness in female friendship dyads. *Human Communications Research, 24,* 564–583.

Wagoner, R., & Waldron, V. R. (1999). How supervisors convey routine bad news: Facework at UPS. *Southern Communication Journal, 64,* 193–210.

Wright, T. J. (1996). *Afrikan American face-saving strategies and friendship embarrassing situations: A qualitative study.* Unpublished masters thesis, California State University of Fullerton, Fullerton.

FOLLOW-UP QUESTIONS AND EXPLORATION PROJECTS

1. Compare the Methods section of the Wright and Orbe article with that produced by Penington. How do you account for the differences in the type of information included in this section in these two articles? Now, compare the ways that findings are presented in these two articles. How is ethnicity included as a component of analysis in each article? How do you account for any differences?

2. While Face Negotiation theory is not generally considered a "Critical Theory," it is definitely applied with a critical theory edge in this instance. To what extent do you think that application is a legitimate extension of this theory?

3. What advantages and disadvantages can you see to a "blind-review" process of journal article review? What implications does this process have for the way you interpret our "knowledge" about communication?

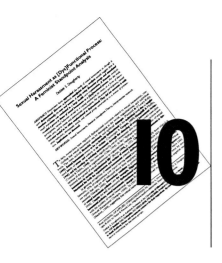

10

It Depends on Where You Stand
Perspectives on Sexual Harassment

Sexual harassment is a rising subject of concern in organizations and there is a growing body of research on this topic (i.e., Lee & Guerrero, 2001). In particular, processes of meaning-making and symbolism regarding sexual harassment as related to privilege and oppression in organizations has been the subject of much communication research (i.e. Clair, 1993). The following article by Dougherty contributes to this literature by exploring why sexual harassment continues to occur despite legal penalties and organizational training designed to reduce it.

Background of Standpoint Theory

To call Standpoint theory a single, unified, theory is somewhat of a misnomer as there are several distinct versions of this approach (Harding, 2004). This said, a uniting premise of Standpoint theories is that we all see the world from a point of view situated in time, space, and social class relations (Harding, 1991). The particular viewpoint that gets transmitted as 'knowledge' tends to be the viewpoint of the dominant group, since members of this group occupy positions of power in relation to the construction and dissemination of knowledge (think back to the last chapter about the peer-review process here). The insight of Standpoint theory is that members of oppressed groups (i.e. women) see the world from a different perspective than members of dominant groups (Hallstein, 1999). Unfortunately, this perspective is often absent from our published 'knowledge.' In addition, symbolism and accompanying assumptions related to gender are deeply embedded in our collective meaning system (Yeo, 2004). The goal of a Standpoint analysis, then, is to call into question our assumptions about the world and to explore ways that power dynamics affect our perceptions.

Article Structure

Daugherty (2001) uses the introduction and literature review section of this article to situate her study in the context of both studies of sexual harassment and work on Feminist Standpoint theories. Next, she describes the methods by which she collected and analyzed her data. The results of this study are presented in the section headed "Analysis: [Dys]Functional Process" (p. 204) where she presents transcribed segments of male, female, and mixed-gender focus group dialogue on themes related to coping mechanisms, therapeutic touch, camaraderie, and consequences. The final Discussion section highlights her argument that sexual harassment does not function in the same way for members of dominant groups (men) and members of oppressed groups (women). The paper concludes with a discussion of the strengths and limitations of this research as well as some implications for organizational practice.

Distinctive Points

A fundamental subject of discussion and controversy with respect to sexual harassment is whether or not a given behavior 'counts' as an example of sexual harassment. Research is clear that women identify more behaviors as sexual harassment than men do (Mongeau & Blalock, 1994) but has not been able to explain why this would be the case. Because Standpoint theory is located in the tradition of Critical theories (Craig, 1999), it highlights ways that power, privilege and oppression affect communication and meaning-making processes. Including group differences in privilege allows Daugherty to understand differences in female and male perspectives on sexualized behavior in an organizational setting.

References

Clair, R. P. (1993). The use of framing devices to sequester organizational narratives: Hegemony and harassment. *Communication Monographs, 60,* 114–136.

Craig, R. T. (1999). Communication theory as a field. *Communication Theory, 9,* 119–161.

Hallstein, D. L. O. (1999). A postmodern caring: Feminist standpoint theories, revisioned caring, and communication ethics. *Western Journal of Communication, 63,* 32–56.

Harding, S. (2004). A socially relevant philosophy of science? Resources from standpoint theorie's controversiality. *Hypatia, 19,* 25–48.

Harding, S. (1991). *Whose science? Whose knowledge? Thinking from women's lives.* Ithaca, NY: Cornell University Press.

Lee, J. W., & Guerrero, L. K. (2001). Types of touch in cross-sex relationships between coworkers: Perceptions of relational and emotional messages, inappropriateness, and sexual harassment. *Journal of Applied Communication Research, 29,* 197–220.

Mongeau, P. A., & Blalock, J. (1994). Student evaluations of instructor immediacy and sexually harassing behaviors: An experimental investigation. *Journal of Applied Communication Research, 22,* 256–272.

Yeo, M. (2004). Harry Potter and the Chamber of Secrets: Feminist interpretations/Junian dreams [Electronic Version]. *Simile, 4,* Article 45. Retrieved May 2, 2005, from http://www.utpjournals.com/simile.

Sexual Harassment as [Dys]Functional Process: A Feminist Standpoint Analysis

Debbie S. Dougherty

ABSTRACT *Researchers have approached the study of sexual harassment as though it were dysfunctional. However, a feminist standpoint theory analysis would suggest that it functions differently for men and women. A study using discussion groups and stimulated recall interviews was conducted in a large health care organization. A thematic analysis revealed a primary theme of sexual harassment as a [dys]functional process. For the male participants, sexual behavior served as a coping mechanism for stress, as a form of therapeutic care, and to create and demonstrate camaraderie. For the women participants, sexual behavior tended to be either nonfunctional or dysfunctional. They did not associate it with stress reduction, therapeutic touch, and viewed group camaraderie as a means of prevention. Implications are discussed.*

KEYWORDS: *Sexual harassment, Feminist Standpoint Theory, Interpretative research.*

To date, researchers have explored dysfunctional outcomes related to sexual harassment, concluding that sexual harassment can be damaging at the social, organizational, and individual levels. The costs include financial, emotional, and spiritual damages (Paetzold & O'Leary-Kelly, 1993). Sexual harassment seems to be particularly dysfunctional at the individual level due to heightened levels of stress and anxiety in its victims (Cartwright & Cooper, 1997; Hemphill & Pfieffer, 1986) and by creating an isolating environment through the silencing of sexual harassment victims (Conrad & Taylor, 1994). Not least significantly, sexual harassment also tends to recreate masculine systems of domination in organizations (Clair, 1994). In fact "dysfunctional discursive practices have fostered the spread of sexual harassment in organizations, leading to the current epidemic of sexual harassment in modern organizational life" (Kreps, 1994, p. 127). Clearly sexual harassment is dysfunctional for both the organization and victims of sexual harassment.

In growing recognition of sexual harassment related dysfunctions (particularly those related to lawsuits), 97% of organizations now report having sexual harassment policies while 84% of employees report that they are well informed about their employer's sexual harassment policy (Sexual Harassment Charges, 1999). Researchers continue to provide insight into improving the effectiveness of sexual harassment policies (see for example, Hippensteele & Pearson, 1999; Keyton & Rhodes, 1999). Despite the well documented dysfunctional nature of sexual harassment and extensive sexual harassment policies, sexual harassment continues to be a problem across the organizational spectrum with the number of sexual harassment charges filed with the EEOC increasing by 127% since 1991 (Sexual Harassment Charges, 1999). In 1997, 11% of claims filed with the EEOC were by men (Markert, 1999), suggesting that sexual harassment affects a broad range of victims in negative ways.

From JOURNAL OF APPLIED COMMUNICATION RESEARCH, Vol. 29, No. 4, November 2001 by D. S. Dougherty. Copyright © 2001 by Taylor & Francis Ltd., http://www.tandf.co.uk/journals. Reprinted by permission.

Debbie S. Dougherty is an Assistant Professor at the University of Missouri-Columbia, Department of Communication, 115 Switzler Hall, Columbia, MO 65211-2310, 573.882.0300, doughertyd@missouri.edu. The author would like to thank Kathleen Krone and anonymous reviewers for their suggestions. Special thanks to Jack Sargent for his assistance in moderating the discussion groups.

Given the dysfunctional nature of sexual harassment, one question emerges: Why does sexual harassment continue to be a problem in organizations? It would seem that if sexual harassment were purely dysfunctional then attempts by the organizational hierarchy to manage the problem through sexual harassment policies and training would have more success. Clearly there is a gap between the intent of sexual harassment policies and the enactment of those policies. Feminist standpoint theories would suggest that men and women experience sexual harassment differently (Dougherty, 1999; Wood, 1994). As a result, sexual harassment may serve different functions for men and women.[1] While research has focused on the dysfunctional nature of sexual harassment, it has largely failed to examine potentially functional components of sexual harassment for the perpetrator of the act. In other words, while sexual harassment is dysfunctional at the individual and social levels, it may be a functional means of organizing—the constant creation and recreation of organizational processes— for some organizational members. The present study uses feminist standpoint theories in an attempt to examine and understand the continuing prevalence of sexual harassment in organizations. I begin with the premise that sexual harassment is discursively constructed and managed (Bingham, 1994; Wood, 1994). Therefore discursive constructions of sexual harassment by men and women will be examined in this study. I will first review feminist standpoint theories followed by an analysis of the sexual harassment literature from a feminist standpoint perspective. Finally, the results of a study examining men's and women's discursively constructed standpoints of sexual harassment will be presented.

Feminist Standpoint Theories

A number of organizational scholars have called for the use of feminist theories in general (Fine, 1993; Marshall, 1993) and feminist standpoint theories more specifically to better understand gendered processes in organizations (Allen, 1998; Bullis, 1993; Buzzanell, 1994; Dougherty & Krone, 2000; Putnam, 1990; Wood, 1994). Furthermore, there has been recognition that feminist standpoint theories provide a unique perspective from which to explore and understand sexual harassment processes (Dougherty, 1999; Wood, 1994). The present study answers this call by exploring men's and women's standpoints of sexual harassment in organizations.

The basic premise of feminist standpoint theories is that some centralized social groups control social structure and cultural expectations, consequently exerting control over more marginalized groups. Men, particularly white heterosexual men, tend to be the dominant social group in organizations. Women, on the other hand, tend to be marginalized and dominated. It is important to note that men experience positions of dominance to varying degrees (Mumby, 1998). However, although their behaviors differ, they tend to reinforce masculine domination in varying ways (Mumby, 1998). Furthermore, different groups of women experience the margins in varying ways both in general (see Bell, Orbe, Drummond, & Camara, 2000) and as related to sexual harassment (see Shelton & Chavous, 1999), suggesting that there are no monolithic standpoints. As a result, any claim of a woman's standpoint is necessarily partial.

A number of feminist standpoint theories have been articulated (for review see Harding, 1991). However, Hartsock (1997) contends that feminist standpoint theories are based on two foundational issues. First, truth is always mediated by an individual's understanding of reality (Hawkesworth, 1989). Consequently, feminist standpoint theorists reject the notion of truth, suggesting instead that truth is understood differently based on the status and related perspectives of the knower (Hawkesworth, 1989). The second foundation of feminist standpoint theories is the focus on political action (Hartsock, 1997). Scholars and managers who use feminist standpoint theories should not only articulate differences, but they must also attempt to mediate positive social change (Hallstein, 2000). Consequently, feminist standpoint research must connect gendered differences to issues of dominance and marginality as mediated within a political, social, and material context. The change orientation of feminist standpoint theories make them ideal for applied communication research.

Two underlying factors shape the present discussion of feminist standpoint theories. First and foremost, standpoints are not based on behavioral differences between men and women. In fact, research suggests that there are very few consistent behavioral differences between men and women in organizations (e.g. Canary & Hause, 1993). Instead, differing standpoints are shaped by material realities that are imposed by external forces and socially constructed through discourse (Hartsock, 1987). Through external and social forces, men and women experience and discursively construct different role expectations (Harding, 1991). These role expectations shape men's and women's experiences when considering issues related to sexual harassment. Men are more likely to form standpoints around the expected role of harasser while women are more likely to form standpoints around the expected role of the victim.

Second, it is important to distinguish between having standpoints and understanding standpoints. All members of organizations operate from various positions of marginality and centrality in organizations. This is called having a standpoint and it generally involves nonreflective discourse and activity in an organization (Dougherty & Krone, 2000). Understanding standpoints, on the other hand, is an active process of organization involving reflective agency in which individuals struggle to achieve an understanding of their positions in an organization in relationship to others (Hartsock, 1987). Consequently, feminist standpoint theory provides an excellent framework from which to view and understand organizing processes. Dialogue is one possible avenue to understanding standpoints. Through dialogue, mutual understanding can occur. Furthermore, dialogue can create systemic thinking (Kellet, 1999), making it a potentially effective means of understanding systems of oppression and different standpoints within those systems. The following study provided men and women the opportunity to engage in dialogue about their sexual harassment related standpoints.

Sexual Harassment and Feminist Standpoints

Scholars tend to agree that sexual harassment is not about sex. It is about power (Bingham, 1994; Bowker, 1993). Like all forms of organizational power, "repression is not necessarily an objective or a prerequisite, but often is simply a by-product of an ideology that maximizes the organization's ability to act" (Hardy & Clegg, 1996, p. 633). In other words, power is not necessarily enacted simply to perpetuate itself. Power in action may have functional implications for the actor. While both scholars and change agents should take care not to allow functional explanations to "gloss over complex sociological, political, and historical issues . . ." (Hawkesworth, 1989, p. 542), it is still important to consider functional explanations as part of a complex array of issues related to sexual harassment. Two standpoint related differences between men and women contribute to the possibility that sexual harassment functions differently for men and women: sexual harassment is normative in organizations and labeling difference in sexual harassment.

Scholars argue that sexual harassment is normative in organizations for both men and women (Dougherty, 1999; Wood, 1994). Feminist standpoint theory would argue that although sexual harassment is normative for both men and women in organizations, there are different gendered experiences of that behavior. Variations in definitional interpretations of sexual harassment illustrate these differences. Although sexual harassment is clearly a serious issue, there is "no widely agreed upon definition" (Gerdes, 1999, p. 12). The courts have recognized the existence of quid pro quo sexual harassment, or when employment decisions are based on submission to or rejection of sexual coercion (Gerdes, 1999). More recently the courts have also recognized sexual harassment as a hostile environment in which sexualized behaviors interfere with a person's work or creates an "intimidating, hostile, or offensive working environment" (Gerdes, 1999, p. 12). Despite the seeming clarity of these interpretations of sexual harassment, the specific behaviors that constitute sexual harassment are consistently interpreted differently by men and women (Berryman-Fink & Riley, 1997). Men, particularly men who identify with the role of harasser, tend to interpret fewer behaviors as sexual harassment than women. For men, because sexual harassment is normative it also tends to be acceptable. Even when men do recognize that their behavior is harassing, they argue that it is acceptable and normal (Sundt, 1996). Many men, however, fail to acknowledge that their behavior is sexual harassment. Instead they use alternative labels, suggesting that sexual behavior is an expected part of the male role in organizations (Berryman-Fink & Riley, 1997). While sexual harassment is also normative for women, it tends to be viewed as less appropriate. For women, sexual harassment creates personal stress and anxiety (Hippensteele & Pearson, 1999), and reinforces dominant structures of oppression (Clair, 1994). Two possible conclusions can be drawn from the discussion of sexual harassment as normative. First, it is possible that the primary function of sexual harassment is to maintain systems of oppression. There is certainly research supporting this position (Clair, 1994). Second, however, it is also possible that sexual harassment serves different functions for men and women beyond the maintenance of systems of oppression. Recent research also provides support for this position, finding that issues of power provide only an additive effect to a larger unknown cause of sexual harassment (De Coster, Estes, & Mueller, 1999). This would explain why sexual harassment persists despite efforts to eliminate it. In actuality, sexual harassment may serve dual functions, both as a self perpetuating system of oppression and as a functional part of the organizing process. This possibility remains unexplored in the literature. Two research questions emerge:

RQ1: How do men and women discursively construct sexual harassment in organizations?

RQ2: How do men and women discursively reinforce and resist constructions of sexual harassment in organizations?

The following analysis is part of a larger study of sexual harassment and provides a partial response to these questions.

Methods

To study how men and women talk about sexual harassment, an interpretive study using discussion groups and stimulated recall interview methods was conducted. Each of these issues are discussed followed by a clarification of the participants, data analysis, and forms of verification.

Interpretive Paradigm

The interpretive research paradigm represents an alternative to the functionalist research paradigm (Putnam, 1983). Instead of focusing on behavior or cognition as the unit of analysis, interpretive research "centers on the study of meanings, that is, the way individuals make sense of their world through their communicative behaviors" (Putnam, 1983, p. 31). Because the purpose of the present study is to examine how organizational members make sense of sexual harassment through talk, using the interpretive paradigm is appropriate.

Methods

To address the research questions, the discourse of groups of individuals in a large health care organization was analyzed. Triangulated methods of data gathering were used. Participants engaged in group discussions followed by individual interviews using a stimulated recall technique.

The organization. Because the study focus is on how sexual harassment is socially constructed, and because social constructions may vary from organization to organization, all participants came from a single organization. The use of a single organization to study organizing processes is a common practice in the field of communication both for qualitative research (see for example Gibson & Papa, 2000; Mattson & Buzzanell, 1999) and quantitative research (see for example Kreps, 1987; Miller, Johnson, Hart, & Peterson, 1999). While this body of work is not generalizable across organizational types, it does enhance our understanding of organizational processes across organizations.

This study was conducted in a large Health Care Organization (HCO) in the Midwest. HCO is a regional, comprehensive health care organization at the center of which is a hospital and medical center. The study was limited to those who worked within the HCO hospital and medical center. Within these components of HCO at the time of this study were 2,201 employees. Of these employees, 447 were men and 1,754 were women. All but 117 of the employees were of European ancestry.

Research participants. Eleven women and twelve men from HCO participated in the present study. Not surprising, given the predominance of employees of European ancestry, all of the participants were European Americans. The average age of the participants was 38. The youngest participant was 19 and the oldest participant was 56. The average number of years of employment at HCO was 7.6 years. Overall, the participants had high levels of education. One participant had a doctorate, nine participants received bachelor degrees, eight participants received associate degrees, two participants had received high school diplomas, two participants claimed some college education, while one participant held a nursing degree but did not specify which type of degree held. Three of the participants supervised between 6 and 70 employees. One employee provided janitorial services, eight provided administrative services ranging from secretarial to managerial, seven were medical technicians, five were working as registered nurses, and two participants provided related medical patient support. Because doctors were not officially employed by HCO, they were excluded from the study.

Participants were selected using theoretical construct sampling (Lindlof, 1995). Theoretical criteria included gender and current employment at HCO. Eleven women and twelve men participated in the men's and women's groups. Ten participants, five men and five women, agreed to participate in the mixed gender discussion groups.[2]

Instead of identifying a sample that is large enough to be representative of the population, interpretive scholars sample until they achieve redundancy, or the point at which no new information is identified (Patton, 1990). Consequently there is no maximum or minimum number of participants' across interpretive studies. In this study, 23 individuals participated in between two and four interactions with the researcher, producing redundancy in this study.

Discussion groups. Three types of discussion groups were conducted: Discussion groups with women participants, discussion groups with men participants, and discussion groups with a mixture of men and women participants. Conducting multiple discussion groups to achieve phenomenological saturation, the point at which little new information is offered by groups, is important (Herndon, 1993). The recommended number of groups is between three and four (Herndon, 1993). A total of nine discussion groups were conducted, three for each gender combination. The themes discussed here were areas in which phenomenological saturation occurred.

Group membership ranged from three to five participants. As a woman, I acted as moderator for the women's discussion groups. Jack Sargent, a colleague and experienced group facilitator, was the male moderator for the men's discussion groups. Both Jack and I facilitated the mixed gender groups.

The discussion groups were video and audio taped. The video tapes were used in the interview portion of the study to stimulate recall of the events in the discussion groups while the audio tapes were used for transcription purposes. Following Morgan and Spanish's (1984) example, immediately prior to the discussion, group participants provided demographic information and wrote briefly about an incident of sexual harassment about which they had heard. They were then asked a series of questions to stimulate discussion (see Appendix). Each group discussion was approximately two hours.

Stimulated recall interviews. One limitation of discussion groups is that the researcher has limited ability to probe deeply into individual responses (Morgan & Spanish, 1984). To account for this limitation, each of the participants engaged in an individual stimulated recall interview following their group discussions. Stimulated recall is used when a conversation is recorded and then played back to the participants to help trigger their memory of the conversation (Frey, Botan, Friedman, & Kreps, 1991). Participants commented about their interactions while watching their video tapes. I conducted the interviews as soon after the participants' discussion groups as their schedules permitted. Participants met with me individually in a private room where they were asked to watch the video tape of their discussion group. They were asked to pause the tape when they wanted to make a comment and fast forward the tape when the discussion centered on issues about which they did not wish to elaborate. I also would push pause to more fully probe an issue.

Data analysis. Both the discussion groups and interviews were transcribed by the author and checked for accuracy, totaling 1011 single spaced typed pages of transcripts. Because the sociolinguistic patterns and technical organization of speech were not the "focal interest" (Lindlof, 1995, p. 211) for the present study, notations were used minimally. A thematic analysis of the social construction of sexual harassment was conducted. A thematic analysis is "the process of recovering the theme or themes that are embodied and dramatized in the evolving meanings and imagery of the work" (Van Manen, 1990, p. 78). In other words, themes are not imposed upon the experiences of the participants. Instead, themes emerge from the context of the experience of the phenomenon. Themes were developed and analyzed using the selective or highlighting approach (Van Manen, 1990) with the reduction explanation, and theory steps suggested by Lindlof (1995).

In the selective approach "we listen to or read a text several times and ask what statement(s) or phrases(s) seem particularly essential or revealing about the phenomenon or experience being described. These statements we then circle, underline, or highlight" (Van Manen, 1990, p. 93). The selective method can be effectively combined with the three steps of analysis suggested by Lindlof (1995): Reduction, explanation, and theory.

Although each step is described separately, they are part of an ongoing process with each phase occurring cyclically as well as simultaneously. Reduction first involves the sorting of data according to potential emerging themes. It is necessary to use reduction to manage the tremendous volume of data. The second step in reduction is conceptualizing possible emergent labels. In this study, the reduction process began immediately following the first discussion group. Notations about possible themes were made in a notebook and the meaning of what the group discussed was contemplated. The reduction process continued throughout the transcription and writing phases of the project. As the data were transcribed, notes about themes and emerging questions were written in a notepad. Once the data were transcribed, colored notes and markers were used to both identify possible themes and to recheck the data to be sure that the themes were strong and persistent. Finally, before writing, the data were reduced further by cutting and pasting together data that both supported and rejected the themes. In this way, 1011 pages of transcriptions were reduced to a manageable level. The labels for the themes constantly evolved until one was identified that captured the essence of the participants' experiences.

The second step in Lindlof's phenomenological strategy involves the explanation of the thematic labels. This is accomplished by combining first order explanations, those explanations used by the participants, and the researcher's experiences and knowledge to create a second order explanation (Lindlof, 1995). The second order explanation is the sense the researcher makes of the experience.

The final step is the interpretation of the themes, or the application of the themes to a theory (Lindlof, 1995). It is essential for researchers to draw on the domain of theory when designing and executing projects" (Lindlof, 1995, p. 72). The present study attempted to contribute to an understanding of both feminist standpoint theories and sexual harassment literature, both separately and in relationship to each other.

Verification. Verification represents a standard of quality in qualitative research (Creswell, 1997). Four forms of verification were used: Methods were triangulated (Lindlof, 1995), a constant comparative method in which alternative themes were constantly compared to identify the best themes for the participants' experiences of sexual harassment, a member check was employed in which one woman participant and one man participant were asked to assess how well the themes captured their experiences (Creswell, 1997), and finally the study uses a form of face validity in which the readers are invited to assess the efficacy of the themes based on the evidence presented (Creswell, 1997).

Analysis: [Dys]Functional Process

One surprising finding of the present study is the discursively constructed functional nature of sexual harassment for some organizational members. While sexual harassment may result in the previously mentioned dysfunctional *outcomes,* it can be a functional part of the organizing *process.* The function of sexual harassment within the organizing process, however, appears to be differentiated along gendered standpoints. For the men, sexual harassment tended to be functional. The same behavior tended to be dysfunctional for the women. Initially, I was resistant to the idea that sexual harassment may serve organizing functions for men. My concern that such a perspective could be used to further marginalize women overwhelmed my willingness to "see" the men's experiences as they understood them. Phenomenological saturation for this theme was so extensive, however, that I began to reflect on these themes.

Of key importance to understanding the following analysis is the use of different labels by men and women to describe similar behaviors. The men would frequently describe a behavior and then claim that the behavior was not sexual harassment. Despite their tendency to avoid the label "sexual harassment" the men did seem to recognize that the behavior was sexualized and that it could be interpreted as sexual harassment. Women, on the other hand, were much more likely to label behaviors as sexual harassment. Consequently, both sexualized behavior and sexual harassment are referred to in this section in an attempt to both remain true to the participants' experiences and to illustrate the perceptual differences in the gendered constructions of sexual harassment. Sexualized behavior is defined as behavior that is verbally or nonverbally sexually explicit or implicit. Examples would be sexual jokes, references to sexuality (Male technician to a patient regarding a female bathing the patient's genitals: "Don't blame me if she can't stop herself"), references to body parts as a sexual evaluation (the size of a woman's "racks"—breasts), touching beyond socially functional behaviors (touching another employees bottom, hugs, shoulder rubs) and threats to touch ("I am the butt checker. You can't leave until I check your Butt"). For the women, the same sexualized behavior referred to by the men tended to be dysfunctional and was more likely to be referred to as sexual harassment, or at least as inappropriate. Three [dys]functional themes emerged from the data: sexual harassment as a coping mechanism, therapeutic touch, and camaraderie. The consequences of these themes will also be discussed.

Coping Mechanism

Coping mechanism refers to the use of sexualized behavior to cope with job related stress. For the men, HCO and other health care organizations tend to produce greater stress in the employee than other work environments. Preliminary research findings indicate that this stress may be a product of reverse sexism in female dominated aspects of health care organizations (Kreps, 1987).[3] Sexualized behavior was these men's means of reducing stress so they could continue to work in the health care environment. On the other hand, the women's groups did not mention stress as an important issue. This is not to suggest that they do not experience stress. To the contrary, women health care providers may experience more stress than men (Ray & Miller, 1994). Consistent with the men's reports, research in general suggests that coworker support is important in managing stress (see Ray & Miller, 1994). However, unlike the male participants, the women did not seem to associate stress management with sexual harassment.

Men. Each of the male participants emphasized the incredible stress they experienced on a daily basis dealing with illness and particularly with life and death. This finding is particularly interesting given that some of the men did not directly deal with patients. Surprisingly, all three of the men's groups spontaneously mentioned stress as an important work related issue. It was surprising because the discussion group protocol was not created to discover this information. The fact that sexualized behavior as a coping mechanism for stress emerged as a strong theme suggests an experiential intensity:

Male A:[4]   I think the important thing about what we would define as sexual harassment, or what anybody else would define as sexual harassment, has a lot to do with familiarity. You know, and I think everybody [indicating group members] brought it up. We all joke with each other, you know, I think particularly in a medical care situation where sometimes it is life and death around here. And that does cause a lot of stress and tension on care givers particularly. I think we tend to step over the line a whole lot more often than in the bank or an insurance office. But being familiar with the people that you work with, you know, and knowing their boundaries and how they've expressed those boundaries to you. I'm not very concerned about sexually harassing any of my co-workers, unless I don't know them and they don't know me. Cause I'll probably on a daily basis say something that's going to offend somebody somewhere. If I, if I know the people I'm dealing with and they know me well, you know then they'll be just as comfortable putting it right back in my face. I was thinking of one person. I'd gotten just a choice insult from one of the security guards. And one of the, one of the cath lab women, she'd been picking on me so I used it on her. God I had to back off and apologize so much I was crawling up the wall, I mean. [laughter]. Something about, what did I say to her? Oh, "how many wrinkles on a pigs butt?" And she said "I don't know, how many?" And I said, "well, smile and I'll count" [laughter]. And she got so mad at me. And I said, "first of all, you don't have any wrinkles."

Jack: Could that be considered sexual-harassment?

Male B: it could be to her.

Male D: I doubt it. I don't see how.

Interestingly, each of the men's groups emphasized the differences separating health care organizations from other types of professions such as banking or insurance. They argued that there is almost a license to enact more sexualized behavior due to the emotional nature of their jobs, particularly as they pertain to stress. Consequently, they argue, the behaviors are unlikely to be interpreted as sexual harassment. Whether it is sexual harassment to compare a woman's face to a pig's "butt" will be dependent upon a number of factors, including the pervasiveness of such behavior. However, by creating an environment in which such behavior is accepted, these men also increase the likelihood that a hostile environment will exist.

Because sexual behavior was functional for the men, it was clear to them that sexual behavior was not sexual harassment. Behaviors that are typically viewed as contributing to a hostile environment were specifically and frequently labeled as "not sexual harassment:"

Jack: Let me ask you this. What is your definition of sexual harassment?

Male B: I think it's more of a, something personal to person. You know?

Male C: Yeah.

Male B: You do something to that person. Um, I tell a dirty joke out loud, I don't think that's sexual harassment. I don't think a funny joke posted on a board is sexual harassment, if I do something either physical or directly toward, directed toward you. If I make a comment about you, or I tell a joke maybe strictly toward you, or I physically touch you in a [sexual] way, yeah, that is. But I think something. I think like [Male C] said, that stress reliever. That's how our department runs. I mean boy.

Jack: Talk about that stress reliever.

Male B: Oh, telling dirty jokes.

Male C: Yeah.

Male A: Something to lighten up the mood.

Male B: Something, something—making a comment about, just about anything. You know, just a general comment like, "did you see the rack [breasts] on her"—or something. I mean not like that.

Male C: Yeah.

Male B: But just general comment made out, that everybody's around. Sometimes you need that.

Male A: Just to pass the time or to get conversation.

Male B: And you're just pumping away. You know. Geez, I know there is some times when you don't have time to even think. And just, something to break the ice later on, or something, you read something in the paper.

Male A: Yeah.

Male B: Or you make a comment. I don't think that is [sexual harassment]. But I think so many times it is taken that way.

The male groups engaged in rather lengthy discussions about the nature of the stress they experienced, the unique nature of that stress in a health care environment, and the importance of sexualized behavior in coping with that stress. It is interesting that these men did not actually say the word "sexual" once during this discussion, although they were responding to the question "what is your definition of sexual harassment." Instead, the participants used vague references such as "it" and "that." The behaviors the men discussed, such as telling or displaying dirty jokes and calling attention to a woman's body parts could clearly contribute to a hostile environment. However, these men were clear that because this behavior serves important stress reducing functions, it was not sexual harassment.

While one male participant, a manager, did not view sexualized behavior such as joking as a functional means of stress reduction, he was later ridiculed during the individual interviews. He claimed that he did not joke with his staff because he did not want to create an environment that tolerated such behavior. Other participants called his comments "managerese" and "anal."

Women.   The length of the men's discussion about the nature of stress becomes particularly important when viewed in conjunction with the women's discussions, or rather, lack of discussion about stress. At no point did the women talk about the stress of their jobs, the unique nature of health care, or about sexualized behavior as functional. This may be because for victims, sexual harassment is highly stressful (Cartwright & Cooper, 1997), offsetting the potential stress reducing function of sexualized behaviors. It is also possible that given the number of women working at HCO, the women in this study may have access to a greater range of coping strategies than the men. As a result, the women may have chosen other alternatives to managing their stress.

Not only did the women not talk about stress or its relationship to sexual harassment, on only one occasion did a woman talk about a behavior that may be interpreted as sexualized as potentially beneficial. The following quotation is from her woman's group discussion:

Female A: I did work with a male surgical tech. If you knew him, he was a very friendly guy. He would not. It didn't bother him a bit to give you a hug. And there are guys now that I work with that, you know, I can walk up to them and say, you know, "I just need a hug today." And they'll give you a hug. Total friends. My husband knows them. I do it in front of my husband, you know, it's nothing.

It is unclear whether the hugging discussed by this participant was a means of stress reduction, affiliation, cohesion, or had some other function. Because the women failed to discuss stress, it is difficult to know if they coped with stress in the same way as the men and if they see health care organizations as unique in terms of sexualized behavior.

The findings of this study are not intended to suggest that women health care professionals do not experience stress on the job. The questions asked, however, did not trigger responses about stress, suggesting that the women experience job related stress in ways not related to this study. So while women may experience stress over the life and death situations of their patients, they do not appear to relate that stress or its reduction to sexualized behavior. Consequently, sexualized behavior tended to be nonfunctional for decreasing work related stress for these women and may even be dysfunctional by increasing work related stress for those who are sexually harassed.

Mixed gender. Stress was discussed in the mixed gender groups, but it appeared to be different from when discussed during the men's groups. While the men's groups tended to talk about sexualized behavior and stress reduction, the mixed gender groups were less likely to do so. For example, two of the men's groups suggested talking about the size of a woman's "racks" (breasts) as an appropriate means of stress reduction. On the other hand a female participant in a mixed gender group talked about "going to Chicago" (in a reference to the death of a patient) and "cussing" (in tense situations) as stress reducers. Neither of these terms were used to refer to sexualized behavior. While the woman in this interaction clearly dominated the discussion, the men's vague references to sexual harassment contributed to the misunderstanding about the gendered differences related to sexual harassment and stress management:

Jack: I'm curious about, you know, stress. People say sometimes under stress, when you were talking about having your hands in somebody's gut or something [laughs].

Female C: That's not stress that's fun.

Jack: Well a stressful case or something like that. Then things are said. And.

Male B: Sometimes there's a different kind of humor involved. It's a different way of dealing with stress sometimes. Other people might be very very offended by something. You know.

Female C: We have a patient die on a certain day and um "yep," you know, "I had a patient who flew to Chicago today." You know and just totally nonchalantly go to Chicago. It's a thing that's said.

Male B: It's a [Uninterpretable].

Jack: Oh.

Female C: Instead of saying "they died," you don't just say you know, "they're dead." Well they go to Chicago. And.

Male B: Which doesn't say a lot for Chicago.

Female C: It doesn't say a lot for Chicago. But I mean, you know we have a way of dealing with it. You have to deal with it. You know when you, we had a tech recently who just had her first patient die on the table. And I'm like you know "I've had four or five of 'em, you know it's not a big deal." And to other people it's like "oh my gosh, somebody dies around you and it's not a big deal?" They're it's [interrupts self]. People can take things way different. You know. So being. It would have to be somebody like you said from the medical field.

Male B: Some people who like to be humorous in that situation to try to get away from stress, and lighten things up a little bit. A lot of other people wouldn't take humor to it. Or if you haven't been around dying very much. "Well how can you make a joke at this point?" Um.

Female C: Yeah.

Male B: It's kind of your own way of dealing with it.

Jack: I'm thinking somebody else could construe sexual harassment as a stress reliever.

Female C: Yeah. Yeah um, there's certain surgeons. One of em in particular who's been warned many times about his, about cussing. And and the heat, in the stress of something happening and he'll just, you know "Blah blah blah blah blah blah blah [for swearing]." And he's going like this. And people come out of there "oh my gosh," making em cry and all this. And I'm "what are you crying for" you know? "He's just. He's cussing at a situation. He's not cussing at you." And until people get to know him they don't realize that. And once they really, get to know him and realize that's how he is, then it doesn't bother them anymore cause they know. He's not cussing at them, he's cussing at a situation. And and he's been written up many times for it. Because people don't get how he is. They don't realize that that's just him and he's not directing it at them. He's been falsely accused, unfortunately. And so now I'll just cuss during a case and tell him I'm doing it for him cause I know he can't [laughter].

Notice that the discussion about stress did not spring naturally from the conversation but was a response to a probe posed by Jack. Furthermore, Female C did not automatically think about sexualized behavior in relationship to stress. Instead she talked about patients going to Chicago, a comment without sexual connotations. This choice is interesting given the nature of the topic being discussed. Because the group was discussing sexual harassment, it would seem natural for discussants to focus on sex related behaviors in response to questions. However, this woman did not. Even when Jack became more specific in his probe, asking the group about the relationship between stress and the construal of sexual harassment, the participant still provided a non sexual example of a doctor who "cusses." It is possible that this participant was simply uncomfortable talking about sex. However, she seemed perfectly comfortable engaging in discussions about reproductive organs during the same group. The most likely conclusion is that she simply did not associate sexualized behaviors with stress reduction. The male participants' tendency to vaguely label references to sexual behavior as "it," "this," and "that" contributed to the lack of understanding achieved by this group of participants. Had Male B more explicitly labeled the "humorous" behaviors he was discussing, then the participants may have reached an understanding of the gendered nature of their discussion. As it was, Male B's meaning remained unclear to the entire group, including both of the moderators.

One common feature of the mixed gender groups when talking about sexualized behavior as stress reducing was the appearance of agreement on the part of the women participants. The appearance of agreement occurred either because the women actually believed that there was agreement, or because despite a dawning realization of differences the women simply failed to articulate those differences during the course of the conversation. The woman who talked about going to Chicago appeared to believe that her perceptions about stress reduction were consistent with the male participants' perceptions. Other women participants also appeared to agree through the use of agreeable language, even after it had become clear to them that there were important differences in men's and women's standpoints on the body. For example:

Male C: The things we do to the human body to make it well. You know, no wonder people are sick [laughter]

Female A: Yeah.

Male C: I mean the things we do to the body. We prick it we prod it we probe it we cut it open, we chop on it. I mean you know we . . .

Female A: We take the covers off and have all the medical students come in. Yes.

Male C: Yeah. Well you know I talked to you [author] about this in the, I work in [unit]. I mean you lose all sense of dignity when you. Because the first time we do it, we strip you naked we stick a [uninterpretable] in you, and we start uh. And everybody comes and checks you out. You do assessments everyday. When they do assessments you are stripped down. You are checked over. Um you know. I mean prop [interrups self], I mean you lose your sense of of of human dignity when you go into a hospital. And I think because of that um, we have a tendency to be more relaxed about the things that we say as far as um, the body goes and how we approach people and what we say to people. I think we're more free with um the sexual inuendos. As far as um.

Female A: When I was a student. One of the. I was working, doing my rotation at the free clinic. And we had uh, an extremely large woman at the OB clinic. And the resident takes a look in, pushes the drape back, comes out, he gets an electrical cord and he puts it in the back of his belt. He said "hold this end [and] pull me out [laugh]."

Male C: Yeah see?

Female A: I mean it's really sad. But yeah, people do that.

Male C: Yeah, I mean and it's uh, it's, I think it's our way of dealing with the stressful day to day things of working in a hospital.

Female A: We make fun of the body.

Male C: Yeah. And um.

Author: You were saying this is the biggest problem with sexual harassment in organizations today?

Male C: Oh very much so.

Author: Tell me what makes it a problem.

Male C: Because we accept it. Because that's the way it is. And. You know we're in this to help people. And we kind of abuse people. More mentally. Not physically but mentally. Because of the things that we do. I mean we just assume that because of where we work at and what we do it's accepted. The public would be very scared. I always said that if I'm going to get worked on I'm going to a different hospital. I'm not going to let my fellow employees take care of me. Cause I know some of the things they do.

Female A: That's exactly what one of the surgery techs said in my other group.

Male C: Yeah. I'll be damned if I'll let some of those women see me naked. [laughs]

Male B: And hell I've offered, but they said no.

Female A actively participated in the discussion about stress and sexualized behavior started by Male C. At one point she even told what she considered to be a funny story about a doctor giving her a cord tied to his belt so she could pull him out of a large woman's vagina. Notice that after this point she continued to participate, but her comments were brief one liners, contributing little in the way of content while clearly suggesting agreement for Male C's perceptions of the body. Furthermore, by claiming that a woman in her women's group had made a similar comment and by the use of the word "we," Female A suggested not just personal agreement, but agreement by women in general. It was not until our stimulated recall interview that her disagreement with Male C became clear:

Female A: . . . And he's expressing a, almost an anger. You know "we prick it we poke it we do this we do this we do this" and he talked about somebody deciding to have surgery in an entirely different hospital so his coworkers didn't see them.

Author: Mmhm.

Female A: And I don't think that was the reaction of the women. Their reaction was more "oh well, my coworkers all know what I look like, you know with my knees up in the stirrups."

Author: Mmhm.

Female A: And it was uh, it was honest. And again, the self deprecation, the kind of funny well, acceptance of it. [Pause. Laughs].

Author: What?

Female A: The uh, the Russian doctor. Russian uh, resident. And again, I think he got away with it because he's a Russian resident and they were like cutting him some slack and [uninterpretable] acceptable behavior. Took an electrical cord, tied it to the back of his belt. Handed it to me and said "here, if I'm not out in a minute, reel me out." It was so rude. And it was so funny.

Author: It made you laugh though?

Female A: Oh it did. I did. I didn't think very highly of him after that. But it was funny.

During the stimulated recall interview, Female A indicated that Male C talked about the body quite differently than her women's group. She perceived the women to be more respectful both of patients' bodies and of health care professionals' jobs of healing those bodies. However, despite the fact that she clearly disagreed with Male C, Female A continued to verbally agree during the mixed gender interaction. It is possible that her intent was to agree with the male participants on one level—there is a great deal of stress at HCO—while disagreeing with the men about the role of sexualized behavior in managing that stress. Male C's repeated used of the word "yeah," following Female A's comment suggests, however, that he accepted her interaction as total agreement with his position. As moderator, this was also my interpretation. The story told by Female A about the doctor who had asked her to pull him out of the woman's vagina was particularly interesting. Female A found humor in the story, despite the graphic and sexual nature of the comment. It is likely that women contribute to the behaviors that make them uncomfortable through participation in sexualized conversations. In this way they actively reinforce the organizing processes that they find so distressing.

In both instances where stress was discussed during the mixed gender groups, the participants failed to reach an agreement about the functional nature of sexual harassment. In fact, the women's responses within the interactions may have reinforced the dominant vision that sexualized behavior is functional in the health care setting. By appearing to agree with the men's perceptions about reducing stress through sexualized behavior, the women gave the impression that sexualized behavior is acceptable, even desirable. However, this was not a position the women advocated or accepted. Clearly there is a meaning gap between the men and women. The men found sexualized behavior to be appropriate means of reducing stress while the women did not associate sexualized behavior with stress. The meaning gap was strengthened by the women's unintentional reinforcement of the men's perceptions of sexual harassment, increasing the likelihood that sexualized behavior will continue to be enacted at HCO. The ongoing enactment of sexualized behavior is very likely to lead to a hostile environment and consequently to sexual harassment.

Therapeutic Touch

Research is clear that touching has important physiological and psychological functions (Caputo, Hazel, & McMahon, 1994). When done appropriately, it can relieve stress and provide comfort and healing. The male participants all discussed the importance of touch in helping both patients and coworkers. They discussed both non-sexualized touch, and sexualized touch as therapeutic. The women failed to refer to any form of touch as therapeutic. Interestingly, the therapeutic nature of touch was not addressed by the mixed gender groups.

Men. It was the men who mentioned the importance of touch in both the healing process and in comforting their fellow employees. The most frequently mentioned forms of physical comforting were back rubs, touching on a shoulder, and hugs. The use of touch as a comforting mechanism by men is not particularly surprising. Wood and Inman (1993) argued that men show emotions and affection through action while women are more likely to show emotions and affection through talk. Consequently, it would make sense that men would find touching to be an important source of comforting. On the other hand, research also suggests that touching is frequently enacted by more powerful others (Henley, 1977) and consequently becomes an enactment of power, or power in action. So while men may intend the touching behavior to be comforting, women may find the same behavior to be uncomfortable and as attempts to control them. This argument is supported by the participant's discussions. For example, on three occasions during the discussion groups and throughout the individual interviews the men talked about their attempts to provide comfort being misinterpreted by a woman. One example comes from a men's discussion group:

Male C: And I think if that is your goal, by touching someone in a particular way by fulfilling a need for you, to me that is sexual harassment. Because it's one sided. Ok. It's you going towards them. And if they pull back. See, I'm a hand talker, you know, [laugh] and so I touch people when I talk um, when I talk to 'em. You know, I go up and I touch people when I talk to 'em. And in my last evaluation. I got one of my highest eval, performance evaluations here I've ever had. But one of the things that was marked against me was I touch people too much. And it's because when I touch some, when I talk to somebody, you know, I'll go up and touch 'em on the shoulder.

Male B: Yeah.

Male C: But it was a female employee that said that on one of my evaluations. Because we have peer evaluations where they submit forms to different employees. And that was the only bad mark on my whole evaluation, is that uh, is that I used my hands too much. I've never touched 'em in, you know, a sexual way. It's just that I might grab 'em by the arm. Or if they are having a bad year or they are having a bad day with a patient, I might go up and put may arm around 'em and talk to 'em. You know, "are you ok?"

Male B: Yeah.

Male C: And it's more of a, hey, I'm here for you if you need to talk.

Male A: Yeah.

Male C: It's just one of those compassion things, where, you know, hey, I'm here for you type thing.

Male A: You don't even think about it, it's

Male C: Yeah, it's just something, that's just the kind of person I am. I don't like to see people hurt and I don't like to see people upset.

Male C clearly intended his behavior to be a source of comfort. However, the female employee found him to use his hands too much, what women frequently refer to as "handsy." This man argued that he never touched his coworkers in a sexual fashion. However, as previously discussed, research clearly indicates that women perceive more behavior, such as a man putting an arm around a woman, as sexual and even as sexual harassment (Berryman-Fink & Riley, 1997; Booth-Butterfield, 1989; Garlick, 1994; Hemphill & Pfieffer, 1986; Mongeau & Blalock, 1994; Thacker & Gohmann, 1993).

Women.   Women seemed to be ambivalent about touch from men. The discussions involving touch in the women's groups suggested that male touch was something to be endured. Rarely was it constructed as therapeutic. In fact, during the women's groups, there was only one instance where a woman seemed to appreciate a man's touch, telling him that she needed a "hug." For the most part, women found men's touch to be uncomfortable, or as merely tolerated. One example comes from a women's discussion group:

Female A: I think its (the definition of sexual harassment) is everybody's opinion. Personally I, nothing bothers me verbally, but when somebody starts touching me, you're in my boundaries. I can blow anything off that's said. I don't care.

Three things are striking about Female A's statement. First, she was the only woman in the group who did not appear to be offended by sexual jokes or comments. Second, she made it clear that touching is invasive. Third, she is the same woman who mentioned that sometimes at work she needs a "hug," indicating that not all touch is offensive. Her comments, as well as the discussions from the women as a whole, suggest an ambivalence to touch as opposed to an aversion to it. This is not to give the impression that women do not like having their shoulders rubbed or that women do not find some touch to be therapeutic. However, it is likely that there is a mixed reaction to such behavior enacted by a man. There is an appreciation for the touching behavior and a simultaneous questioning of the man's motivations. While none of the women talked about receiving back rubs or other forms of therapeutic touch, their silence on this issue reinforces the possibility that they are ambivalent about touch. Furthermore, consistent with the literature, the women participants seemed to view more touching behavior as sexual harassment and as uncomfortable than the men (Booth-Butterfield, 1989; Thacker & Gohmann, 1993). Consequently, for these women, sexual harassment seemed to be simultaneously nonfunctional and dysfunctional.

Camaraderie

Researchers contend that one important component of an effective team is group cohesion (Larson & LaFasto, 1989). Group cohesion is difficult to define because it is more spiritual than concrete. However, some argue that it is a commitment to a common goal (Bormann, 1996). One means of creating and maintaining cohesion is through the enactment of norms and rituals that support a sense of camaraderie (Bormann, 1996).

As the discussion groups and the related individual interviews progressed, an interesting gendered difference emerged in terms of the function of sexualized behavior and camaraderie. For the male participants, sexualized behavior tended to serve a functional and normative role of creating and demonstrating a sense of cohesion for a group to which they felt a strong commitment. For the women, on the other hand, groups were a means of preventing sexualized behavior. So while the men enacted sexualized behavior to demonstrate group cohesion, women used a cohesive group to prevent the enactment of sexualized behavior.

Men. The male participants frequently mentioned the importance of their relationships with their coworkers. They spoke about these relationships using terms such as camaraderie and emotional vulnerability. For example, one group suggested that sexualized behavior as more appropriate at HCO than it would be elsewhere because of the sense of camaraderie:

Male D: What's off-limits at an insurance company, is not off-limits here you know, I mean, it's a different stress level. There's a lot of camaraderie here. And I mean we make digs like that, if somebody comments on their [penis] size I mean, that's just a gag here. If it happens somewhere else it would be [sexual harassment].

Male B: If you're putting a catheter in me it might [be a big deal]...[laughter].

Male D: [Laughter] Actually it would be more appropriate.

Because of the sense of camaraderie experienced among employees, the men argued that sexualized behavior was acceptable at HCO where it would not be acceptable elsewhere. Interestingly, the men made the statement about sexualized behavior and then demonstrated that behavior by joking about whether or not it would be appropriate to joke about the size of a man's penis when inserting a catheter. The male participants seemed to recognize this verbal behavior as a means of establishing and deepening the camaraderie of the group. Given the court's recent recognition of male to male sexual harassment (Markert, 1999), not only is this comment potentially a contributor to a hostile environment, but it also may be distressing for some men. During a stimulated recall interview, one man described different scenarios in which sexualized behavior might be enacted in ways that demonstrate and even create a sense of cohesion through camaraderie. This individual indicated how discussions about patients' sexual body parts and sexual exploits can become a dining table conversation:

Male B: You know and yeah I mean I sat there with people from work, where they all work at, you know, other places. And you know, the stories we tell promote, all of a sudden you realize no one else is saying a damn word at the table. They're all staring at you like. Meanwhile the two of us are laughing. It's like "oh yeah do you remember oh oh oh. It's so funny." And you know, and it does, you know that is a very emotional [bond]. And that's why, in a lot of ways I think people do take more liberties in some ways. Not so much you know physic, well sometimes even physically. You know. I mean I've given out hugs and stuff after someone's died cause it does bother ya. I mean everybody's upset. You know and it does feel good just to have someone that will.

Cohesion between employees can be demonstrated in a number of communication events in a number of settings. Male B provided an example of dinner table conversations in which individuals who were not members of HCO were excluded through the graphic nature of the conversation. In this way, the health care workers were able to establish firm boundaries between their group and "others." It is possible that graphic language provided the male participants with a common code through which boundaries could be established. The men's discussions concur with Conquergood's (1994) finding that not only are boundaries important to the maintenance of a group's sense of itself, but that groups are not located in the center but at the boundaries which define it.

The men constructed sexualized behavior as establishing camaraderie to protect group boundaries from outsiders. Camaraderie was also established within the organizational context through physical behavior, such as hugs and through verbal behavior. These behaviors are both a result and cause of the camaraderie experienced by the men, making sexualized behavior a self perpetuating cycle that produces and reproduces itself as an organizational norm.

Women. The women participants also expressed a sense of camaraderie at work. However, the means of expressing group cohesion as well as the relationship of the group with sexualized behavior was quite different from the male participants. Two important differences emerged. The first difference dealt with the nature of camaraderie at HCO. While the men discussed camaraderie at length, the women participants generally assumed a mutual understanding of the nature of camaraderie in the workplace. The second difference between the men's and women's groups was the (dys)functional nature of sexualized behavior in the creation and maintenance of camaraderie at HCO. Instead of perceiving sexualized behavior as a functional part of the process of establishing and demonstrating group cohesion, the women tended to find such behavior to be unacceptable. Each of the differences will be discussed.

Generally, the women seemed to assume a common understanding of the nature and importance of camaraderie at HCO. As this section will illustrate, they chose not to discuss camaraderie because they assumed that the other group members shared their understanding of the construct. In fact, the importance of group camaraderie and cohesion was not established by the women until they discussed the importance of fear at which point they universally expressed a fear of isolation from their coworkers. In other words, one of their greatest fears was the absence of camaraderie with their coworkers. Explanations of the importance of a group were considered extraneous. For example, when I attempted to probe a group about why isolation was so fearful, they seemed perplexed that I would even bother to ask such a silly question. The following discussion springs from the women's responses to the question "what is your greatest fear related to sexual harassment?":

Author: Ok, I guess, I want to know more. I don't know how to phrase the question. What do you think causes that to be a fear?

Female C: That nobody will believe it?

Author: Yeah.

Female C: What causes it?

Author: I guess that's a good way of phrasing that. Why do you think you would be fearful of that?

Female C: Of not being believed?

Author: Right.

Female A: You feel lonely.

Female C seemed astounded that I would ask this question. Not being believed was such an obvious fear to her with such obvious consequences that there was little sense in discussing it further. She asked for clarification three times before another participant provided a rather blunt response: "You feel lonely." It is possible that the question was poorly phrased and Female C was simply seeking clarification. However, a few moments later a similar conversation was held in which, once again, the women participants seemed amazed that I would ask such an obvious question:

Author: Tell me more about the isolation. What's troubling about being isolated? I'm thinking in terms of the workplace.

Female C: What's troubling about being isolated?

Female A: I'm not sure what you . . .

Female B: If you were accusing?

Author: Right if some people don't believe you, you said you'd feel isolated.

Female C: I think everybody needs interactions with their coworkers. They don't want to feel like they don't belong. I mean it's a mental thing. They have to belong too. You have to have a certain relationship with your coworkers in order to exist. I mean, somebody cannot be isolated forever and continue on I wouldn't think.

Female A: And I think it would make it. If you were accusing somebody and everybody didn't believe you, and it did happen. I think it would become a, they were isolating you. I mean, everybody would be just kind of (tsk sound), you know, it would get to the point where you just want to quit because you were so unhappy.

During this interaction the group as a unit seemed confused and even irritated that I would ask such an obvious question. As Female C explained, everybody needs interaction. In fact, she explained that without interaction or "a certain relationship" with coworkers, a person would cease to exist. It is this sense of cohesion that not only gives work meaning, but also is a source of life. Although this group's reaction to my probes about isolation was the most compelling in terms of the assumed importance of cohesion, the other women's groups were similarly surprised that I would probe such an obvious issue.

While both the men and women viewed camaraderie with coworkers to be important, there were clear differences. The male participants considered camaraderie at HCO to be unique and therefore not assumed. They tended to spend a great deal of time during both the group discussion and the individual interview discussing and clarifying the nature of the group camaraderie and its related sexualized behavior. For the women, the camaraderie they experienced with their coworkers did not seem to be unique to health care organizations. In fact, as one woman indicated "I think everybody needs interactions with their coworkers." Because of the seemingly universal nature of group cohesion and the related construct of camaraderie, the women did not feel a need to discuss this issue with much depth; they assumed a common understanding.

Because the women tended to fear isolation through sexual harassment, they attempted to cope with that behavior through groups of coworkers with whom they had created a close relationship:

Female B: He's not as likely to bawl you out or come after just you if there are several of ya, together as a group. I think it's easier for them to do that on a one-to-one basis. Whether it's sexual harassment or just . . .

Female C: Harassment.

Female B: Harassment [laugh] harassment not with a sexual nature. But it's much easier for them to do it one-to-one than it is to do it in a big, in front of even two or three [uninterpretable].

. . .

Female A: The buddy system. You hear about the buddy system all the time. We just got to be buddies everywhere.

The women in this group viewed close group relationships as one important means of preventing sexual harassment. Clearly for women, sexual harassment tended to be dysfunctional. It had the potential to isolate them from their relationship with coworkers. Interestingly, groups were also women's primary means of preventing sexualized behavior. Consequently, sexualized behavior could isolate women from the very source that could protect them from sexualized behavior. Only one woman indicated that sexualized behavior could help demonstrate and develop group camaraderie. Her experience received the most discussion during her mixed gender group and will be discussed there.

Mixed gender. While the men discussed camaraderie as if it was a unique experience at HCO and the women discussed camaraderie as though it was an absolute condition across work place environments, the mixed gender groups' discussions about camaraderie seemed to be relatively idiosyncratic depending on the personalities of the participants and the directions of the conversation. In one group the importance of group cohesion and camaraderie was not discussed. In a second group, group cohesion was discussed as an environment created by management. This group seemed to have a more feminine orientation to the discussion in that camaraderie and cohesion were assumed to exist and sexualized behavior was clearly not a functional part of the process of creating and demonstrating camaraderie. Interestingly, the third group took more of a masculine orientation. The nature of group cohesion was discussed and sexualized behavior was viewed as important to showing camaraderie. In fact, the one unifying theme that emerged around camaraderie in mixed gender interactions was the tendency of some participants to advocate for the position taken by the other gender. To illustrate this theme, an example of a man and an example of a woman who took positions consistent with the other gender's standpoints on camaraderie will be provided.

In one mixed gender group, the main proponent of the women's orientation toward sexualized behavior and camaraderie was a man. He argued that managers had a responsibility to create a warm environment where sexualized behaviors were viewed as non-normative and as inappropriate:

Male C: . . . But, if that same conversation was taking place and I was in the room, I would be going, "that's enough. That's not where, not an appropriate place to go." Then I, if I let that happen, and me as a manager is in that environment, and I let it happen, and I'm present, then I'm saying this is always ok. I'm setting up an environment that, where things that may not, that shouldn't be acceptable may be perceived as being acceptable because I let it happen. If I'm, if they're having those conversations and they're in the backroom and the person has full right to walk out of that back room and away from that situation and has the full ability to do that, or, to come and talk to me and say, you know, "I feel real uncomfortable with the types of conversations that were occurring back there." Uh, but if they want to stay back there and have that conversation and whatever else, and I'm not present, that's their right to do that. But if I'm back there and I'm in that environment, I'm going to say "no." Because I don't want to set up an environment where I'm saying that this is acceptable.

This man discussed with the other group members how a manager can create a warm and friendly environment for employees. Consistent with the previously discussed women's standpoints on the role of sexualized behavior in feelings of camaraderie, this male participant acknowledged that by allowing sexualized behavior, managers risk destroying the comfort level of a work group. While he recognized that sexualized behavior may happen when a manager is not present, it should never be allowed to happen in the presence of a manager if a comfortable environment is to be maintained.

While in this mixed gender group a male participant appeared to take a feminized view, in a different mixed gender group it was a woman participant who accepted a masculine vision of camaraderie and of the role of sexualized behavior. In fact, her arguments appeared to be more extreme than the positions taken by any of the men in the study, including the men in her mixed gender group:

Female C: . . . I had a fellow RN tell me one time that I needed to watch myself because of jokes that were said and things like that. Because things don't offend me. Verbal things don't offend me. So I, you know, I talk back. And she told me she didn't like what was being said during the, you know. And I don't say anything around her anymore. Because she warned me. But. When we're all standing in our little group and she's way off over there. And we even talk low a lot of times so that certain people don't hear what we are saying. You know, and I think that's a, she should be in trouble for eavesdropping. Cause we're not making her listen to it. I don't know, it just.

After some clarification probes by the moderators and the other group members, Female C offered further clarification of the event in question:

Female C: . . . And all of a sudden she says to me "you need to watch what you say because it can be considered sexual harassment," and I'm going "excuse me?" Another female telling me I was sexually harassing her. I mean it just shocked me."

Clearly this woman viewed the woman who accused her of sexual harassment as an outsider who threatened the boundaries of her group. For Female C, it was the victim of the sexualized behavior who should be punished for violating the group norm of sex talk. In other words, the sex talk was considered appropriate because of the function it performed in the group.

Interestingly, unlike mixed gender discussions about other functions of sexual harassment, this group felt free to disagree with Female C. While the disagreement was polite and non-confrontational, the position of the other participants was clear: They agreed that the victim should not be sanctioned by Female C and other staff members for resisting the norm. In fact, they agreed that the victim's behavior was appropriate and that employees should not engage in sexualized behavior in front of people who find the behavior to be offensive:

Author: I haven't heard from this side of the table for a while. What do you guys . . . ?

Female A: You know, if you're going in there. If it, if it's something that's making the person feel uncomfortable, I think they have a responsibility to say something. That they don't like it. They can't just,

Male D: Mmhm.

Female A: Assume that somebody's going to be able to read their mind and know that whatever's being said bothers them. Cause, you know, if they can't. If they can't express themselves to say hey, I don't like that, then nobody's going to know. It won't change. Unless people are aware of it.

Male: It's a good point.
(unknown)

. . .

Male D: But at least make 'em. Give 'em the opportunity to tone it down while you're around. Or whatever. But yeah. Like you said [Female A], if you don't know you're doing it, how are are you going to correct something?

Male B: Unless it's something really blatant.

Male D: Yeah.

Female C: Mmhm.

Male B: and then you need to be uh, just be concerned for everybody's sake. It's not. Cause then if that person were to speak up, then they're kind of like an outcast . . .

The conversation continued in this vein, with participants asking questions and seeking answers. The participants showed tact by not directly referencing Female C's situation or their disagreement with her. However, it was clear to all group members that Female C's argument was too extreme for the group to accept. This group's interaction suggests that the functionality of sexualized behavior should be balanced with the needs of the individual. The behavior was obviously not functional to the victim and should not be enacted in her presence. Clearly for this mixed gender group, sexualized behavior is functional for some organizational members. However, they seem to acknowledge that the needs of those members should not outweigh the needs of members for whom sexualized behavior is dysfunctional.

Interestingly, unlike mixed gender discussions about other potentially functional components of sexual harassment, participants often spoke in support of the other standpoint during discussions about camaraderie and cohesion. This tendency may be due to the dynamics of the interaction. Same gender groups may be more likely to stifle differences than mixed gender groups. Each of the participants who indicated cross-sex ideas in the mixed gender groups had attempted to do so in the same gender groups but had been shut down in various ways. They were ignored, cut off, or discounted, particularly by the male participants in the men's groups. Mixed gender interactions may provide a more open forum for some participants to explore their understanding of sexual harassment than same gender interactions.

Consequences

As a result of the gendered differences in standpoints of [dys]functional sexual harassment, there are a number of consequences and misunderstandings. Specifically, men were less likely to believe that there was a problem with sexual harassment at HCO and viewed accusations of sexual harassment as misunderstandings or as false accusations.

One repeated theme among the male participants was that because of the functional nature of the sexual harassment, the men did not see sexual harassment as a problem. Male A illustrated this perception during one stimulated recall interview.

Male A: …The men don't perceive sexual harassment as much of an issue around here. I think on a personal. Person to person basis, yes it is. But as a general, a general problem here at HCO it isn't

Author: And that's because of the atmosphere in the hospital?

Male A: It has a lot to do with it. I mean, you know. Tension, stress. How we choose to relieve it, uh. I don't know if it's good or bad, a good or bad example or not. But um, but the old television show M*A*S*H. Certainly exaggerated. But the kind of camaraderie doctors and nurses show, and auxiliary staff showed in that series. That's kind of the feeling I have for around here. There's familiar. Familiarity breeds comfort as well as contempt. And I think the more people interact and joke with each other or, sometimes shock—try and shock each other—which is kind of hard to do with some of the people around here. It is a good way and a healthy way of relieving some of that tension and stress.

Male A combined all of the functional processes for men to explain why sexual harassment was not only not a problem, but was "good and healthy" within the HCO environment. The reference to M*A*S*H is particularly interesting. The only hierarchically powerful woman working at the M*A*S*H 4077 was also the brunt of a number of demeaning jokes and pranks by the male doctors for a large portion of the show's run. In fact, even a casual viewing of M*A*S*H reruns shows that she was humiliated and ostracized by sexual harassment from the doctors. Attempts to correct the problem by reporting to the commanding officer were dismissed and trivialized. On the other hand, the sexual harassment was clearly functional to the harassers. They seemed to enhance camaraderie among the staff through sexual harassment toward the victim of their harassment. M*A*S*H does indeed provide an excellent example of the functional/dysfunctional dichotomy that seems to characterize the standpoints of the men and women who participated in this study.

Because the men tended to view sexual harassment as non problematic, they viewed many accusations of sexual harassment as mere misunderstandings:

Jack: Why do you think sexual harassment occurs?

Male B: I think most the time it doesn't.

Male C: Yeah. I think it's blown out of proportion

Male B: It's blown out of proportion. Either, or it's misconstrued. Or,

Male C: Yeah.

Male A: Misunderstandings.

Male B: Misunderstandings, so . . .

Male C: Yeah.

Male B: And the other times when it does occur, when it is really sexual harassment, it is nothing more
           then someone being just more forward then they should. "No" means "no."

This group of men made it perfectly clear that most sexual harassment is simply a misunderstanding that has been "blown out of proportion." Similarly, many, but not all of the men, viewed most sexual harassment complaints as either misunderstandings or as false accusations. After all, sexualized behavior that was enacted for the good of the organization could not be sexual harassment. Based on this, it is clear that not only is sexual harassment not a problem from the standpoints of the male participants, but perceptions of it must necessarily be misunderstandings or worse, false accusations.

Discussion

Sexual harassment as a [dys]functional process informs our understanding of both sexual harassment and feminist standpoint theories. In terms of sexual harassment, research has suggested that sexual harassment is highly dysfunctional (Kreps, 1994, p. 127). However, the present study discovered that sexual harassment may be a functional part of the organizing process for dominant members of organizations. Specifically, sexual harassment appears to be an effective coping mechanism for work related stress, showing care, and creating and demonstrating camaraderie for the male participants. While sexual harassment may have been a functional part of the organizing process for the male participants, for the most part it appeared to be either nonfunctional or dysfunctional for the female participants. Sexual behavior did not reduce stress, demonstrate caring, or create camaraderie for these women. To the contrary, for most of these women, sexualized behavior was at best endured and at worst sexual harassment. Sexual behaviors were dysfunctional for these women by creating a sense of unease and by isolating victims from their coworkers. These findings are consistent with feminist standpoint theorists' contention that men and women experience and understand sexual harassment differently.

In responding to research question one, "How do men and women discursively construct sexual harassment in organizations?" these findings help explain two consistent conclusions drawn in sexual harassment related research: That sexual behavior is normative in organizations (Sundt, 1996; Wood, 1994) and that men perceive fewer behaviors to be sexual harassment than women (Berryman-Fink & Riley, 1997; Booth-Butterfield, 1989; Garlick, 1994; Hemphill & Pfeiffer, 1986; Mongeau & Blalock, 1994; Thacker & Gohmann, 1993). Clearly, at least for these men, sexualized behavior was constructed as a normative means of organizing. Most of the men easily and spontaneously discussed the functions of sexual jokes, conversations, and touch. The normative and functional nature of sexual harassment for men helps explain why men remain perplexed over women's tendency to find this normal behavior disturbing (Landis-Schiff, 1996). Interestingly, sexual harassment was also constructed as normative by the women. However, unlike the men, they did not seem to view that behavior as either functional or acceptable. They simply tolerated the behavior, possibly because women who object are labeled abnormal (Wood, 1994), or as otherwise defective (Diehl, 1996).

The data also provide some insight into research question two: "How do men and women discursively reinforce and resist constructions of sexual harassment in organizations?" The findings in this analysis provide particular insight into how men discursively reinforce and resist sexual harassment in organizations. First the men reinforced sexual harassment through their tendency to label sexual harassment claims as "misunderstandings" as well as through their failure to label their behavior as sexual harassment. These behaviors support consistent findings in the literature that women label more behavior as sexual harassment than men (Berryman-Fink & Riley, 1997; Booth-Butterfield, 1989; Garlick, 1994; Hemphill & Pfeiffer, 1986; Mongeau & Blalock, 1994; Thacker & Gohmann, 1993). For the men, sexualized behavior that was enacted for the good of the organization could not be sexual harassment. The label "sexual harassment" has negative connotations suggesting that something improper has occurred (Wood, 1992). Based on the men's discussions of the functionality of sexualized behavior, it is clear that behavior is not improper. In fact, it is highly appropriate in the health care setting. Clearly not only is sexual harassment not a problem from the standpoints of the male participants, but perceptions of it must necessarily be misunderstandings or worse, false accusations.

Not only does the present study have implications for understanding sexual harassment, but it also provides insight into feminist standpoint theories. First, and not surprisingly given the literature (see Wood, 1994), men and women do construct different standpoints of sexual harassment. Not only do women perceive more behaviors to be sexual harassment than men, but sexualized behavior in the form of sexual harassment has different process related functions for men and women.

A second implication for feminist standpoint theories is the power of naming claimed by dominant organizational groups (Hartsock, 1987). By controlling what will be labeled as sexual harassment, men, especially white men, create a perverse reality through which organizations operate (Wood, 1992). From this perspective it is understandable why men use alternative language to describe sexual harassment (Berryman-Fink & Riley, 1997).

Strengths and Limitations

The primary strength of the present study was its focus on discursive contexts and the relationship of those contexts to constructions of meaning, specifically the construction of the meaning of sexual harassment. Instead of imposing a definition of sexual harassment on the participants, the meanings of sexual harassment was allowed to emerge from the data. Consequently it was possible to observe the process of meaning construction and the differences in that process for men and women. A second strength was its revelation of the deep structure of functional processes for the male participants. These processes have not been previously discussed in the literature and therefore contribute greatly and uniquely to an understanding of sexual harassment. A third strength of the study is its focus on individuals from across the organization, both in terms of types of positions held and hierarchical positions. This multilevel focus provides a better understanding of processes that cross the organization.

There were also a number of limitations to the present research. While this study does reveal structures that likely cross organizations, the results of the study cannot be generalized. This, of course, is a limitation of all qualitative research and some quantitative research that is conducted in a single organization. A second limitation is that while the study examined individuals from across the organizational spectrum, doctors and high level administrators did not participate in the study. Participation by these two groups could have further enhanced an understanding of the communication processes involved in the construction of sexual harassment. Finally, because it was important to maintain the separate integrity of the men's and women's discussion groups, the same sex groups were not probed regarding issues that emerged during the other gender's interactions. Instead, probes into issues that emerged exclusively during the men's or women's groups were reserved for the mixed gender interactions. While the themes presented in this study did achieve phenomenological saturation, a deeper understanding of the themes may have emerged had issues of functionality been more carefully probed during the women's groups.

Organizational Implications and Application

This section will be introduced with a caution to managers. The inappropriate use of these findings may further marginalize and subjugate women, ultimately increasing the dysfunctions of sexual harassment. Simply informing women about the functional nature of sexual harassment for men in managing stress and creating group cohesion may create pressure in the women to further tolerate unacceptable sexualized behavior. Consequently, the results of this study need to be used more strategically if the study is to help women in organizations. For example, during sexual harassment training, managers may choose to present the functions of sexual harassment in their organizations as sexual harassment "myths." For example, a trainer could discuss "the myth that sexual harassment can help decrease stress." The trainer could then present the arguments made in support of the myth, followed by a thorough discounting of each argument. They might state that "some argue that sexual jokes decrease tension in the work place. However, sexual jokes can have the following effects on the recipients: alienation, distress, disgust, etc." Allowing trainees to participate in identifying the negative effects of sexual behavior may increase their awareness of the harms of sexual harassment. The presentation of myths can be accomplished in a variety of ways, but the key to success is to discredit the myths in a thorough and convincing manner. In this way managers avoid the perception of silent consent to the functions of sexual harassment.

The findings of this study have important implications for managers who are attempting to control sexual harassment in organizations. Sexual harassment policies may fail because of their inability to account for functional sexual harassment processes. While sexual harassment may serve different functions in other organizations, it seems likely that it *does* serve organizing functions. For example, sexualized behavior may serve as a means of relieving boredom in tedious occupations. Consequently, the first step to managing the functions of sexual harassment in organizations is to discover the functions being served by sexual harassment within the context of the organization. Managers can then take a two tiered approach to managing those functions as part of their sexual harassment containment policy.

First, it is important to understand sexual harassment as a complex part of a larger system. Focusing exclusively on the sexual behaviors is unlikely to manage the problem. In other words, merely having a policy and enforcement mechanisms is unlikely to stop sexual harassment. Instead, managers need to understand how sexual harassment is related to other issues in the organizing system. For example, clearly the men in this study had a difficult time coping with stress. This was true even for the men who did not have direct contact with patients. There are a number of effective stress management programs organizations can utilize to help these individuals control stress (see Cartwright & Cooper, 1997; Murphy et al, 1995). Furthermore, given that coworker support is key to managing stress (Ray & Miller, 1994), employees should be taught positive means of providing support. For example, employees can be trained in listening skills that will allow colleagues to share frustrations in a positive, non-sexual way. Whatever the function played by sexual harassment, managers need to discover that function and develop positive alternatives.

A second tier of a sexual harassment containment program would be education about sexual harassment. There appears to be a great deal of gendered confusion about the meaning of sexual harassment. This confusion may stem in part from the fact that in many organizations, training is limited to management. This was true of HCO and is consistent with persistent recommendations that managers and supervisors should receive training, despite the growing recognition that all organizational members need sexual harassment training (Berryman-Fink, 1993). Organizations should train all employees about the definition of sexual harassment, the behaviors that constitute sexual harassment, recourse for victims of sexual harassment, and consequences for harassers. An effective training program will also provide copious amounts of time for questions and answers. Because sexual harassment is a sensitive issue, in order to create an environment open to questions, trainees should be provided with an anonymous means of asking questions. For example, employees could write questions on cards that are then collected and read to the group for discussion. While training will not stop the ongoing discursive construction of sexual harassment by men and women in organizations, it at least provides an opportunity for management's position to be part of that discourse. In this way organizations can better shape member understanding of sexual harassment.

These suggestions will not be a silver bullet solution to sexual harassment. Sexual harassment also performs the function of maintaining systems of domination. Consequently, understanding and addressing the functions of sexual harassment is a partial answer to an ongoing process of managing sexual harassment in organizations.

Endnotes

1. It is probable that men and women experience sexual harassment differently regardless of role expectations. While women are more likely to be harassed and men are more likely to be harassers (Markert, 1999), men who are harassed tend to respond differently than women who are harassed (Diehl, 1996). Furthermore the social ramifications are different based on gender. Women who sexually harass men are unlikely to be viewed as threatening by men who sexually harass women. Furthermore, male victims who resist sexual harassment are more likely to have their sexual identity questioned than women who resist sexual harassment.

2. Some participants decided not to participate in the mixed gender groups for a number of reasons. For some, the times scheduled for the groups was problematic due to prior commitments. At least one participant was unable to participate due to an illness. A number of participants declined to participate in the mixed gender groups because they simply felt uncomfortable speaking about sexual issues in a mixed gender setting.

3. Research in the health care industry seems to view health care organizations as either sexist or reverse sexist. For example, Donald and Merker (1993) found that sexual harassment is widespread in the female dominated field of nursing, while Kreps (1987) found that male nurses were less satisfied with their jobs and perceived a more negative work environment than the female nurses. The conclusion was drawn that this was likely the result of reverse discrimination. It is entirely possible that both sexism and reverse sexism operate simultaneously in the nursing industry. In other words, the existence of one does not preclude the existence of the other.

4. Because of the sensitive nature of the topic being discussed and because of the enhanced vulnerability of participants due to the small sample size, all group members are labeled A, B, C, D, or E. This labeling scheme is designed to prevent tracking individual participants. In so doing, anonymity is protected and potential retaliation is minimized.

References

Allen, B. J. (1998). Black womanhood and feminist standpoints. *Management Communication Quarterly, 11,* 575–586.

Bell, K. E., Orbe, M. P., Drummond, D. K., & Camara, S. K. (2000). Accepting the challenge of centralizing without essentializing: Black feminist thought and African American women's communication experiences. *Women's Studies in Communication, 23,* 41–62.

Berryman-Fink, C. (1993). Preventing sexual harassment through male-female communication training. In G. L. Kreps (Ed.), *Sexual harassment: Communication implications* (pp. 267–280). Cresskill, NJ: Hampton.

Berryman-Fink, C., & Riley, K. V. (1997). The role of gender and feminism in perceptions of sexual and sexually harassing communication. *Women's Studies in Communication, 20,* 24–44.

Bingham, S. G. (1994). Introduction: Framing sexual harassment—defining a discursive focus of study. In S. G. Bingham (Ed.), *Conceptualizing sexual harassment as discursive practice* (pp. 1–14). Westport, CT: Praeger.

Booth-Butterfield, M. (1989). Perceptions of harassing communication as a function of locus of control, work force participation, and gender. *Communication Quarterly, 37,* 262–275.

Bormann, E. G. (1996). *Small group communication: Theory and practice.* Edina, MN: Burgess International Group.

Bowker, J. K. (1993). Reporting sexual harassment: Reconciling power, knowledge, and perspective. In G. L. Kreps (Ed.), *Sexual harassment: Communication implications* (pp. 171–195). Cresskill, NJ: Hampton.

Bullis, C. (1993). Organizational socialization research: Enabling, constraining, and shifting perspectives. *Communication Monographs, 60,* 10–17.

Buzzanell, P. M. (1994). Gaining a voice: Feminist organizational communication theorizing. *Management Communication Quarterly, 7,* 339–383.

Canary, K. J., & Hause, K. S. (1993). Is there any reason to research sex differences in communication? *Communication Quarterly, 41,* 129–144.

Caputo, J. S., Hazel, H. C., & McMahon, C. (1994). *Interpersonal communication: Competency through critical thinking.* Boston: Allyn and Bacon.

Cartwright, S., & Cooper, C. L. (1997). *Managing workplace stress.* Thousand Oaks, CA: Sage.

Clair, R. P. (1994). Hegemony and harassment: A discursive practice. In S. G. Bingham (Ed.), *Conceptualizing sexual harassment as discursive practice* (pp. 59–70). Westport, CT: Praeger.

Conquergood, D. (1994). Homeboys and hoods: Gang communication and cultural space. In L. R. Frey (Ed.), *Group communication in context: Studies of natural groups* (pp. 23–56). Hillsdale, NJ: Lawrence Erlbaum Associates.

Conrad, C., & Taylor, B. (1994). The contest(s) of sexual harassment: Power, silences, and academe. In S. G. Bingham (Ed.), *Conceptualizing Sexual Harassment as Discursive Practice* (pp. 45–58). Westport, CT: Praeger.

Creswell, J. W. (1997). *Qualitative inquity and research design: Choosing among five traditions.* Thousand Oaks: Sage.

Diehl, L. A. (1996). Raising expectations: Institutional responsibility and the issue of sexual harassment. *Initiatives, 57,* 1–10.

De Coster, S., Estes, S. B., & Mueller, C. W. (1999). Routine activities and sexual harassment in the workplace. *Work and Occupations, 26,* 21–49.

Donald, C. G., & Merker, S. (1993). Medical alert: Sexual harassment in the health care industry. *International Journal of Public Administration, 16,* 1483–1499.

Dougherty, D. S. (1999). Dialogue through standpoint: Understanding women's and men's standpoints of sexual harassment. *Management Communication Quarterly, 12,* 436–468.

Dougherty, D. S., & Krone, K. J. (2000). Overcoming the dichotomy: Cultivating standpoints in organizations through research. *Women's Studies in Communication, 23,* 16–40.

Fine, M. G. (1993). New voices in organizational communication: A feminist commentary and critique. In S. P. Bowen & N. Wyatt (Eds.), *Feminist critiques in communication studies* (pp. 125–166). Cresskill, NJ: Hampton Press.

Frey, L. R., Botan, C. H., Friedman, P. G., & Kreps, G. L. (1991). *Investigating communication: An introduction to research methods.* Englewood Cliffs, NJ: Prentice Hall.

Garlick, R. (1994). Male and female responses to ambiguous instructor behaviors. *Sex Roles: A Journal of Research, 30,* 135–158.

Gerdes, L. I. (1999). Introduction. In L. I. Gerdes (Ed.), *Sexual harassment: Current controversies,* (pp. 12–14). San Diego: Greenhaven.

Gibson, M. K., & Papa, M. J. (2000). The mud, the blood, and the beer guys: Organizational osmosis in blue-collar work groups. *Journal of Applied Communication Research, 28,* 68–88.

Hallstein, D. L. O. (2000). Where standpoint stands now: An introduction and commentary. *Women's Studies in Communication, 23,* 1–15.

Harding, S. (1991). *Who's science? Who's knowledge? Thinking from women's lives.* Ithaca, NY: Cornell University Press.

Hardy, C., & Clegg, S. R. (1996). Some dare call it power. In S. R. Clegg, C. Hardy, & W. R. Nord (Eds.), *Handbook of organization studies* (pp. 622–641). Thousand Oaks: Sage.

Hartsock, N. C. M. (1987). The feminist standpoint: Developing the ground for a specifically feminist historical materialism. In S. Harding (Ed.), *Feminism and methodology* (pp. 157–180). Bloomington: Indiana University Press.

Hartsock, N. C. M. (1997). Standpoint theories for the next century. *Women and Politics, 18,* 93–101.

Hawkesworth, M. E. (1989). Knowers, knowing, known: Feminist theory and claims of truth. *Signs: Journal of Women in Culture and Society, 14,* 533–557.

Hemphill, M. R., & Pfeiffer, A. L. (1986). Sexual spillover in the workplace: Testing the appropriateness of male-female interaction. *Women's Studies in Communication, 9,* 52–66.

Henley, N. (1977). *Body politics: Power, sex, and nonverbal communication.* Englewood Cliffs, NJ: Prentice-Hall.

Herndon, S. L. (1993). Using focus group interviews for preliminary investigation. In S. L. Herndon & G. L. Kreps (Eds.), *Qualitative research: Applications in organizational communication* (pp. 39–47). Cresskill, NJ: Hampton.

Hippensteele, S., & Pearson, T. C. (1999). Responding effectively to sexual harassment. *Change, 31,* 48–54.

Kellett, P. M. (1999). Dialogue and dialectics in managing organizational change: The case of a mission-based transformation. *The Southern Communication Journal, 64,* 211–231.

Keyton, J., & Rhodes, S. C. (1999). Organizational sexual harassment: Translating research into application. *Journal of Applied Communication Research, 27,* 158–173.

Kreps, G. L. (1987). Organizational sexism in health care. In L. P. Stewart & S. Ting-Toomey (Eds.), *Communication, gender, and sex roles in diverse interaction contexts,* (pp. 228–236). Norwood: Ablex.

Kreps, G. L. (1994). Sexual harassment as information equivocality: Communication and requisite variety. In S. G. Bingham (Ed.), *Conceptualizing sexual harassment as discursive practice* (pp. 127–138). Westport, CT: Praeger.

Landis-Schiff, R. (1996). Sexual harassment: Why men don't understand it. *Initiatives, 57,* 15–26.

Larson, C. E., & LaFasto, F. M. (1989). *Teamwork: What must go right, what can go wrong.* Newbury Park, CA: Sage.

Lindlof, T. R. (1995). *Qualitative communication research methods.* In J. G. Delia (series Ed.), *Current communication: An advanced text series: Vol 3.* Thousand Oaks: Sage.

Markert, J. (1999). Sexual harassment and the communication conundrum. *Gender Issues, 17,* 34–52.

Marshall, J. (1993). Viewing organizational communication from a feminist perspective: A critique and some offerings. In S. A. Deetz (Ed.), *Communication Yearbook 16,* (pp. 122–143). Newbury Park, CA: Sage.

Mattson, M., & Buzzanell, P. M. (1999). Traditional and feminist organizational communication ethical analyses of messages and issues surrounding an actual job loss case. *Journal of Applied Communication Research, 27,* 49–72.

Miller, V. D., Johnson, J. R., Hart, Z., & Peterson, D. L. (1999). A test of antecedents and outcomes of employee role negotiation ability. *Journal of Applied Communication Research, 27,* 24–48.

Mongeau, P. A., & Blalock, J. (1994). Student evaluations of instructor immediacy and sexually harassing behaviors: An experimental investigation. *Journal of Applied Communication Research, 22,* 256–272.

Morgan, D. L., & Spanish, M. T. (1984). Focus groups: A new tool for qualitative research. *Qualitative Sociology, 7,* 253–270.

Mumby, D. K. (1998). Organizing men: Power, discourse, and the social construction of masculinity(s) in the workplace. *Communication Theory, 8,* 164–183.

Murphy, L. R., Hurrell, J. J., Sauter, S. L., & Keita, G. P. (Eds.). (1995). *Job stress interventions.* Washington, D.C.: American Psychological Association.

Paetzold, R. L., & O'Leary-Kelly, A. M. (1993). Organizational communication and the legal dimensions of hostile work environment sexual harassment. In G. L. Kreps (Ed.), *Sexual harassment: Communication implications* (pp. 63–77). Cresskill, NJ: Hampton.

Patton, M. Q. (1990). *Qualitative evaluation and research methods* (2nd ed.). Newbury Park: Sage.

Putnam, L. L. (1983). The interpretive perspective: An alternative to functionalism. In L. L. Putnam & M. E. Pacanowsky (Eds.), *Communication and organizations: An interpretive approach* (pp. 31–54). Beverly Hills: Sage.

Putnam, L. L. (1990). *Feminist theories, dispute processes, and organizational communication.* Paper presented at the Arizona State University Conference on Organizational Communication: Perspectives for the 90s, Tempe, AZ.

Ray, E. B., & Miller, K. I. (1994). Social support, home/work stress, and burnout: who can help? *Journal of Applied Behavioral Science, 30,* 357–373.

Sexual Harassment charges (and Dismissals) escalate, (April 1999). *HR Focus, 76,* 4.

Shelton, N. J., & Chavous, T. M. (1999). Black and white college women's perceptions of sexual harassment. *Sex Roles: A Journal of Research, 40,* 593–615.

Sundt, M. (1996). Understanding the characteristics of the sexual harasser. *Initiatives, 57,* 27–36.

Thacker, R. A., & Gohmann, S. F. (1993). Male/female differences in perceptions and effects of hostile environment sexual harassment: "Reasonable assumptions?" *Public Personnel Management, 22,* 461–472.

Van Manen, M. (1990). *Researching lived experience: Human science for an action sensitive pedagogy.* State University of New York Press.

Wood, J. T. (1992). Telling our stories: Narratives as a basis for theorizing sexual harassment. *Journal of Applied Communication Research, 20,* 349–362.

Wood, J. T. (1994). Saying it makes it so: The discursive construction of sexual harassment. In S. G. Bingham (Ed.), *Conceptualizing sexual harassment as discursive practice* (pp. 17–30). Westport, CT: Praeger.

Wood, J. T., & Inman, C. (1993). In a different mode: Recognizing male modes of closeness. *Journal of Applied Communication Research, 21,* 279–162.

Received May 12, 2000
Accepted February 6, 2001

Appendix

Group Discussion Questions

1. Discuss each of your stories about sexual harassment. What would you do if you were the victim in this story?
2. What is your definition of sexual harassment?
3. What is the biggest problem with sexual harassment in organizations today? At HCO?
4. Describe your greatest fear related to sexual harassment. What do you think are men's [women's] greatest fears related to sexual harassment?
5. Why does sexual harassment occur?
6. Why do some men sexually harass women?
7. How can people effectively respond to sexual harassment?
8. Describe an ideal sexual harassment policy.

FOLLOW-UP QUESTIONS AND EXPLORATION PROJECTS

1. Daugherty takes a critical theory perspective on communication and meaning-making with regard to sexualized behaviors. Bevan takes a more traditional social-scientific (objectivist) perspective on ways people might respond to resistance to sexual invitations. Compare the ways that these two authors approach their research. How might the difference between critical and objectivist perspectives affect the following aspects of the research?

    a. What questions do the authors ask?

    b. What sorts of sexualized behaviors do they look at? How do they gather their data? How do they measure or examine communication relating to sexual behaviors?

    c. How do they analyze their data?

    d. Where do they apply their conclusions (to theory, to a practical application, etc.)?

2. Look up the article by Mongeau and Blalock (1994), cited in the references for this chapter, and compare their approach to sexual harassment with Daugherty's approach. What might account for the differences in the approach taken in these two articles?

3. If an organization took Daugherty's findings seriously, what might they need to do in their trainings around the issue of sexual harassment? What might they need to do in their organizational policy and or structure?

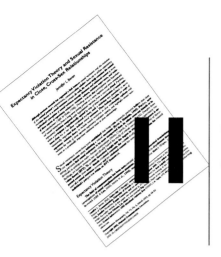

Making More Connections: Summarizing and Integrating

II

We began this book asking you to take an inquisitive stance toward your exploration of communication and communication theory. We also asked you to explore connections between theoretical material, research, and practical applications. In between then and now we have journeyed through a variety of theories and journal articles and you may have lost track of where you started in this process. Now, usually this is the point in a book where readers tend to expect authors to provide a summary of the material covered and draw some conclusions about it. This kind of analysis might be valuable in letting you know about the connections *we* make with regard to this material. It might be valuable in giving you an example of *our* journeys to understand the theories and articles covered here. But ultimately, you are the one who will be using this material. It is the connections that *you* are making, the questions *you* are asking, and *your* journey that should be the focus here. So, rather than give you our conclusions, we will be providing some structures that you may find helpful in reviewing the material you read in this book and making connections between different theories and articles. Our goal, in this section of the book, is to help you make your own map of communication theory and research. Hopefully, you will be able to extend this process to include other theories and articles not covered here. While understanding the content of this book may be valuable, developing skills in reading, interpreting, and using theory and scholarship will take you farther, last longer, and be more flexibly useful to you in a variety of circumstances.

Summary Exercise 1

This activity is intended both as a review of the articles you have read in this book and as a way of helping you make connections between them. In order to accomplish these goals, we will ask you to fill in the information requested on the charts on the next 2 pages. The following descriptions should help you figure out what kind of information is being asked for in each section of the charts. Once you have filled out the charts, continue the exercise on the following page.

Theories Used: In this space you should identify all theories referenced as being important in the development of the article.

Type of Assumptions: Here you can identify articles as objectivist or interpretive (or you can use whatever labels for assumptions you have been using in your class).

Type of Data: The basic distinction here is between qualitative or quantitative data.

Design: Is this analysis based on an experimental design, a grounded approach, a case study, a rhetorical analysis . . .

Purpose: One basic distinction in the purpose section is between applied research (intended to have an immediate practical application or solve a real-world problem) versus theoretical research (intended to test a theory or improve understanding of a topic area).

Context(s): Choices here include: interpersonal communication, organizational communication, rhetoric, health communication, culture, diversity areas such as ethnicity or gender, public communication . . .

	BEVAN—EXPECTANCY VIOLATION AND SEXUAL RESISTANCE	PEARCE & PEARCE—COMMUNITY DIALOGUE PROCESS	PENINGTON—CONNECTION/AUTONOMY BETWEEN MOTHERS AND DAUGHTERS	FREEMAN & SPYRIDKIS—CREDIBILITY OF ONLINE HEALTH INFO	KIRBY & KRONE—WORK/FAMILY POLICIES
Theories used					
Type of assumptions					
Type of data					
Design					
Purpose					
Context(s)					

ARTICLE

231

	SCHEIBEL—IF YOUR ROOMMATE DIES YOU GET A 4.0	KENNY—TOWARD A BETTER DEATH	ARTICLE WRIGHT & ORBE—FACEWORK STRATEGIES OF EURO-AMERICAN REVIEWERS	DOUGHERTY—SEXUAL HARASSMENT AS A [DYS]FUNCTIONAL PROCESS
Theories used				
Type of assumptions				
Type of data				
Design				
Purpose				
Context(s)				

Given the information on these charts, map where each article fits on the space below. You should put articles you see as being more similar closer together and articles you see as being more different farther apart. You should also mark on the space the dimensions you are using to map the articles. If you prefer to use a different shape, you are welcome to do so—simply use the back of this page.

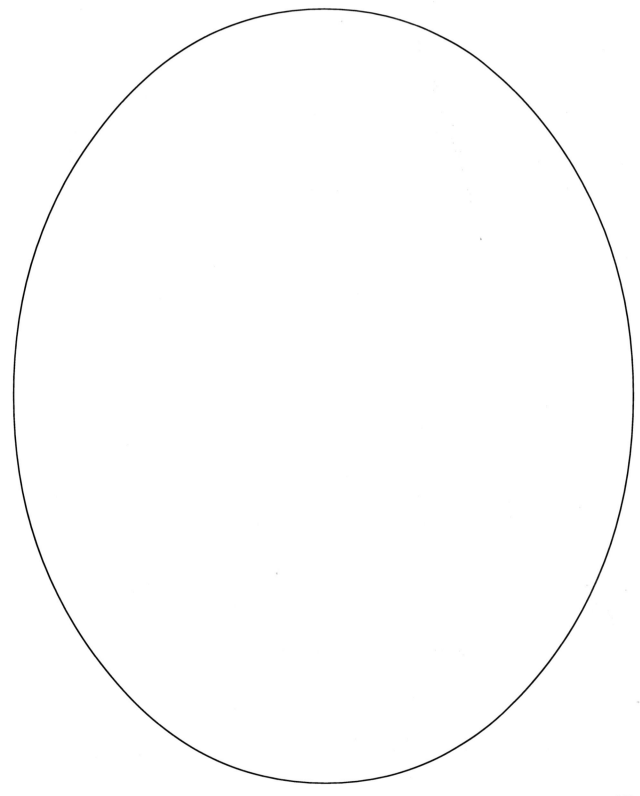

1. Why did you choose the dimensions you did to map the articles? What seems particularly significant to you about those dimensions?

2. How do you think your mapping would change if you used different dimensions? Under what conditions might you want to use different dimensions?

3. Why did you put the articles where you did on your map? What does this set of relationships suggest to you about these articles and about the theories on which they are based?

Summary Exercise 2

1. Communication can be seen in a variety of ways. For example, most of you will have seen the sender-receiver model of communication in which a communicator (sender) selects a message, encodes it, sends it over a channel where another person receives the message and must decode it. How do each of the articles in this book conceptualize communication? How does each article see communication as being important? What do the authors see communication as having an impact on?

   a. Bevan—Expectancy Violation and Sexual Resistance

   b. Pearce & Pearce—Community Dialogue Process

   c. Penington—Connection/Autonomy Between Mothers and Daughters

   d. Freeman & Spyridkis—Credibility of Online Health Info

   e. Kirby & Krone—Work/Family Policies

   f. Scheibel—If Your Roommate Dies You Get a 4.0

   g. Kenny—Toward A Better Death

   h. Wright & Orbe—Facework Strategies of Euro-American Reviewers

   i. Dougherty—Sexual Harassment as a [Dys]functional Process

How might this analysis on conceptualizations of communication change your mapping of the articles from the prior activity?

2. What sort of conversation might Kenny have with Freeman and Spyridkis about health communication? What might they agree on? What might they argue about? What do they have to learn from each other? What do they each have to teach you about your own communication with health-care providers and/or family members about health-related topics?

3. What sort of conversation might Dougherty and Bevan have about ways we communicate on sexual topics? What might they agree on? What might they argue about? What do they have to learn from each other? What do they each have to teach you about your own communication with co-workers and romantic partners on sexual issues?

4. What sort of conversation might Penington have with Wright and Orbe about the role of ethnicity in communication? What might they agree on? What might they argue about? What do they have to learn from each other? What do they each have to teach you about your own understanding of ethnicity and its role in your life and communication processes?

5. What sort of conversation might Pearce and Pearce have with Kirby and Krone about government, public policy, and the ways communication affects perceptions and implementation of policy? What might they agree on? What might they argue about? What do they have to learn from each other? What do they each have to teach you about communication processes in government, organizations, and/or communities you are involved in?

6. What sort of conversation might Scheibel and Kenny have about the work of Kenneth Burke? How might each critique the work of the other given their respective understandings of Burke? What might they agree on? What might they argue about? What do they have to learn from each other? What do their points of agreement and disagreement tell you about Burke's theory specifically and about the ways scholars use theories in general?

7. Which article did you like the best? What made this one so compelling for you? What does this say about your theoretical orientation, your assumptions, your conceptualization of communication, and/or your areas of interest?

8. Of all the theories covered here, which one seems to fit your experiences the best? How did that "fit" affect your understanding of the theory? Which theory fit your experiences the least well? How did that lack of "fit" affect your understanding of the theory?

9. Having covered all the material in this book, what is your understanding now of how journal articles and communication theory are related? In the future, for what purposes might you want to read journal articles? For what purposes might you want to use communication theory?